CULTURAL STUDIES IN INDIA

This volume discusses the development of cultural studies in India. It shows how inter-disciplinarity and cultural pluralism form the basis of this emerging field. It deals with contemporary debates and interpretations of post-colonial theory, subaltern studies, Marxism and post-Marxism, nationalism and post-nationalism. Drawing upon literature, linguistics, history, political science, media and theatre studies and cultural anthropology, it explores themes such as caste, indigenous peoples, vernacular languages and folklore and their role in the making of historical consciousness.

A significant intervention in the area, this book will be useful to scholars and students of cultural studies and theory, literature, history, cultural anthropology, sociology and media and mass communication.

Rana Nayar is a Professor in the Department of English and Cultural Studies, Panjab University, Chandigarh.

Pushpinder Syal is a Professor in the Department of English and Cultural Studies, Panjab University, Chandigarh.

Akshaya Kumar is a Professor in the Department of English and Cultural Studies, Panjab University, Chandigarh.

CULTURAL STUDIES IN INDIA

*Edited by Rana Nayar,
Pushpinder Syal and
Akshaya Kumar*

NEW DELHI LONDON NEW YORK

First published 2016
by Routledge
2 Park Square, Milton Park, Abingdon, Oxon OX14 4RN

and by Routledge
711 Third Avenue, New York, NY 10017

Routledge is an imprint of the Taylor & Francis Group, an informa business

© 2016 Rana Nayar, Pushpinder Syal and Akshaya Kumar

The right of Rana Nayar, Pushpinder Syal and Akshaya Kumar to be identified as the authors of the editorial material, and of the authors for their individual chapters, has been asserted in accordance with sections 77 and 78 of the Copyright, Designs and Patents Act 1988.

All rights reserved. No part of this book may be reprinted or reproduced or utilised in any form or by any electronic, mechanical, or other means, now known or hereafter invented, including photocopying and recording, or in any information storage or retrieval system, without permission in writing from the publishers.

Trademark notice: Product or corporate names may be trademarks or registered trademarks, and are used only for identification and explanation without intent to infringe.

British Library Cataloguing in Publication Data
A catalogue record for this book is available from the British Library

Library of Congress Cataloging-in-Publication Data
A catalog record has been requested for this book

ISBN: 978-1-138-89254-5 (hbk)

Typeset in Sabon
by Apex CoVantage, LLC

CONTENTS

List of figures ix
Prologue xi
Notes on contributors xxxiii

PART I
Cultural studies and Indian context

1 Culture and English studies in India 3
  KAPIL KAPOOR

2 The return of the silenced oral: culture and study
  in our time 19
  G. N. DEVY

PART II
Cultural studies and literary studies

3 The relevance of classical Indian aesthetics for
  contemporary culture studies 35
  SAUGATA BHADURI

4 Popular culture studies in India today: issues
  and problems 45
  SIMI MALHOTRA

CONTENTS

5 Postcolonial cultural studies at the crossroads: theoretical approaches and practical realities 52
RUMINA SETHI

6 Dalit autobiographies in the Punjabi context 65
AKSHAYA KUMAR

PART III
Cultural history and local traditions

7 Indianness: a battlefield 99
SUSHIL KUMAR

8 Cultural studies in Indian history: dominant models from South Asia 117
MAHESH SHARMA

9 History, historiography and Punjabi folk literature: issues of canons and cultures 139
ISHWAR DAYAL GAUR

10 Uses of the folk: cultural historical practice and the Guga tradition 170
ANNE MURPHY

PART IV
Cultural politics and mass media

11 (In)visible publics: television and participatory culture in India 201
ABHIJIT ROY

12 Transformative energy of performance: 'Budhan Theatre' as case study 222
TUTUN MUKHERJEE

13 Reinvention and appropriation of the folk in Daler Mehndi's pop videos 237
PUSHPINDER SYAL

CONTENTS

14 Subverting the male gaze: a case study of *Zindagi Na Milegi Dobara*   247
VIVEK SACHDEVA

PART V
Cultural imagination and new identities

15 New cultures of remembering: the Indian memory project   265
PRAMOD K. NAYAR

16 Romantic imagination: science and empire in the works of Amitav Ghosh   273
SAKOON N. SINGH

17 Cultural economy of leisure and the Indian Premier League   286
RAJ THAKUR

Index   297

FIGURES

8.1 'Hindus bathing in the early morning during a festival in Kashmir' watercolour painting by William Carpenter 120
8.2 Watercolour painting by William Carpenter of a Varanasi ghat 123
12.1 Budhan Theatre, 'Choli ke Peechhey kya hai', 6th Jan 2009 at Nizam College, Hyderabad 230
12.2 Budhan Theatre, 'Choli ke Peechhey kya hai' 'doubling' effect 230

PROLOGUE

Cultural studies in Indian context: problems and challenges

Before I start elaborating on the subject in hand, let me strike a personal note. It was in April 2009 that we decided to change the nomenclature of our department, which, like so many other departments across the country, was earlier known as the Department of English. It certainly begs a question, which is why we decided to go through this act of re-christening ourselves. It was not a quirky decision, but a well thought out one.

Over the years, following the drift of theory, we have slowly tried to dismantle the all-powerful and hegemonic monolith of English studies by creating more and more space for Indian literatures (in English as well as translations), post-colonial studies and world literatures in translation. As this drift became more focused, our students, for purposes of research, began to branch off into the areas of literary theory, post-colonial studies, translation studies, media studies, popular culture, etc. This is what necessitated the change in nomenclature.

No wonder, when we thought of applying for the University Grants Commission (UGC) Special Assistance Programme (SAP) in October 2010, the theme we chose for our proposal was 'Cultural Studies in the Indian Context', which incidentally was the defining focus of the conference, too, whose proceedings are now being published in the form of this anthology. Our proposal to UGC was finally accepted by September 2011, and that is how we were able to organize the National Conference in March 2012, the first in a series of conferences we propose to organize on different aspects of cultural studies over the next five years. This anthology is the outcome of the first conference.

Now, as I turn to the subject, I find myself confronted with two interrelated, though dissimilar terms, both of which I have hypothesized in my title, and these are 'culture studies' and 'cultural studies'. My purpose in bringing these two terms into the purview of our discussion is not really to give any kind of *semantic twist*. Browsing through a list of different departments across the country (where the focus is almost identical to ours), I came across these two terms in different contexts, which nearly had me flummoxed. I started wondering if these two could actually be used synonymously. On little investigation, I found that it certainly wasn't possible for us to do so. So now the question arises: what is the essential difference between these two terms? The difference, I'm afraid, is not merely grammatical in nature, as in the first case, 'culture' is used as a 'noun' and in the second, as an 'adjective'. The difference is also not to be perceived either in terms of *nomenclature* or *emphasis* alone; it is primarily a difference of *focus, methodology, ideology* and also that of *institutional practices*.

When we refer to 'culture studies', it willy-nilly becomes a study of the culture within which we are either located or implicated. In other words, 'culture studies' may set up multiple perspectives on a singular, amorphous formation called 'culture'. However, 'cultural studies', by its very nature, extends to a whole range of cultural practices, and so is a 'plural formation' that presupposes a variety of approaches/disciplines for studying it, as much as it emphasizes the pluralistic notion of culture, something we owe to the redoubtable Raymond Williams. (Do I need to emphasize here that in our case, at least, 'cultural studies' carries a definite resonance of the Centre for Contemporary Cultural Studies (CCCS) that was set up at the University of Birmingham in 1964, through the mediation of Richard Hoggart and finally closed down in 2002, merged as it was with the Department of Sociology, with David Marsh as its head). How far this notion of 'cultural pluralism', so essential for the survival or continuation of 'cultural studies', could possibly be treated as a set of living practices or merely as an ossified myth in the Indian context, is a question that still remains to be addressed.

Let me point out, however, that in our case, 'cultural studies' has only been suffixed to the Department of English, and as such no independent centre has been set up yet, the way it was done at Birmingham. Though this does raise certain basic questions about the terms

PROLOGUE

of reference on which the inter-relationship of English studies and cultural studies must ultimately be premised or negotiated, I shall refrain from raising any such questions at this juncture. The reason being that the future course of cultural studies, I presume, shall depend largely upon the direction it takes in our department or the other departments, for that matter. But I shall certainly not refrain from asking some more pressing, immediate questions about the location of this discipline, which I think, can well be raised here with some profit. For instance, it'd be pertinent to ask: where is 'cultural studies' meant to be located, first within the academic boundaries, and then within the societal boundaries? The question of location, to my mind, is an extremely significant one, as it shall not only determine the direction 'cultural studies' as an academic discipline would take in future, but also help in delimiting or demarcating its range and scope, possible areas of operation, methodology and ideological underpinnings, even shifts.

To my mind, there are three possibilities one could speculate about in this regard. One, 'cultural studies' may, at some point of time, emerge as an independent, autonomous discipline, with a discourse of its own. In his chapter, 'Cultural Studies in the Indian Context' (which included in this anthology), Bhaskar Mukhopadhayaya has made three very significant observations, which I would like to reiterate (Mukhopadhayaya 2006).First of all, he says that cultural studies in India is, as yet, an emerging discipline, not an evolved one. He further says that it began to emerge in the 1980s, with the publication of *Journal of Art and Culture*, a left-wing journal, in the post-Emergency phase. He is also of the view that this 'cultural turn' is the second major contribution of the political Left to India, after the Progressive Movement of the 1940s, which incidentally introduced 'modernism' in India, much before it was modernized through the post-Independence industrialization. Therefore, it would not be wrong to say that at present, 'cultural studies' only exists at the intersection of several disciplines such as English, psychology, sociology, anthropology, political science, mass communications, theatre/film studies, philosophy and religion; it borrows its methodology from these disciplines and follows a situation-specific, context-specific or occasionally an eclectic approach to build its methodological apparatuses. Interdisciplinary nature of the 'cultural studies' and the great possibility of transgressing the disciplinary boundaries it so generously offers is what makes it truly into a fascinating and absorbing field of study. However, if it does manage to create its own discourse or define its academic boundaries, it, too, shall probably have to contend with the questions of *power/knowledge* in relation to itself, and also other discourses, just the way Edward Said's 'Orientalism' once had to.

Secondly, 'cultural studies' may turn into what Bhaskar Mukhopadhayaya calls the 'political cultural studies'. In that case, it shall have to look into, as he suggests, the history of the Emergency in India, the first ever concerted political attempt at suppressing civil liberties, which not only triggered off a series of mass movements across the country, but also brought 'political society' into direct conflict with 'civil society'. Though the political landscape of our country has changed dramatically since, and so have the political fortunes of various political outfits or the character of Indian democracy (from a single-party dominance, it has become a multi-party coalition), this confrontation between 'political society' and 'civil society' has remained the only unchanging, common factor. If the rise and fall of the Anna Hazaare movement in our country in 2011 is anything to go by, then it has actually brought this confrontation to a head. Without going into the reasons for its success or failure, let me say that, among other things, it has clearly demonstrated that the trust deficit between the civil and the political societies is at an all-time high, something that doesn't augur well for the future of political or representational democracy in our country. (The trust deficit is so high that the civil society doesn't even want the political society to legislate in matters of Lokpal and Lokayukta.) Regardless of how we choose to think about its consequences, one thing is clear that if 'cultural studies' does take a 'political turn', it may well turn out to be study of the mass movements in India, starting from the linguistic movements of the 1960s, the Left-led protest movements of the 1970s, JP-led student movement of the 1970s, churning of Indian society on account of its Mandalization, politico-religious movements and RathYatras of the 1980s and 1990s or several attempts by the political Left or the political Right to engineer radical or even communal mass-mobilization programmes, purely for their own political ends. And if it were to happen, I don't know, if it'd be possible for us to demarcate boundaries of what we have chosen to call 'cultural studies'. If the collapse of boundaries is what we are consciously seeking right now, tomorrow, we may find ourselves in a position where 'cultural studies' becomes another amorphous, all-subsuming discipline, with no clearly defined boundaries of its own. My worry is if that were to happen ever, 'cultural studies' may meet the same fate in India – its nemesis – that the Birmingham Centre met in England, more than a decade ago. The third possibility is that 'cultural studies' may continue to exist, as it presently does exist, as a necessary adjunct to 'English/literary studies', within whose spatial boundaries it has often been located. Of course, at one level, it may seem to pose no problems, whatsoever. But if we look hard enough, then, a whole range of questions begin to trouble us. For instance, we ask ourselves: Within the domain of English studies, will it exist as a minor or as a major partner; as an ally of the discipline or as a counter-discourse, an alterity to it? And further, will it be a counter-discourse to the hegemony of English studies and/or British studies alone or also seek to challenge, if not pose a real threat, to the hegemony of the Western theories/ideas/systems of knowledge? Will it emerge as a counter-discourse parallel to the one that was created by such Western thinkers as Adorno, Horkheimer, Marcuse, Raymond Williams, Richard Hoggart and Stuart Hall et al., thus legitimizing the hegemony of the Western theories/apparatuses; or become truly Indian, an alterity, a nativist enterprise, with its distinctively Indian ways of constructing systems of knowledge. We also need to ask ourselves: do we have access to such systems of knowledge in our tradition that could effectively help us build a parallel Indian response to the discourse of 'cultural studies' in the contemporary context? And finally, we may turn around and ask: what is this brouhaha about nativism and counter-discourse when all that 'cultural studies' does is to remind us of our inseparable links with the globalized, digitalized world which thrives on the principles of consumerism and commodification.

Of course, there is no denying the fact that universalism is one of the many undeniable myths of our times. More globalized and digitalized we become, more we tend to become aware of our localism. Emphasizing the need for both rootedness and change in culture, Gandhi had once said, 'I want the winds from every corner to blow through my house, but I refuse to be swept off my feet by any of them'. In our times, when it is almost fashionable to invoke global prescriptions for local maladies, I'm convinced in my mind that Indian traditions, histories and cultures (I insist on using the plural form for each) demand a very different kind of understanding from the one that the Western theories have either offered or tend to promote. For instance, the Marxist theories may not be serviceable, if we have to probe into the dynamics of 'caste' and its tenacious hold upon our collective, cultural psyche. Similarly, what sense would post-modernism make in a society which continues to thrive on the concept of kinship culture, strong, durable sense of community and filiations or a society that easily reconciles the 'paternalistic model of governance' or 'feudal notions of dynasty' and *'mai-baap* culture' with the modern ideals of democracy and secularism? Our secularism, let us admit, is not based upon the denial or suppression of multiple religions in our social/cultural space, rather it derives its legitimacy from the co-existence of these competing religious identities. Our Bollywood, too, has less to do with Hollywood and more to do with the tradition of Parsi theatre from where it has always drawn its sustenance, even strength. Our soap operas may seem to borrow the format from the American or British Television, but our stories are very much our own, and their characters, our next-door neighbours. While dealing with 'cultural studies' in the Indian context, we may have to address some of these contradictions and their spin-offs.

For instance, 'cultural studies', in actual practice, may turn out to be a serious, academic engagement with 'popular culture', and also with the cultural/literary/semi-literary or even non-literary texts from the perspective of popular culture. If such is the premise, then somewhere down the line, we may also have to negotiate this question of what constitutes 'popular culture' in the Indian context and understand its multiple negotiations, especially with the practices and/or methodologies of literary studies. Before we begin to hypothesize about the Indian variant of 'popular culture', it is important to ask ourselves as to what it really is, and also how it came into existence. There is no denying the fact that 'popular culture' is a contested category, and so it deserves to be examined very closely. If one were to look into the definition of the term, one would certainly be confounded not only by the sheer range, variety and versatility of its meanings, but also by their self-contradictory, self-annihilating postures and possibilities.

For instance, some of us may think of popular culture as something of a people's culture (which is a very broad way of defining the term, as 'people' is too generalized and amorphous a term to be used here), while others may associate it with a certain class of people, say, the 'working class', or the 'rural people' or the 'urban masses' or sometimes, even a confused aggregate or conglomerate of urban and rural consumers. Going further, one may talk of popular culture as a post-industrial (or post-technology) culture (whose beginnings coincided with the proliferation of the technology, that is, the printing press, photography, cinema, television and now Internet) or one may continue to see it as re-articulation of essentially agrarian feudal/folk cultural forms (original or pastiche) in our contemporary world.

Though popular culture has now come to mean everything, from 'common culture' to 'folk culture', from 'people's culture' to 'mass culture', it has, undoubtedly, been all of these things at various points in history. In the post-war period, America linked popular culture to a strong commercial culture and all its trappings: movies, television, radio, cyberspace, advertising, toys, or for that matter, any commodity available for purchase; several forms of art, photography and even games. While humanities and social science departments before the 1970s would rarely have imagined including any of the above-listed items in their curricula, 'popular culture' is now a well-established discipline, enmeshed in a complex set of institutional practices. Though 'pop culture' is, today, one of the US' most lucrative export commodities, making everything from Levi's jeans to Sylvester Stallone movies popular in the international market, it should not be analysed or studied exclusively from the perspective of the US material, economic and political culture. Americanization, or if I may say so, MacDonaldization of 'popular culture' being a fairly recent phenomenon (going as far back as the early decades of 20th century), only tells half the story. Globalization of this phenomenon has resulted in the blurring of fault lines, masking the contradictions of its cultural history, erasing the specificities of its multiple variants in vastly different cultural contexts.

In order to capture the plurality, multiplicity and differentiated variety of 'popular culture', it is necessary to look into the specificities of its nature, function and even history in different cultural contexts. Let us now evaluate some of the definitions of 'popular culture' in their historical context so as to understand some of the complications inherent in this process. In his extremely well-written chapter, 'What Is Popular Culture', John Storey has discussed six different ways of defining popular culture, all of which deserve our attention (Storey 2009: 1–15). One of the starting points, according to him, is the quantitative index, through which everything 'cultural' such as concerts, sporting events, festivals, books, CDs or DVDs that gain numerical popularity qualify as popular culture. He further points out that such a 'quantitative index' may sometimes prove to be misleading, as it is not always easy for us to determine the exact quantity or number of what constitutes the 'popular'. Even if we were to do so, it may often prove to be transgressive, knocking off the distinction between 'high culture' and 'popular culture' in the process.

In the second definition, he says, 'popular' may be perceived as a 'residual category' which may accommodate texts and practices that otherwise fail to qualify as expressions of 'high culture'. In this respect, 'popular culture', he suggests, may only be seen as the 'left over' culture and thus also inferiorized in comparison with 'high culture'. John Storey insists that such definitions are advanced on the premise that 'popular culture' is the 'Other' of the 'high culture' and so can only be understood in relation to it. He suggests that often we forget that these two categories are not trans-historical in nature, but keep shifting and evolving over a period of time. In other words, what is an expression of 'popular' at one point in time may also become 'classical' at another. These categories are, therefore, not fixed or immutable, but porous or permeable. Regardless of whether we talk of Shakespearean plays or the novels of Dickens, Margaret Mitchell's *Gone with the Wind* (1936) or its *film version* (1939), Francis Ford Coppola's *The Godfather* (1972) or Mario Puzo's novel of the same name (1969) from which it drew inspiration, the fault lines between the 'classical' and 'popular' often tend to collapse and merge into each other.

The third definition of 'popular culture', Storey contends, treats it as an extension of 'mass culture', which is meant primarily for the mass consumption of its willing or unwilling consumers. This notion of mass culture raises some fundamental questions regarding discriminating, active participation or non-discriminating, passive response of its consumers; the presence or absence of its historical contact with organic, folk community/culture in the past, hegemonic influence of America or Americanization and also homogenization of popular culture; or the possibility of interpreting it either as a collective dream world (Maltby 1989: 14) or as an ideological machine that reproduces the existing structures of power, the way some Foucauldian critics would do. Another question that such a definition of popular culture must contend with, of course, has to do with what, who and in what manner this category called 'mass' or 'people' is to be constituted, which is not so much of an academic question as a political one. In this respect, Graeme Turner has rightly pointed out: 'Popular culture is a site where the construction of everyday life may be examined. The point of doing so is not only academic – that is, as an attempt to understand a process or practice – it is also political, to examine the power relations that constitute this form of everyday life and thus reveal the configurations of interests its construction serves' (Turner 1996: 6).

The fourth definition, according to Storey, looks upon popular culture as an authentic expression of the people's culture. In this case, he suggests, it is extremely difficult to say whether the term 'people' is to be used for representing the 'folk' or the 'working class', as both the meanings are inherent in it. At the same time, there is another related problem regarding what is to be included and/or excluded from the purview of the term 'people', and further, what should the basis of these inclusions or exclusions be. The fact that the culture is not created in a very spontaneous manner, but is essentially complicit with certain forces/processes of production that are inherently commercial in nature, further complicates our understanding of the term 'popular culture'. Under these circumstances, we may not be able to say in very clear and emphatic terms as to where the people's culture ends and the 'mass culture' begins.

The fifth definition, Storey avers, derives itself largely from the Gramsci's notion of hegemony, and as such it should neither be seen as an imposed mass culture of the cultural theorists nor as the oppositional culture of people emerging from below. He contends that if it is approached from Gramsci's ideological position then it becomes 'a site of struggle between the 'resistance' of subordinate groups and the forces of incorporation operating in the interests of dominant groups' (Storey 2009: 10). Popular culture, in this particular case, becomes a contested terrain of negotiation and exchange between two warring groups, with conflictual interests. It is another matter that the boundaries of the 'dominant' and the 'subordinate', both of which are tied to the historical processes, also keep shifting in the same manner as those between the 'classical' and the 'popular' often do. If we follow the logic of this argument, then at any given point in time, we may have three or more than three variants of 'popular culture' that is, *dominant, emergent* and *residual* operating in a given society, in much the same way as Raymond Williams postulates about different forms of Culture.

John Storey suggests that the sixth definition, however, could be seen as a by-product of our post-modern culture, As post-modern culture refuses to recognize any distinction between the high and the low, the sacred and the profane, the classical and the modern, it neither despairs over the end of elitism nor celebrates the emergence of the working class. In such a situation, he contends, our real challenge is twofold: to sift the 'authentic' from the 'commercial culture' and then to decide as to whether the 'authentic' is governed by the 'commercial' or the vice versa. My purpose in enumerating all these definitions of John Storey in some detail is merely to establish this fact that when we start thinking we have understood the term 'popular culture', it begins to face in exactly the opposite direction, thus revealing its Janus-faced character. One of the major semantic, or should I say, theoretical worries about it is that it can't easily be pinned down or demarcated. Often, it is difficult to decide as to what should be included in and/or excluded from the purview of this eminently 'slippery' term.

Let me now turn briefly to the question of how this 'slipperiness' may create its own share of complications, were we to invoke this term 'popular culture' in the Indian context. It could quite easily be used to describe anything from a Shobha De novel to a Talk Show on the television, from a popular mass movement like the one Anna Hazare started last year to a popular Tamil song 'Kola Veri Di', from a Sufi song of Nusrat Fateh Ali Khan to a dance number 'Ooh la la' picturized on Vidya Balan in *The Dirty Picture*. Interestingly, a Shobha De novel becomes an instance of 'popular literature' only if it sells some 10,000 copies (which may be around 001 per cent of the total number of English literates in the country), and 'Kola Veri Di' enters the realm of a 'popular song' only after it is heard by some ten million people across the world. All I'm saying is that when we often describe something as 'popular', do we ever pause to ask ourselves as to how 'popular' is this 'popular' or what is the extent of popularity this 'popular' really enjoys? Or for that matter, what is 'popular' or how and under what conditions does it become 'popular'? Or is it that whatever often fails to qualify as the 'classical' becomes 'popular' by sheer default? After all, when we do look through the history of literature, don't we find that all those who are being feted today as the 'classical' writers such as Homer, Sophocles, Dante, Shakespeare, Cervantes, Dickens and Margaret Mitchell were once extremely popular in their own times. Doesn't it mean then that the divide between the 'classical' and the 'popular' is only context-specific, even porous, and that the notions of 'popular' and the 'classical' not only keep shifting and changing, but are interchangeable, too?

Otherwise, too, the real negotiation in Indian context is not between the 'classical' and the 'popular', but between the 'margi' and the 'desi', which unlike the West do not constitute an oppositional discourse, but a mutually reciprocal or a symbiotic one. This may also create

PROLOGUE

another set of problems with regard to our understanding of the 'folk culture'. In his extremely well-researched book, *Inventing Popular Culture: from Folklore to Globalization*, John Storey suggests how the 'folk culture' had actually begun to emerge as a subject of academic inquiry and investigation among the 18th-century European intellectuals (2007). (It is ironic, isn't it that 'folk culture' was not the invention of the people, but that of the intellectuals, a fact that Roger Cartier, a French historian has also corroborated). John Storey further emphasizes that there were mainly two reasons for this growing trend: one, the collapse of a sense of community owing to industrialization and urbanization; two, a surge of nationalism sweeping through most parts of Europe, culminating into a genuine need for a very specific cultural identity. My point is in what way do we contextualize our own efforts at academization of folk and/or tribal history, literature and/or culture; or in what way do we construct and legitimize our own public sphere(s) in this regard?

One way of looking at it is that all these questions of Indianness are really spurious in a context where our identity is part real, part reel, and most of it, only virtual. After all, aren't we living through the times, when the theatres of war have moved from the grim barrenness of outside to the plush comfort of our drawing rooms; where the battles are not only shown but actually fought on the television screens? Aren't we living through the times when theatre has quietly moved out of the four walls, and moved surreptitiously into daily, quotidian life, threatening now to make spectacle(s) out of our humdrum grind, turning everydayness into a carnival of black humour? We are, indeed, living in the times when art doesn't imitate reality, but lived reality seems to be more of a vulgar reproduction of cinematic life; where we criticize capitalism in one breath and sing hosannas to MacDonaldization of our life and culture, in the other; where the rapid spread of consumerism has made little, regressive children out of us all, perpetually dissatisfied with whatever we have or get. I suppose, such are the dilemmas and such the paradoxes of our post-modern life and culture, and to a lesser extent, perhaps of the 'cultural studies', too.

In this chapter, I have simply outlined some of my concerns, worries, confusions and problems that the emerging discipline of 'culture studies/cultural studies' either throws up or is likely to throw up in future. I do not know how far I have succeeded in articulating the theoretical as well as practical issues connected with this discipline. If nothing more, at least, we now have a tertiary map of the direction cultural studies could possibly take in our context. I'm happy to say that to a large extent, the chapters included in this book have not only successfully problematized some of my worries and concerns, but also offered far reaching pointers and answers for them. The scholars and thinkers (whose chapters are included here and who are drawn from an amazing range of diverse disciplines) have covered a vast hinterland of theoretical issues. This may well prove to be a starting point for a multi-disciplinary, academic dialogue/debate of an enduring nature.

An overview of anthology

It is with this assurance that we now go into the plan of the anthology, and also its rationale. The anthology has been divided into five parts, namely 'Cultural Studies and Indian Context', 'Cultural Studies and Literary Studies', 'Cultural History and Local Traditions', 'Cultural Politics and Mass Media' and 'Cultural Imagination and New Identities'. Though cultural studies in India is the common theme running through this anthology, it also explores the notion of multiple conjunctures that different disciplines develop, once the disciplinary boundaries collapse. It is an attempt to see how and in what different ways inter-disciplinary dialogues could possibly be set up between cultural studies and a host of other disciplines such as literary studies, history, politics, mass media and cultural imaginary.

In his chapter, 'Indianness: A Battlefield', Prof. Sushil Kumar argues that Indianness is not an absolute term but a contested territory. Prof. Kumar defines it as a historical process that is constantly constructing and de-constructing itself, both from inside and outside. This raises, according to him, certain fundamental questions about whether this ever-changing, ever-evolving Indianness could also become compatible with relatively static notions of order and justice. Building up on Rawls' notion of justice, he asks several questions: Do people really author their self or write their identity? Does this invert the goal of just order and just citizenship? Does the rise of a power-seeking state a defeat of Indianness? Or, is power-seeking state a case of transcending Indianness, its cant of difference and ambiguity? He further argues that it was in the post-Nehruvian phase that a new brand of popular culture emerged, in which Dalit mobilization developed its own set of performative grammar. This bottom-up discourse was based on real and imaginary memories of 'otherness' and it sought to empower subalterns from the outside. But the social impact of subaltern domestics continued to be a neglected concern in sociology and cultural studies. In the recent times, however, social sciences have entered into an interface with literary and cultural studies, thus filling the gap. Though these studies are themselves in quest of relevance, he claims, their output on popular culture is certainly deserving of attention and examination.

In order to unmask multiple dilemmas of culture studies in Indian context, Prof. Kapil Kapoor in his chapter, 'Culture and English Studies in India', examines India's relationship with the English language. According to him, this relationship is twofold and has historically functioned both as a language of liberation and a language of subordination. While as a language of liberation, it may have brought the equation of language-employment-consumerism into play, as a language of subordination, it has certainly turned us into a de-intellectualized community, a community that is constantly in search of its own relevance, and continues to make sporadic gestures in this direction. He is of the view that the 'culture studies turn' in literary studies is predominantly an expression of this anxiety of de-intellectualized community, which has internalized Arnold's logic of propagating culture through literature (which Macaulay had also bought wholesale, once). This community, according to him, is a by-product of the conflict between two traditions; Hebraic and Pagan, which have irreconcilable differences between them. He further demonstrates the cultural differences between the two traditions, Western and Indian in terms of man's relationship to other species, man's relationship to environment, man's relationship to knowledge systems (which encourage plurality of thought in Indian context at least), man's relationship to time and God, notion of oneness versus notion of difference, etc. His main contention is that this situation has led to the collapse of such time-honoured Indian values as *dharma*, *niyam*, *sanyama*, *niyata karma* and *shraddha*. His contention is that in Indian society, culture studies must address these questions of how and why de-intellectualized communities have proliferated and how this has led to the collapse of our value system.

In his chapter, 'The Return of the Silenced Oral: Culture and Study in Our Time', Prof. Ganesh N. Devy recognizes that one of the major challenges confronting us today is the decolonization of Indian Aesthetics and Indian Linguistics, without a regressive turning back to the past. This, according to him, has brought us into direct confrontation with the question of how the taxonomies of knowledge ought to be perceived in relation to language as well as orality. Prof. Devy's main emphasis is on analysing this problem and discussing the possibilities of proposing an approach relevant to cultural and ecological contexts in India from his own perspective. Of late, he has been engaged with the struggles of the adivasis and the nomadic communities in India, both as an activist and a professional theoretician. In the pre-colonial epistemologies, linguistic diversity was an accepted norm and internal or external hierarchy of languages was not common. During the colonial period, with the introduction of print technology, the concept of literature underwent a dramatic change. New norms were introduced that privileged the written over the oral, the monolingual over the multilingual, thus silencing the tribal languages, which were primarily oral in nature. This tendency towards aphasia and marginalization of the tribal languages continued unhindered in the post-Independence phase, which meant a slow neglect and gradual erasure of their world view as well. It was Verrier Elwin who foregrounded the languages/literatures of adivasis in the early part of 20th century, and his work was further consolidated through the interventions of the Dalit writers. Prof. Devy suggests that in the last twenty years or so, different *adivasi* communities in India have witnessed a remarkable resurgence in the literary activity. It is this resurgence that would ultimately define the cultural ecology of our literatures in the times to come.

In his chapter, 'The Relevance of Classical Indian Aesthetics to Contemporary Culture Studies', Saugata Bhaduri has examined the possibility of symbiosis between Classical Indian Aesthetics and the contemporary discipline of culture studies. His basic premise is that it is possible to discover complex connections across the notions of the *loka-dharmī*, the *laukika* and the *lokāyata*, and read all kinds of texts from the standpoint of *rasa*, *dhvani* and *alankaar*. He also suggests that it is the *lokayata* that accommodates the folk and the popular within its fold. Prof. Bhaduri argues that there is practically nothing that falls outside the purview of 'culture', and that it also renders the Kantian distinction between mechanical art, agreeable art, and fine art (with its own aesthetic hierarchy) completely irrelevant. Culture studies, he says, necessitates methodological shift from reflection to mediation which has two corollaries. First, if culture is to be ideological, then one must focus on its simulatory and illusory-affective aspects, a shift from realism to stylization; and second, for it the alter-real, the counter-normative, the disruptive, the subversive, can become cherished objects of study. With illustrations from the aesthetics formulations of Bharata, Bhāmaha, Daṇḍin, Vāmana, Kuntaka, Bhaṭṭalollaṭa,

PROLOGUE

Bhaṭṭanāyaka, Śaṅkuka, Prof. Bhaduri shows how these four features have been well-discussed in classical Indian aesthetics, and a perusal of the same could also help us understand and appreciate the project of contemporary culture studies.

In her chapter, 'Popular Culture Studies in India Today: Issues and Problems', Simi Malhotra has focused her attention on the problems and issues that the prospect of pursuing popular culture studies in India tends to offer today. This chapter looks at this enterprise in terms of four of its aspects – terminology, or how the Indian term for the category itself may be deeply problematic; ontology or what should comprise the corpus of popular culture studies in India is debatable; methodology or how it is difficult to decide as to what should be the appropriate tools for such a discipline, especially in a post-colonial and neo-imperialized context like India; and ethics or how to determine the import of such a discipline for the rather stratified Indian society in general and the Indian academia in particular. Dr Malhotra points out the problems we encounter while defining 'Indian Popular Culture' especially through the use of the terms like *kṛṣṭi*, *saṁskṛti*, *loka*, etc., in a multilingual, multi-ethnic, multi-religious, multicultural context like India. She further argues how difficult it is to adopt either the scientific/ethnographic or the socio-politico-economic approach, or even evolve an 'Indian' approach, for such a field, given the history of the contemporary Indian cultural and academic formations. Moreover, she suggests that the questions about the relevance of this 'cultural turn' in liberal arts in India today are in no way different from the issues and problems that popular culture studies itself faces, and also raises before the academic community.

In her chapter, 'Postcolonial Cultural Studies at the Crossroads: Theoretical Approaches and Practical Realities', Rumina Sethi has offered a critique of postcolonial cultural theory by seeking to re-define 'postcolonialism' as a condition of living, a practice, a political belief or set of political beliefs that come into effect in a situation of oppression or marginalization. She further analyses how 'postcolonialism' exists pretty much in the world in which we live, but literary studies (particularly since the United States turned postcolonial) focus less and less on such politics. Global pressures on universities and correspondingly, on literary sensibilities, have reduced praxis and encouraged ideas of diffusion and difference even as binary oppositions continue to exist in the world as seen in the US aggression upon Iraq. The prioritizing of global capitalism over praxis corresponds with the decline of Marxism and Marxist studies. By citing differences between 'postcolonialism' and 'postcolonial studies', Dr Sethi goes far beyond the hermeneutics of mutation, hybridity and intermixture, which ignores the facts of contemporary history and the terror of late modern cultural and economic repression. She emphasizes that in the terrain of anti-capitalist struggles and political upsurge in the Afro-Asian world, postcolonial protest and resistance must evolve global socialist politics. If postcolonial studies are released from 'theory', we might still have postcolonial moments that find correspondence with the world outside theory.

In his chapter, 'Dalit Autobiographies in the Punjabi Context', Akshaya Kumar has made a plea for the indigenization of the project of cultural studies, especially in the embattled postcolonial situations. In the Indian context, the rhetoric of mass culture or consumer culture will have to engage itself with the deep-seated cultural imperatives of caste, which would require an investigation into the life-narratives of the subaltern. He focuses on the possibilities as well as the problems of deploying Punjabi Dalit autobiography as a tool of mobilization of scheduled caste population in the state of Punjab. Punjabi Dalit autobiographical expression is not as virulent and violent as it is in other parts of India, partly because of the emancipatory discourse of Sikhism, relatively better levels of economic prosperity, diasporic distractions of the Punjabis. It is certainly different from what surfaces in the autobiographers or the radical discourses of Marathi Dalit panthers. As self-narratives of well-known writers, Punjabi Dalit autobiographies evince authorly aesthetics which lend a degree of sophistication to their expression, idiom and architectural design. In these autobiographies, despite caste-based identity rhetoric, the protest of the Dalit writers as protagonists stands negotiated, if not postponed. The chapter offers a close textual reading of six autobiographies to underline the predicament of Punjabi Dalits in terms of the cultural ambivalences they inherit and share.

In his chapter 'Cultural Studies in Indian History: Dominant Models from South Asia', Mahesh Sharma has examined different possibilities with regard to a pre-eminently complex negotiation between history-writing and culture. He points out how in the past few decades, there has been a discernible shift from the objectivist notion of history to the idea of cultural history. It is in this context that he examines some Indic-cultural models used by both historians and anthropologists. He contextualizes these models with the help of a case study from Kashmir with inscriptional inputs from Chamba (Himachal Pradesh).

PROLOGUE

The purpose of this case study is to understand how cultural space is contrived in historical texts; how abstract notions are concretized and given the form of ritual, space or object; and alternatively, how the concrete is reduced to abstraction. In order to buttress his argument, he draws upon his reading of *Nilamata Purana*, a sixth- to tenth-century text of Kashmiri provenance, and also that of the inscriptions from Chamba. His reading of *Nilamata Purana* emphasizes how alternative cultural space is devised, replacing the earlier Buddhist/Vedic ethos that prevailed in Kashmir; while in case of Chamba, he argues, Puranic cultural ethos established itself by replacing the indigenous ethos.

In his chapter, 'History, Historiography and Punjabi Folk Literature: Issues of Canons and Cultures', Ishwar Dayal Gaur interrogates belief in *rational* understanding of history that has led many historians to exclude folk and its multiple voices from their craft of history-writing. He is of the view that historians have a widespread tendency to ignore folk literature, folk culture or collective memory as authentic and uncontaminated sources of history. This mainly happened, according to him, owing to George Wilhelm Friedrich Hegel, who, in the early 19th century sought to exclude folklore from the discipline of history, disparaging it as 'dim and hazy forms of historical apprehension'. Prof. Gaur, however, is of the view that folk community evolves and organizes its archives through various processes of socio-cultural and language contacts, displaying the characteristics of a syncretic ethos or cultural fusion. It has its own authenticity claims and its lore constitutes an archival discourse, different from the official or the elite one. He argues that folk literature needs to be judged from the view point of its historical, cultural and social locations, functions and effects, rather than merely in terms of its aesthetic essence. Following this argument, he offers a sustained critique of the way in which identity of the Muslims and the Sikhs has been projected in traditional historiography. In the last part of the chapter, he discusses the implications of this argument for the construction of cultural folk history around Bhagat Singh, specifically in the context of Punjab.

Much in the manner of I.D. Gaur, Anne Murphy also believes that the folk tradition has multiple lives. In her chapter, 'Uses of the Folk: Towards a Cultural History of the Guga Tradition', she raises a series of very pertinent questions such as: How do we write the cultural history of the fringe and the centre, of that which is both inside and outside? Do we treat the tradition of Guga Pir, a deity popular across northern India for protection against snake bites, as an artefact or remnant or contemporary, hybrid and new? She legitimately asks: 'Is it low, or high; does it uniquely express aspects of Indian tradition, or a form of subaltern religious experience. And further, if it is the popular, how does it relate to the cultural production in more elite quarters?' Her contention is that variants of this particular tradition are as much to be found in the folk culture as in the elite or quasi-elite culture. In order to establish this point, Dr. Murphy goes into the history of different variants of Guga tradition, found in several northern regions of India. She is of the view that the Guga tradition stands at the crossroads of the oral and the written, the elite and the popular, the pre-modern and the modern. She uses this particular theoretical frame to locate different variants of Guga tradition commonly found in literary as well as performative texts.

In his chapter, '(In)visible Publics: Television and Participatory Culture in India', Abhijit Roy argues that his primary interest is to investigate the structures and ideologies of Indian tele-visual publics in post-liberalization India, with special reference to the pan-Indian participatory culture around news television and Reality TV. At a time of increasing 'Reality TVization' of all infotainment, public participation in media seems to point towards a specific contour of popular culture, where the inter-media (print, cinema, television, radio, internet, mobile phones, along with other traditional modes of communication) dynamics of consumerism enters into a complex relationship with issues of citizenship, democracy, identity, class, gender and sexuality. Drawing upon a wide range of instances of public participation through studio presence, live SMS polls, phone-in programmes, web-interfaces, contests or other forms of voting and participation, the author has demonstrated how continuous staging/performance of a 'democratic' order, in the sense of what Graeme Turner calls the 'demotic turn', has become a major imperative for the post-liberalization satellite television. Both the State and the Market lend their powers to this site of performance, demonstrating the historical liaison between democracy and capitalism. All the three estates of Legislative, Executive and the Judiciary seem to be more or less influenced by the Fourth Estate's foregrounding of 'public demand', thus calling for a close reading of the blurred boundary between these institutions of democracy and correspondingly between the legal and the ethical realms of the media. By looking at the under-researched area of participatory culture around television in India, cultural studies promises to analyse the changing and diverse forms of media-citizenry in India and to break new grounds in popular culture research.

In her chapter, 'The Transformative Energy of Performance', Tutun Mukherjee argues that theatre is essentially our way of saying that we are alive. It's a way of telling our people, we count; even if we are poor or illiterate, we have a voice. She follows the trail of Richard Schechner, who has pointed out that unlike other art forms such as painting, sculpture, or even writing, performance offers actual behaviour as it is being behaved. For the performer the process of embodiment of ordinary behaviour framed within the particularity of 'a performance' often arouses ineffable dimensions of experience which augment expression. This chapter focuses on performance that emerges as a 'secondary formulation' that comments on the 'primary process' of representing existential angst. The process, however, of reflecting upon significant experiences through performance is not always easy. By not just intellectually but viscerally reflecting upon experience through performance, the actors must discover and communicate latent meaning from their own lives. The performance by Tejgarh tribals led by Daxin Bajrange Chhara exemplifies this complex process of moving from the primary realization to the secondary stage of expressivity that lends transformative energy to their performance.

Pushpinder Syal in her chapter 'Reinvention and Appropriation of Folk in Daler Mehndi's Pop Videos' argues that one of the culturally significant phenomena in the Indian context is the manner in which folk forms are being transformed in new environments and for new audiences. Hybridity is the order of the day, though hybridity assumes complex configurations depending on specific situations and popular perceptions and needs. A pop phenomenon of the 1990s in Punjab, the singer and performer Daler Mehndi achieved immense popularity, not only in Punjab, but across India, with his songs and song-picturizations in television music videos. Mehndi represents a move in Punjabi culture where folk is being reinvented in the forms of emergent television culture, involving the introduction of imagery that reflects the moods and perceptions of people at a particular point in history – after the period of terrorism, the attempt to erase disturbing memories, reintroduce rhythms of dance and celebration, reinstate the 'happy' Sardar and the Punjabi as a hedonist reveller, through reconfiguring the lyrics and rhythms already resident in Punjabi folk songs. Integral to this process is the appropriation of the folk by the music industry, the apparent playfulness and insouciance of Mehndi's performance and the underlying political ideologies and economic forces at work.

In his chapter 'Subverting the Male Gaze: A Case Study of *Zindagi Na Milegi Dobara*', Vivek Sachdeva mainly argues that often camera becomes a tool of subversive politics in the hands of women filmmakers. His contention is that if the eye behind the camera changes, it brings about concurrent changes in the way subjectivities are constructed or the politics of representation is negotiated. Operating within the theoretical frame of Gaze Theory, Vivek focuses his attention upon such changes as they manifest themselves in the representation of both men and women. By alluding to other visual arts, he also offers a historical review of the representation of women in Indian cinema. He works around the hypothesis that in popular Hindi cinema, women have primarily been portrayed to provide voyeuristic pleasure to the male members of the audience. He further seeks to trace linkages between the gaze theory, culture and the power politics of machismo. Going beyond the domain of psychoanalysis, this chapter raises some basic questions about whether the female gaze could actually exist in a male-dominated system (industry) and phallocentric medium of creative expression (films and camera). Having explored some of these issues, this chapter goes on to address the question of how far such narratives as *Zindagi Na Milegi Dobara* be made to bear the burden of the changing cultural reality of India.

In his chapter, 'New cultures of memory: the Indian memory project', Pramod Nayar examines and critiques the Indian memory project initiated by Anusha Yadav in 2010. It is an online curated, visual and oral history based archive that traces a personal history of the Indian Subcontinent, its peoples, cultures, professions, cities, development and traditions. Nayar argues that such a digitized collection of private memories produces a whole new way of thinking about citizenship and national/community identity itself. Proceeding on the assumption that memory is always mediated, he postulates that new technologies of remembering not only constitute publicness of private memory but also lend a new shareable and transmittable materiality to memories. These 'travelling memories' use mulltimedia formats, thus also emphasizing the mortality of materiality. At this point, he wonders, if all private memories that morph into cultural memory have the potential to challenge the limits of official history. Within the space of digital archives, a new geography of affinity is forged, thus paving the way for memory citizenship. Memory citizenship, according to him, creates new ways of belonging as much as it offers an opportunity for radical decentring of 'official' history. This is how the local and the personal get instituted as new ways of creating history in a post-national or trans-national territories.

In her chapter, 'Romantic Imagination: Science and Empire in the works of Amitav Ghosh', Sakoon K. Chhabra has argued that in the process of being transplanted to India, the Western science underwent a definite transformation as a discipline. In this chapter, she traces the influence of the Romantic Movement on the practice of the science of Botany, as seen through the works of Amitav Ghosh. The Romantic Movement in the early 19th century is seen as the larger context of the culture of knowledge that was being practiced in the metropole. She argues that Ghosh shows through his latest novels such as *The Sea of Poppies* (2008) and *The River of Smoke* (2011) that there was a class of scientists who were inspired by the romantic ideal of close correspondence between man and nature, and how this, in turn, influenced the fledgling science of Botany. She further argues that there was an ascending mechanistic science, too, which was purely utilitarian in its view as it used Botany to bring material gains to the Empire.

Raj Thakur in his chapter 'Cultural Economy of Leisure and Indian Premier League' puts forth this argument that in the late capitalist societies, cricket has taken over the function that Marx believed religion fulfilled in the 19th century as an opiate for the masses. From 1980s onwards, the fortunes of Indian cricket have been inextricably linked with the economic reforms, deregulation of satellite networks and creation of large middle class. Hybridized, neoliberal trend in cricket represents final victory of the modern ideas of nation-state and market. Deconstructing the neo-liberal confluence of corporate sport, Indian Premier league (IPL) in particular and mass culture in general reveal that it is consumed within the realm of leisure economy as a popular culture sport. The shift from pre-industrial to post-industrial society had facilitated pitching in of the 'game' as a 'sport', a shift from ritual to record and from artefact to performance. The development is towards faster spectacular events, through the packaging and presentation of events for audiences with much shorter attention span. The Industrial Revolution changed the concept of time, including free time, the gate way of leisure. Leisure-sport practices like IPL are deftly inscribed in the performative codes and grammar of spare time spectrum. Cultural consumption is viewed as centring on fascination with the spectacular surfaces of media forms and the economy of signs and space. A symbiotic relation between leisure industry and media-sports complex serves as an extension of the culture industry, where mass culture takes IPL into custody. Leisure time comes to represent segmented portion of time or activity or fleeting states of mind contrary to the philosophical ideals of leisure linked to contemplation or ethics. We hope do that the readers of all shades, lay as well as specialized, shall be able to engage with some of the questions this anthology throws up.

Rana Nayar

References

Maltby, Richard (ed.)1989. 'Introduction', in *Dreams for Sale: Popular Culture in the Twentieth Century*. London: Harrap.

Mukhopadhayaya, Bhaskar. 2006. 'Cultural Studies and Politics in India Today', *Theory, Culture & Society*, 23 (7–8): 279–92.

Storey, John (ed.) 2009. 'What is Popular Culture', in *Cultural Theory & Popular Culture: A Reader*, 5th ed, pp. 1–15. Harlow: Pearson.

———. 2007. *Inventing Popular Culture: From Folklore to Globalization*. London: Blackwell.

Turner, Graeme. 1996. *British Cultural Studies*, 2nd ed. London: Routledge.

CONTRIBUTORS

Abhijit Roy is associate professor of film studies, Jadavpur University, Calcutta. A member of the editorial board of *Journal of the Moving Image*, he writes on television, popular culture and politics.

Akshaya Kumar is a professor in the Department of English and Cultural Studies, Panjab University, Chandigarh. His areas of specialization are comparative Indian literature and contemporary literary and cultural theory. Besides other publications, he has published two important books: *A. K. Ramanujan: In Profile and Fragment* (2004) and *Poetry, Politics and Culture: Essays on Indian Texts and Contexts* (2009).

Anne Murphy is associate professor and chair of Punjabi Language, Literature, and Sikh Studies at the University of British Columbia. Her research interests focus on the historical formation of religious communities in Punjab and northern South Asia, with particular attention to the Sikh tradition.

Ganesh N. Devy is a renowned literary critic and activist and is currently Chairperson, *The People's Linguistic Survey of India*. His publications include *Critical Thought* (1987), *After Amnesia* (1992), *Of Many Heroes* (1997), *India Between Tradition and Modernity* (co-edited, 1997), *In Another Tongue* (2000), *Indian Literary Criticism: Theory & Interpretation* (2002), *Painted Words: An Anthology of Tribal Literature* (editor, 2002), *A Nomad Called Thief* (2006), *The G.N. Devy Reader* (2009) and *Tribal Arts in India* (2012).

CONTRIBUTORS

Ishwar Dayal Gaur is professor of history at the Multi-Disciplinary Research Centre, Department of Evening Studies, Panjab University, Chandigarh. His research pertains to Punjab culture, folklore and literature.

Kapil Kapoor is former professor of English at the Centre for Linguistics and English, and Concurrent Professor, Centre for Sanskrit Studies, Jawaharlal Nehru University, New Delhi. His teaching and research interests include literary and linguistic theories, both Indian and Western, philosophy of language, 19th-century British literature and Indian intellectual traditions. His recent book is *Rati-Bhakti in India's Narrative Traditions* (2011).

Mahesh Sharma is professor of History at Panjab University, Chandigarh. Fellow, IIAS (Shimla) and Fulbright Senior Fellow (UCLA), besides being Visiting Faculty at UNF, Jacksonville, he has worked extensively on the history and culture of the Western Himalayas and early medieval India.

Pramod Nayar is associate professor at the Department of English, University of Hyderabad, Hyderabad. Among his newest books are *Frantz Fanon* (Routledge 2013), *Colonial Voices: The Discourses of Empire* (2012), *Writing Wrongs: The Cultural Construction of Human Rights in India* (Routledge 2012) and *Digital Cool: Life in the Age of New Media* (2012). He is currently working on a book on transnationalism in English literature and a book on surveillance cultures.

Pushpinder Syal is a professor in the Department of English and Cultural Studies at Panjab University Chandigarh. She has a PhD from the University of Lancaster, UK, and a number of research publications in the areas of stylistics and language teaching, and on literatures in English, including African, Indian and Australian Literature in English. She has also taught and guided research in these areas.

Raj Thakur is assistant professor in the Department of Comparative Literature, Central University, Jammu. He is currently pursuing his PhD on 'Cultural Economy of Leisure and Its Media Representation: A Case Study of Indian Premier League'. His areas of interest

CONTRIBUTORS

include cultural studies, leisure studies, cricket literature, media and sports, visual culture, postcolonial literature and popular culture.

Rana Nayar is a professor in the Department of English and Cultural Studies, Panjab University, Chandigarh. His main areas of interest are world drama/theatre, translation studies, literary theory and cultural studies. A practising translator, he has rendered around 10 modern classics of Punjabi into English, including the works of Gurdial Singh, Mohan Bhandari, Raghbir Dhand and Beeba Balwant. His most recent book is *Gurdial Singh: A Reader* (2012). He has published more than 80 articles and translations in national and international journals.

Rumina Sethi is professor of English at Panjab University, Chandigarh. She is the author of *Myths of the Nation: National Identity and Literary Representation* (1999) and *The Politics of Postcolonialism* (2011).

Sakoon K. Chhabra teaches English literature at DAV College, Chandigarh. Her area of specialization is Indian writings in English and postcolonial theory, focusing on the works of Amitav Ghosh.

Saugata Bhaduri is professor and chairperson at the Centre for English Studies, Jawaharlal Nehru University, New Delhi. His areas of interest are literary and cultural theory, popular culture studies, classical Indian and Western philosophy, comparative literature, and the theory and practice of translation.

Simi Malhotra is professor at the Department of English and European Languages at Jamia Millia Islamia, New Delhi, and the Media Co-ordinator, International Relations, and Co-ordinator of the Outreach Programme of the University. Her areas of research interest include postmodernism and globalization, literary and cultural theory, popular culture studies, and religion and theology, especially Sikhism, in all of which she has taught, conducted research and published extensively.

Sushil Kumar is former professor of international politics at Jawaharlal Nehru University, New Delhi. Earlier he taught political science

CONTRIBUTORS

at the University of Rajasthan, Jaipur. His forthcoming publication is *Liberal Humanism and the Non-Western Other.*

Tutun Mukherjee is professor and head of the Centre for Comparative Literature and also joint professor at Theatre Department and Centre for Women's Studies at the University of Hyderabad, India. Her specialisation is Literary Criticism and Theory and research interests include Translation, Women's Writing, Theatre and Film Studies. On theatre, some of her edited anthologies are *Staging Resistance: Plays by Women in Translation; Girish Karnad's Plays: Performance and Critical Perspectives; Plays by Mahesh Dattani: An Anthology of Recent Criticism*; book chapter 'Women's Theatre' in *OUP Encyclopedia of Indian Theatres*; and other papers in journals. Forthcoming is her translation of plays by Mridula Garg.

Vivek Sachdeva is associate professor at GGS Indraprastha University, New Delhi, where he teaches literature and cinema. He is also a poet and a translator and has published two books of translation so far. He has been associated with the Ladakh International Film Festival (LIFF) as member, Selection Jury.

Part I

CULTURAL STUDIES AND INDIAN CONTEXT

1
CULTURE AND ENGLISH STUDIES IN INDIA

Kapil Kapoor

It is all too well known that the introduction of English in India in the mid-19th century had a clearly stated socio-political and cultural purpose. English has a long history in India of more than 150 years; before it became a subject of study in the UK, English literature became, for reasons of employment and social distinction, a subject of study with the establishment of the 'presidency' colleges. This had far-reaching consequences – on the positive side, it facilitated an interaction both with contemporary Western thought and with Western classics (writings of Plato, Aristotle, Homer, Virgil and Dante) and extended the horizons of the Indian mind by foregrounding socio-political thinking (Locke onwards) and the values of equity, social responsibility and honour. This was accompanied by the founding of new civilization institutions – the post office, the railways, the macadam road, the public hospitals and the municipality.

The new liberal thought also ushered in the much-needed social reform, and many Indians, for example Ishvarachandra Vidyasagar and Raja Ram Mohan Roy, distinguished themselves by introducing reform measures in Hindu society, according to their own understanding. In this sense, the English language may be called a language of liberation. But on the flip side, English became a language of subordination. The astounding material values bedazzled the educated, and the best Indian minds busied themselves acquiring these ideas, uncritically, while the Indian languages became recipient/borrowing languages and the Indian mind became 'a translator's mind' and a 'translated mind'. This subordination of the Indian mind (*a*) created a de-intellectualized community completely in disjunction with its own thought and its own self becoming, in the end, cheap labour, cheap soldiers and cheap 'cyber-labour'. Above all, it (b) induced a conflict between the new civilization institutions and the inherited, sedimented cultural values. A duty-centred society began to think in terms of *rights*, the inherited values of restraint (*sanyam*), discipline (*niyama*), and reverence (*shraddha*) conflicted with Utilitarian values of 'indulgence', 'freedom' and 'dispose-off'. India became 'two-nations' (Disraeli's phrase for the rich and the poor 19th-century England) – those who know English and rule and those who do not know English and are the ruled. In such a divided society, the language pyramid debars the ruled masses from the higher echelons of the judiciary, the administration, the education and the media. Furthermore, it has excluded the rich Indian languages from many legitimate spheres of use, by initializing a process of pushing them down and out.

Of late, we have discussed the nature, role and teaching of English in India – both language and literature. English has become the *second language* in education in both Hindi and non-Hindi areas and in serious business has a role that rightfully would belong to an Indian language, regional or any other, and its scope and domain have extended beyond this and it often functions as L-1 in certain communities and classes. It is now being increasingly taught at early primary classes while a larger class even uses it as a mother tongue or as an alternative mother tongue. Though the changes in the language situation, as a whole, are very complex, given the spread and the 'jeansification' of English and the numerically large number of students being taught English, there is a need to reflect once again on its role and its impact on the society and the individuals. The same holds true for English studies, particularly the study and teaching of English literature which was the original agenda of English education. The Departments of English in the universities have of late been in flux, striving to relate English studies meaningfully to the Indian context, moving first to non-British literatures then to 'theory' and then to what is now called 'culture studies'.

A realization of the need to disseminate 'culture' right down to the 'populace' was in fact the original impulse for introducing English literature even in England. Given the 19th-century pervasive social divisions in the English society in the background of the violent French Revolution, Matthew Arnold had articulated the developing climate of ideas that sought to assuage class conflict by promoting 'culture' through the teaching of English literature. (Arnold 1869). In the aftermath of loss of faith in the face of the onslaught of empirical sciences, Arnold offered literature as a new faith, a support for 'culture' that he thought needed to be maintained for social harmony, the Western Christian culture.

Lord Macaulay saw this as a useful project for the colonies also, albeit redefined for a colonial agenda. He saw the incorporation of English Language and literature in Indian Education for the spread of Western Christian culture that gradually took the form, *avatara* of the much touted 'modern culture' alienate the people, particularly the restless and intelligent Hindus from their own cultural roots. His views about producing 'educated Indians' who look Indian but feel English and about the great value of English literature as an instrument in this enterprise are too well known to be repeated, but the following letter that Macaulay wrote to his father from Calcutta, 23 years before he drafted his famous Minute, is a tell-tale document:

> Our English schools are flourishing wonderfully. We find it difficult, – indeed, in some places impossible, – to provide instruction for all who want it. At the single town of Hoogly fourteen hundred boys are learning English. The effect of this education on the Hindoos is prodigious. No Hindoo, who has received an English education, ever remains sincerely attached to his religion. Some continue to profess it as a matter of policy; but many profess pure deism and some embrace Christianity. It is my firm belief that, if our plans are followed up, there will not be a single idolator among the respectable classes in Bengal thirty years hence. And this will be effected without any efforts to proselytize, without the smallest interference with religious liberty; merely by the natural operation of knowledge and reflection. I heartily rejoice in the prospect.
> (Macaulay 1836)

The world is in the middle of the neo-English empire. The English language is evolving from its status as the language of one empire among others to its current position as the only fully globalized language. Scholars have agreed that this poses a threat to the other cultures and the local languages. It has been suggested that the language policies of the third world countries continue to serve the interests of Western powers and contribute to preserve existing inequalities between the 'first world' and the so-called 'third world'.

More importantly, this policy assumed that India has no worthy knowledge or 'culture' that deserved to be preserved or maintained.

'A single shelf of a good European library', said Macaulay, 'was worth the whole native literature of India and Arabia' (ibid.). Not surprising, the Bengali middle class and other local elites were interested in English language education as a means of access to social and political power. Today, for the same class, it is the road to employment and the means of upward mobility for those who are not yet in that class. It is the link established between education-English-employment that gave pace to English.

As of today a large mass of Indian people are becoming or have become adherents and admirers of Western culture. Linguistic monism is at variance with the extremely varied cultural contexts and conditions of and is actually inimical to local cultures. It is only to be expected that this cultural intellectual centralism in the end shall be resisted by communities particularly those that have a strong long-lived cultures.

Resistance to English in India, howsoever isolated and weak, stems from the danger that English poses to India's culture – its long-held values and ways of life and thought. Sri Aurobindo way back reflected on the cultural loss that followed the imposition of English in Ireland and India:

> Ireland had its own tongue when it had its own free nationality and culture and its loss was a loss to humanity as well as to the Irish nation. For what might not this Celtic race with its fine psychic turn and quick intelligence and delicate imagination, which did so much in the beginning for European culture and religion, have given to the world through all these centuries under natural conditions? But the forcible imposition of a foreign tongue and the turning of a nation into a province left Ireland for so many centuries mute and culturally stagnant, a dead force in the life of Europe. Nor can we count as an adequate compensation for this loss the small indirect influence of the race upon English culture or the few direct contributions made by gifted Irishmen forced to pour their natural genius into a foreign mould of thought. Even when Ireland in her struggle for freedom was striving to recover her free soul and give it a voice, she has been hampered by having to use a tongue which does not naturally express her spirit and peculiar bent. In time she may conquer the obstacle, make this tongue her own, force it to express her, but it will

be long, if ever, before she can do it with the same richness, force and unfettered individuality as she would have done in her Gaelic speech. That speech she had tried to recover but the natural obstacles have been and are likely always to be too heavy and too strongly established for any complete success in that endeavour.

Modern India is another striking example. Nothing has stood more in the way of the rapid progress in India, nothing has more successfully prevented her self-finding and development under modern conditions than the long overshadowing of the Indian tongues as cultural instruments by the English language.

[. . .] Language is the sign of the cultural life of a people, the index of its soul in thought and mind that stands behind and enriches its soul in action. (Sri Aurobindo 1997)

It is the cultural invasion, subtle and manifest that concerns us directly here.

Cultures, dynamic cultures and societies are always changing but they change faster in periods of cultural contact with others. While India has had cultural intervention since virtually the 11th century and therefore has been undergoing processes of deep cultural interaction and change, it has, along with most of the Asian and African world, undergone another phase of colonization, the colonization by the West. In these last two or three centuries, there has been a marked change due to the presence of a superior political and military culture. Indian life and mind really started getting restructured radically in this phase in the name of 'modernization' and 'progress'. The 'Modern Culture' of the West as a matter of policy was seen as an instrument of pushing what was believed to be a 'pre-Modern', traditional culture out of its 'backwardness'.

The introduction of English studies became the medium of modern culture and has had far-reaching consequences on the Indian civilization and culture. There was so much visible change in Indian life and it made so much difference to the external, material conditions that the young Indian, completely sold on working for comfort and for good life, was virtually swept off his feet and filled with deep admiration for the West. The astounding material benefits that accompanied Western thought bedazzled the educated Indian so thoroughly that he began to admire without reflection. The best Indian minds busied themselves acquiring these ideas, uncritically, and disseminating them in the languages of the people. It is thus that the Indian languages became recipient/borrowing languages, lost their status and came to be looked upon as simply mediums for spreading borrowed thought. The Indian academy in a recipient–donor relationship with the Western academy created a de-intellectualized community completely in disjunction with its own thought and its own self. It started producing, and continues to produce, young people who at best are ignorant and at worst have contempt for themselves.

In the process, the Indian mind became 'a translator's mind' and the best Indian minds that were earlier exegetes of great distinction became mere 'translators'. Today, the educated Indian's mind is at best a translator's mind.

The Indian mind became docile and dependent, and given the innate good quality of our mind, our ability to learn, our obedience and our low economic expectations made us 'ideal employees' – the Indians became 'ideal ruled people' and forgot how to rule and are proving 'bad rulers' as far as good governance is concerned. Of late, a change is seen to be in the offing due to the world becoming increasingly a dangerous and an intolerant place. We are beginning to see 'The Return of the Native'. Now the erstwhile colonized people have started critiquing the 'Modern Culture'. This Modernity, a fact of the European history of ideas, is claimed to have its basis in science and reason in opposition to religion and faith. Through the Enlightenment Project, it sought to realize the ancient Western hope of the Millennium, 'the Second Coming' but it has landed the Western society into its present crisis. It sought to promote comfort and material well-being through maximum exploitation of nature and maximum industrial production, both facilitated by technology, but forgot the imperative of human happiness. The 19th-century 'individual' became first a citizen and then a mere number in the 20th century on a variety of cards – Pan Card, Identity Card, Ration Card and Adhaar Card. So much for the dream and the reality!

Latin American intellectuals have led the way in this and have since the nineties been discussing, among others, the issues of traditional–modern cultural relationship and the transformation of oral cultures into written, scriptal cultures, phenomena that we have also experienced, and have thus initiated a process of recovery of the 'traditional' cultures which are no longer seen as 'backward'.

'Modern' period in European history began with the Renaissance and was characterized by the ontological shift from God to man and the epistemological shift from the verbal authority to reason. In the Indian history of ideas, Buddha in the sixth century BCE had decisively shifted the Indian mind from ritual to reason but the Indian mind did not prestige reason to the exclusion of other means of knowledge though reason, *anumana*, and reasoning, *tarka*, always remained high in the cline of epistemology. India's is, and has been, a 'non-modern', *not* a 'pre-modern' culture and it has been invaded in the last 200 years by this Modern Culture and for more than a thousand years by the other monotheistic Semitic Cultures, each with its own foundational assumptions. What kinds of conflict have this confrontation of foundational beliefs and ideas generated in the Indian mind and to what consequences?

Two kinds of knowledge cultures are recognizable – the Hebraic and the Pagan. The Hebraic subsumes, with internal differences, the Judaic, the Christian and the Islamic sub-cultures, all marked by a belief in a personal God. The Pagan is represented by the I gvedic culture and subsumes with internal differences in different degrees of relationships, Sanatana Dharma, Jainism, Buddhism, Sikhism, the early Iranian (Zoroashtrian) and the Greek sub-cultures. The two cultures differ foundationally and the difference has produced the fragmented self, the splintered, fragmented mind (*vikshiptamana*) of the modern 'educated Indian'.

What are the foundational differences? There are in fact basic differences in the drivers of the two cultures:

(*a*) In respect of man's relationship with other species, Indians believe that all life is one; now, in the 19th century we have the man-centred worldview, the principle of man's centrality in the universe. God had remarked (Genesis 1.26) He had created man in His own image and all fruits and birds and plants and trees and fish and fowl are for him to enjoy. Now this privileges man over nature and the animal world – 'human rights' not rights of all living beings. If the elephants intrude into farms, kill the elephants. But the core driver in our minds is that man is just a link in a chain of beings and has no more right to exist than the meanest of creatures. This explained the philosophy of *ahimsa* and the practice of vegetarianism. This grand idea has this concrete gross reflex – refusal to kill a mouse or a snake or a housewife getting up in the morning, feeding birds, dogs, cows and ants. This impulse is now weakening and the other driver, man's centrality, is promoting a philosophy of self-indulgence, a philosophy of comfort, the search for comfort, to individualism, imperialism, everything – because 'you' are the lord and master. You have to pander to yourself, not cater only. We are today submerged in this philosophy in the cities at least.

(b) This is also related to a very different relationship with the environment. Nature is at your disposal. So, Descartes in *On Method* says the goal of knowledge is to bend nature to man's purpose. And the modern civilization has been harnessing nature till it has brought about a virtual ecological disaster.

How do we, or how *did* we, look upon Nature – what is our basic system? In our view, there is no separateness of reality and we are a part of reality. Our metaphor for Nature is one of 'mother' as one that nourishes. I remember from my childhood that in the evening if a child plucked a flower, the grandfather would stop him by saying 'the flower is also sleeping'. There is a whole different relationship with the environment. You worship the tree; you worship the river and all bodies of water. All this affinity with everything, this sanctity of everything in Nature (to raise things to the level of a god, to perform worship, to light the lamp) that has been dismissed as mere ritual is an expression of and a recognition of the need of man to be one with Nature. Just as the self can be your friend as well as your enemy, so too Nature is your friend and can be your enemy. Now with denudation, Nature is becoming your enemy with floods and other forms of natural disaster. So this philosophy leads to a different thinking about environmental relationship. The Pauranic King Prithu ruled over a town now known as Pehova, the then called Prithudaka, near present-day Karnal. Five times he 'milked' (*dohna*) the earth. A severe drought followed and the river Saraswati dried up. This is the consequence of exploitation of land. In earlier times, for three months the land was left fallow to rejuvenate. Because we must give back to the land something we have taken from it. We give it back. That was the cycle. Now with pesticides, new seeds, intermediate crops, we are exploiting the land because we have now a different economics generated by the new principles, the economics of surplus. Not the economy of need but of surplus. So, for the first time saline lands are appearing in otherwise fertile Panjab on account of over-exploitation. It leads to a different economics. 'Freedom *from* replaced by freedom *to*' as noted by the Venezuelan scholar, Jorge Armand (2000).

(c) Indian thought systems support a kind of pagan pluralism and make plurality a ground reality of Indian intellectual life – it is *inherently pluralistic* and not pluralistic by the accidents of history such as invasions and foreign interventions. This also includes atheism such as that of the Carvakas and ethical materialism such as that of the Buddhists and Jains. Three of the six theistic systems do not have God as an ontological category. The chief marker of the *Hebraic-Vedic* opposition is the One Formless Personal God presiding over a separate material universe as the object of knowledge (and devotion), an unqualified monotheism, versus polytheism of an informing principle immanent in the material universe and taking *forms* as so many 'gods'. In Indian thought, there is no room for uncompromising monism/monotheism, or for One Given Truth and, therefore, a plurality of 'truths' is allowed. While allowing for the fact that there must always be a truth out there, the Indian thinkers are sceptical about the possibility of accessing or recognizing it. They allow therefore 'several/multiple paths' to truth. The great differentia of world views, ontologies and epistemologies in Indian thought stems from this foundational principle. The indeterminacy, this relative unknowability, makes for tolerance of the other. There is no requirement, therefore, to conform and the individual is not subjected to the societal or the communal. Lord Krishna's discourse to Arjuna may be erroneously interpreted as the societal voice. But, it may be noted, this voice is not imposed on Arjuna. Lord Krishna after completing his statement tells him, 'I have shared with you the most substantial doctrine; meditate on this and *do exactly as you want to*' (*BG* 18.63).

In the 19th century, this imperative of monism triggered many reform movements and many young men today are sceptical about polytheism and pluralism.

(*d*) With respect to relationship with God, the Hebraic God, adversarial and seeking obedience from man, punishing him (Old Testament, Deuteronomy, 4.10. 43) and forgiving him, is different from the Indian gods who are seen as friends. Man no doubt is the special creation of God but then man defied God and shall seek redemption. The adversarial, conflict mode is legitimized by this. And since man is a fallen creature, he needs to be reformed/enlightened, even proselytized. The Indian mind considers man as a spark of the divine ('sparkles of divinity floating in time' as Carlyle said in *Sartor Resartus*) and has to seek perfection through his own effort.

(*e*) This is reinforced by the notion of time – the modern mind operates with the notion of linearity of time. The notion of 'progress' is built into this notion of linearity in the sense that whatever comes later is better and everything 'evolves' in time.

So progress, development and reform are the keystones of all modern socioeconomic political philosophy.

The Indian thought rests on cyclicity as against linearity. The Indian mind operates not with pre-X-post apparatus but with the configurational model. This means that Indian mind does not accept the principle of evolution, does not believe that with the passage of time, progress necessarily takes place. The direction of human change is towards decay rather than progress. This however does not lead to a life-negating philosophy. In that representative text of Hindu thought, the Bhagavad Gita, all are called upon to commit themselves to a philosophy of action. But this action is to maintain equilibrium, *rta*, an innate balance of the given, not 'development'.

So we did not set out to reform or enlighten others.

(*f*) Faced with immense variety and multiplicity so characteristic of Indian geographical and social reality, the Indian mind developed synthesizing transcendental knowledge framework and concluded that the highest form of knowledge is the knowledge of Oneness of all, *abheda*, of non-difference, of transcending the opposition between the Self and the Other(s). But this *ekatvabudhi*, synthesizing intellect, is not in opposition to the different points of view – *ekatvabuddhisarvavadaavirodhini* (*Vakyapadiya* 1.9).

The Western tradition, on the other hand, in its effort to break through the strait jacket of monism, built theories around *difference,* and today all Indian research in social sciences and humanities is almost totally ethnographic and is proving divisive. We are now identity oriented and all identity is in terms of how we are different from others and is contingent on *bheda*. Hence we see social fragmentation and tensions in contemporary Indian life. For good reason, in view of the multiplicity and diversity, in our system *bhedabuddhi*, the intellect that legitimizes *difference* is referred to as *avidya*. Why? Why should we rise from *bheda*, difference, to *abheda*, non-difference? Bhartrhari asks us to think about it. Or as Plato while addressing his disciples in *Cratylus*, recalls what Heraclitus says: 'Everything is in a flux. There is nothing to be known and there is no knowledge'. 'I am too old to investigate this', says Plato to his students and asks them to 'go out into the world. Find an answer. If you get one, come back and tell me'. In the same way one posits Bhartrhari's statement – *ekatvabuddhisarvavadavirodhini*. *Ekatva* is superior because it is opposed to no *vada*. It is in opposition to no *vada*, no point of view – it is a grand synthesis or tolerance if you please. But today divisive ideologies and conflict models hold a sway.

Modernity has in this way altered or affected the modes of thinking of the educated Indians who are role models or trendsetters of our society. The ontological man-centred world view and the imperative of progress have shifted for us, as they did for the West, the focus of individual life and sociopolitical theory to the *promotion of comfort and material well-being*. It is almost the Utilitarian pursuit of pleasure, this official philosophy. It is almost as if the *Carvakas*, the *Lokayatas*, are back in full form.

As a consequence, there is a visible value-collapse.

(*a*) Our society has always had a time honoured balanced framework of the four ends of life – righteousness (*dharma*), material well-being (*artha*), fulfilment of desires (*kama*) and freedom from worldly bonds (*moksha*). Our worldview required an equilibrium to be maintained in these four. Today, the brackets of righteousness and freedom have been removed.

(*b*) *Niyama* was a key concept of Indian life. *Niyama* is a concept from *Mimamsa*. It is best translated as *norm*. It means that if there are two ways of doing something, one of them is to be preferred. If I am thirsty, I can shout at someone and demand water – that is one way; the second way is to ask gently if I can have some water – which is the preferred way of asking for it. If you are hungry you can feed your appetite with anything but you are told 'eat this, not this' (*niyama*). It is a governing principle of all aspects of life from dress to food to actions. When in my childhood I used to go out with my top shirt button open, my mother used to say – 'Tie up this button'. Even now, though I like it open, when I go to the class, the first thing I do is to tie this shirt button. Compare this with two kinds of nakedness – one that I saw in Singapore in public and the other of a Jain Digambara ascetic. One is naked, the other is not. The other *you see* as naked; he is not naked. But the other ones are naked because they want to be seen naked. Freedom without norms, self-willed expression, linguistic or physical, is becoming a part of public life. In all the four ends of life, *purushartha*, *niyama* was the overarching principle. It is no longer so – travel in the train, go to a public place, have an evening walk in the lawns or gardens, it hits you the absence of *niyama*.

(*c*) The third key value of Indian life is sanyama or sanjam. It is best translated as restraint, self-control. I used to be told that if I have hunger for three chapattis, I should eat two. If something is very delicious I should eat it less than what I would normally do. So in earlier days the richest man in the locality and the poorest wore the same dress, spoke the same language and ate substantially the same kind of food. Today, one speaks Panjabi, the other English; one wears expensive cotton trousers or jeans, the other his *tahmat* or pyjama; one eats chapatti, the other chicken. There is unrestrained display of what one possesses and unrestrained consumption. Self-indulgence, and not sanjam, rules our lives. Some people say these are the values of a poor people; others say these are the values of a happy people.

(*d*) The fourth value is *dharma* in the sense of enjoined duty, *niyata karma*. The essence of *dharma* is to think about others and not about oneself when deciding on any course of action. The key question in Indian philosophy has been how to be happy (contrary to the understanding that Indian philosophy is very metaphysical), *dukhnivritti*. The answers are as diverse as the systems. One important School, *Mimamsa*, says, do the enjoined duty, your *dharma*. One of the later answers is the one that Krishna gives to Arjuna when he asks him to transcend this opposition between the self and the other and to do his allotted duty for the welfare of the people – *niyata karma* – for *loksamgraha*. The whole structure or network of human relationships is founded on the key concept of *duty* as against *rights* in the Western society and in our Western-inspired constitution. Duty is a parameter that places equal disabilities on all men and all women. It sustains the family network and the larger network of human relationships – it is an ancient system, the family, and the *biradari*, and its survival over thousands of years is the proof of its value as necessary conditions of human happiness.

The theory of *rights* is inimical to human relationships. A *right* is directed towards your own self. Therefore 'rights' is in the conflict mode. Rights are always in the conflict mode, just as the notion of progress is in the conflict mode, because you progress by shedding the 'garbage', you clean up and let only the best and the clean to survive. Against 'rights' our culture's driver is *duty, dharma*. The eldest son in our families does not think of what he wants for himself; he always thinks of what he has to do for his parents and for his brothers and sisters. And he does not become neurotic by doing that, by not bothering about his own rights. Duty is directed towards the other; therefore it is in the harmony mode.

But our political system, our Constitution, contrary to the genius of our society is based on the rights and enunciates the fundamental rights but duties are only in the directive principles. It should have been the other way round which would be more in tune with our drivers.

But the way things are, our institutions, family etc., are already showing strain under the impact of the theory of rights. The Joint Family, a time-honoured Hindu institution, the guarantee of social security of the old and the infirm, has already practically broken down, and the other cardinal institution, marriage, is under palpable thoughtless legislation and so-called liberalism.

(e) The fifth time-honoured value is reverence, *shraddha*, for objects, people and relationships. It is a very valuable, almost indispensable individual and social principle that provides psychic stability to individuals and social stability to the community. It is a principle of loyalty and as such it is almost an aesthetic principle as the artist in the Indian tradition is a *sadhaka*, a devotee who manifests the unmanifest, gives *rupa* to *dravya*. For him, beauty is not something pertaining to form, something of appearance, but beauty is in the object to which your mind attaches itself with *reverence*. It may be your old grandmother. She is beautiful because your mind attaches to her with such reverence. It is the quality of reverence that in the socio-economic framework is opposed to utility. So you had a Lambretta and now you have graduated to Mitsubishi Lancer. But the Lambretta still stands in your courtyard – 'We have seen very good days. The Lambretta has made me what I am'. This is loyalty, this is reverence and this is beautiful. We don't dispose of things and people when they are no more of use to us. So there is no anxiety or fear that one will be abandoned.

But in the new order of freedom and self-fulfilment (*not* self-realization), things and people suffer from in-built tiredness with staying on with something too long.

We are also headed that way and at the end of it let no one say that we took a 'road not taken'. It is a much-travelled road. The Western society had moved far on this road, and though 'going over is as difficult as coming back', the Western society is in the beginning of a U-turn.

What facilitates the dispose off economy and dispose off society is the modern explanatory psychology that explains all failures and wrong doing either on the society or on the circumstances and the wrong doer and one who fails to be loyal is never held responsible – 'Ah, you see he comes from a broken home', they say. But the Indian *Karma* theory squarely holds the agent/instrument responsible for the act and allows no getting away from responsibility.

But this inhibits *freedom* and freedom is the key word. However, it is no ontological freedom of the will; it is the freedom to gratify one's senses and one that is indifferent to any moral responsibility to others or to the society. In ultimate terms it becomes an argument for unbridled sexuality – witness the 'intellectual' and 'social activist' attacks on models of monogamy: Rama, Sita and Savitri. Unbridled sexuality loosens the hinges of the social order, of the institutions such as the family. This abandonment of the ethical frame of reference weakens and finally destroys the values and basic social conventions that have existed since time immemorial. These values have determined the nature and quality of human relationships especially the family and gender roles that gave coherence to society. Those relations lose their authority and force. A vacuum is left for the new order has not put in place any alternative set of values. In this onslaught of modernity, traditional socio-religious beliefs and practices that were valid until recently are overcome by untested belief in power, money and freedom to indulge. These are transient pleasures meaningless in the long run when age sets on one self and one is left alone and without friends or companions.

If happiness is the goal of life, and one agrees with Aristotle that it is, then one has to evaluate the new ideologies and social modes in that light. In this frame of unbridled sexuality women are more vulnerable and pay a higher price. This unbridled sexuality is more harmful when the institutions of family and marriage are weak or are growing weak. We see in our times all kinds of non-conventional modes of living together designed for transient pleasures and satisfactions. This is also in tune with the consumer economics, the 'use and discard' economy. Nothing endures about these relationships. And when the core family has dissolved, there is no question of any larger network of relationships or social roles. In this framework, the woman loses her bio-social identity as a mother or as a wife and there is no question of any larger meaningful identities.

The denial of what are, in fact, bio-social roles intrinsic to womanhood has no substance. It is easy to argue that these are just empty words.

The Indian context is totally different. The Hindu family is recognized by sociologists the world over as a recognizably different and a vibrant institution, recent change nonetheless – sociology texts devote separate chapters to this institution. The Hindu family structure extends in varying degrees, depending on the intensity of Western influence, to widening concentric circles of relationships. Both men and women therefore have complex identities in terms of these human relationships besides the identity they may have or claim in terms of their profession or personal achievement. As much honour attaches to the achievement of excellence in these bio-social roles as to professional roles and there is individual, collective and psychiatric evidence that these bio-social roles well-performed yield deep satisfaction and are important, perhaps necessary, components of happiness. Talking of the conceptual method of functional relationship or role definition, Yaska, the ninth-century BCE semanticist, gives the example of the same lady being identified as mother, daughter, wife, sister, *bhabhi, mausi, chachi, nanad, mami, bhua*, and so on. The existence of innumerable kinship terms in the Hindu social system – and their absence in the West – tells its own story of cultural density in the area of human relationships. For an average adult Indian, there are infinitely many answers to the question 'Who am I?' And this applies to both men and women. This over-identification, if one may use the term, has a deeply useful psychic-moral effect of curbing your *ahamkara*, of taking the focus away from your own self and enabling you to seek satisfaction by doing things for others.

So the bio-social roles are very real and substantial and are not just linguistic constructs. Their reality is ensured by the concomitant conduct, acts and expectations and the deep sense of identity they provide.

Again, India has handled sexuality differently. Its reality and its power have been more explicitly recognized than in any other culture (no other culture has a *sastra* devoted to it) and no other culture has honoured sexual union as our culture has done (witness its place in temple sculpture). But from reality of the urge to an honoured fact of life, there is a movement through a rigorous ethical framework, both institutional and general. Sex is an appetite and its gratification, like that of other appetites such as hunger, has to be regulated as is required by the general Indian philosophy of self-imposed restraint and abstemiousness (*sanyama*). Again, unlike other appetites, its gratification has social, beyond-the-individual consequences. Therefore apart from the personal, there is the need for social regulation. And the Indian sociological thought therefore restricts sex to marriage and procreation. 'I am also the sexual desire attended by a desire to procreate', says Sri Krishna to Arjuna. These constructs are deep-rooted and immanent and provide the necessary strength and character to the institutions of marriage and family, violations notwithstanding.

Therefore as one sees it, the most damaging cultural change in recent times is the one that has affected the institution of Family. The breakdown of the joint family system has had deleterious effect on our relatively stable social framework and has reduced that much the quantum of human happiness in the Indian society. To recall an old poem:

'Ill fares the land, to hastening ills a prey/Where wealth accumulates and men decay'.

As we begin to boast of our rapid economic development, our enlarging GNP and our becoming the second largest market, we should repeat to ourselves Carlyle's the Spirit of the Age question – 'Is the wealth of a nation the happiness of its people?'

The Centre also does not remain the same in the long run. The dynamics of colonization and what is happening to Europe now – the weapon (of thought, liberalism) turning back on the propounder. Don't we have another Frankenstein's monster on the table? Proto-explanatory models are the Lord Shiva–Banasura legend and the Pauranic narrative of *rakta-bijarakshas*.

There were civilizations that focused on the mind, such as the Greeks, civilizations that focused on conduct, such as the Confucian Chinese, and civilizations that focused on the self, such as the ancient Hindu. The contemporary civilization is built around the *stomach* – let us hope it will move away from the gullet and the gut.

References

Arnold, Matthew. 1869. *Culture and Anarchy: An Essay in Political and Social Criticism* (First Edition). London: John Murray Publishers Limited.

Macaulay, Lord. 1930 [1836]. 'From a letter written by Lord Macaulay from Calcutta on October 12, 1836 to his father Mr. Zachary Macaulay', in V. Downs and G.L. Davies (eds), *Selections From Macaulay. Letters, Prose, Speeches and Poetry*. London: Methuen and Co. Ltd.

Sri Aurobindo. 1997. *The Ideal of Human Unity* (vol.25), in *The Complete Works of Sri Aurobindo*, pp. 516–19. Pondicherry: Sri Aurobindo Ashram,

Selections From Macaulay. Letters, Prose, Speeches and Poetry. 1930. Edited with Introduction and Notes by E. V. Downs and G. L. Davies. Methuen's English Classics. Methuen and Co. Ltd. London.

2

THE RETURN OF THE SILENCED ORAL

Culture and study in our time

G. N. Devy

Colonial taxonomies

Since the times of Sir William Jones, major attempts have been made to propose and formulate conceptual categories for describing the bio-cultural diversity and knowledge traditions in India. The corresponding process of decolonization, too, has produced attempts at synchronization of traditional knowledge with the colonial production of knowledge within the context of the Western modernity. While the clash as well as collaboration between what is seen as knowledge compatible with the western cognitive categories and knowledge traditions rooted in the lives of predominantly oral communities continue to occupy the imaginative transactions in India, the mainstream institutions of knowledge – such as schools, universities, hospitals, courts, etc. – have acquired forms that often leave out the complexities involved in the 'great transition of civilization in the Indian sub-continent'. This situation poses an intellectual challenge that thinkers in the 21st century need to negotiate. Probably, the most important among the cognitive categories that continue to carry the stress of this 'transition in civilization' belong to the field of creative expression in language and language description. Decolonization of Indian Aesthetics and Indian Linguistics, without an obscurantist turning back entirely to the past, is the larger task at hand for the contemporary Indian intellectual, attempted several times over but not yet accomplished. In the recent times, there have been moves towards opening the question of descriptive categories in relation to language and orality. I intend to analyse the nature of the problem and discuss the possibilities of proposing an approach relevant to cultural and ecological contexts in India from the perspective of my direct engagement with the struggle of the adivasis and the nomadic communities in India.

The changed epistemology of language

In the pre-colonial epistemologies of language, hierarchy in terms of a 'standard' and a 'dialect' was not common. Language diversity was an accepted fact of life. Literary artists could use several languages within a single composition, and their audience accepted the practice as normal. In most of the celebrated literary classics of ancient India followed this practice. Great works like the epic *Mahabharata* continued to exist in several versions handed down through a number of different languages almost till the beginning of the 20th century. When literary critics theorized, they took into account literature in numerous languages. Matanga's early medieval compendium of styles, *Brihad-deshi*, is the most outstanding example of criticism arising out of the principle that language diversity is normal. During the colonial times, many of India's languages were brought into the print medium. Previously, writing was known and numerous scripts were already used for writing. Paper too was used as a means for reproducing written texts. However, despite being 'written', texts had been circulating mainly through the oral means. The print technology diminished the existing oral traditions. New norms of literature were introduced, privileging the written over the oral and bringing in the idea that a literary text needs be essentially monolingual. These ideas, and the power relation created by the colonial context, started affecting the stock of languages in India. The languages that had not been placed within the print technology came to be seen as 'inferior' languages. After Independence, the Indian states were created on the basis of languages and are known as 'linguistic states'. If a language had a script, and if the language had *printed* literature in it, it was given a geographical zone as a separate state within the Union of India. Languages that did not have printed literature, even though they had rich tradition of oral literature, were not given such states. Further, the State official language was used as a medium of primary and high-school education within a given state. Similarly, a special Schedule of Languages (The Eighth Schedule) was created within the Indian Constitution. The Constitution is divided into several parts such as the Preamble, Fundamental Rights, Articles, and Schedules. One of the Schedules, the eighth one, contains a list of languages to be used for administration. It is generally described as 'the Eighth Schedule of the Indian Constitution'. In the beginning, it had a list of fourteen languages. At present, the list has twenty-two languages in it. It became obligatory for the government to commit all education-related expenditure on these languages alone. The 1961 Census of India had a list of 1652 'Mother Tongues'. In the figures of the next Census (1971), the figure was substantially reduced, and only 108 languages spoken by more than 10,000 were officially acknowledged. Thus, nearly 1500 'Mother Tongues' were silenced. Most of these languages are spoken by nomadic communities and the indigenous communities. Most of these languages are on way to a rapid extinction, if they are not already gone. The 'Margins' of Indian literature, coming from the Indigenous peoples and the nomadic communities, are thus marginalized mainly due to the 'Aphasia' being systemically imposed on them.

Marginalization and aphasia

The existential pathos of the peoples whether identified from outside, or through self-identification as 'marginalized, minority, indigenous', has common features in all continents. The indigenous have been facing deprivation and dispossession of their natural resource base, denial of access to quality education, healthcare, and other citizenship rights, and have come to be seen as 'a problem for the development project of modernity'. Going by any parameters of development, these communities always figure at the tail end. The situation of the communities that have been pastoral or nomadic has been even worse. Considering the immense odds against which these communities have had to survive, it is not short of a miracle that they have preserved their languages and continue to contribute to the astonishing linguistic diversity of the world. However, if the situation persists, the languages of the marginalized stand the risk of extinction. Aphasia, a loss of speech, seems to be their fate.

It may not be inappropriate to assume that people all over the world are paying a heavy cost for a 'global' development in terms of their language heritage. This linguistic condition may be described as the condition of 'partial language acquisition' in which a fully literate person, with a relatively high degree of education, is able to read, write and speak a language other than her/his mother tongue, but is able to only speak but not write the language she/he claims as the mother tongue.

Between the collective consciousness of a given community and the language it uses to articulate the consciousness is situated what is described as the 'worldview' of that community. Preservation of a language involves, therefore, respecting the worldview of the given speech-community. If such a community believes that the human destiny is to belong to the earth and not to offend the earth by claiming that it belongs to us, the language of that community cannot be preserved if we invite the community to share a political imagination that believes in vandalizing the earth's resources in the name of development. In such a situation, the community will have only two options: it can either reject the Utopia that asserts the human right to exploit the natural resources and turn them into exclusively commercial commodities or it can reject its own worldview and step out of the language system that binds it with the worldview. It takes centuries for a community to create a language. All languages created by human communities are our collective cultural heritage. Therefore, it is necessary to ensure that they do not face the global *phonocide* let loose upon the world.

The emergent voice

The first decade of the present century is marked in Indian literature by the emergence of the expression of the voice of the indigenous communities. Throughout the first decade there has been a remarkable manifestation of this voice through little magazines in various languages. Previously, the literary creativity of the indigenous communities came to us solely through the recordings made by anthropologists, linguists and folklorists. Besides, the translations through which the folklore was rendered were largely unreadable. Perhaps, the only exception was of the works by Verrier Elwin. In a way, the imaginative life of the 'janajatis', as the official term likes to describe them, or the adivasis of India has remained inaccessible to the rest of India.

The social isolation and marginalization of the adivasis began during the colonial times. When the Portuguese arrived in India they developed a descriptive apparatus for referring to Indian communities by coining the term 'tribe'. The term was drawn from ancient Roman practice of describing the speakers of peripheral languages as 'tribes'. The British refined the concept further and started using the term only for those communities that did not show state formation as the central feature of social organization. Understandably, these 'tribes' were the forest dwellers, untouched by capital economy and without urbanized habitat. In the 1870s, communities singled out by the colonial British were enumerated and a list of Indian tribes was created. Another list pertaining to nomadic communities was drawn up as the list of Criminal Tribes (1871). As the colonial rulers had inadequate understanding of the nomadic sections of Indian working classes and pastoral communities, they came to be branded as 'criminal' resulting into the Criminal Tribes Act (CTA) of 1871. The CTA was perceived by the colonial rulers as a reformatory measure, but for the branded communities, it resulted in untold misery and injustice. Prior to the colonial intrusion in the life of these communities, they had a close engagement with the rest of the Indian society in terms of cultural production. Many of India's major dance styles originated among them. It is believed that an epic like the *Ramayana* was composed by a forest dweller; and as far as the origin of fiction writing in India is concerned, it is a historical fact that the *Ocean of Stories* or *Katha-saritasagar* of Gunadhya was written in Paisachik, or what the colonial British would have described as a tribal language. This dialogical cultural relation was snapped forever due to colonial anthropological engineering.

During the early part of the 20th century when the Dalits started registering their voice in Indian literature, the adivasis kept themselves entirely within the confines of their oral tradition of epics, stories and songs. In fact, it took a sympathetic observer like Verrier Elwin to articulate on behalf of the adivasis, for they themselves remained quiet. Even after Independence, the fiction of the adivasis had to find expression through the writings of Gopinath Mohanty and Mahasweta Devi, who were tremendously sympathetic to the plight of the adivasis but were not adivasis themselves. It is in this context that Malayalam author Narayan's *Kocharethi* acquires a tremendous historical significance. *Kocharethi* written in 1988 and published in 1998 in Malayalam is decidedly the first tribal novel in India. Indian literature has reason to celebrate the work not only as the first tribal novel but also as a remarkable literary achievement. It is important both as history and as literature. It is even more important to look at how it paves the path for emerging voices of adivasis all over the sub-continent. In our times, when the larger society is content with looking at the adivasis as perennially marginalized, and when the state is in a way demonizing the discontent among the adivasis, Narayan no doubt has accomplished the important work of building a bridge much needed and hence most welcome.

In the amazingly rich tapestry of Indian literary creativity, an important strand has been the lyrical and dramatic traditions of adivasi communities and the picaresque narratives constructed by the nomadic communities. If the visibility of tribal languages has remained somewhat poor, those languages need not be blamed for the want of creativity. The responsibility rests with the received idea that literature in order to be literature has to be written and circulated in a printed form. In most cases the literary works in the languages of India's adivasi communities have been oral in nature. The number of languages in which Indian tribal communities have been expressing themselves is amazingly large. After the print technology started impacting Indian languages during the 19th century, the fate of the oral became precarious. A gross cultural neglect had to be faced by the languages which remained outside the print technology. The reorganization of Indian states after Independence was along the linguistic lines. The languages that had scripts came to be counted for. The ones that had not acquired scripts, and therefore need not have printed literature, did not get their own states. Schools and colleges were established only for the official languages. The ones without scripts, even if they had stock of wisdom carried forward orally, were not fortunate enough to get dedicated educational institutions. It is in this context of gross neglect that one has to understand the creativity in the languages of India's adivasi communities.

Just as the initial construction of histories of the ancient and modern Indian languages was carried out by the colonial scholars engaged in Asiatic studies, the initial portrayal of the adivasis and their literary traditions comes to us through the works of Verrier Elwin. From 1932 to the very end of his life, Elwin spent over three decades living among the adivasis, serving them, learning their languages and culture, documenting oral traditions, preparing policy documents, advising the Government on tribal issues and writing about them. The turbulent years of the freedom movement and the world war formed the backdrop of Elwin's work. After arriving in India, Elwin did not return to England for any long spells, and all these other sides of his life increasingly kept becoming far less significant for him in comparison to his profound attraction for the tribal communities and his deep emotional ties with them. He liked to describe his life philosophy as the philosophy of love:

> Love and duties it imposes is the real lesson of the forest . . .
> Among very poor and exploited people there was the need to

maintain those imponderable values that give dignity to the life of man; to restore them their self-respect, the feeling of being loved . . . There was the need for reverence, reverence for all life. (*The Oxford India Elwin* 2008: 348)

It was the sequential unfolding of his many-sided love for the adivasis through an intimate engagement with them that led to Elwin's production of such mighty works as *The Baiga, The Agariya, Maria Murder and Suicide, Folk-Tales of Mahakoshal, Folk-Songs of Chattisgarh, The Muria and the Ghotul, The Tribal Art of Middle India, The Myths of Middle India, Songs of the Forest, Folk-Songs of the Maikal Hills, Leaves from the Jungle* and *The Aboriginals and Bondo Highlanders*. Had Elwin's style possessed no literary charm, had his prose not reflected an alluring personality, had he not lavished such profound love on the communities that he researched, and had he not belonged to an exciting era, even then just the wealth of information that Elwin's numerous works contain would have made his contribution phenomenal. His involvement with them went far beyond an anthropological dedication, aesthetic fascination or altruistic community work.

However, Elwin's works were all in English, and while they made an impact on the government's 'tribal' policy, they did not result in initiating any 'adivasi language movement'. Some four decades ago, when Dalit literature started drawing the nation's attention towards it, it was usual to include adivasis and nomads among them as part of the Dalit movement. In Marathi, for instance, Atmaram Rathod, Laxman Mane and Laxman Gaikwad, who were from nomadic tribal communities, were seen as Dalit writers. At that time, the north-east was no more than a rumor for the rest of India.

During the early 1990s, I decided to approach the languages such as Kukna, Bhili, Gondi, Mizo, Garo, Santhali, Kinnauri, Garhwali, Dehwali, Warli, Pawri and so on, expecting to find at the most a few hundred songs and stories in them. As a beginning of the work, my adivasi colleagues and I launched a series of magazines in adivasi languages. These languages included various sub-groups of the Bhili family and a couple of languages of nomadic communities such as the Bhantu spoken by the Sansis and the Gor-Banjara spoken by the Banjaras. I was quite surprised by the popularity these e-magazine acquired in a very short time. Not only did they attract a large number of contributors from the respective speech communities, but the copies sold in large bulks. Within a few years, a community of adivasis and nomads deeply interested in creative writing and documentation of oral traditions in their own languages emerged out of this experiment.

Having documented over a ten thousand printed pages with the help of the newly emergent literary community of the adivasis, publishing a dozen magazines and fifty odd books containing tribal imaginative expression, I am now aware of how painfully little of the vast literary wealth my humble efforts have managed to tackle. If a systematic publication programme were created to document tribal literature in India, easily several hundred titles can be launched containing the oral traditions. The story does not end there. In the recent years, the adivasis and the nomads have taken to writing. A few of the languages such as Santali and Mizo had previously created their orthographic conventions; in the recent years, many more adivasi languages such as Gondi and Bhili have devised their own scripts or resorted to the state scripts.

During the last twenty years, various tribal voices and works have started making their presence felt. Thus, *Kochereti* from Kerala and *Alma Kabutri* from the north surprised the readers almost the same time when L. Khiangte's anthology of *Mizo Literature* and Govind Chatak's anthology of Garhwali literature appeared in English and Hindi translation, respectively, making it possible for me to bring out *Painted Words* (2002), an anthology of the literature of adivasis and nomads. The last two decades have demonstrated that tribal literature is no longer nearly the folk songs and folk tales. It now encompasses other complex genres such as the novel and drama. Daxin Bajarange's Budhan Theatre in Ahmedabad has been producing thought-provoking plays, modern in form and contemporary in content. Little magazines such as *Chattisgarhi Lokakshar* and *Dhol* started appearing during these decades. There is now a greater understanding among tribal activists all over the country that tribal identity and culture cannot be preserved unless the tribal languages and literature are foregrounded. Over the last four decades, a mainstream writer like Mahasveta Devi has been writing on behalf of the tribals. That situation has changed now. The voice of the tribals themselves is now beginning to be heard.

Literature as resistance

The colonial disruption of cultural history left the social fabric changed considerably. Old professions that were seen as useful during the course of the early phase of colonialism started being seen as menacing, harmful professions during the post-1857 years. For

THE RETURN OF THE SILENCED ORAL

example, the soldiers of the defeated princes marooned to their isolated existence came to be seen as dangerous to the state. Many such groups were brought under a common law by the British. In 1871, the colonial government passed an act called The Criminal Tribes Act (CTA).

Coin making, traditionally, was not a prerogative of the state. It was outsourced because kings changed very frequently. Currency stayed fairly stable in medieval and ancient India. The coin makers came to be seen as doing something illegal and were brought under the purview of this Act. They were described as 'counterfeiters'. The 'hijras' were traditionally trained to guard the royal harems. They too were covered by the CTA. Not all of them were *criminal* by habit or occupation. Special 'settlements' were created for keeping these communities in detention.

The colonial town planning provided for the 'city', the cantonment with the civil lines and the military barracks, and beyond the cantonment, the settlement. The 'criminal communities' were restricted to the settlement areas. They were taken to work sites in the morning, in handcuffs or tied with ropes, and likewise brought back in the evening. Their labour was unpaid in most instances. Somewhere along the history of the settlements, the assumption that not just some individuals in the community but the entire community is criminal crept in and became an accepted social stereotype.

There was of course the other part of the Indian society involved in the freedom struggle, modernization through English education, in developing agriculture and acquiring upper caste social status, moving from villages to cities, and building the modern Indian nation. All those communities, too, started viewing these people as born criminals. From 1871 to 1924, when the last modification of this Act came about, 191 communities were brought under the purview of this Act, beginning with the North-West Frontier and going up to the Nizam's state in the south. In 1952, these communities were finally 'freed' through the annulment of the CTA. When the earlier notifications were annulled, these people came to be known as the 'denotified communities'. Most of them had been nomadic in habit in the past. They were wandering singers, entertainers, rope-walkers, snake-charmers, medicine men, and such others. Because they were nomadic in habit, they came to be known as the denotified and nomadic communities or tribes, very different from the Adivasis. So for short we now call them the denotified tribes (DNTs).

In 1952, when they came out of the settlement, after about 70 years of imprisonment, several generations had passed from the time of their initial branding. By the time they became 'free', they were fully stigmatized. The communities outside had been looking at them as 'criminals', and in the textbooks of the police academy, they were listed by caste and community names as the are criminal tribes. So a whole field of knowledge was built round this wrong notion that everyone in these communities is a 'born criminal'; these are the people who kidnap children and sell them, the ones who engage in theft and illegal activities. The earlier Criminal Tribes Act had been replaced by what is known as the Habitual Offenders' Act. 'Habitual Offenders' Act' is the title of an Act implemented in various Indian States. It allows the police to bypass the normal criminal investigation procedures in the case of a person brought under police scrutiny more than three times within a given period. The police took advantage of this act and criminalized innocent people who wanted to come out and educate themselves, get into some profession. Not having land, they had to learn a variety of new professions. The total population of such people in India is at the most conservative estimate 6 crores.

In Purulia, West Bengal, there was a custodial death of a young man called Budhan in 1998. Budhan was born on Wednesday (*Budhwar*), hence his name. He was not a criminal but was taken to the police custody, beaten up and then kept as under-trial prisoner for a few days where he was further tortured. He died in the prison cell there. The police and the jail officials tried to depict his death as a suicide. But the piece of cloth, the *gamcha* with which he reportedly tried to hang himself didn't belong to him. Mahashweta Devi had filed a case in the Calcutta High Court seeking compensation for Budhan's widow. The Calcutta High Court gave a favourable judgement in this case. When the case was being heard in the Kolkata High Court in the meanwhile Mahashweta Devi had come to Baroda for a lecture. She spoke on denotified tribes, with pain in her heart, tears in her eyes. Some of us felt very deeply moved by what she said and we decided to form a Denotified and Nomadic Tribes' Rights Action Group in June 1998. A few weeks later, the Kolkata High Court judgement came. In these intervening weeks, she and I had made a journey to Chharanagar in Ahmedabad, a *busti* of the Kanjar community that has come up in and around the former settlement for 'criminal tribes'. There, we got a group of young people together and set up a small library. Bhupen Kakkar, the painter joined us in this. He came and inaugurated the library. Noted film-maker Kumar Shahani came and read out literary takes there.

Thus, many artists and writers started going to Chharanagar where a group of Chhara young men and women started interacting with them. When the judgement came out, I decided to print the entire High Court judgement in a magazine which I had started under the title *Budhan*. Inspired by the text of the court judgment, the young boys in Chharanagar decided to create a play based on Budhan's life. They were not professional or trained actors but the production became effective as it was the story intimately related to the life of their own community. When I saw the production for the first time, I was so deeply moved that I decided to invite some other writers and artists from Ahmedabad to view the play. This play was then staged in various cities, such as Bhopal, Delhi, Hyderabad, Bangalore, and Bombay. Somebody made a video show and it was taken to the United States of America. It was produced there by some Americans. And somebody in St. Xavier's College in Bombay decided to produce the English version of 'Budhan'.

When I put together an anthology of tribal literature and literature of the denotified communities, I decided to include a written version of this play in English translation. That went out to a few other countries and it was produced. When all this was happening, we had been building committees of people among the Chamtas, Vadis, Vispadas, Turis, Dafers, Bajnaias, Dauri Gosawis, and such other communities. In Baroda, about 4–5 km from Chhani, one Bhikabhai Bajana was caught by people in the society, tied to a tree with a rope, beaten to pulp and he died. When I saw the news, I asked the police if they were investigating the case and found out that they were not. So I had to go and sit on a 'dharna' outside the Police Commissioner's office. Finally, after several days, the Commissioner agreed to visit the place incognito. He came in plain clothes with me to visit the Bajania area and the place where the murder was committed. Subsequently, the killers were arrested. But in the process, the 'Bajania' wanted to celebrate their little victory and they called up one evening, with drums and singing 'bhajans'. Then I started taking other people to listen to their songs of joy.

These committees of different communities that we had made, I noticed, were exhilarated and inspired by any artistic activity. They responded very spontaneously to dance, song or drama – a performance. So we decided that we should bring all of them together to watch each other's performances of this agony. We were looking for a suitable place in Gujarat. I didn't want everything of the song and the story to be transcribed and printed. I wanted to go about it in a slightly different manner. We located a place called Kaleshwari in Panchmahals, which is an archaeological site and since it is called Kaleshwari, derived from *kala* meaning art, the art element is also present. This place was not used by any other religion or ritual. So we decided to call the communities to Kaleshwari for expressing their performative and literary skills. A few thousand artists were present there – people walking on ropes, playing with drums, dancing, bringing all kinds of musical instruments with them. They came and performed throughout the day in the Kaleshwari campus. Next year they went there again. Fifteen years later, they still keep going to Kaleshwari to express their 'imaginative' energies, their 'literature', their culture.

The future of cultural studies

Gradually, the Kaleshwari 'mela' also became a place where charters of people's demands started getting drawn. A few of these were presented to various district officers, the state government and the national government. In 2006, the Government of India appointed a National Commission and a Technical Advisory Group to look into the condition of the DNTs. The Budhan Theatre and the Kaleshwari mela had a major role to play in the creation of the National Commission. All this partly as the expression of art, drama, literature, song, music was coupled with a human rights campaign.

In our time, the potential of 'culture' as a means for mobilizing the 'voiceless' needs to be seen differently than one used to view the 'agit-prop' literature of the mid-20th century. This is particularly necessary as the nation state has ceded most of its ground to the market forces. Even if the Constitutional guarantees exist in letter, the state itself is passing through a very severe identity crisis. And its ability to deliver the substance of the guarantees is less than guaranteed. Therefore, creating spaces for the cultural presentation of the marginalized through art, literature and human rights awareness becomes all the more necessary. When a faceless, completely concealed agency starts governing our destinies, not through elections or parties, but through the use of high-age technology and very advanced, complicated legal structures which are beyond the understanding of the common man's grasp, the 'silenced oral' cultures people have to be at the front line facing the 'structured genocide'. If, somehow, the great cultural diversity can be kept alive, the impact of the devastation can be reduced. Therefore, in our time, culture study must necessarily verge on activism in favour of conserving and promoting cultural diversity. Probably, the desire for theorizing can be kept on hold in the interest of keeping the 'subject' of cultural study alive. The discipline should neither move closer to history nor to theory; it needs the force of passion that goes into reforestation of the hills and planes. Revitalization has to be our approach to 'study' culture.

References

Devy, G. N. 2002. *Painted Words*. New Delhi: Penguin.
Narayan. Tr. Catherine Thankamma. 2011. *Kocharethi*. New Delhi: Oxford University Press.
The Oxford India Elwin. 2008. Introduction by G. N. Devy. New Delhi: Oxford University Press.

Part II

CULTURAL STUDIES AND LITERARY STUDIES

3
THE RELEVANCE OF CLASSICAL INDIAN AESTHETICS FOR CONTEMPORARY CULTURE STUDIES

Saugata Bhaduri

One of the lines of query that a seminar on 'Cultural Studies in the Indian Context' can lead us into is how classical Indian aesthetic theories and propositions may be relevant to the discipline of culture studies in general and with regards to contemporary popular culture studies in particular. An initial speculation in this direction can yield some ready answers. I can think of three 'obvious' lines of connection between classical Indian aesthetics and contemporary popular culture studies. First, there can of course be an 'instrumental' connection, where classical Indian categories like *rasa, bhāva, dhvani*, etc. may be used as critical tools to analyse certain texts of contemporary popular culture. A second and less instrumental, but equally obvious, connection may lie in the fact that the classical Indian tradition was, in its articulation and circulation, primarily 'oral' in nature, and the focus in contemporary popular culture studies is also often on non-literary, extra-literary or para-literary modes of discourse, with orality being one of its major areas of inquiry. A final and more categorical connection can lie in the fact that within the classical Indian tradition a lot of emphasis has been put on the *loka* – with the *laukika* being an oft-repeated topic of discussion in the tradition, *lokadharmī* texts being considered as appropriate subjects of academic deliberation and the *lokāyata* being one of the primary branches of classical Indian philosophy – and this paradigmatic engagement with the folk or the popular may well make classical Indian aesthetics fit to accommodate within it a study of popular culture. However, like all things obvious, if these three points alone were to constitute the connection between the two, the link indeed would be rather tenuous, and probably not able to withstand the load of the two heavy universes that hang on either side of its slender fabric. There is a need therefore to go beyond the three points made earlier – the oral nature of the classical Indian tradition, the focus in it on the *loka* and the possibility of using its analytical categories – as the sole grounds of connecting classical Indian aesthetics to contemporary popular culture studies, and look for how instead of these generalities, the very ontological and methodological bases of the latter may have strong resonances in postulations of the former.

Talking of the ontology of culture studies in general, and popular culture studies in particular, the most salient feature that strikes one is its multimedial character – that multiple cultural forms can be studied under this one rubric – as opposed to the monomedial focus of insular disciplines like literary studies, performance studies, visual culture studies, film studies, etc. More importantly, and especially within popular culture studies, the catholic possibility of this feature has two theoretical implications. First, it follows that within the domain of the discipline, everything can be potentially read as 'culture', a presumption that itself has two corollaries. Culture studies presume that everything is 'cultural', and the classic distinction between nature and culture is a specious one. It is not that certain things are 'natural' or 'real' and certain identifiably textual entities alone are 'cultural'; everything, even material objects that populate our lived universe are valid as objects of culture studies – there is nothing that falls outside the purview of 'culture'. The second corollary of the first implication is that, furthermore, there is nothing sacrosanct within the definitional parameters of this all-encompassive category of 'culture'. For culture studies, and especially popular culture studies, any object is potentially an art object if the context labels it as such, if certain conventions or certain modes of institutionalization decide that it is indeed so. Some common examples would be how kitsch, found objects, objects of everyday use, even Duchamp's inverted urinal or bottle-rack – any object in short – can become legitimate cultural objects if and only if there is a consensual owning of the same by some school, some stylistic establishment. Of course, this is not novel to contemporary culture studies, though it may have been significantly accentuated by postmodernist positions on art. From as early as Kant at least, Western aesthetics has let it be known that the definitional onus of what is art

THE RELEVANCE OF CLASSICAL INDIAN AESTHETICS

cannot be left to the vagaries of the essentially subjective experience and assessment of the individual viewer alone; aesthetic judgement truly appears, an object actually qualifies as an art object, when its subjective appreciation becomes objectively consensually agreed upon by a convention-sharing collectivity, when the 'synthetic', so to say, becomes 'a priori'.

Very interestingly, this first implication of the ontology of culture studies, and both its corollaries elaborated previously, have significant resonances in classical Indian aesthetics. Talking of the first corollary, that everything is potentially cultural, that there is nothing that can be seen as natural and outside the purview of culture, one cannot but recall what Bharata (indeterminate dates, but before fifth century CE) says in verse I.116 of his *Nāṭyaśāstra*:

> *na tat-jñānaṁ na tat-śilpaṁ na sā vidyā na sā kalā*
> *nāsau yogo na tat-karma nāṭye'smin yat-na dṛśyate* (Bharata 2001: 7)
>
> there is no knowledge, no craft, no discipline, no art, no skill, no work, which does not fall within the purview of *nāṭya* (translation mine)

Evidently, for the very founder of classical Indian aesthetics everything can thus be potentially interpreted as belonging to the domain of culture (*nāṭya*, literally 'drama', being but a metonym for all cultural forms within the tradition).

Similarly, as for the second corollary explained earlier – that any object qualifies as an art object, provided it follows certain conventions and gets acknowledged as belonging to an established mode or style – one can note some strikingly similar observations within classical Indian aesthetics. For instance, Vāmana (eighth century CE) talks in his *Kāvyālaṅkārasūtra* of *prayogikā*-s or conventions that an object must follow to qualify as 'art'. Before him, Bhāmaha (seventh century CE) had already discussed in his *Kāvyālaṅkāra* the notion of *rīti*, or established stylistic modes or schools which an object must adhere to and be accepted by to qualify as art. It can be noted, though it may not be very significant for our current discussion, that for Bhāmaha, there are two *rīti*-s, the Gauḍīya (east-Indian) and the Vaidarbhī (central Indian), to which Vāmana adds a third, the Pāñcālī (north-west Indian) and suggests that works of art have to necessarily correspond to the precepts of these different schools. In fact, Daṇḍin (late seventh–early eighth century CE) goes a step further in his *Kāvyādarśa* and says that belonging to a *rīti*, or *mārga* as he calls it, is the primary essence and defining feature of art, being thus the founder of the *mārga* mode of aesthetics, or that to be considered an art, an object, any object, must adhere to and be identified with a school or a set of established stylistic conventions.

One can now move on to the second implication of the primary ontological feature of culture studies in general, and contemporary popular culture studies in particular, that for it, the erstwhile distinction between 'high' art and 'low' art collapses, and rather than the former alone being worthy of academic engagement, the latter – the popular, the profane – also gets admitted legitimately into the hallowed portals of scholastic discourse. The classic Kantian distinction between mechanical art, agreeable art and fine art – and the hierarchy amongst them as the lowest to the highest form of art – simply does not hold for the multimedial and pluriformal field of culture studies. Rather than restricting itself to studying austere and serious forms of art alone, culture studies dares to foray into the non-serious, the inutile, the Dionysian, the marginal, the merely entertaining. Interestingly, in classical Indian aesthetics, in a similar vein, equal validation has been given to both the high canonized forms and the odd, the marginal, the queer forms of art. For instance, Kuntaka (early 11th century CE) shows in his *Vakroktijīvita* how cultural texts belonging to both the *sukumāra-mārga* and the *vicitra-mārga* are equally legitimate as objects of aesthetic reflection. Of course, more importantly, entertainment has been put a far greater premium on in classical Indian aesthetics than instructive or even realistic art, putting it more in consonance with popular culture studies, but more of that later, at a more appropriate place in this article.

Let me move on to methodological features of culture studies, which also have two major implications. First of all, culture studies, through innovations of Raymond Williams's 'cultural materialism', tell us that rather than the mimetic presumption of art being merely an inert and passive 'reflection' of pre-existing social conditions, one needs to talk about art in terms of 'affect', or how art brings about, constitutes and negotiates those very conditions. The focus accordingly shifts in culture studies from what art 'is' – the content of the art work – to what it 'does' – the effects it causes. This in itself also has two methodological corollaries. First, cultural texts start getting read as 'ideology', or that rather than representing truthfully what is 'real', art creates 'illusions' that convince the viewer of its reality – the classic Marxian thesis of ideology as 'false consciousness', the Althusserian suggestion that ideology constitutes 'false representations of real relations', whereby, as Gramsci would put it succinctly, the hegemonic function of power legitimizing itself through consensus building would work.

Second, this implication also entails that methodologically, the focus in culture studies would shift from 'realistic' modes of representation to 'stylization', because ultimately if art is not a true representation of reality but an illusion aimed at affect, it is not its reality quotient but the stylistic devices it adopts to pretend to be real that count more.

The second implication of the methodological shifts that culture studies bring about in the ways we look at texts is what may appear to be at contradistinction with the ideological point made earlier, but is indeed but an extension of it. The ideology thesis entails that while culture becomes the means through which a power structure perpetrates its sway by indoctrinating the masses and making them internalize and consent to its forms of normativity, it is precisely through culture itself that counter-hegemonic forms can be generated, leading to resistance to and subversion of the norm. This becomes especially crucial for popular culture studies, where the focus shifts from studying texts as austere documents of the times, bearing within them marks of the order of the day, to studying them as potentially disruptive and subversive organs that, through their Dionysian foregrounding of enjoyment, can undercut and challenge the austere Apollonian norm. The shift in methodological focus in popular culture studies to entertainment rather than instruction being the prime function of art, transgressing rather than upholding the norm being the more cherishable purpose of culture, is what I have in mind here. Methodologically, contemporary popular culture studies enable us to read the popular *qua* the popular, nay it even suggests that enjoyment is a category that we need not brush under the carpet of highbrow instructive academicity, but actually cultivate as the prime goal of art.

Needless to say, these features also find resonances within certain postulations of classical Indian aesthetics. Coming to the first implication first – that the focus in reading a cultural text shifts in culture studies from the content of the work to the effect it creates in the reader/viewer/audience's mind – it can be easily noted how the pre-eminent category of aesthetic analysis in the classical Indian tradition is *rasa*, or the effect created in the spectator, rather than any of the formal or contentual elements of the work itself. More specifically, if we move to the first corollary of this first methodological implication – that rather than being a slice of reality, art operates through illusion, by convincing the viewer of its reality – we can find direct references to similar theoretical propositions in classical Indian aesthetics. For instance, Bhaṭṭalollaṭa (ninth century CE) clearly says that art is of the order of illusion, and it works by convincing the viewer and almost cheating him into believing it is real. Though Abhinavagupta (11th century CE) refutes this view in his *Abhinavabhāratī*, in suggesting that it is not that the spectator is dumb enough to be really conned into believing that a work of art is indeed real, but that he consciously, knowing fully well that it is 'art', participates in the aesthetic process, surely this is not as resounding a refutation of the 'illusion' thesis, as is Abhinavagupta's rejection in the same breath of Śrī-Śaṅkuka's 'imitation-inference' theory. Śrī-Śaṅkuka (ninth century CE), whose work, like Bhaṭṭalollaṭa's, is not extant any more and is known only through Abhinavagupta's refutation of him, suggests that works of art are imitations of reality and the aesthetic act lies in the viewer being able to infer what they represent. Abhinavagupta resoundingly proves that it is quite to the contrary, and that the prime function of art is not imitation of reality, as indeed is not it getting inferring as such.

The second corollary of the first methodological implication of culture studies elaborated earlier – that the focus, therefore, is on stylization rather than realistic reflection – has even more vocal takers in classical Indian aesthetics. Bharata says that there are two kinds of plays – *prakaraṇa*, or realistic plays that describe real-life incidents, and *nāṭaka*, or stylized plays with imaginary content – and he proposes that the latter is the superior form of drama. Similarly, he suggests that there are two kinds of acting – *anukaraṇa*, or the mimetic mode, and *anukīrtana*, or the adulatory, celebratory, stylized mode – and, once again, for him the latter is superior to the former. Similarly, Mammaṭa (mid-11th century CE) says in his *Kāvyaprakāśa* how *citra-kāvya* or mimetic, realistic poetry is the most inferior form of poetry. As I stated earlier, since in classical Indian aesthetics, *nāṭya* and even *kāvya* are metonyms that do not signify drama or poetry alone but can stand for all art, it is clear that for the tradition, much like contemporary culture studies, stylization as a mode of representation is preferred over mimetic realism. Furthermore, the focus in the tradition, by Bhāmaha to begin with and by Kuntaka in great detail, on *vakrokti* – literally, deviant or crooked statement – as the very essence of art, further highlights how deliberate stylization rather than realistic representation is what classical Indian aesthetics values in art. Coming to the second methodological implication – that the primary function of art is 'entertainment' that can transgress and subvert the norm, rather than 'instruction' that upholds the norm – one can again see what sort of a premium is put on the same in classical Indian aesthetics. The origin myth of *nāṭya* that Bharata narrates is a case in point here. Bharata tells us that the gods invented the art and taught it to him to be passed on to humankind so that people could entertain themselves at the end of their tiresome days and relieve their stress and boredom. Thus, rather than having the austere function of being instructive, the purpose of art in the classical Indian tradition is to provide entertainment. What is also interesting is the direction in which art flows according to this myth – from the gods to the humans, from the sacred to the profane – the purpose of art thus not being of human beings trying to propitiate the gods above them, but the gods trying to amuse the mortals – a transgressive reversal indeed. The entertaining function of art is best borne out in verse I.114 of *Nāṭyaśāstra*:

duḥkhārtānāṁ śramārtānāṁ tapasvinām
viśrāntijananaṁ kāle nāṭyametad bhaviṣyati (Bharata 2001: 7)

To the ones troubled by sadness, hard work, self-castigation,
At the instant of giving birth to relief, *Nāṭya* thus happens
(translation mine)

There could not have been a bolder statement as to the rather mundane task of art – to provide relief through entertainment to tired, bogged down souls.

While I have already discussed the resonances of both ontological and methodological features of contemporary culture studies in classical Indian aesthetics, and thus the relevance of the latter for the former, this chapter would be incomplete if I did not issue at the end a few words of caution, things that one should be careful about while engaging in such a comparatism. Lest we presume that every category of classical Indian aesthetics suits the agenda of contemporary culture studies, we should note how there are important divergences between the two. First, while contemporary culture studies focuses majorly on dissensus, discordance and diversity, classical Indian aesthetics is often caught up with models of concord, homogeneity and unity. The

Sanskrit word for 'literature', or for art in general, following the metonymic logic presented earlier, is *sāhitya*, literally meaning 'togetherness' (*sahit* means 'together', *sāhitya* is its nominal derivative), and the stress therefore is on the perfect balance and stable unity that must be established in art between *śabda* and *artha* – form and content – with there being no scope for fault-lines, fissures, dissonant open ends, that contemporary culture studies so looks for in texts. The model of togetherness or *sāhitya* is extended in classical Indian aesthetics to the relationship between the text and the reader too, so much so that Ānandavardhana (ninth century CE) says in his *Dhvanyāloka* that the aesthete has to be a *sahṛdaya*, or sharing one's heart with, totally in empathy with, the work of art. This surely compromises the possibility of any subversive, against-the-grain reading, which is so often the cherished ethics of much of contemporary culture studies. Second, classical Indian aesthetics puts a lot of premium on *aucitya*, or 'propriety', with it being suggested as an absolute requirement for an object to qualify as art, first by Ānandavardhana and later in greater detail by Kṣemendra (late 10th–early 11th century CE) in his *Aucitya-vicāra-carcā*. Evidently, with popular culture studies often focusing on texts that may be considered 'improper' by many codes of propriety, this insistence of classical Indian aesthetics may not aid the cause of culture studies much. Third, while contemporary culture studies encourages us to take up for analysis marginalized, subjugated, delegitimized texts, classical Indian aesthetics often argues – as in Vāmana's suggestion that only *vivekin*, or discerning, poets need to be taught, or Abhinavagupta's suggestion that not everyone can be a *rasika*, or an appreciator of art – that only certain poets and certain readers are capable of participating in the aesthetic process, a far cry from some of the democratizing bids of contemporary culture studies. Finally, and most significantly (also because this is the ground on which our comparatism began), the history of classical Indian aesthetics shows that it began in the para-literary domain of *nāṭya* or dramaturgy, but it soon got appropriated, almost exclusively, to the literary discourse of *kāvya*, thus posing a challenge to its applicability to something that is as definitionally multimedial and trans-literary as the discipline of culture studies.

In the final analysis, it should be also understood that like any exercise in trans-historical and trans-cultural comparatism, there may be a danger in the current exercise, of being appropriated into a resurgent nativism that may have some legitimacy in certain academic circles, or

THE RELEVANCE OF CLASSICAL INDIAN AESTHETICS

falling prey to the usual suspicion on the part of the other circles of being nativistic, especially when one attempts to talk about anything 'Indic'. An exercise like the current one has to state it objectives clearly, and there could not be a better note to end it on. An attempt like this has to steer clear from the possibility of it being construed as a jingoistic statement in how Indian sages had thought of all this centuries before 'Western' critics could theorize them, and that we are therefore the original cradle of civilization, and so on and so forth. The objective has not been to establish that classical Indian aesthetics has in any way influenced or been a predecessor to contemporary culture studies, but rather to show how one – conversant as one is in both traditions – can find very interesting resonances between the two. And, herein lies the second and more important danger that one has to steer clear of – the squeamishness or political discomfort that one often has in dealing with things that are classical Indian in origin, under the threat of being branded a regressive obscurantist by virtue of just doing that. The most avid postmodernist or Marxist in the West is not shy of delving into the treasure trove of his or her Graeco-Roman philosophical heritage; in fact his or her theorizations will more often than not be contingent upon the same. We as an intellectual nation are not likely to make any significant contribution to knowledge if we have to be caught between the two extremes of either, in the name of modernity or secularism, eschewing our classical knowledge systems altogether, or delving in it with a clearly nativistic, supremacist agenda. The need is to avoid both of these reductive approaches and rather make a progressive and radical cultural ethic emerge that is not ignorant of but rather draws from one's cultural past. This attempt to look at how classical Indian aesthetics may be relevant to contemporary culture studies is nothing more than such an effort.

References

Abhinavagupta [*Abhinavabhāratī*]. 1997. *Abhinavabharati: Abhinavagupta's Commentary on Bharata's Natyasastra Chapter-XXVIII*, trans. and ed. by *Anupa Pande*. New Delhi: Raka Prakashan.
Anandavardhana and Abhinavagupta. 1990. *The Dhvanyaloka of Anandavardhana with the Locana of Abhinavagupta*, trans. by Daniel H.H. Ingalls, Jeffrey Moussaieff Masson, and M.V. Patwardhan, ed. with an introduction by Daniel H.H. Ingalls. Cambridge/London: Harvard University Press.
Bhāmaha [*Kāvyālankāra*]. 1970. *Kāvyālankāra of Bhāmaha*, trans. and ed. by *P. V. Naganatha Sastry*. Delhi: Motilal Banarsidass.

Bharata. 'Nāṭyaśāstram Adhyāya 1' (in Sanskrit). 2001. Encoded by Padmakar Dadegaonkar. Web. http://sanskritdocuments.org/all_pdf/natya01.pdf. Accessed on 28 February 2012.

Bharata [Nāṭyaśāstra]. 1950. *The Natyashastra of Bharata Muni*, trans. and ed. by Manomohan Ghosh. Calcutta: The Asiatic Society.

Daṇḍin [Kāvyādarśa]. 2004. *Mahākavi Daṇḍī's Kāvyādarṣaḥ*, trans. by Premachandra Tarkavagisa, ed. by Kumudranjan Ray and Subhash Jain. New Delhi: Oriental Book Centre.

Kṣemendra [Aucitya-vicāra-carcā] in *Minor Works of Kshemendra*, trans. and ed. by Shrinivasa Varakhedi, et al. Hyderabad: Osmania University Sanskrit Academy, 2009.

Kuntaka [Vakroktijīvita]. 1961. *The Vakrokti-Jīvita: A Treatise on Sanskrit Poetics by Rājānaka Kuntaka*, trans. and ed. by Sushil Kumar De. Calcutta: Firma KLM.

Mammaṭa [Kāvyaprakāśa]. 1967. *Kāvyaprakāśa of Mammaṭa with English Translation*, trans. by Ganganath Jha. Varanasi: Bharatiya Vidya Prakashan.

Vāmana [Kāvyālaṅkārasūtra]. 2005. *Kavyalankarasutra Vrtti of Vamana*, trans. by K.K. Raja. Chennai: Kuppuswami Sastri Research Institute.

4
POPULAR CULTURE STUDIES IN INDIA TODAY
Issues and problems

Simi Malhotra

The objective of this chapter is to see what are the issues and problems in doing popular culture studies in India today. To begin with, in order to examine the academic category of popular culture studies in the contextual parameters of India, one has to necessarily examine at least four categories or aspects. The first of these four aspects concerns the very category of 'popular culture' itself and its attendant terminology. The second of these aspects would be the ontology of popular culture studies and consequently the protocols of including/ excluding 'texts' within the ambit of popular culture studies. The third aspect worth exploring in this context would be the methodologies or approaches adopted while practising popular culture studies today, while the fourth category would entail examining the ethics of doing popular culture studies in India today and exploring its implications for us. In this chapter, I will take up each of these above categories one after the other and try and outline the issues and problems associated with them.

The first of these problems has to do with the term 'popular culture' itself, which is a problematic compound construction in itself. The term 'culture', which is etymologically related to cultivation, stands in opposition to 'nature'. This opposition between 'culture' and 'nature' is well documented: culture or cultural is often seen as contrived, non-organic, even manufactured, full of artifice, which puts it in opposition to what is otherwise thought of as natural, organic. If in this so-called opposition between 'nature' and 'culture', one were to presume for nature all that is autochthonous and organic, and for culture all that is contrivedly non-organic, it still does not help us make a distinction between what is art and culture on the one hand and what is science and technology on the other. For often, science and technology, which is also contrivedly non-organic, is presented in opposition to all that is art and culture. Moreover, there is a further problem with the term 'culture' – how does an individuated subjectivized expression of culture come to stand for and cohere into a collective expression of culture. Therefore, the question that arises is whether culture inheres in the individual or in the collective. If it inheres in the collective, what route does it take from the individual enunciation to become a part of this collective? How is consensus achieved around 'culture'? How does this apparent consensus around 'culture' respond to potential fault-lines which may develop?

This problem gets further compounded, when one tries to think of the term 'culture' in the Indian context. Culture, as has been discussed above, etymologically stands close to cultivation. In Indian languages, the same sense would have ideally got resonated by the word *kṛṣṭi*, which would take it closer to *kṛṣi* or cultivation. However, in the Indian context, the term usually used is not *kṛsti* but *saṁskṛti*, derived from the word *saṁskāra*. *Saṁskāra* incidentally stands for the act of rectification or reform, and *saṁskṛti* thus for that which is rectified or reformed. As is evident, this use presumes for culture the role of being a corrective, if not being out-rightly didactic. This aspect of culture willy-nilly brings us face to face with the question of the very administration of culture and how culture becomes a tool to control and administer, to hegemonize. So much about the word 'culture'.

The term 'popular' is as contested, if not more. Morag Schiach's essay 'A History of the Changing Definition of the Term Popular' documents well the history of the term 'popular'. It traces how from its origins in legal and political discourse, the term comes to stand as a qualifier for culture, and how from its early use as a term which was used pejoratively, it becomes an acceptable one down centuries. Thus, the term 'popular' defies easy definition. There has been enough written about not equating 'popular' with numbers or assessing it numerically, or even equating 'popular' with the formulaic. Moreover, in the Indian context, the term used for 'popular' is *lokapriya* which implies being favoured by the public. But *loka* is a contested term itself because *loka* has the semantic baggage of the 'folk' and interestingly folk, more often than not, stands in contradistinction to what may be thought of as official or normative culture. This sense of the *loka* as counter-publics is not the sense conveyed by the term 'popular' which stands more on the side of affirmation than resistance. In fact, the term *loka saṁskṛti* as an Indian equivalent of 'popular culture' is an oxymoronic assemblage. Whereas *loka* may well stand for what is counter-public, *saṁskṛti*, as explained above, stands for what is didactic or corrective. This term therefore holds within itself both these competing impulses – of being counter-public while at the same time being prescriptive. Having thus problematized the term 'popular culture' itself, let me now turn to the issues related to the ontology of popular culture.

When one considers the ontology of popular culture in India, there are several problems which crop up. The first of these is that it is extremely difficult to talk about a shared common 'Indian culture', popular or otherwise. India being a multicultural, multilingual, multi-ethnic entity, it is rather impossible to think of a common set of shared texts as paradigm cultural texts which can represent it all. This poses a problem for the very subject matter of popular culture studies in India, since the paradigm texts are impossible to define. Moreover, unlike in the 'West', where theorizations on culture make a sharp distinction between high culture (or what may be considered as classical), folk culture (seen as autochthonously popular) and mass culture (seen as part of culture industry) – and this theorization is the key to defining the contours of the very discipline of culture studies itself – in India this distinction does not always hold.

In fact, India and many such countries, which have faced an epistemic violence because of colonial modernity, have had to grapple with this categorization itself. The epistemic violence may have rendered all that was high or traditional or classical into 'folk' in contexts such as ours. This process of delegitimation of cultures which various nations have had to suffer at the hands of colonial modernity multiplies the very problem of defining texts of culture. Colonial modernity often renders traditional native high cultural forms, emerging from institutionalized religions, into folk and equable with folk. This is not the experience of the 'West'. This issue gets further compounded by the fact that mass culture appropriates the high and the folk, without discriminating between the two, for its own ends.

Furthermore, the term 'Indian culture', because of its deployment by the political right in recent years, cannot be embraced without accompanying unease. One cannot but be conscious of the fact that 'Indian culture' has been deployed by the rightist forces in recent years and it has come to stand for many majoritarian, fascist, obscurantist tendencies of our times, if not being directly associated with upper caste Hindu culture of a certain kind. It becomes therefore difficult to sustain the term 'Indian culture' or *bhāratīya saṁskṛti* in a context such as ours.

Therefore, it is difficult to speak about popular culture ontologically in the Indian context, because India's multicultural fabric does not allow building a unified corpus of paradigm cultural texts. The multiplicity poses a serious problem in defining the objects of such an enterprise. Further, the tripartition of culture into traditional/folk/mass in the Indian context gets mediated and problematized by colonial modernity since it ends up delegitimizing various forms and treats them as the 'other' of modernity. Moreover, mass culture ends up subsuming both the classical and the folk, and therefore posing the question of resistance becomes more and more difficult. It is also ontologically difficult to speak about Indian culture because of the recent politicization of the Indian polity by *hindutva* forces. One has to be conscious of all these problems while dealing with popular culture studies in India.

One can now move to the third set of issues and problems related to the domain of popular culture studies in India that concern its methodology. No doubt there is a general mistrust of the Western colonial epistemic baggage, but what we need to grapple with is the question that, is taking recourse to imported epistemologies necessarily problematic. If so, how?

One of the modes of doing cultural analysis is the one practised by anthropologists or ethnographers, where culture becomes an object of scientific analysis, much as in Malinowski, where one draws upon the empirico-rational model to study culture. However, the adoption of such a model in the Indian context raises a problem. Is studying Indian culture using the method adopted by an anthropologist or ethnographer valid, or is it rendered problematic by the fact that the ethnographer here does not enjoy distance from the culture s/he seems to be analysing since s/he is embedded in it. Another method of cultural analysis, that of performing a socio-political analysis, much like the one adopted by the likes of Pierre Bourdieu has its own drawbacks. The chief being that it sees all expressions of culture as nothing but instruments of hegemonic power. This method has held sway for a fairly long time, right from statements about 'Culture Industry' by members of the Frankfurt School to the more pessimistic assertions by the likes of Jean Baudrillard or Paul Virilio. However, this needs to be revisited, especially in the Indian context, in the light of formulations such as 'dominance without hegemony' by the subaltern historiographer Ranajit Guha and others. Does culture as a tool of hegemony enjoy the same legitimacy in India as elsewhere? A third set of methods comprises those by Marxist cultural theorists such as Raymond Williams, who see culture as a potential tool of resistance or a site of counter-hegemony, and affirmative and optimistic takes by the likes of Marshall McLuhan, who see enabling potential in mass culture. However, in the Indian context, one would need to see whether culture enjoys such agency or not, the potential to operate as a tool of resistance or not. Furthermore, stepping away from the ethnographic and political critique, can one study the site of popular culture in India as a site of enjoyment? What pitfalls does such an analysis have?

Also, if one is generally suspicious of all that is imported from the West because it is removed from one's own context, one needs to be equally suspicious of evoking classical Indian aesthetic categories while studying contemporary culture since they too are far removed from one's context. Moreover, in the age of Globalization, where location itself is hardly a marker of rootedness, one cannot simply harp on colonial modernity but has to be more attendant towards current forms of imperialism and its impact on culture.

Finally, one must also examine issues related to ethics while doing popular culture studies in India. In doing popular culture studies in an Indian classroom, one needs to take into account the highly stratified, if not utterly disparate, social structure of the student body in such a classroom and its different levels of access to cultural capital. With policies of social inclusion being adopted more and more by Indian universities, which in itself is laudable, one needs to be mindful of the heterogeneity that makes for an Indian classroom today.

Furthermore, in India, popular culture studies does not enjoy the independently existing disciplinary space as it does in many other areas. Either it is part of the more manualistic training programme of a media studies department, or has a marginal position in an English department. Either way, it is treated rather suspiciously since it is often seen as part of the global academic machine which plays into the hands of global capital. Also a question is raised as to why do popular culture studies at all. Is it that in the face of utter redundancy, the humanities tries to find a foothold for itself by latching on to the latest fad? In the face of a legitimation crisis, is doing popular culture studies a bid by the humanities to somehow stay relevant?

In conclusion then, in this rather sketchy chapter, I have examined the issues and problems in doing popular culture studies in India, under four heads: those to do with terminology, ontology, methodology and ethics. Terminologically the Indian term for popular culture, that is, *lokasaṁskṛti* is rendered problematic because it at the same time espouses alterity, a counter-public, as it also does normativity. Ontologically, too, a multicultural India makes it difficult to arrive at a stable of paradigm texts of popular culture for study. Moreover, colonial modernity has sufficiently blurred the clear distinctions between traditional/folk/mass culture in the Indian context. Furthermore, 'Indian culture' is rendered politically problematic because of some elements of recent history and their fallout, making it a suspect object of study. Methodologically, the usual methods of field study (here, studying one's own culture), ideology critique (both of the hegemonizing kind as also of those espousing resistance), or being seen as an affirmation of globalization, or making a case for enjoyment, among others, are all questions that practices of popular culture studies in India today need to pay heed to. As does one need to ethically take into account the heterogeneity of our lived reality while doing culture studies and reflect on whether this current focus on popular culture is a mere survival strategy for humanities today. These are, to my mind, some of the preliminary problems and issues that we, who engage in popular culture studies, need to be cognizant of, especially in country like India.

References

Adorno, Theodor W. 1991 [1963]. 'Culture Industry Reconsidered', in J. M. Bernstein (ed.), *The Culture Industry: Selected Essays on Mass Culture*, pp. 53–92. London: Routledge.

———. 1981. 'The Schema of Mass Culture' ('Das Schema der Massenkultur'), in Adorno, trans. by Nicholas Walker, *Gesammelte Schriften III: Dialektik der aufklärung*, pp. 299–335. Frankfurt: Suhrkamp Verlag.

Baudrillard, Jean. 2001 'The Masses: The Implosion of the Social in the Media', in Mark Poster (ed.), *Selected Writings*, pp. 210–22. Cambridge: Polity Press.

———. 1993. 'The Work of Art in the Electronic Age', in Mike Gane (ed.), *Baudrillard Live: Selected Interviews*, pp. 145–51. London and New York: Routledge.

Bourdieu, Pierre. 1993. 'The Field of Cultural Production, or: The Economic World Reversed' (trans. Richard Nice, *Poetics*, vol. 12, nos. 4–5, 1983, pp. 311–56), in Randal Johnson (ed.), Bourdieu, *The Field of Cultural Production: Essays on Art and Literature*, pp. 29–73. Cambridge: Polity.

Guha, Ranajit. 1998. *Dominance without Hegemony: History and Power in Colonial India*, Cambridge MA: Harvard University Press.

Malinowski, Bronislaw. 1944. *A Scientific Theory of Culture and Other Essays*, Chapel Hill: University of North Carolina Press.

McLuhan, Marshall. 1964. *Understanding Media: The Extensions of Man*, London: Routledge and Kegan Paul.

Schiach, Morag. 1989. 'A History of Changing Definitions of the Popular', Chapter 1 in *Discourse on Popular Culture: Class, Gender and History in Cultural Analysis, 1730 to the Present*, London: Polity Press, pp. 19–34.

Virilio, Paul. 2000. *The Information Bomb* (*La bombe informatique*, Paris: Éditions Galilée, 1998), trans. Chris Turner, London and New York: Verso.

Williams, Raymond. 1961. 'The Analysis of Culture', in *The Long Revolution*, pp. 57–88. London: Chatto & Windus.

———. 1981. *Culture*, Glasgow: Fontana Chapterbacks.

5
POSTCOLONIAL CULTURAL STUDIES AT THE CROSSROADS
Theoretical approaches and practical realities

Rumina Sethi

In any discussion on cultural studies in India, it would be prudent to both narrow down the field a little to bring the focus on the postcolonial potential of cultural studies, and at the same time, widen the gaze so that one may look beyond India to other countries of the developing world. I am interested in examining postcolonial realities with particular reference to rapidly globalizing economies of the world. Even more significant is the other issue that I want to raise – how effective is postcolonial studies in the academy as a site of confrontation and intervention.[1]

I would like to begin by examining the meanings postcolonial studies has for us today: the trouble with postcolonialism lies in its indiscriminate application to subjects that would never be perceived collectively. Its original focus on colonial politics extends from issues of minority-ism under European rule to the hegemony of the US in turning the world global and from the marginality of women and blacks to the exile of those of us settled outside our nations.

For years now, postcolonial theorists have been occupied with finding alternatives to this ill-fitting nomenclature. The term 'postcolonial' has been under a great deal of scrutiny ever since it was used to include 'all the culture affected by the imperial process from the moment of colonization to the present day' (Ashcroft, Griffiths and Tiffin 1989: 2). Such an all-embracing definition not only posits colonialism as some sort of continuum with hazy beginnings and no end, but also places the literatures and politics of practically the whole world within its ambit. In the attempt to 'world' postcolonialism, an emphasis on border crossing and an inclusion of 'diasporic communities' and ethnic minorities was added (Williams and Chrisman 1993: 373). With the new imperialism of the superpowers, it seemed that colonialism's obituary had been rather prematurely declared.

At the outset, I would like to make certain terms quite clear: 'postcolonialism', to my mind, represents a philosophy, rather than just an academic discipline, that seeks to encourage radical politics and engagement with people's struggles, which includes the study of the history of colonialism that always exists as a reminder of anti-imperialist politics.[2] 'Postcolonial theory', on the other hand, has its own baggage and tends to get related to Western theories and is thus termed elitist by many people in academia. Having said that, it is not as though theory does not have its application in issues relating to almost every aspect of postcolonialism such as gender, race, migrancy, diaspora, nation, English studies and so on. Finally, 'postcolonial studies' is the discipline that has still not embraced many of the economic and political issues relating to postcolonialism largely because it is taught in the English departments of universities where emphasis on cultural studies is predominant (Loomba 1998: 40). As a discipline, it includes the study of postcolonial theory and postcolonial literature.

The institutionalization of postcolonial cultural studies began with the assertion of freedom and justice as witnessed in Sartre's preface to *The Wretched of the Earth*. The critique of the Enlightenment tradition cannot be any more incisive than when Sartre quotes Fanon: 'Europe has laid her hands on our continents, and we must slash at her fingers till she lets go' (1967: 11). Fanon, who worked for the Algerian resistance movement against France; Césaire, the West Indian poet, his fellow-companion who inspired him; Senghor, later President of Senegal, whose emancipatory statements urged activism among black people; Gandhi, who in India was leading the masses to a non-violent revolution against the British, are prominent spokespersons of the colonized cultures of the world and would become the foundational heroes of postcolonialism. Their best-known literary descendants today are Edward Said, Gayatri Spivak and Homi Bhabha whose writings and commentaries are regarded as intrinsic to what is known as colonial discourse analysis. Significantly, the inclusion of the cultural effects of colonialism within postcolonial studies becomes apparent by the late 1970s when 'post' begins to stand for more than simply the historical passing of time signifying 'after'. This coincides with the publication of Said's *Orientalism* which deals with issues of colonial representation and cultural stereotyping.

Following decolonization struggles across the world, the power of the US grew phenomenally, and so did the legitimacy of the monopoly of reason appropriated by institutions like the International Monetary Fund and the World Bank. Postcolonial studies, at this point, is regarded to have exhibited a marked complicity with the market economy by not making neoliberalism its target. Liberal capitalism, through the spread of multinational corporations, on its part, contributed a great deal in undoing the borders of nation-states. With the growth of market capitalism, postcolonial studies appeared to have a singularity of purpose: from the promotion of revolutionary pedagogy, it began to follow the trajectory of cultural criticism in its critique of nations and nationalisms. The demise of the nation, although in textbooks, bore the risk of taking away the very sentiment revolutionaries had fought for. The discipline of postcolonial studies, instead of pioneering a focus on historical Marxism underpinned by popular struggles of dissent in the third world, began to scrutinize the cultural aspects of issues of race, gender, class and, of course, the nation.

The turn in postcolonialism made redundant one of the most significant categories of identity politics – the nation. In academic curricula, the decline of the nation and the corresponding expansion of the metaphor of marginalization have led to the embrace of concepts like diaspora, hybridity, difference and migrancy, which are all related to the growth of a global economy and have come to be perceived as new configurations of dominance. The prioritizing of global capitalism over praxis corresponds with the waning of Marxism and Marxist studies. The success of information technology and the internet, the transnational corporations and the flows of global capital make us wonder where labour is currently located. Whereas labour and trade unions had been the primary focus of Marxist struggles, they are now lost in the maze of global exchange.

The triumph of globalization over labour and the nation, categories that were quintessentially significant to decolonizing struggles, has led to protests among the opponents of postcolonial studies who object that there appears no historical or materialist trajectory in such writing, just as there exists an enormous rift between its anticolonial 'intellectual antecedents' such as C. L. R. James, Fanon, Cesaire, Gandhi, Nyrere, Senghor, Memmi, Cabral and others and the more contemporary breed of intellectuals known as postcolonial theorists (Sharpe 2000: 109).

Postcolonialism is placed in a particular predicament today: it purports to be a liberatory practice but it is coeval with forms of domination particularly after its appropriation by the university curricula of the United States. The crisis results from its origins that are both political and historical – postcolonialism emerged out of struggles against colonization, and being part of that history, must confront authority and aggression. Today, the end of European subjugation does not imply the end of the existence of Western superpowers and their neocolonial tendencies. The increasing pressures of the West have led to the institutionalization of postcolonial studies in universities all over the world which is no doubt seen as a subversive discipline, but also perceived to be implicated in Western hegemony, particularly because of its compatibility with other contemporary theoretical approaches such as postmodernism and poststructuralism, a relationship that is used to trump up the apolitical nature of postcolonialism.[3]

Viewing the current condition of global capitalism and the rise of 'new' imperialism from the point of view of postcolonial writing, one is confronted by issues that draw attention to the fact that what started off as a deeply versatile discipline for introducing more activism into the academy ended up in mere codification, creating a schism between 'postcolonialism' and 'postcolonial studies'. The former, as explained earlier, is taken as a condition of living, a practice, a political belief or set of political beliefs that come into effect in a situation of oppression or marginalization and that can help counter that oppression through protest, resistance and activism; while 'postcolonial studies', and its accomplice, 'postcolonial theory', is a discipline that was set up to examine the literature of political protest and resistance among people of the third world but has come to represent university curricula that abounds in issues of hybridity and multiculturalism that is taught in elite institutions of the world. Although there are obvious limits to what literary studies can accomplish to change the new economic and political realities, these prescriptions are imposed, consciously or unconsciously, and hegemonically, through global pressures to fashion a university curriculum that blunts postcolonial sensibilities.

In fact, this issue can be taken up by identifying two camps – the Marxist and the postcolonialist. Marxism is linked to praxis whereas postcolonialism to textual analysis. Marxists are worried about the closeness of postcolonial studies to poststructuralism because, for them, the histories of colonialism, decolonization and freedom struggles cannot be separated from the all-important part played by the people. In other words, Marxists would like postcolonialism to be an instrument of people's politics. The postcolonial practitioners, on their part, consider postcolonialism as a necessary intervention in the dominant discourse of European humanism which stretches into contemporary globalism. What is common to both views is the platform across which their critical commentaries are mounted – that postcolonial thought as well as Marxism are Eurocentric having originated in the Western academy. Unfortunately both Marxism and postcolonial studies maintain a distance from each other to their mutual cost.

The academic manifestations of postcolonialism, predominantly postcolonial theory and postcolonial studies, can be criticized for developing right-wing tendencies and severing links with what was to be their responsibility after decolonization struggles, that is, to maintain an adequate historical representation of the condition of the formerly oppressed and support the creation of an equitable, anti-Eurocentric world through public-spirited debate rather than textual obscurantism. Postcolonial studies has received its strongest criticism as a result of its 'textualism' which disallows it from making an intervention in the real politics of the people through its academic methodologies. In their analysis, for example, both Bhabha and Spivak have tried to recover postcolonial identity by recounting cases of ambivalence or by articulating the simultaneous presence of sameness and difference instead of emphasizing historically specific acts of resistance. These 'acts' could include debates about movements resisting colonial powers, national integration movements or resistance to new imperial controls over recklessly globalizing economies. Postcolonial studies, by addressing representations of alterity and the ambivalent relations between centre and periphery, loses its historical-material reality and begins to exist merely in theoretical terms. As 'theory', constituting strategies of reading and textualism, sweeps aside the political expression of a transformative history, silencing the subalterns that need more than ever to speak, postcolonial studies leads to a marked disappointment among exponents of Marxism as it begins to rely more and more on poststructuralist methodologies. Bhabha's idea of the Self-as-Other and the Other-as-Self, both of which serve to make colonialism a very problematic category in which 'slippage', 'excess' and 'difference' between binaries cannot be easily dismissed (1994: 86), is convincing in many ways, but has provoked his critics to allege that if identity can be perceived only as a process of rapidly eroding self-images, how can identity be visualized at all? Where would one locate the politics of struggle and resistance which are necessary parts of decolonization movements? Instead of rejecting Marxist criticism, effort should be made to relate academic teaching with third-world societies and peoples' struggles so that it remains connected with the problems that emerged from the colonial encounter.

Outside the academy, local struggles continue in their specificity, but inside the academy, national identity and native locations are lost. By its very dismissal of foundationalism, postcolonial studies lose sight of the world of real events such as those real national struggles and local identities which it is worth every nation to preserve.[4] There arises, thus, an increasing rift between postcolonial *theory* on the one hand, which forms the vanguard of postcolonial studies, and what can be called postcolonial *practice* on the other. The former is underwritten by the 'high' theory of Derrida, Lacan and Foucault, incorporated by their disciples in the academy (especially Spivak and Bhabha) and the latter espoused by a host of others who condemn the encroachment of French theory into postcolonial criticism.[5] Real struggles have become so suspect that those who insist that terms such as 'nationhood' and 'Marxism', 'citizenship', 'constitutionality' and 'revolution' are acceptable even today are curiously not called 'postcolonial' critics even as they inhabit a postcolonial world.[6] Indeed, only those critics are 'postcolonial' who are also 'postmodern' (Ahmad 1995: 10).

The other issue I wish to draw attention to is the relationship between postcolonialism and global capitalism, the fact that postcolonial studies developed side by side with the growth of neocolonialism. Swept as it is by the wave of Western poststructuralism, 'postcolonialism' fails to counter imperialism in the guise of its new avatar, globalization, and with it tends to conflate the local experiences of particular countries with a sweeping postcolonial sensibility acquired by postcolonial theorists as they migrate to centres of the global corporate world (Dirlik 1994: 340). That postcolonial intellectuals, furthermore, promote 'multiculturalism' and 'cultural hybridity' is a sign of complicity in sponsoring postcolonial corporatism. Postcolonial studies in the US is evidently related with the growing ascendancy of a cultural studies programme and its own advancement as a global power by the end of the Cold War. As the politics of location is changed, so is the displacement of the Third World by the term 'postcolonial'. Correspondingly, it may be inferred that postcolonial intellectuals would be those who participate in the discourse of postcolonialism rather than those who actively pursue third-world concerns (Dirlik 332). Postcolonialism as a discursive construction, freed of its third-world location, is then easily transferred across the Atlantic to reside in the classrooms of advanced capitalist countries that have a homegrown postcolonial population of their own – the ethnic groups and migrants.

The disaffiliation with the third world not only releases postcolonialism from its commitment to anti-eurocentrism, but also marks a change in its orientation as third-world identity begins to reside in traces and transitions, diaspora flows and migrancy. Instead of originating in the third world, postcolonial studies has flourished in Britain, Australia, Canada, New Zealand and now the US. Having become global in its conceptualization, the 'third world' becomes a cultural category of Western academic criticism, thus making the distinction between postcolonial theory and postcolonial practice even more marked.[7] The Third World, which was a place where radical alternatives to the First World were available, develops contagion with the latter in its global give-and-take, leading us to say with Aijaz Ahmad that 'we live not in three worlds but in one' (1993: 103).

Yet those who live and practice in the 'real' postcolonial world are seldom part of the rubric of postcolonial studies. An even more devastating effect of the 'hybrid' version of contemporary postcolonial studies has been its utter neglect of the people. Its refusal to engage with the politics of the people leads to the charge of a collaborative intent between postcolonialism and globalization. Thus, Miyoshi writes:

> We witnessed a full-scale genocide in Rwanda as the world stood by. Many areas in the former colonies in Africa, Eastern Europe, the Middle East, Central America, the Indian Subcontinent . . . in short a vast majority of the world, are threatened with unmediated disorder resulting from overpopulation, poverty, and civil violence. Forsaken by the industrialized elites as unprofitable, the majority of humanity faces a bleak future. As we talk about postcoloniality . . . in metropolitan academia, we ignore those billions outside our ongoing discourse for whom life has nothing 'post' about it. (1997: 54)

In the same spirit, one can make a list of the aborigines in the Americas, the New Zealand Maoris, the child prostitutes in India, Thailand and other countries, the plight of the refugees in Africa, Chechnya, the erstwhile Yugoslavia, the Mayan Indians, the people of East Timor, and so on and question the commitment of postcolonial studies to the representation of the underprivileged of the less-advanced countries of the world.

As we can see, Marxists and postcolonial theorists have not been the best of friends. Where the former privileges actual historical struggles between two unevenly matched sides, the latter is hostile to its reductive vision, promoting instead the mutual contagion of binary entities. The logic of Marxist ideology is the presence of 'material unevenness' and the need to resist exploitation; the postcolonial approach is culturalist emphasizing 'the intermixing of cultures' whereby we may never be able to distinguish the exploiter from the exploited (Bartolovich 2000: 140). Although a definition of the postcolonial in terms of cut-and-dried closed categories would amount to doing great disservice to the interplay of politics and power relations in any given situation, it cannot be denied that the national urge remains that of unconditional freedom and pure origins. One look at the speeches of Nehru or Nkrumah can dispel the academic beneficence of cultural translation. Who can deny the power politics that still exist in the world between India and Britain, Grenada and the United States, or Palestine and Israel? Can India, Grenada or Palestine exist comfortably in the knowledge of mutual contagion? The global interchange between China and India, notwithstanding, the slightest build-up of arms on the Indo-China border immediately summons the categories of 'us' and 'them' even as Indian and Chinese academics write their scholarly articles on the 'transnational' politics of postcolonialism.

Theory undoubtedly remains an abstraction unless its proponents succeed in nudging it towards concrete instances of economic and social exploitation or at least in fashioning an agenda full of acts of resistance towards Western-dominated discourses. If postcolonial studies were released from 'theory', we might still have postcolonial moments that find correspondence with the world outside. In order to become interventionist, postcolonial studies per se does not need to become politically active; on the contrary, it should shed its 'thin' textualism in favour of 'a richer critical and historical analysis' (Loomba 1998: 42) that would contain questions of identity, struggle and change intermixed with the politics of our times. It is worth asking the question why the classroom cannot establish a connection with the real history of people or university teaching breed the kind of responsible intellectual Edward Said speaks of? Why do we have to deal with the so-called reality in literary studies today? Clearly, this has to do with the abiding link between postcolonialism and anti-foundationalism, a link postcolonial theory has done much to promote. If social, economic and political concerns are to remain at the heart of postcolonial studies, it needs to continuously struggle against the crisis introduced by rapidly changing teaching practices as much as by the rising cosmopolitanism of the world.

There has, correspondingly, been a pressure on postcolonial studies to illustrate its usefulness in the context of globalization against apologists of free-market economy and to take a passionate stance for the defence of the marginalized and the powerless. An important part of such an academic study would have to be its relatedness with political activity to the extent that it can become a medium that supports resistance movements across the world. Postcolonial studies, for example, must include a critique of the forces that prop up manufacturing units of Pepsi or Coke that prevent people from using running streams of water. There are voices that are growing against multinational seed giants who dictate which genetically-modified crops should be grown, and against US agribusinesses that regularly indulge in seed-tampering and patenting which affects natural farming all across the global south by preventing farmers from re-planting existing seeds cheaply. Few people realize that the Ganges itself has been privatized by the Suez, a global water giant, resulting in the suspension of all public water supply schemes by the government of India. In order to give 635 million litres of Ganges water to Delhi's elite, at least 100,000 people will be forcefully evicted from their homes owing to the construction of the Tehri Dam that will aid the venture (Shiva 2005: 78–79). More notably, in connection with the threat to land rights, the Zapatistas, Mexican rebels of the Chiapas highlands, revolutionized themselves into an army for 12 full days in 1994 fighting the Mexican government's strategies of *neoliberalismo* (Notes 2003: 22). In the real world, there are women who clung to trees and prevented deforestation (known popularly as the Chipko Movement).[8] There are other instances such as that of the tribals protesting on the banks of the river Narmada who were evicted by the construction of big dams or even that of the Maoist 'terrorists' of Chhattisgarh, who are presently militating against the mining of their forest land as hundreds of MoUs amounting to billions of dollars are being signed with transnational corporations. All of them, in their limited ways, are engaged in civil insurgency against their own state for speaking the language of global capital and endeavouring to reclaim their nation.[9] All such acts of dissent and activism against infrastructural projects initiated under the aegis of resistance to corporate globalization should be included in the term 'postcolonial'.

The concerns that have been outlined are real (rather than hyperreal) in the lives of marginalized communities of the postcolonial world. The inability to account for neocolonialism and the inadequacy in relating theory with actual resistance, thereby, become the shortcomings of postcolonial analyses.[10] To my mind, postcolonial critics will have to put their feet back on the ground and link the postcolonial once again to the political activism by which it has always been inspired. Too often, postcolonial studies has advanced as an academic discipline while remaining deaf to the roaring turmoil of global resistance to domination and exploitation. That struggle must continue, and if postcolonial critics are to align themselves with it, they must begin by returning to the place where the people dwell.

Notes

1. This chapter is a reworking of some of the views expressed in my book *The Politics of Postcolonialism: Empire, Nation and Resistance* (London: Pluto, 2011).
2. Young's definition in *Interventions*, a journal of postcolonial studies which is dedicated to understanding the implications of postcolonialism today, covers most aspects: 'Postcolonialism has come to name a certain kind of interdisciplinary political, theoretical and historical academic work that sets out to serve as a transnational forum of studies grounded in the historical context of colonialism, as well as in the political context of contemporary problems of globalization' (1998: 4).
3. In the 1995 'Afterword' to *Orientalism*, Said distinguishes postcolonialism as it-used-to-be from postcolonialism as it-has-evolved, having moved from the writings of 'distinguished thinkers as Anwar Abdel Malek, Samir Amin, C.L.R. James's to those of its more postmodernist practitioners, and from themes of struggle and liberation to a detachment from urgent political goals: 'The earliest studies of the post-colonial . . . were based on studies of domination and control made from the standpoint of either a completed political independence or an incomplete liberationist project. Yet whereas post-modernism in one of its most famous programmatic statements (by Jean-François Lyotard) stresses the disappearance of the grand narratives of emancipation and enlightenment, the emphasis behind much of the work done by the first generation of post-colonial artists and scholars is exactly the opposite: the grand narratives remain, even though their implementation and realization are at present in abeyance, deferred, or circumvented. This crucial difference between the urgent historical

and political imperatives of post-colonialism and post-modernism's relative detachment makes for altogether different approaches and results' (1995: 351).
4. For John McLeod, postcolonial theory has 'conceded too much ground by questioning oppositional discourses such as nationalism and Marxism *at the very moment* when we need these discourses more than ever to combat conflicts around the world' (2000: 252). The inverse is as true. As Young puts it: '[I]n practice postcolonial studies can be strongly foundationalist, grounded in an epistemology which gives primacy to an authentic historical reality (a position decisively mapped out in the founding text of modern postcolonial studies, Edward Said's *Orientalism* of 1978)' (1998: 7–8).
5. See Moore-Gilbert (1997: 1).
6. As Ahmad writes: '[Only] those critics, who believe not only that colonialism has more or less ended but who also subscribe to the idea of the end of Marxism, nationalism, collective historical subjects and revolutionary possibility as such, are the *true* post-colonials, while the rest of us, who do not quite accept this apocalyptic anti-Marxism, are not postcolonial at all' (1995: 10).
7. Eagleton defines two kinds of postcolonialisms: one that recognizes that most parts of the world had been colonized and that domination still continues in economic, if not political, ways; and the other which is affiliated to Western critical theory from where it takes its origin. He writes: 'For myself, it is not that there is no postcolonialism, rather that there is something called postcolonialism and . . . something called "postcolonialism" too. That is to say, there is obviously a lot of the globe which used to be colonized directly and is now colonized by other means, a distinction which involves (though it doesn't reduce itself to) one between the political and the economic. At the same time, there is a particular theoretical agenda known as "postcolonialism", which has its roots in a highly specific western intellectual history and is a much more controversial phenomenon altogether. The first kind of postcolonialism has the advantage of being fairly self-evident, along with the drawback of being blandly unarguable; the second kind reaps the benefit of contentiousness, along with the disadvantage of being more easily questioned' (1998: 25).
8. The Chipko agitation is associated with the Garhwal area of the Himalayas. In 1971, women courageously resisted the felling of trees by clinging to them, thus stalling the work of sawing and chopping. 'Chipko', which literally means 'sticking', was a means to this end. This led to a ten-year ban on the felling of trees.
9. As Arundhati Roy puts it, the areas infested with the Maoist rebels should be called 'MoU-ist corridor' and not the 'Maoist corridor' (quoted in Lakshman 2010: 9).
10. Said had pointed out as early as *Orientalism* that ' . . . an openly polemical and right-minded "progressive" scholarship can very easily degenerate into dogmatic slumber . . . ' (1978: 327). Young has also expressed anxiety over the rapidity with which postcolonialism is becoming

'stagnated' and 'reified' in its approach mainly because 'we have stopped asking questions about the limits and boundaries of our own assumptions' (1995: 164). This is not helped by the fact, as Moore-Gilbert indicates, that one of Bhabha's essays, 'The Postcolonial and the Postmodern' was published three times under three different titles in quick succession with scarcely a change, signalling an exhaustion. There is also very little textual dependence and cross-referencing between the three major critics of postcolonial theory – Said, Spivak and Bhabha (1997: 186–9).

References

Ahmad, Aijaz. 1993. *In Theory: Classes, Nations, Literatures*. New Delhi: Oxford University Press.
———. 1995. 'The Politics of Literary Postcoloniality', *Race and Class*, 36(3): 1–20.
Ashcroft, Bill, Gareth Griffiths and Helen Tiffin. 1989. *The Empire Writes Back: Theory and Practice in Post-Colonial Literatures*. London and New York: Routledge.
Bartolovich, Crystal. 2000. 'Global Capital and Transnationalism', in Henry Schwarz and Sangeeta Ray (eds), *A Companion to Postcolonial Studies*, pp. 126–61. Oxford: Blackwell.
Bhabha, Homi K. 1994. *The Location of Culture*. London and New York: Routledge.
Dirlik, Arif. 1994. 'The Postcolonial Aura: Third World Capitalism in the Age of Global Capitalism', *Critical Inquiry*, 20 (2): 328–56.
Eagleton, Terry. 1998. 'Postcolonialism and "Postcolonialism"', *Interventions: International Journal of Postcolonial Studies*, 1(1): 24–26.
Fanon, Frantz. 1967. *The Wretched of the Earth*, trans. by Constance Farrington. Harmondsworth: Penguin.
Lakshman, Narayan. 2010. 'Too much Representation, too little Democracy', *The Hindu*, 4 April.
Loomba, Ania. 1998. 'Postcolonialism – or Postcolonial Studies', *Interventions: International Journal of Postcolonial Studies*, 1(1): 39–42.
McLeod, John. 2000. *Beginning Postcolonialism*. Manchester and New York: Manchester University Press.
Miyoshi, Masao. 1997. 'Sites of Resistance in the Global Economy', in Keith Ansell-Pearson, Benita Parry and Judith Squires (eds), *Cultural Readings of Imperialism: Edward Said and the Gravity of History*, pp. 49–66. New York: St. Martin's Press.
Moore-Gilbert, Bart. 1997. *Postcolonial Theory: Contexts, Practices, Politics*. London: Verso.
Notes from Nowhere, ed. (2003) *We are Everywhere: The Irresistible Rise Of Global Anticapitalism*. London and New York: Verso.

Said, Edward W. 1978. *Orientalism*. London: Routledge.
———. 1995. 'Afterword', in *Orientalism*. New Delhi: Penguin.
Sharpe, Jenny. 2000. 'Is the United States Postcolonial? Transnationalism, Immigration, and Race', in C. Richard King (ed.), *Postcolonial America*, pp. 103–21. Urbana and Chicago: University of Illinois Press.
Shiva, Vandana. 2005. *Globalization's New Wars: Seed, Water and Life Forms*. New Delhi: Women Unlimited.
Williams, Patrick and Laura Chrisman (eds). 1993. *Colonial Discourse and Post-Colonial Theory: A Reader*. Hertfordshire: Harvester Wheatsheaf.
Young, Robert J.C. 1995. *Colonial Desire: Hybridity in Theory, Culture and Race*. London and New York: Routledge.
———. 1998. 'Ideologies of the Postcolonial', *Interventions: International Journal of Postcolonial Studies*, 1(1): 4–8.

6

DALIT AUTOBIOGRAPHIES IN THE PUNJABI CONTEXT[1]

Akshaya Kumar

The rhetoric of 'counter-aesthetics' or the polemics of 'subaltern historiography' did provide enabling critical take off to approach the rise of Dalit autobiography in its initial stages, but as the portfolio of this form of literature increases, it calls for a more nuanced and calibrated reading of its region- and language-specific character.[2] In this chapter, an attempt has been made to critically read Punjabi Dalit autobiography in terms of its distinct pre-and post-production politics, its culture-specific structural configuration, its corresponding sociological make-up, and more importantly its participatory/activist potential in Dalit mobilization in north-west India. Marathi Dalit autobiography, written primarily by the young Dalit Panthers, of course, forms the necessary critical baseline for it is in this language that this genre of self-expression makes its headway in a very substantial way.[3] Dalit Panthers radicalize the form of autobiography which had hitherto been spiritualized by the nationalist elite beyond human recovery.[4] Not only do they transform this into a genre of activist commitment with its threefold purpose of 'revolution', 'transformation' and 'liberation' of the low caste, but they also alter its very character.[5] From being a self-reflexive account of an achiever, autobiography in the hands of young Marathi Dalit writers becomes a broken, angry and vituperative account of the non-achiever, one who is perpetually defeated and even decimated. The fact that they choose autobiography as an authentic or a natural genre of the 'socially excluded/discriminated' constitutes in itself a major turn-about in the history of literature. It is against this backdrop that this chapter makes an attempt to evaluate Punjabi Dalit autobiography not just in terms of its distinct subject matter, but also in terms of its extra-textual implications.

Post-90s phenomenon

While chronicling the contribution of Dalits to the making of Punjabi discourse, Punjabi Dalit historians research back into the medieval past to track Dalits among writers. Rajkumar Hans in his article 'Rich Heritage of Punjabi Dalit Literature and Its Exclusion from Histories' traces 'Punjabi Dalit literary tradition' (2010: 73) from Bhai Jaita alias Jeevan Singh onwards, who composed a devotional epic 'Sri Gur Katha' on the life of Guru Gobind Singh around 1699–1700. Sadhu Wazir Singh (1790–1859), Giani Ditt Singh (1852–1901), Sadhu Daya Singh Arif (1894–1946) are other Dalit writers who form the Dalit tradition much before the arrival of Gurdas Ram Alam (1912–89), often hailed as first Punjabi Dalit poet. Hans merely considers the caste background of the writers, but is not at all concerned about their Dalit-consciousness. The fact of the matter is that Punjabi Dalit autobiography arrives on the critical scene only in mid-1990s. Here is a quick recount of the year of publication of various Dalit autobiographies. Lal Singh Dil's *Dastan*, Prem Gorkhi's *Gair Hazir Aadmi* and Balbir Madhopuri's *Changiya Rukh* were published around 1995; Gurnam Akida's *Kakh Kande* and Atarjeet's *Akk da Dudh* were published in 2007 and 2008 respectively. Giani Gurbakhash Singh Rahi's *Jini Rahi Mein Turiya* came in 2002.[6]

The rather late arrival of this form of literature in Punjab is indeed baffling because economically, demographically, culturally and historically, Punjabi Dalits enjoy a position which in a relative frame is much better than that of Dalits elsewhere in India. In terms of percentage, Punjab has the maximum SC population (about 30 per cent of the total population of the state), of which some sections had exposure to Western education during the colonial times. Mazhabis, for instance, were recruited in the British Indian army, and had separate regiment, later named as 'Sikh Light infantry'. During World Wars, they happened to have a first-hand experience of Western modernity. Such a concentration of Dalit population having awareness of the outer world gives Punjabi Dalits a clear advantage in the days of electoral politics. By virtue of their number, and also because of their political awareness, Punjabi Dalits, ideally speaking, always have a chance to dictate their terms in the political arena. It is not out of place to underline that Kanshi Ram, the founder of Bahujan Samaj movement, was a Punjabi Dalit Member of Parliament from Hoshiarpur. In terms of economic resources, Punjabi Dalits are definitely at disadvantage vis-à-vis other upper castes and middle-level castes of the state, but still there are pockets of relative Dalit affluence in Punjab. Doaba region of Punjab, which has a high concentration of Ravidasiyas, thrives with rare prosperity, thanks to large-scale migration of its low-caste youth to First World and Gulf countries.

The undivided Punjab, right from the days of pre-Partition, has witnessed some 'serious' movements aimed at the social amelioration of the Dalits in the region. From Ad-dharm movement led by Mangu Ram to present day dera-culture, Punjab has seen Dalit consolidation through what may be termed as quasi-religious mobilization. Dalits in Punjab therefore are not just contained to backwaters or that they are not cut off from processes of culture – be it sanskritization, Westernization or modernization. Punjabi Dalits, despite being victims of caste-biases, have never been as passive or helpless, as Dalits are in the rest of the country. Despite so much to speak in favour of Punjabi Dalits, Punjabi Dalit autobiography does not come about in a visible way. Even till date the total number of Punjabi Dalit autobiographies does not go beyond double digits.

While the chapters in the subsequent sections would unfold the micro-level reasons that can possibly account for the delay in the arrival of Punjabi Dalit autobiography, what is more pertinent to observe is that its sudden arrival in mid-1990s does correspond with some macro-level developments in Punjab and outside. One macro-level development that coincides with the arrival of Punjabi Dalit autobiography is the rise of bahujan politics in cow-belt, particularly Uttar Pradesh. The imperatives of identitarian politics along caste lines, which bahujan phase of Indian politics augmented in a very urgent way, seem to have its cascading effect on Punjabi Dalit literature, which hitherto mired or somewhat obscured by the Marxist rhetoric and begins to acquire patently casteist hues in mid-1990s. The availability of the translations of Marathi Dalit autobiographies in Punjabi and Hindi also opened new vistas of expression. Though it would be critically simplistic to surmise that Punjabi Dalit autobiography is not organic enough in its intent and experience, it is not remote to think that it models itself after Marathi Dalit discourse. In any case it seems to 'follow', historically if not structurally, Marathi Dalit autobiography.

Absence of non-writers as authors[7]

The question of authorship is central to the understanding of Dalit discourse. In strict fundamental terms, the authorship of Dalit writings has to be exclusively Dalit; and despite dissensions among Dalits, such a position has now been more or less accepted with a rider that the Dalit author must have a sense of caste-consciousness. Punjabi Dalit autobiographers fit in the frame for they do evince a degree of caste-consciousness. But still the issue of authorship remains highly skewed in case of Punjabi Dalit autobiographers because all of them, without exception, happen to be well-known writers, who publish in mainstream Punjabi journals and magazines. Gorkhi had published his stories, Dil had established himself as a poet, and Madhopuri had also made his place as a poet through his collections *Maruthal da Birakh* and *Bhakhda Patal*. Akida had a novel *Katal Hoya Hatth* (1995) to his credit, Atarjeet had published as many as seven collections of short stories and a novel besides a few edited volumes and literature written for children. Punjabi Dalit autobiographer is by no stretch of imagination an obscure and unknown 'other' – one who has not been exposed to the public realm, already.

Here, it is significant to observe that autobiography in general has been one such genre that has hitherto enjoyed a wide array of authorship. Activists, entrepreneurs, leaders, scientists, painters, bureaucrats, diplomats and a whole range of other professional have penned down their autobiographies without any formal foregrounding into literature. In fact, non-writers have more often resorted to this form of self-articulation. But when it comes to Punjabi, there is not a single Dalit non-writer who writes his autobiography. In the context of Dalit literature/aesthetics, where literariness is presumably not as important as the veracity of experience, the absence of non-writer as autobiographer becomes very crucial. Most of the Punjabi Dalit autobiographers first establish themselves as writers and later as Dalit autobiographers. In case of Marathi and other language-writings the trajectory is often the reverse. It is for this reason that Punjabi Dalit autobiography remains at best a side-pursuit, a by-product, or an after-product of a literary career. Punjabi Dalit autobiography still needs to undergo beyond the authorly world – a world wherein any ordinary Dalit, literate, semi-literate or even illiterate is able to record his/her life history.

Autobiography, it so appears, does not come naturally to the Punjabi Dalit writer as his chosen genre of self-expression. Most of the Punjabi Dalit writers are literally cajoled, persuaded and even sponsored by the publishers to write their life accounts. Gorkhi is persuaded by Amrita Pritam, Dil is persuaded by Amarjit Chandan and Madhopuri gathers the confidence to write his autobiography after reading the autobiography of a Hindi Dalit writer Seoraj Singh Baichain. Apparently

Punjabi Dalit autobiography, unlike the Marathi one, is not compulsively organic enough for it is prompted from outside. Besides a host of authorly Punjabi autobiographies, the Punjabi/Hindi translation of autobiographies of Dalits elsewhere provide Punjabi Dalit autobiographer two readymade models/frames for attempting his own hybridized model of autobiography. Punjabi Dalit autobiography is a very inadequate description of its actual character; it is in fact a corpus of Punjabi Dalit writers' autobiography. It is in this sense it is a hybridized genre in which Dalit experiences are mixed with authorly practices of the mainstream Punjabi autobiography.

The age at which an autobiographer chooses to script his own life history is very significant. In a canonical frame, autobiographies tend to be reflective and are generally attempted towards the fag end of life/career, when there is either a sense of accomplishment or a satisfaction of some achievement. For a more activist and immediate account of personal life, should the writing of autobiography not preferably be coincidental with the active life of the writer? Bakhtin approaches testimonies as discourses 'still warm from the struggle and hostility, as yet unresolved and still fraught with hostile intentions and accents' (Bakhtin 1998: 331). Some of the Marathi Dalit autobiographies are written by activists when they are very young and are feverishly involved in some kind of activism. *Akkarmashi* (1984) is written by Sarankumar Limbale when he is just 25. Laxman Mane writes his *Upara* (1980) at the age of 31. Laxman M. Gaikwad's *Uchalya* (1987) was published when the writer was just 31. Daya Pawar's *Baluta* (1978) was published when the writer was 43 years old. Most of the Black Panthers write their autobiographies while they are very much into the vortex of struggle.[8]

Practically all Punjabi Dalit autobiographers attempt their life-accounts at a much later stage in their life. Gorkhi, Atarjeet, Dil wrote at the ripe age of 60+; Giani Gurbakhash Singh Rahi chronicled his account when he was around 90 years old; Madhopuri and Gurnam Akida were relatively young and they wrote their life histories when they were around 50 years old. For want of a better word/terminology, we can say these autobiographies are the autobiographies of people who are well into their post-retirement phase of life. In her preface to *The Daughter of the East* (1988), Benazir Bhutto, when she was in her early 30s, challenges the notion of writing autobiography at a later stage in life. Punjabi Dalit autobiography as a whole operates within the canonical frame of post-facto reflection/analysis. Unlike Marathi

Dalit autobiographies, Punjabi Dalit autobiographies written as they are by the mature Dalit writers of overripe subjectivities, lack that activist edge which is otherwise supposed to be salient to its very being. The authorship of Punjabi Dalit autobiography suffers imbalance at another level. There is not a single Dalit woman, writing in Punjabi. By way of contrast, there are a number of woman Dalit autobiographers in Marathi who in their own distinct ways express their anguish against both gender and caste-oppression. Shantabai Kamble (*Majhya Jalmachi Chitarakatha*, 1986), Babytai Kamble (*JinaAmucha*, 1986), Mukta Sarvagod (*Mitleli Kavaade*, 1983), Kumad Pawde (*Antasphot*, 1981) and Urmila Pawar (*Aaidan*, 1945) are well-known Dalit women's autobiographers in Marathi. Most of them published/serialized their autobiographies in early 80s. In fact most of these have already been translated into English. Punjabi still waits for an autobiography by a Dalit woman. This is all the more glaring in the sense that within mainstream Punjabi autobiographical tradition, there have been formidable female autobiographers. Amrita Pritam's *Rasidi Ticket* (translated as *The Revenue Stamp*), Ajeet Kaur's *Kura Kabara* and Dilip Kaur Tiwana's *Nange Pairan da Safar* have been hailed for their radical feminist fervour.

Not only all Punjabi Dalit autobiographers are male, even in their accounts, the females are hardly lent any significant voice. Grandmothers and mothers are objects of veneration; due to lack of sustained love affair, even the beloveds make short appearances and disappear. In most of the autobiographies, the father–son duo holds the centre stage. In Gorkhi's *Gair Hazir Aadmi* it is the 'father' who overshadows the son in terms of his sheer presence on the pages of the autobiography; in Gurnam Akida's *Kakh Kande*, more often it is the dialogue between the father and the son that provides the structural fulcrum to the narrative. In *Dastan* too, Dil often remembers what his 'Bapu' used to say about social discrimination. Madhopuri's *Changiya Rukh* is unthinkable about 'Bhaia'. In Marathi 'male' Dalit autobiography, the father is not necessarily valourized. Daya Pawar in his *Baluta* has no words of unqualified reverence for his 'dead' father, he asks his mother, 'What prompted you to marry him?' (Pawar 2010: 42). He resolves not to be like his father. Even Limbale, not sure about his paternity, takes exception to paternal interference: 'I stood like a cactus plant. I used to abuse kaka as well who hit me, when my mother told him of my behaviour. I boldly told him, "Patil you are in no way concerned with me. You can't touch me; I felt I would explode with wild rage" (Limbale 2003: 63).

Operational dialectics

(*a*) Purity-Pollution Divide: Normally, it the purity-pollution polarity that constitutes the central dialectics of protest in any Dalit discourse – autobiographical or non-autobiographical. Punjabi Dalit autobiographers do recount first-hand experiences of discrimination on account of their being treated as 'impure'; yet what distinguishes their autobiographies is the predominant operation of another binary which has more to do with economics than with caste alone. The binary of the landed versus the landless in Punjabi Dalit autobiography overtakes purity-pollution syndrome which is otherwise more pronounced in the Dalit writings that come from other parts of India, particularly Maharashtra and UP. Ronki Ram, a keen scholar of Punjabi Dalit politics, also observes that 'Since cultivation involves Dalits in its various operations, it was not feasible to strictly follow the system of untouchability based on the principle of purity/pollution, as in many parts of India' (Ram 2004: 898). This is not to say that purity-pollution politics is altogether negligible or absent from the Punjabi landscape.

Balbir Madhopuri, for instance, would refer to politics of defilement thus: 'Defilement – I had confronted this word time and again. . . . I would think of the care the zamindars took of their animals – scrubbing and bathing, and tending them tenderly . . . Bhaia and others like him have to carry their own tumblers' (Madhopuri 2010: 33). Most of the Punjabi Dalit autobiographies do refer to separate Dalits habitats, located on the western fringes of the villages, named variously as *vehras* or *chamarlis*. Madhopuri explains the reasons of their localities being on the western side thus: 'the dirty water of the village flows towards the west, which is only the lower part of the village; and it is believed that not only should they not pollute clean water but also that these people should live in dirt, mire and slime' (ibid.: 9–10).

At places, one does come across rather poignant poetics/politics of 'touch' in Punjabi Dalit autobiographies. In Gurnam Akida's *Kakh Kande*, the protagonist has a very intimate encounter with a young married non-Dalit woman who is ready for everything except mouth-to-mouth kiss. This is how the description goes:

> I started licking her body . . . but she got little nervous. I asked about her unease, she in a tinkling voice replied, 'please, don't do this.' I asked, 'What?' She said, 'Do not bring your mouth close to my mouth.' . . . She said, 'Do not do this. Do whatever else you want to do.' Pointing towards her salwar which

she had lowered down, she said, 'For what else did I untie my salwar? Tell me.' . . . I inquired about her objection to my kissing. She revealed that some Baba Sita Ram had forbidden this. I kept wondering what the Baba had asked Shanno not to do. She could not answer. I asked her, 'Tie up your salwar'. She responded, 'Today it is time Gama, such occasions rarely come about. I am right here, undressed. I love you too much. But please do not insist on kissing. Do not defile my faith, do whatever else you want to'. (2007: 37–38)

It is indeed intriguing that the sexual act is kept out of the purity–pollution taboo; it is, however, the external touch or the kiss that upsets the sacred caste order. Among most of the hypergamous relations depicted in mainstream Punjabi literature, it is generally the upper-caste male landlords who force themselves on the women of the lower castes.[9] Akida's account does bring about a reversal in the sense that it is the lower-caste male who is all set for a sexual encounter with a consenting upper-caste woman, but the politics of purity-pollution does dampen the passion.

In Dil's autobiography *Dastan*, young Lal Singh too suffers the ignominy of being looked down as impure by the so-called twice born. In the instance quoted here, the possibility of caste-clash is hinted at the very site of caste intermixing: 'The Brahmin boys did not like that we could see them playing. Once a Brahmin came from the ground hit his shapeless hockey made of a tree-bough on my legs, I was just watching him play. Next day I waylaid him with a stick in my hand, he just deviated from the path and went back to his home' (Dil 1998: 30).

The pitch of the protagonist becomes aggressive, but the confrontation is postponed. At one more place the Brahmin–low caste divide comes to the fore but there is no pronounced rancour: 'Jai Dev master was a man of average height, just like a small orange . . . He would never release his anger by way of explicitly showing his Brahminism, while other Brahmin teachers would take it as their first duty to assert their caste-identity either before or after they would beat their students' (ibid.: 36). In the same passage Dil would refer to the poverty among brahmins too. He mentions about one poor Brahmin teacher who used to play the role of Ravan in Ramleela. He was despised by people of his own community for accepting such an 'unholy' role.

Atarjeet also recounts experiences of discrimination right from childhood. In school, he ventured to dip the tin-can inside the container to take the water; also with a sense of rebel, he would go to the big village well, and take water to quench his thirst (Atarjeet 2008: 44). His misdoings do invite backlash, yet he would repeat them. He remembers with a lot of anguish how his friend's mother would offer him a tea in a separate utensil which he was supposed to carry with himself (ibid.: 45). While inside the home of his upper caste friends/classmates, Atarjeet would continuously suffer discrimination; in the outer spheres of public life, however, the situation was much more bearable: '[He] had stopped practicing untouchability not as much inside the house, as outside it. He used to take me to his relations. Sitting on the same coat, we would sip tea' (ibid.: 46).

(*b*) The Landed versus the Landless: But the central polarity operational in Punjabi Dalit autobiography is not that of purity-pollution; rather it is that of the landed versus the landless, which in terms of caste-politics translates easily itself into a kind of perpetual feud between the rural jatt landlords and the Dalit landless peasants.[10] Noted political analyst Harish K. Puri observes: 'So the history of the oppression of Dalits in Punjab was related more to the structure of economy, ownership of land, and the politics of power relations, rather than the Brahmanical worldview' (Intro. to Madhopuri's *Changiya Rukh* 2010: xvii). The actual and more immediate oppressor of the Punjabi Dalit is jatt, and not as much the brahmin. In Akida's *Kakh Kande*, one of the characters Atam Prakash says in so many words: 'What kind of Dalit leaders are these? They keep on saying down with Brahmanism. Where is Brahmanism? Now it is jattism, brahmins themselves are menial in the villages' (Akida 2007: 55). In most of the Punjabi Dalit autobiographies, brahmins are fringe players of the social set up and are referred to rather sparingly in the narratives.

Gorkhi's autobiography *Gair Hazir Aadmi*, for instance, is hardly 'Dalit' in the sense that in about 200 pages, the caste remarks appear twice-thrice. It is more like an account of a son of labourer/mason who has the talent to write and whose writings are accepted by mainstream Punjabi journals for publications, and who rises from village Ladowali in Jalandhar to find an editorial position in a newspaper office at Chandigarh. *Gair Hazir Aadmi* is not fiercely Marxist, but at a very moderate level, there are ideological underpinnings. Time and again, more than caste-discrimination, the father of the protagonist bemoans the situation of landlessness that his family is in. He would think that once even a small patch of land is given to his family, everything else would be taken care of.

In Madhopuri's *Changiya Rukh*, the rare poetic flashes that surface in the narrative pertain more to life in agricultural fields than to life in Dalit ghettos. The image of Persian wheel recurs frequently: 'My thoughts spun like the Persian wheel and the clear and pure water of the pond turned into mirror' (Madhopuri 2010: 63).[11] Young Madhopuri wants to plant mango saplings in the limited yard of his house, and this is how his father reprimands him:

> It was when I was digging in our courtyard to plant the sapling that Bhaia snatched the hoe from my hand, and said, 'Maama, you are trying to ape the Jats! They have large lands and large havelis! We only have this much space where we can sit and relax! . . . My heart wilted like the plant. A storm had blown away the flowers of my desire. (ibid.: 13)

The landlessness continues to be a major source of deprivation. Another image of calf being asked to plough the field is typically agricultural: '. . . "I am like the calf which is still not used to the yoke, and Bhaia is impatient to put me to the plough of responsibilities. . . My feet were being scorched like the corn in Mala's furnace" (ibid.: 51). One policeman constantly chastises Dil inside the torture-cell of the police station for the desire of chamars to own the land. As he tortures Dil, he would say 'let us give you chamars more land!' (Dil 1998: 114).

Discourses of distraction/co-option

Despite suffering discrimination on account of their being dependent on jatt landlords, landless Punjabi Dalits fail to consolidate their ranks so as to launch a concerted counter-offensive. Punjabi Dalit autobiographers do suffer agony and pain, yet the sense of injustice before it ossifies into a potential emotion for a sustained rebel gets distracted into discourses of reform and ideological appropriation. What distinguishes Punjabi Dalit autobiography most, therefore, is its rather contained character; it reveals discontent, yet it does not simmer with it. Multiple discourses intervene and possibly postpone a unified Dalit backlash.

(*a*) Sikhism: The most pronounced discourse that blunts Dalit backlash is the discourse of egalitarian theology within Sikhism itself, and this is despite practices of patent discrimination among Sikhs at the level of praxis.[12] Since Sikh Dalits did not receive equal treatment in gurudwaras, they were compelled to have their separate gurudwaras. The rise of dera-culture outside the scope of Sikhism also has much to do with the sense of alienation that Sikh Dalits undergo within institutionalized Sikhism. About this hypocrisy or duplicity in Sikh behaviour, Atam Prakash, a character in Akida's *Kakh Kande* makes a cryptic statement thus: 'Loud philosophy, nil implementation' (Akida 2007: 153). It is pertinent to observe that caste not only continues to survive even in Sikhism but also it acquires more denominations. Besides the standard north Indian caste categories of chamars and chuhras, there are number of distinct religion/region-specific caste categories such as those of Ramdasiyas (mostly julahas, i.e. weavers), Ravidasiyas (mostly leather workers, i.e. chamars), Mazhabis (mostly sweepers, i.e. chuhras), Rangretas (mostly sweepers, also chuhras) etc. Atarjeet as a Ramdasia Sikh, ironically enough, suffers discrimination at the hands of other jatt and non-jatt Sikhs. In his *Akk da Dudh*, he narrates an instance when some Giani Bhagwan Singh who happened to be a head *granthi* of a historic gurudwara at Dhamot, impressed by his spiritual wisdom, asks him to come to gurudwara. The protagonist expresses his inability to do so on account of being a Ramdasia, Giani Bhagwan Singh persuades the estranged protagonist into the discourse of Sikh emancipation, thus:

> Giani Bhagwan Singh embraced me with a passionate pull. 'Gurus have placed you on a higher pedestal Gianiji [Atarjeet]. Now you must come to the gurudwara.' Holding my hands, he took me to gurudwara. In his room, on the hard-bed, his own seat, there was a white sheet, on which he asked me to sit. There were cans of dry fruits near the wall, and he served me these into a bowl. As long as I was in Dhamot, I had established deep relationship with these dry fruits and Giani Ji. Here under the inspiration of Giani Bhagwan Singh, along with another gentleman science-master Sawarn Singh, I took the holy *amrit*, and thus became as a follower of the gurus, which I probably was not before. (Atarjeet 2008: 65)

As Atarjeet is arrested for his naxalite activities, on his way to jail, he is on the seventh sky for he casts himself in the line of Sikh martyrs: 'The history of Gurus, the arrest of young sons, Guru Tegh Bahadur and his Sikh followers, their arrest and martyrdom and other such glorious pages of past appeared to enlighten my path to jail' (ibid.:

104). The grandfather of the protagonist used to be one among 'punj piaras' in Sikh processions, yet he did not have the permission to sit in the queue for *langar*.

Most of the Punjabi Dalit autobiographers are Sikh Dalits, while they continue to draw spiritual sustenance from *gurbani*; however, at the level of day-to-day discourse they are not part of mainstream Sikhism. SGPC, the supreme body of the Sikh religious affairs, is dominated by jatts. Giani Gurbakhash Singh begins his life history by quoting a hymn from *Guru Granth Sahib*. He actually takes on the responsibility of professional preacher/sermonizer (*pracharak*) of Sikhism from 1941 to 1945. Such is his abiding faith in *Guru Granth Sahib* that once there was a feud between the Ravidasiyas and local jatts, and to resolve the stalemate he takes recourse to the recitation of the holy text along with the fellow chamars, and prays for the demise of Zaildar Singh, the local jatt trouble-maker, and as he informs, rather dramatically, the prayers are answered and the culprit dies within two months (Rahi and Singh 2002: 148). He recounts with fervour of a Sikh devotee, his visits to all the major gurudwaras right from Damdama Sahib to Hem Kund.

(*b*) Dera Culture: Punjabi Dalit Sikhs, in the first instance, seek solace from Sikh religious institutions, and as they fail them, they increasingly gravitate towards local saints (*siddh*s or *pir*s) who form their own *dera*s. The *dera*s provide an alternative tradition of guru-bhakti outside the institutionalized religion of Sikhism. The number of deras runs into thousands. There are deras such as Radha Soami (Beas), Sacha Sauda (Sirsa), Nirankaris, Namdharis, Divya Jyoti Jagran Sansthan (Nurmahal), Dera Sant Bhaniarawalla, Dera Sachkhand (Ballan), Dera Sant Phuriwala, Dera Baba Budha Dal, Dera Begowal and Nanaksarwale that enjoy mass following among Dalits in particular. Gurnam Akida's illiterate father would sing aloud *Japuji Sahib* – the holy text of Sikhs, but he would also visit the *smadhi* of a local pir:

> Bapu was illiterate, yet he would recite Japuji Sahib which he had learnt by heart. Early morning he would take bath, sit with folded legs, and then would start singing Japuji Sahib aloud, but I could also see him bowing his head on the occasion of festivals at the *smadhi* of *siddhbaba*. . . . Every Sunday we used to light lamps at the *smadhi* of *siddh baba*. (Akida 2007: 110–11)

Even the fiercest of a Punjabi Dalit tends to seek social as well as spiritual solace from either Sikhism or local dera culture. Akida is so enamoured by the dera at Sirsa that he despite being dissuaded by his ailing father not to go to dera, decides to go ahead. As he returns, his father collapses without uttering a word. He later on repents his decision (2007: 140–41).

Such is the pull of local pirs and saints in Punjab that besides the larger institutional frames of organized religions, a host of cults exist at sub-regional level. Dil's *Dastan* refers to a dera of *nath*s (Dil 1998: 53), whose very presence was resented to by the local brahmins and the jatts. Most of the Punjabi Dalit autobiographers, in their childhood, seem to believe in the existence of ghosts, apparitions of the dead, witches etc. Madhopuri expresses his fears thus: 'Thoughts of the ghosts jostled about in my mind throughout the night. Frightened I would close my eyes. . . . When the flame trembled, my heart also sank, and I would think, "If only I could get Suleiman's cap!"'(Madhopuri 2010: 14). Baba Sidh Chano or Baba Sidh Wali also figures in the narrative a local chamar diety. The myth of the valour of the Sidh Wali is recounted in terms of his prolonged wrestling match with Lord Krishna who defeats ultimately through deception.

(*c*) Communism: Punjab has been the epicentre of Marxist movements, and in mid-1970s, in post-Green Revolution period, Punjabi youth, disgruntled as it was, with the growing levels of economic disparity, was driven towards naxalite movement. Dil, Atarjeet, Gorkhi and other Dalits writers (Sant Ram Udasi, a people's poet, in particular) joined the ranks of a radical naxalism and suffered prolonged bouts of extreme police torture. Except for not believing in the existence of God, Atarjeet observes, that 'the ideology of communism is not beyond Gurbani'(Atarjeet 2008: 85). At one point, he regrets for not being able to live to the ideals of a true comradeship, and that in the face of police torture he proved to be a very weak comrade. Yet he makes a distinction between being a weak comrade and a traitor one, thus:

> Lal salam! Lal salam my dear comrade!! I salute your sacrifices!!! I proved to be a weak one, but I did not betray. I remained an incomplete being, unfinished half a being. I shall try to become a complete being. I shall try to overcome my weaknesses my dear comrade Bhola! (ibid.: 110)

Punjabi Dalit autobiographers seek fulfilment in communism and remain under its spell for a considerable part of their lives. The autobiographies of Punjabi Dalit read more like the memoirs of underground armed naxal revolutionaries than fragmented accounts of vulnerable and directionless Dalits. Dil recounts his rather engaging days with one Lala Des Raj who was a comrade, thus:

> In the shop he used to feel happy while taking food with me from the same utensil, and we used to mix dal and dahi in one box of the tiffin, rather than keeping them separately. With him I used to feel some kind of companionship. (1998: 88)

In a marriage party, when Dil is offered liquor, he refuses it, saying that 'We are comrades, to claim that one is comrade in itself an intoxication of a kind, which I was experiencing again at that moment' (ibid.: 96). Young Madhopuri is also driven towards communism. He is impressed by the knowledge of fellow comrades and seems to share their vision of revolution in favour of social equality, thus:

> I wanted to be as knowledgeable as the comrades. I also wanted to be able to speak as impressively and passionately as the comrades did when I grew up. When I heard people talk about social equality, and the rapid development in the USSR, I was filled with a warm filling of a bright future. (2010: 113)

It is however very significant to note that almost all the Punjabi Dalit autobiographers, after their tryst with communism or naxalism during their youth, in their latter phase of life, feel betrayed more by the practitioners of the ideolog than by the ideology itself. Gorkhi's following remarks explain Punjabi Dalit's initial fascination and subsequent disillusionment with communism, thus:

> I often think that had the comrades not come in my life, it would have been an empty vessel, mere mud in a waterspring . . . These comrades also showed me their meanness and rotten thinking, even among them the walls of casteism are as high as ever before. (Gorkhi 2007: 194)

Atarjeet is literally abused along the caste-lines by the comrades when he decides to quit the party: 'We'll tell that mother-fucker, that sister-fucker chamar that resignations are not received in the party. . .' (2008: 171).

(*d*) Relatively Better Levels of Prosperity: The protagonists of Punjabi Dalit autobiography, unlike their Marathi counterparts, are not victims of abject poverty, though they do undergo many phases of struggle and economic hardships. The economic profile of Dalits in Punjab is rather checkered. The Ad-dharmis of the Jalandhar region control the leather business and industry and are relatively well off as compared to other Punjabi Dalits. A small number of Dalits also has landholdings, which is around 0.40 per cent of the total holdings in Punjab. Some Punjabi Dalits have gained important administrative positions due to affirmative action of the state. Madhopuri, being an Ad-dharmi of Doaba region, is not as poor as a shudra Gorkhi is. Also Madhopuri's maternal uncle is in Indian Administrative Service. Most of the Punjabi Dalit autobiographers are either journalists or teachers. Except for Dil, all lead a life of middle-class aspirations.

Atarjeet provides an extended genealogy of his family (called *kursinama*), suggesting thereby a formidable background of his past (2008: 12–14). He observes: 'The people of the *vehra* had started competing with the *swarn* at the level of economics and the exchange between the two had increased' (ibid.: 12). Akida also enjoys relatively comfortable childhood: 'My dear mother, daily in the morning would serve me pranthas, a bowl full of curd, butter . . . . In our house milk used to be freely available' (2007: 51). Marathi Dalit autobiographers, by way of contrast, undergo what may be termed as 'bastardization of the self' as they have their mothers or females of the house working in he red-light areas as prostitutes. Daya Pawar's *mausi* (mother's sister) is a prostitute in Golpeetha, a red-light area in Mumbai, and Limbale's mother too was a mistress of some Hanumanta, local chief.

The anger quotient of Punjabi Dalit autobiography is relatively less as compared to what one comes across in the Hindi or Marathi Dalit autobiography. Due to general prosperity and stability of relationships, the possibilities of vertical oppression of the low caste are also reduced. At one place Madhopuri's father runs into poorbias (also bhaiyyas) – the migrant labour from eastern UP. They share with him tales of vertical caste oppression in their *desh*. This is what one bhaiya tells: 'You are talking of land, I believe that even our daughters and daughters-in-law are common possession' (Madhopuri 2010: 74). This is how the protagonist's father responds: 'It is better you people live here, than undergo the humiliation you have on to that side' (ibid.:

73). The observation of 'bhaiya' is equally important: 'We want to stay here in Punjab where things are not as bad. There is less rigidity about untouchability also . . . We have been living here for the last three-four years and have observed things' (ibid.: 73).

(*e*) Division/Dissensions among Punjabi Dalits: Punjabi Dalits are a highly fragmented community, and as suggested in the second section of this chapter, due to the impact of Sikhism, a host of new and well-hierarchized categories of Dalits have emerged among them. There is a definite divide between Hindu low castes and Sikh low castes, between Punjabi Dalits and Dalits that have migrated from eastern UP to Punjab. Also there is a divide between *amritdhari* and *non-amritdhari* (or *sahajdhari*) low-caste Sikhs; and among Sikh chamars there are all kinds of differentiation.[13] Atarjeet, a Sikh chamar, provides ample hints of subtle hierarchies within Sikh chamars thus:

> Many other families of the *vehra* were engaged in agriculture with jatts as partners. There was a set of four-five houses, different from those of us who used to deal with leather. There were some families which used to do with raw leather and its tanning. (2008: 13)

And as he clarifies his intentions of not to highlight hierarchies within a caste, he ends up doing exactly the opposite thus:

> It is not my intention to show the superiority of my family, but from purely a historical angle, it is not at all irrelevant to tell that on the basis of the nature of work that people did within their caste, many layers could be seen. (ibid.: 13)

At another place in his autobiography, Atarjeet foregrounds the fact that high-caste Sikhs (primarily jatts) did not discriminate with *amritdhari* Sikh chamars as much. As he takes a temporary shelter in a gurudwara at Chak Fateh Singhwala, he feels that the entire town and also other town in the vicinity had a special blessing of the tenth guru: 'in these thirty villages, I could not see any discrimination on the grounds of purity-pollution with the low caste, especially with the *amritdharis*' (ibid.: 78). Akida and his brother have different take on their caste-status. While Akida does not hesitate to declare himself as a chamar, his brother Dev Singh however avoids the embarrassment of being a low caste by way of hiding his caste (Akida 2007: 62). He declares himself to be a mason, belonging to the caste of Ramgarhiya (ibid.: 43). In *Changiya Rukh*, a sense of strangeness as well as sympathy is shown towards the low-caste poorbiya (bhaiyyas) by the local Dalits. There is another divide that is fast emerging among Dalits not just in Punjab but all over India. The ordinary Dalit who has not benefited from the policies of affirmative action of the state in the form of reservation also feels alienated from Dalit officers. Taaya in *Changiya Rukh* makes an intervention: 'People say many things, that the officers have formed a separate category of their own and are ignoring even their closest relatives' (Madhopuri 2010: 122).

(*f*) Some Enlightened Jatts/Other Upper Castes Families: Despite adversarial relationship with jatts, most of the Punjabi Dalit autobiographers do run into some enlightened jatt families with whom they subsequently enjoy a degree of cordiality. Madhopuri devotes one full chapter which he rather poetically entitles as 'An Oasis in the Desert' to a jatt family of Taaya Jeet with which he had familial bonding. The protagonist fondly remembers:

> Tai would give me roti with jaggery or molasses, sugar or butter. She would give me dal, dahi and saag. If I wanted pickles, then I would take some from the chatti in the small room next to the kitchen. Nor would she let wash the vessels I had used. (ibid.: 153)

The chapter concludes on this note: 'Now, whenever I think of the love and affection given to us by this Jat family, it seems to me that their love, which made our lives beautiful and colourful as the spring, had been an oasis in the barren desert of our life' (ibid.: 162). Dil also observes that his father also earned respect from the jatts: 'Every jatt used to treat my father with respect' (1998: 56). But this respect stemmed from the fact that without the cooperation of the chamars, rural jatt peasantry was often helpless: 'Jatts cannot breathe without chamars; without them, they cannot survive, but they were to behave in ways which were highly unnatural' (ibid.: 56).

Atarjeet, despite facing discrimination on account of his being a low caste, acknowledges those people from higher caste who stand by him in moments of distress. While inside the jail, facing inhuman police barbarism, he is reminded of 'a sympathetic jatt family of the Mahina village and Bai Balwant who trusted me so much' (2008:

106). Towards the end the scenes of social harmony in way de-fang Dalit backlash:

> There were some Brahmin Hindu families on whose beds I could relax. I could eat with them as one of their relatives . . . Daily I could see that boys and girls, making fun of some Manu, used to eat from each other mouths without any sense of caste discrimination. Where was casteism? Where was untouchability? (ibid.: 214)

Even Akida acknowledges one Sadhu Ram, a brahmin, as his 'dharam bhra' [adopted/foster brother] (2007: 144).

Authorly aesthetics

(*a*) Palpable Design: Due to its peculiar sociology, enunciated above, Punjabi Dalit autobiography therefore evinces a negotiated texture, which does not let it splinter in unpredictable directions. The narratives do not collapse; nor are there any loose ends; the omniscient narrator of each autobiography gallops towards a destination in a planned manner. The distribution of time across different phases of life is more or less conventional, and the sequencing of events is linear. The early self-portraits are followed by later ones; the description of memories of discrimination suffered in early childhood is followed by a vivid account of hardships endured during the intermediate phase of life. First 80–85 pages of Dil's autobiography are devoted to his pre-college phase of life; Madhopuri's describes his childhood (till high school) in the first half of the book; *Jini Rahi Mein Tooriya* by Giani Gurbakhash Singh Rahi is divided rather fastidiously into four phases of almost equal time-spans, that is, 1912–34, 1935–56, 1957–78 and 1979–2001.

Prem Gorkhi's *Gair Hazir Aadmi* has all the trappings of a formal literary narrative in which the author takes precedence over the persona (protagonist) in a very obvious way. The selection of events/situations (in 1994 edition) is such that the continuity of the narrative remains intact. His search for decent and stable livelihood, his frustration with women, and a build-up towards his final decision of remaining unmarried, his slow and steady rise as a short-story-writer – everything is mapped with relentless authorly control. What is more important is that there are hardly any sustained outbursts or scathing harangues against the caste-order. Divided into 36 chapters, with each spread over 4–6 pages, the autobiography is evenly laid out in terms of its temporal design. Some of the titles of the chapters – such as 'Kande ton Phul tak', 'Kalje da Diva', 'Noor di Pand', 'Kandhan hee Kandhan' – betray literary sophistication, though of a conventional kind.

There is another very baffling aspect of Gorkhi's autobiography. It appears in two editions – 1994 edition was brought out by Sapta Sandhu Publications, Delhi, and a later edition in 2007 published by Lokgeet Prakashan Chandigarh. The two editions are ostensibly different. In the new edition published by Lokgeet Prakashan in 2007, there is a deliberate attempt to disturb the linearity of time as new chapters (7) are added quite literally towards the end. This is uncalled for, and such additions only reveal total disregard for the 'original' form. It reminds of *Akkarmashi* which was also revised by Limbale as *Poonah Akkarmashi (Again Akkarmashi)*. Santosh Bhoomikar, translator of Limbale's autobiography, despite requests from the author does not include the new additions in his translation because, as he observes, there is a distinct lack of vigour and sincerity in the newer version. The same can be said about the new additions made in *Gair Hazir Aadmi*. The original autobiography undergoes strict editorial controls, the latter one brings back the edited out matter in a rather mechanical manner.

Neatly divided into twenty chapters, Madhopuri's autobiography also follows a linear trajectory without distractions. Like any standard autobiography it opens with a detailed account of the village of the protagonist, followed by 'the inscriptions on a tender mind' and the days of his youth are recounted in the middle chapters. The titles of the middle chapters are poetical, and the images used are too authorly. Here are some of the titles: 'Kore Kagaz te Guhri Likhat', 'Registan wich Vagda Dariya', 'Kandiyaale Rahan de Rahi', 'Tirke Sheeshey de Vithiya' and 'Baddlan wich Jhakda Sooraj'. The imagery employed by the author by no stretch of imagination constitutes 'alternative idiom'. The authorly propensities pre-empt the possibilities of raw flow. Very often, the author lapses into offering extented explanations which in the latter chapters turn quite polemical. Even the narrative illusion of 'let the events speak for themselves' is given up. The names of chapter 16 and 19 as 'Literature and Politics' and 'The Humanist Slap', respectively, point towards overt politicization of personal history.

Gurnam Akida is critically aware of authorly seductions, and therefore in his introductory remarks, he would say, 'For two years continuously I did not read any literary book, except keeping a track of daily news because I believed that after having read so much, the writer many a times tends to allow his reading to influence his creative output' (2007:10). Structurally, *Kakh Kande* is seemingly very different and is conceived in a dialogue form. The protagonist recounts his experience/memory, which besides other minor characters, his father and one Atam Prakash respond to by way of extended advice/analysis. The autobiographer himself informs that the book was literally dictated to his graphic-designer friend Baljinder Singh:

> With my eyes closed, I used to dictate orally Baljinder the matter of the book every morning and he in his swift speed would type and compose the matter simultaneously. The book was complete, but between its dictation, and its final publication I had to pass through a difficult passage. (ibid.)

He obviously refers to the arduous author-function of controlling the narrative. He would change the names of some of the characters and would also fabricate some events to escape the displeasure of those about whom he had made some uncharitable comments. The oral informality (that one comes across in an autobiography, like that of Viramma, an anonymous illiterate Dalit woman from Tamilnadu) is conspicuously missing. *Viramma* is replete with native wisecracks, songs, description of rituals and raw laughter.[14] The prose used in Akida's narrative is formal and follows very much the protocols of print capitalism. Even the sequencing of dialogues in each chapter is very predictable. First the author as protagonist speaks, the other characters react thereafter. Most of the chapters begin and end with poems in four lines. Of course most of these poetic epitaphs tend to be prosaic and are loaded with lot of preaching, but the regularity with which they appear hint towards the planned nature of Akida's autobiographical account.

Atarjeet's *Akk da Dudh* oscillates between two kinds of experiences – experiences of discrimination and experiences of social harmony; at practically every turn in his life, the protagonist suffers social biases, yet before the experiences of suffering mount, some source of partial comfort or momentary redemption appears. The autobiography follows a pattern which holds it back from being an account of a veritable sufferer. In various schools to which the protagonist is often transferred, if some set of teachers, students or parents pillory him for being a low caste, there are others who acknowledge his teaching prowess. The major portion of the autobiography is given to his encounter with communism and his subsequent arrest and torture by the Punjab police, the latter half of the autobiography is devoted to his stint in schools as teacher.

Lal Singh's Dil's autobiography *Dastan* does not depart radically from the general rubric of Punjabi Dalit autobiography. It too operates within the authorly grid. The opening suggests the methodology of writing:

> the poets have to pass through fire, to keep their inner light burning. They negotiate with mischievous processes with caution so as to survive for writing. It is god's miracle that I am thrown into the fire repeatedly, and yet I am saved from its heat. Had it not happened with me, I wouldn't have been what I am. (1998: 13)

An abstract philosophical observation precedes the image of experience. Each fragment of memory, before it is recorded in its empirical details, is summarized in the first line or couple of lines. For instance, first he would write – 'There is not such an environment in the school, which could have suited me' (ibid.) – and this would be followed by details of discrimination within the school precincts. While reading Punjabi Dalit autobiography it so appears that at times the 'experience' is prefaced by authorial directions. The proclivity to represent, rather than to enfigure, makes Punjabi Dalit autobiography more authorly, than writerly. Prem Prakash while eulogizing the literary qualities of Dil's *Dastan* writes: 'It is not just an autobiography; at some places it is a great poem, at other it is a high quality narrative, and at yet other it is good prose' (1998: 175). Such an observation only confirms the authorly presence in the autobiography, and for mainstream autobiographies, such a critical endorsement is indeed laudable; but in case of a Dalit autobiography, classical poetic grandeur is counter-productive.

Despite being very much authorly, *Dastan* is not very cohesive and is not even divided into self-contained chapters. And the reasons of its being slightly patchy and discontinuous could be that parts of its manuscript were lost in a storm. Prem Prakash, a close associate of

Dil and one who was instrumental in the publication of *Dastan*, in his afterword to the book supplies very useful information.

Another unfortunate thing that happened was that some pages (of the manuscript) were blown in the storm. Some could be taken hold, while some could not be. We were left with an incomplete form. About two years ago someone pursuing his MPhil took from me those pages, and he did not return these for two years. When I put pressure on him, he sent them back. He did one good thing. He asked Dil to rewrite the lost pages, and those rewritten were inserted back into the draft. We have tried to edit this draft to put things in some sequence; even then disorderliness could not be helped (ibid.).

The distribution of time is also not even. Some memories extend rather vividly into 20–30 pages without break, while some just last for three to four lines. There are hints of waywardness and in the latter half such waywardness increases. Dil's autobiography grapples with multiple variables and it undergoes radical shifts of character which tend to lend an element of instability in the narrative linearity. The debates of economic disparity, caste-discrimination, oppression of the state, US imperialism, Vietnam War etc. that comrades used to indulge in, in their hide-outs, instil in Dil a rare sense of activism. His rather effusive naxalite phase and his relapse into an easy-going Imam later on and finally his return to Samarala as a tea vendor make him acquire a rather checkered profile that he as an autobiographer fails to cope up with. His conversion to Islam and the intellectual dilemmas that he undergoes point towards the complexity of his personality. He confronts the question of reconciling Marxist atheism with the credo of faith that Islam inheres and offers his own half-baked working solutions. This is how he accounts for his conversion:

> How could one be a Communist, with being a Muslim? I used to believe that Islam is quite akin to Communist culture. The only difference is that the former is theistic and the latter is atheistic. I thought that till Communist culture is not achieved, I should convert to Islam but at the same I should stick my atheism. This was a strange idea that I should become a Muslim, and yet remain an atheist. (Dil 1998: 130)

The cultural atlas of Gorkhi's autobiography is limited. The last post in his case is Chandigarh. Dil's escape to UP following brutal police torture and his interaction with Islamic workers and labourers leading to his conversion into Islam show his destiny not different from that of 'a runaway slave'. Dil is a man on run, geographically, ideologically and religiously. As compared to Gorkhi's cogent autobiography, Dil's is more irregular and broken. Gorkhi writes his autobiography as much as his autobiography writes him. Dil fails to write his autobiography as much as his autobiography fails him. Gorkhi's persona is focused and reveals a trajectory of evolution – a ready stuff for a conventional autobiography. Dil's persona meanders and survives from moment to moment. There is no destination, nor is there any precise sense of arrival. Struggle and squandering the wages of this struggle is the only constant in the life of Dil. The autobiography is replete with bouts of disillusionment, humiliation, third-degree torture, bohemian bravadoes and escapades that till the very end keep the protagonist instable.

Except for Dil's *Dastan* which is relatively more unorganized and fragmentary than other Punjabi Dalit autobiographies, overall, there does emerge a palpable tropological constitution of this form of writing. Neither the degree of deprivation is exceptional, nor the degree of achievement phenomenal, yet there is a trajectory of evolution. Since the discourses of redemption intervene on and off, the evolution is never dramatic or radical to hold the interest of a general reader. Some of the autobiographies tend to foreground father-son relationship, locked as they are, in the lop-sided socio-cultural set up; the father usually represents the submissive Dalit character of the older generation, and the son stands for the aggressive and assertive Dalit present. The protagonists end up achieving reasonable status in civil society and thus operate very much within the metaphysics of arrival/cognition. The autobiographies tend to open with a detail caste-wise, scholarly and even well-researched sociological description of the native village of the respective protagonists, and culminate on a note of overt and conscious Dalit assertion. Unlike Marathi Dalit narratives, where there is a relentless description of tragic suffering, Punjabi Dalit autobiography does not attain lofty tragic proportions.

What stand out in Punjabi Dalit autobiographies are the scenes of police torture. The autobiographers bring out with graphic vividness their experiences inside the jail, police stations and interrogation-centres of the state. In Marathi autobiographies, the protagonists are too weak or insignificant to take on the might of the state. Punjabi Dalit prisoners do find caste-discrimination no less oppressive inside the police stations. In fact, Dil refers to a caste division within police force thus: 'There was a special-staff, and there was a non-special staff. One vessel, two stomachs' (1998: 109). But the encounters with police often remain as encounters between stubborn comrades on the one side and ruthless state on the other; the narrators display a rare streak of stoicism. The resistance shown by different rebellious protagonists to state-oppression provides them one of the primary motivations to lapse into autobiographical writing. The autobiographies are chronicles more against the state than against the excesses of jatts. The autobiography of Dil, Atarjeet and Gorkhi in particular tend to foreground their naxalite leanings as against their anti-caste-tirades.

(*b*) Chapters as Well-made Stories: Not only do the autobiographies evince a degree of aesthetic tautness but even the chapters in which these are divided tend to have the autonomy of well-made stories. No wonder some of the chapters of the autobiographies of Prem Gorkhi and Madhopuri had been published as independent stories in various little magazines of Punjabi literature. Madhopuri's 'Meri Daddi – Ek Itihas', and Gorkhi's 'Arjan Safaidi Wala' retained as chapters in their autobiographies had already earned a lot of critical acclaim. The beginning and end of most of the chapters of Gorkhi's self-narrative for instance have all the attributes of classical story-telling. This is how one chapter ends:

> Dark dense night, with rain lashing, I was alone that night, but now I had alphabets, I had words, I touched the edges of the letters with my lips, the turbulence that had set in mind subsided. Next morning I gave my reply to the uncle: 'I have become a coward now. You excuse me. I do not require your money.' (2007: 96)

The lines constitute a melodramatic climax, which also becomes a befitting take off for the succeeding chapter. The play of darkness and light, gloominess and brilliance, sound and silence, eternity and moment relates one chapter with another. The next chapter though is a follow-up of the preceding one, has its own self-contained, well-conceived moment of beginning: My sky had become very clear, dirt-free, stretched over hundreds of miles – milky white. As though the jungle of lines etched on my hand and forehead had receded far back. As though the sand had spread – bright-golden, radiating and shining from one end of my life to another, and as though the strings of a silent veena had reverberated in the entire eternity (ibid.: 97).

The poetical overtakes the empirical and the stereotypical narrative tropes temper with the depiction of reality. Neither 'dark dense night', nor 'clear' sky, nor even 'the strings of silent veena' take the reader closer to the ghettoized interior Dalit landscape. The narrator is too conscious of the classical requirement of providing a dramatic setting for the action to take off.

Here is yet another illustration of what can be termed as anxiety of authorship that Punjabi Dalit writing is deeply mired in. The death of the beloved in Gorkhi's autobiography is lamented thus:

> And then Gorkhi started moving along with me. I gazed at stars, the rays of light, the bubbles rising due to air, and then towards white milky moon. I know it; it is my belief that she did not become star, she would become moon whose cool light always spreads across the yard of my heart. (ibid.: 139)

It is either the white milky moon up in the sky or the outstretched loneliness right in the courtyard of his house that Prem Gorkhi finds himself invariably in. The 'star' and the 'moon' are exhausted or over-determined romantic images, which the Dalit writer frequently re-invokes without replenishing them with fresh semantic possibilities. From an overtly romantic register, the autobiographer moves to an existential register:

> I could see at a stretch everything around me was unfulfilled, half-realized, broken, fragmented.
>
> – What life did Chaina have? Undergoing the nights of anguish and pain, ironing clothes she was heading towards death inch by inch.
> – Where did I stand? There was neither a bank nor any anchor/stay. What kind of employment did I have? The situation forces me virtually to beg.
> – And Mukhtar on the far end of the border is cut off from the family, teaching in backward schools in the villages
>
> And my lovely cat the entire courtyard around me and the lame people inhabiting within it . . .
> Everything was incomplete, lame and infirm. (ibid.: 152)

It so appears that most of the Dalit writers, across languages and regions, tend to express their despair through given existential frameworks used hitherto by the writers of absurd and anti-story movement within mainstream literature. While in Marathi Dalit writings, the limits of absurdity have been transgressed with an unprecedented language of violence, in Punjabi Dalit writing, the limits seem to have been rehearsed.

(c) Lack of Virulent Idiom: While Dil's autobiography is most cataclysmic of all the Dalit autobiographies written in Punjabi, yet it does not let his anger fly uncontrollably. Dil's preferred term is 'thanda gussa' [cold rage] (ibid.: 161). Madhopuri gets angrier, but there are hardly any sustained vituperative diatribes. His ironic explanations and counter-questions however do add pungency to his narrative. Dil's prose is descriptive and there is a lack of rhetoric in his style. The passage quoted below from *Changiya Rukh* is at best an example of intellectual anger (hatred): 'How could Brahmaji give birth to four at once? Who would have assisted him at their birth and helped him clean up, the way Gango the midwife did in the village? How would he have suckled four babies at his breasts? And did his body swell like my mother's and how had he walked about?' (Madhopuri 2010: 94) The questioning is relentless, and the sadhu who narrates the birth of four *varna*s from the body of Brahma is pilloried thus: 'Then you explain to us how Brahma could give birth through his mouth, arms, stomach, and feet? How can anyone enjoy his own body? How would he have menstruated like a woman? You tell us – has a man ever delivered a baby?' (ibid.: 95).

Such a mood of uneasy questioning permeates throughout Madhopuri's autobiography. But most of these interrogative interventions seem to have a sophisticated intellectual syllogism, seen at play in Jotibha Phule's *Gulamgiri* or even in the writings of Ambedkar.[15] Such theoretical interpolations defeat the very purpose of writing an autobiography. In fact it is the failure of the abstract theorizations that necessitates the arrival of autobiography as a discourse of ultra-naked personal experience. Rather than recording childhood memories without ideological filter, most of the Dalit autobiographers seem to invest lot of latter-day mature understanding of caste-discrimination into situations of childhood.

There is a lack of autobiographical candour and forthrightness, which otherwise is a hallmark of Dalit aesthetics. The autobiographer Gorkhi, for instance, has multiple love affairs (three) but the sheer carnality of experience is lost/postponed in poetic obfuscations such as 'moh da ugiya boota moorjha gaya' [the plant of love withered away]

(2007: 50) or narrative indirections as 'usne mera hath phar ke bullan naal ghut liya/par agle dina bare sanoo sar nahin se' [Holding my hand, she kissed it fiercely, but for the days to come we had no clue] (ibid.: 35). Also, since there is not so much of a free play of carnality or raw physicality, the most intimate encounters get sublimated into rather sophisticated tropes. Marathi Dalit autobiographers expose the grammar of the body without camouflage thus: 'No passenger alighted from the bus nor did anyone board it. It came and went empty without passengers, like the foetus of a barren woman. Yet we kept our hopes alive like a womb cared for after an abortion' (Limbale 2003: 41). The mother's womb, which is hitherto spiritualized under nationalist hangovers, is used as physical fact of life without any rarefied claptrap.

Madhopuri does at time tend to reach to the ground zero of a provocative situation, but then the opportunity is lost as the situation is described in either passive voice or in an indirect speech. Instead of retaining Daadi's volley of invectives which she hurls on those who destroy the banyan tree of the chamars, the author ends up offering just a prosaic description thus:

> My Daadi showered expletives on those responsible for this destruction and went on till the next morning, 'May you be destroyed! You have hurt me! God will do the same unto you!'
> Daadi had seen those twin trees grow and flourish before her eyes ever since she had come here as a bride. She was deeply upset that the tree planted by her husband. (2010: 146)

The expletives are too decent, and there is nothing abusive about them. The socialist and the religious fervour that underlies the life-narratives of Punjabi Dalits does generate an expression of transformation and reform, but it precludes the possibility of a violent and vituperative idiom. In Rahi's autobiography, for instance, the very language is couched in the *bhakti* ethos of surrender: 'smarpan de sabad' [words of surrender] (Rahi and Singh 2002: 5), 'mattha tekda han' [bow my forehead] (ibid.: 7).

In Marathi Dalit life-narratives 'Hunger is bigger than man' (Limbale 2003: 50), in Punjabi it hardly overtakes the sufferer.[16] At the level of idiom, therefore, there are hardly any flashes of 'Dalit brilliance'. The romantic and the gristly happen simultaneously in the surcharged Marathi Dalit idiom thus: 'Our affair was known to the people in my house, while our love spread like a patch of rash on a leper's skin' (ibid.: 27).

The idiomatic depth that Marathi Dalit autobiography evinces is a direct function of the suffering that the protagonist undergoes. The poetic images/metaphor used in Punjabi Dalit narratives remain more or less agrarian in nature; there is nothing gothic or monstrous about them. It requires an intense Dalit gaze or experiential veracity to transform a broom into a witch thus: 'The broom of the corner looked like a widow who practiced witchcraft' (ibid.: 14).

Notes

1. The quotes inserted in the text of the paper from Punjabi autobiographies have been translated by the author of the chapter himself, and the translations are only of working nature. Except for Madhopuri's *Changiya Rukh*, which is available in its English translation, all other Punjabi Dalit autobiographies are yet to be translated. Only quotes from *Changiya Rukh* are not translated by the author and have been taken from the available translation. Also the author of the paper gained a lot from the works of Manjit Singh, Surinder Jodhka, Gian Singh Bal and other Dalit activists and scholars. It is just a matter of chance that their works go unquoted in the paper.
2. Most of the Dalit and non-Dalit critics, across various Indian languages, continue to approach Dalit autobiography in terms of its oppositional aesthetics. Rejecting classical aesthetics, Sarankumar Limbale, for instance, declares: 'Satyam, shivam, sundaram is a foolish concept' (2003: 22). Dalit literature, he argues is 'all about the sorrows, tribulations, slavery, degradation, ridicule and poverty endured by Dalits. This literature is but a lofty image of grief' (ibid.: 30).
3. First Marathi Dalit autobiography that received critical recognition was that of Daya Pawar's *Baluta* (1978). It was followed by a host of other autobiographies such as Laxman Mane's *Upara* (1980), Sharankumar Limbale's *Akkarmashi* (1984) and Laxman Gaikwad's *Uchalya* (1987). Most notably these autobiographies came from Maharashtra, were written in Marathi and were subsequently published in Hindi and English translations by the leading publishing houses of the country.
4. In the Indian context, most of the leaders who were in the vanguard of struggle for Independence wrote their autobiographies. Tilak, Lajpat Rai, Nehru, Rajendra Prasad, Maulana Abul Kalam, Rajaji and of course Gandhi, along with many local level leaders brought out their autobiographical accounts during or just after the Freedom Movement. Their autobiographies speak less about their personal details and are more geared towards the pronouncement or re-iteration of their sublime nationalist goals. The private self becomes the locus of national self and *vice versa*. Ranajit Guha's critical observation that 'The history of Indian nationalism is thus written up as a sort of spiritual biography of the Indian elite' (1952: 2) in a way sums up the over-arching intent of what may be termed as 'nationalist autobiography'.

5. Sarankumar Limbale, as Alok Mukherjee points out, characterizes Dalit literature as 'purposive' and describes its purpose variously as 'revolutionary', 'transformational' and 'liberatory' (2003: 14).
6. Though the autobiographies were published around mid-1990s, it was not the precise period of their take off. They must have begun about five to ten years ago as some of the chapters/portions included in them happen to have been published in leading Punjabi journals and magazines much earlier. Lal Singh Dil's *Dastan* was published much after the completion of its manuscript. As Prem Prakash informs, Dil's friend and a compatriot, some of the pages of Dil's *Dastan* were lost in the wind. Even Madhopuri's *Changiya Rukh* had its parts published much earlier in the form of short stories or memoirs in journals. Most of the Punjabi Dalit autobiographies have been serialized in local journals and newspapers before they are compiled into a book form. The fact that these autobiographies were serialized in a way 'tones' down the revelatory potential that they pretend to carry. The publication of a Dalit autobiography in Punjabi does not constitute an event in itself for substantial part of it is already published in the vernacular press.
7. Roland Barthes makes a distinction between the writers and the authors. While authors 'represent', the writers 'enfigure'. In his *The Pleasure of the Text*, he observes that 'figuration is the way in which the erotic body appears... in the profile of the text. [T]he text itself, a diagrammatic and not an imitative structure, can reveal itself in the form of the body split into fetish objects, into erotic sites... Representation, on the other hand, is embarrassed figuration, encumbered with other meanings that that of desire; a space of alibis...' (1976: 57).
8. Huey P. Newton, the founding leader of Black Panthers, wrote his autobiography *Revolutionary Suicide* (1973) at the age of 31. George Jackson penned down his *Blood in My Eyes* (1971) at the age of 30. Jamil Abdullah Al Amin (aka H. Rap Brown) wrote *Die Nigger Die!* (1969) at the age of 26. Eldridge Cleaver wrote his personal memoir *Soul on Ice* (1969) from prison at the age 30. Assata Shakur, a female Black Panthers, wrote her *Assata* (1987) at the age of 40. L. George 'Bobby' Seale's *A Lonely Rage* (1978) was published when he was 42.
9. One of the major Punjabi kissa named *Kissa Pooran Bhagat* hinges on the hypergamous relationship for its thematic take off. In the kissa, Luna is a young luscious low-caste woman (a tanner's daughter), whom King Salwan marries following his disenchantment with his first wife Icchran. She is morally pilloried for showing her attraction towards her step-son Pooran. Shiv Kumar Batalavi rewrites the kissa and entitles it as *Luna* (1965). In the rewritten form, instead of Luna being deprecated as a morally depraved mother, her sexuality is celebrated, and she gathers agency to act and express herself.
10. Probably for this reason, Punjabi fiction, written by progressive writers like Gurdial Singh, Sohan Singh Sital or Ram Sarup Ankhi remains formidable for its representation of not only of social realism but also of what may be termed as Dalit realism. Social realism and Dalit realism tend to coincide in the predominantly agrarian context of Punjab. Dalit

characters that appear in fiction written by Dalit as well as non-Dalit Punjabi writers suffer more on account of their being more as landless labourers/workers/peasants than as low-caste beings. In Gurdial Singh's critically acclaimed novel *Marhi da Deeva* (1964), hailed as the first 'Dalit' novel in Punjabi, the tragedy of Jagseer, a low-caste farmer working at the fields of his landlord Dharam Singh, remains the tragedy of an agricultural labourer, the fact of his being a low caste is not foregrounded in the narrative.

11. This is how Madhopuri would repeatedly use the metaphor of Persian wheel: (a) 'The wheel of destiny would seem to be on its perpetual journey like the Persian wheel. It seemed that the new buckets strung on the wheel were full of water, like the symbol of the good deeds of the tales of holy men, and the old hole-ridden buckets were empty like the stories that could not be articulated' (2010: 15), and (b) 'These thoughts jostled about in my mind, rotating like the buckets of the Persian wheel in school' (2010: 102).

12. While, the discourse of Sikh Gurus aimed at universal brotherhood and the practices of 'sangat' and 'langar' (community kitchen) and of offering 'karah prasad' by any one irrespective of caste do lend Sikhism a rare quality of being caste-less, but the fact remains that low-caste Sikhs are discriminated even inside the gurudwaras, forcing them to open their own. In a survey of 116 villages in Amritsar, undertaken by Harish K. Puri, 68 villages had separate gurudwaras of the Dalits, and there were separate cremation grounds for Dalits in 72 villages (2003: 2700).

13. Sikhs who are formally baptized and initiated into *khalsa panth* are called *amritdhari* Sikhs. Those who do not follow the Sikh vows, they are called *sahajdharis*.

14. *Viramma* (1998) is an unusual autobiography because it is co-authored by Josaine Racine and Jean-Luc Racine – Tamil-born ethnomusicologists educated in France. Viramma narrates her story in the first person to them, and they reproduce the tape-recorded version of it in French and English translation. *Viramma* is thus the first person account of an illiterate Dalit woman from Tamil Naidu.

15. In his *Gulamgiri* (Slavery), for instance, Jotirao Phule argues along the same lines:

Now from this you can observe for yourself that since Brahma had genital organs at four places – mouth, arms, groins and legs (for the four varnas were born out of these four organs according to *Manusmriti*) – each of them must have menstruated at least for four days each, and he must have sat aside in seclusion, as an untouchable person, for sixteen days in all, each month. (1873: 49)

16. Limbale in his *Akkarmashi* creates shocking counter-aesthetics of hunger thus:

Bhakari is as large as man. It is as vast as the sky, and bright like the sun. Hunger is bigger than man. Hunger is vaster than the seven circles of hell. Man is only as big as a bhakari, and only as big as his hunger. Hunger is more powerful than man. A single stomach is like the whole earth. Hunger seems no bigger than your open palm, but it can swallow the whole world and let out a belch. (2003: 50)

References

Akida, Gurnam. 2007. *Kakh Kande*. Barnala: Vishwabharati.
Atarjeet. 2008. *Akk da Dudh*. Bhatinda: Balraj Sahni Yaadgari Prakashan.
Bakhtin, M.M. 1998. *The Dialogic Imagination: Four Essays*. Trans. by Caryl Emerson and Michael Holquist. Austin: University of Texas Press.
Batalavi, Shiv Kumar. 1985. *Luna*. Trans. by Sant Singh Sekhon. *Bharati Journal of Comparative Literature*, 1(1): 55–158.
Barthes, Roland. 1976. *The Pleasure of Text*. Trans. by Richard Miller. New York: Hill and Wang.
Bhutto, Benazir. 1988. *The Daughter of the East*. London: Hamish Hamilton.
Dil, Lal Singh. 1998. *Dastan*. Ludhiana: Chetna Prakashan.
Gorkhi, Prem. 2007.*Gair Hazir Aadmi*. Chandigarh: Lokgeet Prakashan (revised publication).
Guha, Ranajit. 1982. 'On Some Aspects of the Historiography of Colonial India', in Ranajit Guha (ed.), *Subaltern Studies: Writings on South Asian History and Society*, Vol. 1, pp. 37–44. New Delhi: Oxford University Press.
Hans, Rajkumar. 2010. 'Rich Heritage of Punjabi Dalit Literature and Its Exclusion from Histories', *Beyond Borders*, 6(1–2): 73–81.
Limbale, Sarankumar. 2003. *Akkarmashi* (Outcaste). Trans. by Santosh Bhoomikar. New Delhi: Oxford University Press.
———. 2004. *Towards an Aesthetic of Dalit Literature: From Erasure to Assertion*. Trans. by Alok Mukherjee. New Delhi: Oxford University Press.
Madhopuri, Balbir. 2010. *Changiya Rukh* (2002), translated as *Against the Night: An Autobiography*. Trans. by Tripti Jain. New Delhi: Oxford University Press.
Mukherjee, Alok. 2004. 'Reading Sharankumar Limbale's *Towards an Aesthetic of Dalit Literature: From Erasure to Assertion*' in *Towards an Aesthetic of Dalit Literature: From Erasure to Assertion*. New Delhi: Oxford University Press.
Pawar, Daya. 2010 [1978]. *Baluta*, translated in Hindi as *Acchoot*. Trans. by Damodar Khadse, New Delhi: Radhakrishan Paperbacks.
Phule, Jotirao. *Gulamgiri* 2002 [1873]. Trans. by Maya Pandit, *Selected Writings of Jotirao Phule*. Ed. by G.P. Deshpande, pp. 23–99. New Delhi: Leftword.
Prakash, Prem. 1998. 'Udno Bachaye Varke', in *Dastan*. Ludhiana: Chetna Prakashan.
Puri, Harish K. 2003. 'Scheduled Castes in Sikh Community: A Historical Perspective', *Economic and Political Weekly*, 2693–701.

Rahi, Giani Gurbakhas Singh. 2002. *Jini Rahi Mein Tooriya*. Barnala: Rahi Sahitya Prakashan.
Ram, Ronki. 2004. 'Untouchability in India with a Difference: Ad Dharm, Dalit Assertion and Caste Conflicts in Punjab', *Asian Survey*, XLIV(6): 895–912.
Singh, Gurdial (ed.). 2000 [1964]. *Marhi da Diva*. Chandigarh: Lokgeet Prakashan.
Viramma, Josiane Racine and Jean-Luc Racine. 1998. *Viramma*. New York and London: Verso.

Part III

CULTURAL HISTORY AND LOCAL TRADITIONS

7

INDIANNESS

A battlefield

Sushil Kumar

India is a constitutional state. The moment of its formation was the moment for exploring India's moral universe in terms of principles and ideals as they crystallized in recent and distant past, with a view to position them in a 'reflective equilibrium' and in relation to the thinking and practices of other states, their principles and ideals. John Rawls describes it as a process for constructing 'a theory of justice' (1973: 48).

> I now turn to the notion of reflective equilibrium [*sic*]. From the standpoint of moral philosophy the best account of a person's sense of justice is not the one which fits his judgment, but rather the one which matches his judgments in reflective equilibrium. As we have seen this state is one reached after a person has weighed various proposed conceptions and has either revised his judgments to accord with one of them or hold fast to his initial conviction (and the corresponding conception).

The Rawlsian concept of reflective equilibrium is a mode of theoretical intervention in contextually defined relationship between order and justice. It is generally not a matching relationship. The conditions of order do not generally match with the requirements of justice, and so the mode of intervention has to be tailored appropriately. Putting it differently, the intervention is not a mechanical application of the ideals conceived in universal terms, whether these ideals are historically given or rationally conceptualized. Such an intervention has an imperative. It should be based on relevant ideas in literary, political and international theories and generally in other branches of humanities and social sciences, and, after configuring them in reflective equilibrium, test whether they produce delightful sounds against elements in the context. As such, reflective equilibrium as a theory of justice is a point of reference which cuts across disciplinary boundaries. The aim is to articulate a conception of reason which is simultaneously universal and contextual, normative and emancipatory, without being specifically religious or narrowly transcendental. It is a kind of 'intellectual endeavour' which 'involves a blend of exegesis, conceptual analysis, ideology critique and constructive theorizing based on scrupulous attention to empirical realities' (Kulkarni 2011: xvi). Changing parameters of the international context are also incorporated in the processes of reflective equilibrium. For example, the post-Cold War drive towards neoliberal globalization is changing the parameters for defining regional, national and local contexts. This has evoked sharply polarized reactions from supporters and opponents of globalization. Each of these reactions is centred and theoretically dense. It leaves little scope for dealing with its negative effects in terms of its own methods. You cannot take care of these effects by extending greater support or greater opposition to globalization. This brings in social sciences and cultural studies and defines the social context for their exertions. The only way out is to examine the emerging social realities for identifying spaces where the values of justice, equity and democracy can be strategically located.

The vision

Indianness is a comprehensive vision of justice for the Indian people for themselves and for the world. Other people can share it or contribute to it. In relation to the existing ways of thinking and action, the vision is destructive and reconstructive at the same time. It is destructive of ideas and ideals which deny sovereign consciousness to people and aim to manipulate them, or silence their voice. It is reconstructive of institutions for extension of love and care, freedom and equality across social differences. It does not matter whether these ideas and ideals are contained in classical or other texts of India itself, or in the social practices of its own people. It does not matter whether these ideas or ideals are contained in the texts and practices in other cultures and civilizations. The people who undertake such destruction and reconstruction in specific social contexts command neither guns nor big finance. They generally have only discursive capital to invest. This is where they locate their efforts.

Nehru's spiritual pilgrimage in *The Discovery of India* (1989 [1946]) was an articulated discourse of reconstruction.[1] He was puzzled by the fact that India, 'with a rich and immemorial past' (ibid.: 49), should find itself in a condition of such poverty and degradation. He said: 'The present for me, and for many others like me, was an odd mixture of medievalism, appalling poverty and misery and somewhat superficial modernism of the middle classes' (ibid.: 57). His stance was a little ambivalent as between polarities, between India's past and the present, or between India's middle class and the rest. He appreciated India's historical continuity: 'the whole of the past belonged to me in the present' (ibid.: 23). He was optimistic, that India would 'find herself again' (ibid.: 36).

At the same time, he distinguished between 'the old and the new'. A people whose history goes back to thousands of years cannot be constituted into a form which is culturally empty, that is, devoid of high ideals and principles. India was full of such ideals and principles but these were conceived in pre-modern times. Their contemporaneity with ideals and principles of modernity was missing. India appeared to Nehru as half full and half empty. For him India was a naturally grown phenomenon but could not grow further this way. It could not brush aside the international context and the forces emanating from there. A modern nation did not grow like an oak or a tree. It had to be fabricated. It was like a building; it was planned by people and built on a particular foundation. And like a building it could undergo modifications through time or as well fall. Ernest Gellner in his book *Nation and Nationalism* argued that 'nations are not inscribed on the nature of things' (1983: 49). A modern nation was just an idea, an imagined community. Its members felt themselves as part of a greater collective and shared a 'deep, horizontal comradeship'. Nehru as a re-constructionist had a bifocal vision. Such a vision refers (Brennan 1990: 45) 'both to the modern nation-state and to something more ancient and nebulous – the *natio* – a local community, domicile, family, condition of belonging'.

In Nehru's view, a nation required an emotive foundation for the organization and membership of the state which served as its political agency. During his tenure as head of government, he gained first-hand experience of the kind of insurmountable problems that this agency encountered in a decentralized social order. He realized how difficult it was to give precedence to the issues of justice over all others. The issues of justice appear as scratches on the emotive foundation and evaluate their coincidences with various narratives, rituals and symbols meant to stimulate a sense of national belonging. They examine the images personifying the nation, *bharatmata* or Bhakra Dam or both put together. They examine linguistic and cartoon stereotypes used for representing the nation. They celebrate simultaneities of time and place in everyday life. When I pick up *The Times of India* in the morning, I know that so many others are doing the same. Such unities of time and place bridge social differences. The national history too plays a part. It aims to posit a common archive and a common past. National historians choose a defining moment in the past and put on the same pedestal nation-builders from diverse social backgrounds selected for their role and inspirational qualities.

Nonetheless, the relationship between representation and reality is problematic. Different people chose different representations of the nation. For Nehru, India's past was to be revived in terms of its flavour only insofar as it was consonant with a creative present. Andre Malraux (1967: 329) rightly put it, 'there was an English Nehru. But there's also the other'. Nehru perceived an enormous gap between the modernity for which he strove and the cultural heritage, rich and beautiful though, but a burden. A perfect cocktail was difficult to mix. The differences were difficult to transcend as for example between the followers of Swami Dayanand and those of Raja Rammohan Roy. Malraux spoke of his 'tired smile' (ibid.). Gunnar Myrdal in his *Asian Drama* (1969) describes his approach as verging on the tragic. He found that difference and ambivalence were rooted in the very structure of Indianness. Should we therefore conclude that any representation of India should feature difference and ambivalence as its defining characteristics? Has it not led to a tendency of defining India through negations, what India is not? Was it not the tenor of Nehru's domestic and foreign policies? Was it not the source of his disillusionment also? After Chinese aggression he did confess the unreality of the world of his imagination. Those concerned with the future of India pose the question, is it possible to transcend ambivalence between pre-modern and modern, order and justice?

India's policy-making elite took this page out from Nehru's life and re-read it for lessons in building post-Nehruvian India. They learnt that hovering between the two worlds was wasteful and that the vision should be so reconstructed as to push modernization with a firm determination modelled on the practices of such futurists as Mustafa Kamal Ataturk. This signalled the battle between a democratic and egalitarian India, its roots going back to the movement for independence, and the post-Nehruvian drive for power cloaked as imperative for a strong government and a strong Centre. This was interpreted as sacrifice of democracy on the altar of statism. The transition was effected by the forty-second amendment. The way for this amendment was paved by the political debates during the seventies (Kogekar 1976).

After the end of the Cold War, India faced an empty treasury and a rising crescendo of caste and religious differences. After a 40-year cycle, the debates of the 1970s are being revisited and strategies reinvented for laying a path for a major constitutional amendment for re-establishing an order which could drive progressive change. During the seventies, the rising power of the former Soviet Union could not be overlooked. This time, in a unipolar world, Fukuyama's advice to go the way of the West in culture and institutions is, Hobson's choice. Earlier it was a transition from democracy to statism. There were proposals for moving over to presidential form of government and shifting the seat of power from prime minister to the president. Now, when the Cold War ended, the transition was from statism to neo-liberalism and there are proposals to shift the seat of power from the people to parliament.

This evokes the remark, Indianness is a brew distilled in the first world. But, in reality, the post-Cold War transition is dictated, not by international conditions alone, but equally and more importantly, by domestic circumstances, a context when 'the tall poppies' are out and their successors have to make a choice between a weak and vulnerable India and an India which is strong and equipped with economic and military power. Does the world take this seriously? 'Hegemon China' and 'Terrorist Pakistan' are one set of contextual responses to the ongoing discourse of 'Rising India'.

Are these responses adequate for transcending the issues of freedom and justice? Do they represent 'we the people' as sovereign subjects in our history and politics? Probably they don't. No doubt, we fought against colonial domination. The fight was successful and India won independence. Is the struggle for independence adequate to infuse the people with sovereign subjecthood?[2] If it does, then how do we bear witness to the agency of those representations which constitute consciousness of 'being Indian' by shifting discourses of power which 'speak through' us and situate and re-situate us in particular positions and relations. Sovereign subjecthood appears to be a distant goal. Indianness is de-centred in that it is constructed from positions outside of itself. Power and knowledge are intertwined in its discursive constitution. Caught in this cross-fire of forces external to the self, it is questionable whether the people do really author their self or write their identity. Does this invert the goal of just order and just citizenship? The question is this: does the rise of a power-seeking state a defeat of Indianness? Or, is a power-seeking state a case of transcending Indianness, its cant of difference and ambiguity?

The post-Nehruvian shift brought to surface certain uneasiness with intellectual modes of representing Indian reality. One reaction to this uneasiness was a movement towards popular culture as the preferred mode of expression. How do we interpret this? Is it because the intellectuals became 'official' and represented Indianness within frameworks of hegemonic domination? Is it because the representative institutions are caught between peoples' interests and the mounting pressures contingent on the shift? Both intellectuals and institutions produce discordant sounds against elements in the context, the negative consequences of forced, top-down progressive change. There is not enough resonance with the social realities of those who are excluded and feel alienated. They speak in the idiom of 'foreign' discourses – imperial, colonial or patriarchal. For example, inclusive development is pursued by inviting the subalterns to join the Delhi marathon? Or should we interpret the subaltern performative acts as an option exercised by them in their sovereign consciousness to become a part of the market by accepting the opportunities offered by it? The manner of posing these questions reveals a normative position that justice is dispensed in terms of your value in building national power or consists in matching your market worth with your price.

Popular culture articulates rebellion and resentment against these metanarratives. A performative act hides the rage within. The intellectuals give voice to this rage by making theoretical interventions designed to render the hegemony more just and egalitarian. The Sarva Shiksha Abhiyan puts up an advertisement, *bare bares apne*. A poor little girl figures in it. Can she be credited with that level of autonomous consciousness? The dilemma is that a school dropout in her place will take no time in countering the claim. The subalterns are therefore not impressed with political slogans in favour of child rights, social and gender justice. The subalterns no longer endorse them as alternatives to the ruling ideas, norms and practices of otherness and hegemonic control.

Antonio Gramsci gave theoretical articulation to subaltern performative acts. His idea was to establish an alternative hegemony of the subalterns including the working classes. In a society where social and political constraints forestall class consolidation, the subalterns are impatient to change the game by digging trenches beyond Marxist materialism. A neo-Freudian expression of resentment, along the lines indicated by Herbert Marcuse's 'the return of the repressed' in his *Eros and Civilization: a Philosophical Inquiry into Freud* (1955), catches their imagination. Repression, according to him, is contingent on 'a hierarchical organization of work' and on 'the monogamic–patriarchal family'. The subaltern imaginings along neo-Freudian lines found support in Max Horkheimer (1947: 100–6). The modern man, according to Horkheimer, submits himself to the authority of civilization and the suppression of instinctual human nature without fully resigning to it. The subalterns feel that Horkheimer is talking about them. Forced adjustments do involve 'an element of resentment and suppressed fury', and so the repressed urges lie in wait 'to break out as a destructive force'. The subalterns have seen an opening here for them. They do not mind letting repression break out as a destructive force, not in violence but through subversion in stealth. Stealth for them is now the road to justice.

The bottom up discourse is located in popular culture and its oppositional stance is based on real and imaginary memories of otherness. The intellectual production, on the contrary, positions subaltern consciousness in economic inequalities and cultural specificity, not in otherness. This means that the texts and images are not a disinterested mediator in giving voice to subaltern subjectivity. It seeks to empower subalterns from the outside. The design of these strategies depends more on mobilization than participation.

The empowerment strategies located within hegemonic discourses have exhausted themselves. They could not subvert the moral universe of political and economic power. These discourses had the limited effect of extending the neoliberal acquisitive drive and possessive individualism to middle class subaltern youth. Some of them succeeded but a vast majority looks for small gains through legal or illegal methods. Beyond this they could not go. The subalterns were not empowered as an autonomous political agent. The subalterns can be empowered only through the subversion of the moral order which leads to their marginalization and otherness, both political and cultural. Hence, they are opting for activities which are within the range of their competence and where they excel the middle classes.

The subaltern consciousness to be so constructed needs to be retrieved from the texts and images claiming to represent it. Gayatri

Spivak underlines the mistake of attributing a centred-consciousness to subalterns in their expression of resistance. Their identity continues to be written and rewritten by those who hold political and economic power, whether in modern or traditional sectors, whether in state, market or pulpit. Whether the discourse is colonial or post-colonial makes no difference. The representations continue to be similar. This means that, in subaltern perception, the splits in the architecture of citizenship continue to be wide. *Aam adami* continues to be colonized and silenced. A reconstructed inclusive vision of Indianness based on *sarvodaya* is not yet there.

How then do we know what is Indian? The post-modern emphasis on difference and ethical relativism draws one away from hegemonic definitions. You tend to misspell words and forget your 'loved accent'. You find your luminous wings beating in vain. How should one understand the situation? The study entitled *Learning to Labour: How Working Class Kids Get Working Class Jobs* (Willis 1977) gives an answer. It underlines the resignation of these kids to their 'inevitable' fate through expression of oppositional racist and sexist values and by celebrating their own failure in academic attainment with 'a laff' (p. 76). In neo-Gramscian understanding the social processes including the cultural impact of educational institutions promote the subjective identification of these kids as 'factory fodder'. In a hegemonic setting, educational institutions, their culture and curriculum, are designed for easy movement of Hegemon's children to the West for subsequent return home into elite jobs. A chief minister recently remarked that equality of opportunity, a metanarrative of liberal modernity embodied in the Constitution of India, would not get subverted if, by chance or design, the children happened to occupy the jobs of their successful parents, in politics and the civil services.

The social sciences and cultural studies, without turning their focus on those who are not able to make the grade in the so-called open competition for the jobs, high and low, will not be able to see the extraordinary in the ordinary social contexts. The Althusserian moment seems to have arrived. The normative and ideological mechanisms are failing to secure the consent of the subaltern and so more coercive approaches are being adopted to secure social and political order. Playing religious music especially *bhajans* in public places like parks is soft persuasion, short of police coercion. Cognitive dissonance is slowly creeping in and distorting the relationship between hegemony and dissent, or between order and justice within the panoramic view of Indianness.

A cognitive project

As a cognitive project, Indianness divides between two streams. The first is religious and mythical and the second is scientific and secular. Each stream has huge literature explicating its point of view. Even a cursory familiarity with it is difficult. A cognitive grasp of Indianness through this literature is confounded by wide gaps between representation and reality, or between idealized descriptions of India and the situation on the ground. The idealized narratives are embellished with beautiful and exotic imagery of people and their surroundings. This is so in calendar art and animation films or in media texts on economic development and national power, or on such national events as the Republic Day parade. The art genres and official texts complement the discourses of hegemony. The whole enterprise is to appropriate the symbols of popular art forms for the benefit of hegemony.

The predicament is not peculiar to us. It was so in the West also. Reconciling the idea of the West with endorsement of universal human values was possible only during periods of economic prosperity. The subsequent collapse of prosperity and clash among forms of government leading to violence, even war, did not incline the West to take commitment beyond humanism and democracy, at least in public sphere. Any such extension was perceived as subversive to their civilizational project. Such linking of science to civilizational project was misconceived.

Science was no respecter of differences between humanism and fascism or between Western and other civilizations. In fact, science and technology developed faster under fascism, so also in non-Western settings, at least in certain sectors. The non-Western political thinking therefore easily veers round to the view that the technologies of war need to be developed and perfected against attempts to dislodge them from their cultural base. The recent induction of the F-word in politics is attributed to 'the failure of traditional religion to encompass modernity', not science. The effect is to de-centre non-Western politics and push it away from concern for widening chasms between the mythical ideals, rhetoric and reality. The more the reality slips from under the feet of the ideals, the more the ideals are vocalized as weapons of opposition. The ideals, whether secular or mythical, are reduced to words, empty words, and mere language games.

Nehru situated himself in this battle of reconstituting the Janus-faced Indianness for consolidating the hard won independence for the nation-state by trying to reconcile its mythical ideals of the past with building its future through science. Several illustrious scholars inspired by Nehru, or on their own, came together in an academic enterprise called the History of Indian Science, Philosophy and Culture. Those who know the scholars associated with this project will feel blessed in bowing down to their high scholarship and commitment. Huge effort and scholarship went into it. But the reality of Indianness continued to be ambivalent. This can be attributed to the fact that science offers no choice between values. Mythical ideals, on the other hand, prescribe no absolute standards for judging their claims. This opens flood gates for scientific and mythological relativism.

Indianness can therefore be conceived as composed of features which have limitless possibilities of extension from potentiality to actuality. Within the present post-structural normative framework, it can be translated into multiple narratives. An actuality can be defined as Indian which in the absence of any standard of Indianness cannot be disputed. Indianness may take forms which may evoke their description as un-Indian but if they are defined as Indian, they become Indian. Definitions thus acquire ontological significance. The designated name constitutes a designated reality. Thomas Hobbes says that names are 'signs of our conceptions' and manifestly 'not signs of the things themselves'. This is an effect of an epistemological revolution, a legacy of scientific rationality. The 17th-century philosophy replaced a structurally rigid cosmos of substances (as theorized by classical thinkers like Aristotle) by a substantially empty and homogeneous spatial cosmos.[3]

This led to a new understanding of the role of language in society. This understanding departed from the role of language in theological thought which in some ways converged on classical thought. The Aristotelian world was a verbal world. It was a noun-oriented world. In such a world, the heterogeneity of words could do justice with the heterogeneity of reality. The attempt was to use a separate word for a separate reality. An accurate definition revealed the essence of the reality represented by that word. The word embodied the reality. Change the word and you refer to another reality. This attributed an explanatory function to language. Interrogations of any reality could be answered by referring to the meaning embodied in the noun used to name it. The view rested on the belief in the efficacy of final causality. The definition and the cause were united in the *telos* of the reality in question. This led to excessive concern with the subtleties of definition.

All this changed under the impact of a scientific worldview. The use of nouns and definitions in characterizing reality now became casual and arbitrary. The assignment of names was no longer the discovery of a structural aspect of reality but instead an arbitrary designation of the intellect. Everything exists in singular. This is a kind of logical atomism associated with Bertrand Russell and the thought of Wittgenstein. Just shift words in relation to one another and the meaning changes. It is like rearranging furniture in your drawing room. In this sense Indianness is like redness which names a range of objects that are united by some common form or feature but are otherwise separate. It is an invention, a creation of the mind. No wonder a large number of intellectuals label India as an idea, an essence or an archetype, or an invention, a constructed device meant to achieve a given goal. How should one define the archetypical India? And how is India being contrived to achieve a predetermined goal? Both represent Indianness not as discrete entities but as representations of relative reality, of an India unfolding itself. For reconstructing Indianness not in absolute but in relative terms, the common tendency is to spread it on a scale ranging, say, from one to ten from each end. Each point marks out relative Indianness. Stand somewhere in the middle, equidistant from the two ends, and look from one end to the other. This is not what is intended by reconstruction. It is just a caricature of it. Such caricatures appear now and then. For example, some people used scientific principles to make a statue of Lord Ganesha drink milk. Or, the government code named nuclear explosions as 'Buddha Smiling'. Architects design a separate temple room in houses owned by people who do not practice any religion. Even the practice of religion is relativized with respect to market availability of artefacts needed for such practice. Religion has gone commercial like bridal dress which is available on hire. A bride is a bride, hired or married. The difference is only a linguistic expression. Re-enactment of an image is what matters. These caricatures show that Indianness as a cognitive project is getting disconnected from its mandate.

Nehru's 'tired smile' is leading the succeeding generations to shut the door on his dream. There lurks a danger here. Social sciences and humanities, conceived in universalistic framework, are enabling the power elite to control the social environment so as to make it congruent with their needs and wants. In the *Division of Labour in Society*, Durkheim says that man can escape nature not merely by controlling it but also by creating another world where he himself is at home and secure; this world is society. We must not forget that it is only in the political realm that the vision of Indianness can be articulated and pursued. When the engineering capabilities of humanities and social sciences are being harnessed in formulation of public policies for consolidating neo-liberal hegemony, then the realization of alternatives is a political and cultural enterprise and depends on creation of discourses for generation of symbolic capital and networks of alternative discourse communities.

An emancipatory project

There are broadly two approaches for addressing Indianness as an emancipatory project, the rational approach and its other. Reason understands itself in opposition to its other, through negations. Indianness as a rational category has come to understand its emancipatory content in opposition to colonialism. Anti-colonial stance is emancipatory. But reason as an emancipatory project does not end there. Reason continues to wage war against the irrational, that is, against that which does not yield to the freedom, independence and autonomy of the thinking self. Reason calls on people to reflect on their experiences and actions, and thereby change the ends they seek and the means for achieving them. A nation is emancipated when its members make such deliberate efforts to order, direct and control their collective affairs and activities. Such participation and consequent determinations imply emancipation. Hence it is only by determining the conditions of their lives that a people enjoy freedom through self-determination. This means that Indianness prescribes expansion of democratic control on the collective life of the people by creating conditions for a real rather than demagogic political development. In terms of this imperative, intellectuals have an important role in deconstructing the dominant and subaltern discourses to advance emancipation. Only organic intellectuals can guard against appropriation of subaltern discourses by hegemonic intellectuals, national or international. Only they can lead projects for development of sovereign consciousness among people.

One way of doing it is to build political capability within subaltern groups. At a time when the hegemonic intellectuals are zealous about guarding national independence and sovereignty, the masses find that the real conditions of existence in terms of livelihood adequacy and security are deteriorating. The masses also find that their ability for participation in political process as empowered citizens on egalitarian basis is on decline. High electoral turnout and use of cell phones and other products, or drinking cola straight from the bottle, are not good indicators of the aam adami's ability to be him. *Aam Istri* ranks still lower on this scale. The link is not so much with the material conditions of life as with social practices aimed at the cognitive insulation of *aam adami* or *istri* from market mechanisms, so that a choice between prices and products is not a personal but a political one. By turning political into personal, you surrender agency and become an object of scientific manipulation.

This is not to blame individual social scientists that they intentionally make plans for manipulating the subalterns. Their social commitments are transparent and above board. Social manipulation at the behest of science is not an empirical but a theoretical question. The scientific enterprise rests on *a priori* assumptions and the practitioners of science work within these assumptions. Unless they make a conscious effort to dig into the theoretical foundations of their work, they would not be able to know the conceptual linkages between the idea of a policy science and the idea of a positivist theory of social science. To know an event is to understand the events which produce it. To know this is to have the ability to produce the event in experimental situations. This is intimately connected to the notion of control.

An instrumentalist and engineering conception of knowledge and its relation to social action defines social science. Nehru's 'tired smile' while fitting Indianness into his vision loaded the stakes of scholars in favour of policy sciences and they struggled to increase their visibility for co-optation into the hegemonic discourses of national and international outfits. The effect was to put Indianness as an emancipatory project on the back burner. As social sciences never yielded monological laws of applied value, the co-optation process succeeded only in changing the rules of the game on the campuses.

Nehru's reconstructive project, conceived by him at Gandhiji's feet, was no longer a take away from the classroom to the library. The 'outs' envy the 'ins' for what they munch, while the 'ins' perversely enjoy what the 'outs' are missing. Such embattled relationship of the 'ins' with the 'outs' has turned Indianness into a political battlefield foregrounding self-interest not an enlightened citizenry. Their mutual oppositions are articulated as speech acts based on contrasting narratives which empty Indianness of all substance. In the absence of a metanarrative as a point of reference, Indianness is relativized and given a postmodern flavour. It is narrated through banners, add-ons to life style and similar displays. Such displays constituting Indianness are presented as polarized indicators along several axes: traditional and modern; domestic and foreign; material and cultural; democratic and hegemonic; national and local; elite and subaltern; sovereign and dependent subjectivity; and the like. Indianness, in such a context, is over-determined. No single factor or variable can describe it fully. Like *a la carte*, it allows one to have his or her pick from among them. We, therefore, come back to Rawls' concept of 'reflective equilibrium' as a process of adjustment among the constitutive factors of a configuration, which, as an effect of this process, is inherently ambivalent, and, as a mechanism for holding the diverse factors together, retains its difference from other such configurations. Such ambivalence and difference come out loudly in political speeches. This can be illustrated with reference to secular – democratic and communal – fundamentalist formations. Both are ambivalent from inside but oppositional from outside. The diverse factors within a configuration are held together by what Isaiah Berlin (1970: 37) calls 'moral gravity' which, as he says, gives the nation its 'unique character'.

Such grounding of Indianness on opposite and mutually balancing factors situates it within what are known as the structuralist approaches to culture. Indianness so situated is advanced as an authentic and authoritative point of reference. It continues to be so advanced even when it meets its own negations. The Constitution of India, for example, represents a great tradition but governance at local levels shows signs of disconnect with it. The reality at the lower levels of governance is represented by the age old tradition of using office for personal benefit. There is nothing new about it. The practice can trace its roots to practices in colonial and pre-colonial times, in official and non-official institutions, public and private spheres. The practice reinvents itself as a little tradition. The presence of this tradition at the high table is subverting the moral universe of political hegemony while at lower levels it was only a gesture of consideration. It is the same story in other spheres of hegemony.

Great traditions are transmitted by the elite to the masses. The meanings inscribed in the elite messages to the masses interact with different lived experiences of the people. The two do not necessarily integrate in everyday life. The gaps between the two constitute welcome spaces for bottom-up little traditions to position themselves strategically for subverting the moral universe of the great traditions. Surface appearances of hegemonic depth hide the empirical reality of dynamic undercurrents. The subalterns know that resort to violence can activate the coercive machinery. Hence, they socially integrate with middle classes by avidly taking to consumer preference along market trends. This helps in breaking the barrier of otherness in looks and expressive behaviour and in securing easy access into the households of the hegemonic classes as domestic workers especially for child care. The social impact of subaltern domestics has been a neglected concern in sociology and cultural studies. These disciplines originated in concern for other societies and cultures. This has generated an imperative for insulating the knowing subject from the object of study. This blinkers the social context of what they study. The context is taken for granted and is even trivialized or denigrated. The knowing subject positions himself or herself on a higher pedestal, more or less in coalition with the ruling classes and representing their interests in hegemonic discourses. This leads to the production of high-end meanings palatable to these classes. The social reproduction of these meanings through formal institutions and their practices does not offer a fuller understanding of India's social existence. There is now an eagerness on the part of social sciences to make up for this shortfall through interface with academic output in literary and cultural studies. It is interesting to find that these studies are themselves in quest for relevance. But still their output on popular culture is vast and interesting.

The post-disciplinary interface between social sciences and cultural studies has the potential of contextualizing the emancipatory dynamics of Indianness within a post-structuralist framework. Suppose a great tradition invites a little tradition as guest for dinner. The guest has a strange presence. The dinner table symbolizes the space where the meaning of Indianness as represented by the little tradition is contested by the great tradition. And the little tradition is puzzled that the great tradition feels secure by grounding the meaning of hegemonic practices on foundations which are just linguistic constructs and empty signifiers. The little tradition is able to 'see through' the great tradition. This reassures it in implementing its hidden agenda. For a moment suppose that the little tradition is reinvented as item dances in Bollywood films.

The item dances as social discourse

The subaltern domestics in middle-class homes did not like the practice of 'othering' by their employers. This practice was reinforced by casting household women in opposition to the domestics. The maid–wife polarity is perennial. The subordination and othering of the domestics has motivated them to discover cracks in the moral fibre of the people in the household. Such discoveries encouraged the workers, the maids, to learn erotic arts for attracting men in the household. The maids, in a way, discovered their bodies, their sexuality or their 'interiorized subjecthood'. They discovered their ability to entertain men. The consequent transgressions through intimacy and fantasy and their social and political effects have been theorized by Michel Foucault in *History of Sexuality* (1976) and by Sigmund Freud in his writings on the Oedipus complex and related subjects. The maid and family romance soon emerged as a serious intellectual concern.[4] Dipesh Chakrabarty (1994) describes it as 'difference–deferral'. The maid as slave and seductress was able to transcend social difference and created new communities. Their pronounced eroticism and aggressiveness was able to cross prescribed social boundaries and subvert middle class morality. Like the maids, the item dancers are probably aiming to reinvent female eroticism as a dissident sub-culture, with the aim of bringing it to the centre-stage of social discourse of inequality and marginalization. This little tradition is amenable to transformation and extension. The moral order of this dance form is immanent in the social context and is probably conscious of its location in the political order. This is evident from the growing engagement of lower classes with sexuality.

What is the aggregated effect of such erotic extravagance? There is no perceptible trend yet towards polarization of polity or society. There is no threat yet to social hegemony and domination. The meaning of the item dances need to be understood as a sub-culture of upward mobility and assimilation.[5] The generational gap is getting superimposed on social and class distinctions in choice of style and method for achieving goals. They are seen as alternative roads to advancement when honesty, integrity and hard work and even good citizenship are seen as new myths and less credible in this respect. Tapping sources of wealth and forging family connections with upper classes are more decisive pathways to good life. Petty corruption, song and dance sequences represent subaltern helplessness and as such should melt hearts and cause catharsis. When, therefore, you find that the sites of hegemonic control are a black market of morality and collapse with an erotic touch and the body language of *ooh la la*, you celebrate.

Notes

1. Jawaharlal Nehru wrote *The Discovery of India* when he was in Ahmednagar Fort prison during the years 1942–45. The book was first published

in 1946. The Centenary Edition was published by Oxford University Press in 1989. The references here are from the 1961 Bombay edition.
2. The question whether autonomous subjecthood is a contention or reality has been there since colonial times.
3. Thomas Hobbes's science of politics grabbed so much attention that his materialistic theory of language and the working of the human mind were almost eclipsed. See Philip Pettit. 2008. *Made with Words: Hobbes on Language, Mind and Politics*. Princeton: Princeton University Press. Pettit refers to a skilful orator who, while battling with his many enemies, denounces the rhetoric of his opponents but uses the most powerful tool of rhetoric under the guise of scientific orthodoxy. This Hobbesian insight has become everyday experience in domestic politics and international relations. Indianness represents such uses of language across political battle lines. For further details, reference may be made to Thomas Hobbes, 1839–45. *The English Works of Thomas Hobbes of Malmesbury*, Vol. 1–11, Ed. by Sir William Molesworth, London: John Bohn, Rpt, in The Elibron Classics. Vol. 1–6, 2004.
4. Some studies in the colonial context construct domesticity as a 'dangerous sexual terrain' where hegemonic and counter-hegemonic practices interface. See Stoler, Ann Laure. 1995. *Race and the Education of Desire: Foucault's History of Sexuality and the Colonial Order of Things*. Durham: Duke University Press.
5. A few item dances can be listed here. 'Choli', *Khalnayak*, 1993; 'Kajra Re', *Bunti Aur Babli*, 2005; 'Beedi', *Omkara*, 2006; 'Munni Badnaam Hui', *Dabangg*, 2010; 'Sheela Ki Jawani', *Tees Maar Khan*, 2010; 'Ooh la la', *The Dirty Picture*, 2012. There are several others also.

References

Berlin, Isaiah. 1998. *The Crooked Timber of Humanity*, ed. by H. Hardy. Princeton: Princeton University Press.

Chakrabarty, Dipesh. 1994. 'The Difference–Deferral of a Colonial Modernity: Public Debates on Domesticity in British India', *Subaltern Studies*, VIII, pp. 50–80. New Delhi: Oxford University Press.

Gellner, Ernest. 1983. *Nation and Nationalism*. Oxford: Basil-Blackwell.

Horkheimer, Max. 1947. *The Eclipse of Reason*. New York: Oxford University Press.

Kogekar, S. V. 1976. 'The Constitution Amendment Bill', *Economic and Political Weekly*, 9(42): 1659–64.

Kulkarni, M. (ed.). 2011. *Interdisciplinary Perspectives in Political Theory*. New Delhi: Sage.

Malraux, Andre. 1968. *Antimemoires*. London: Hamish Hamilton.

Marcuse, Herbert. 1955. *Eros and Civilization: A Philosophical Inquiry into Freud*. Boston: Beacon Press.

Myrdal, Gunnar. 1968. *Asian Drama*. New York: Pantheon.

Nehru, Jawaharlal. 1961. *The Discovery of India*. Bombay: Asia Publishing House.

Rawls, John. 1973. *Theory of Justice*. Oxford: Oxford University Press.
Spivak, Gayatri. 1988. 'Can the Subaltern Speak', in Cary Nelson and Lawrence Grasberg (eds), *Marxism and the Interpretation of Culture*, Urbana: University of Illinois Press.
Timothy, Brennan. 1990. 'The National Longing for Form', in Homi Bhaba (ed.), *Nation and Narration*. London and New York: Routledge.
Willis, P. 1977. *Learning to Labour: Working Class Kids Get Working Class Jobs*. Farnborough: Saxon House.

8
CULTURAL STUDIES IN INDIAN HISTORY
Dominant models from South Asia

Mahesh Sharma

The past two decades have witnessed a discernible shift in history-writing in South Asia from the objectivist model that emphasized the socio-economic determinants as the sole or primary causal relationship driven by the intention[ality] motive. The culture concept was also a product of such social conditioning. The shift today is to understand the social and cultural processes on their own terms, liberated from the causal connections between each other and the underlying structures. This is a huge leap forward from the notions furthered in the social sciences or history textbooks of earlier years – which invariably contained a chapter on Indian culture as a part of Indian society or even as an achieving glory of the period polity – to underscore today the role that culture plays in shaping social practices and historical processes. One reason for this shift is the appreciation of the fact that culture is not simply a function of the social, but constitutes the interpretative and moral, religious and symbolic, abstract and absolute, which interact with their socio-economic expectations. The interaction, thus, between the symbolic spaces with its social reality and cultural sensitivity brings forth fresh perceptions on questions like identities, experiences, meanings and interests, among others (see Cabrera 2001; Frecchia and Lewontin 1999; Sartori 2005).

In this article, I play upon this shift to explore some Indic cultural models used as explanatory tools by historians and anthropologists. I shall contextualize these models in a case study from Kashmir with inscriptional inputs from Chamba (in Himachal Pradesh), in order to understand how cultural space is contrived in historical texts; how abstract notions are concretized and given the form of ritual, space or object; and alternatively, how the concrete is reduced to abstraction. How the 'social' is conditioned by the cultural conditions may be constructed by our reading of the 16th-century text of Kashmiri provenance, the *Nilamata Purana*, and the copper-plate and stone inscriptions from Chamba. The example of *Nilamata Purana* is significant in understanding how an alternative cultural space is devised, replacing the earlier Buddhist/Vedic ethos that prevailed in Kashmir; while in Chamba, we argue that Puranic cultural ethos was established replacing the indigenous ethos.

Kashmir: devising alternative cultural space[1]

Nilamata Purana (hereafter NP) is the glorification of Kashmir, the infusion of Puranic cosmos to make it a sacred territory. It was, therefore, conceived as the place of Prajapati, the creator (NP: 226–27). The territory itself is organically conceived as the body of Sati (ibid.: 245), nurtured by river Vitasta (river Jhelum), which is likened to Uma (ibid.: 67, 257–53). The cultural geography of Kashmir was similarly devised by co-opting the entire range of Vedic-Puranic goddesses by associating them with rivers, creating thereby a divine hierarchy. That the goddess motif was used for regional sacrality is not unusual as has been discussed, for instance, by Chakrabarty in the case of Bengal. Chakrabarty (2000; 2001) concludes that the brahmanic ideological dominance was created by assimilating the local goddesses within the larger Puranic fold. The divisibility of the goddess' form and the multiplicity of myth, held together by the conception that all forms are of one goddess, aided assimilative flexibility (Chakrabarty 2001: 54–55). Further, the sacred-centres were devised on the banks of these rivers. For instance, the meandering Candrabhaga (river Chenab) housed such redemptive *tirtha*s as Guhyesvara, Satamukha, among others. Significantly, some of these centres were considered particularly auspicious, equated 'in holiness' to Varanasi and considered 'even higher than that' (NP: 120–25). For instance, the *tirtha* of river Pavana, Cirapramocana, was considered as 'a gateway to heaven', just like Kasi (ibid.: 1380). Like Kasi, it was considered auspicious to die and to be cremated at this place. Likewise, the river Mayuri was as holy as Mathura (ibid.: 1400); while the *tirtha* at the confluence of Vitasta with Dhanadharini was 'as holy as Prayaga' (ibid.: 1357–58). The text abounds in such semantic strategies, using similes for creating deft linkages with the pan-Indian pilgrim centres, and metaphors to parochialize them. Thus, an added dimension is provided to the conception of sacrality and the spiritual meaning of the regional pilgrimage by adopting such textual manipulations. This was, however, not an exclusive phenomenon and was a dynamic process. Such linkages, appropriations and networking to construct a parallel sacred geography may also be gleaned elsewhere in the hills, particularly Kangra, as late as mid-19th century (Sharma 1999: 41–56; 2001: 145–70). That the authors were sensitive to the spiritual and ritual needs of the locality is thus demonstrated.

Ritual cleansing by bathing in the consecrated waters was considered the most auspicious act, a prelude to offering homage and worship at these pilgrimage centres. Ceremonials were devised in which the local practices were subtly adopted, sometimes changed along with prescribed rituals. For instance, bathing in Vitasta was considered highly auspicious; its water was also ritually administered to the dying, like the water of river Ganga, to ensure a passage to heaven (NP: 1432).[2] Similarly, bathing in Vipasa[3] provided absolution and eternal bliss to the pure who visited the Kalikasrama centre that it housed (ibid.: 107–9), while Devahrda granted exoneration and heaven (NP: 109). In this way the local *tirtha-ksetras* (sacred territory), as well as the tirthas (pilgrim centres), were constructed/legitimized on the banks of rivers or their confluences.[4]

The tirthas were the centres where religious rites were performed. Usually such rites consisted of fire-oblations (*homa*), liturgy (*puja*), *vratas* (vows), *upavasa* (fasts), *dana* (charity), *snana* (bathing), *tarpana*-libations, *pinda-dana* (offering of funeral cakes to the manes), *sraddha* (ancestral rites), *tapas* (austerities), scriptural study or recitation, and rites-de-passage – particularly tonsure, death-cremation and funeral rites – accompanied by appropriate honorarium (*daksina*) and donation (*dana*) made to the presiding priests of various brahmanic ranks (Dubey 2001: 74). The merit/rewards of ritual praxis were also worked out. Providing salvation was the most significant characteristic of a *tirtha* or pilgrim centre on the riverbank. So much so that *Skanda Purana* ordains salvation even to birds and animals living on these riverbanks. Cessation from the cycle of rebirth, redemption and freedom from bad *karmas* or sins, the gaining of merits, heaven etc. prioritized the pilgrimage (Kumar 1983: 232–70). This is also evident in the copper-plate inscriptions issued by the rulers of the neighbouring state of Chamba. We can hence map the development chronologically. For instance, the Kulait inscription refers to the Chamba ruler of

Figure 8.1 'Hindus bathing in the early morning during a festival in Kashmir' watercolour painting by William Carpenter, ca 1885, V&A Museum London, South and Southeast Asian Collection. No. IS.113–1882 (2006AH4265). Copyright: Trustees, V&A Museum London.

early 10th century, Sahila Varman's visit and patronage to ritualists at Kuruksetra (Vogel: 182–87). Jasata, another Chamba ruler, undertook a pilgrimage with other chieftains to Kuruksetra (*Kalhana* VII: 319, 1512–4; VIII: 1083–6, 1443). Pratap Singh undertook a pilgrimage to Badrinatha in the early 13th century, where he distributed jewels among the *pujari*-priests. At Kedaranatha, land grant was made to a brahmana after performing a penance as well as purifying fast for six nights – *sada-ratropositena* (Chhabra 1957: 48–50). Subsequent rulers or princes of Chamba undertook pilgrimages to purify self and family, particularly after death. For instance, Anirudha undertook a pilgrimage to Prayaga, carrying the mortal remains of his mother (ibid.: 102–3). Ganga, as a repository of mortal remains (*ast/u/i* or bones and ash), had already gained currency among Chamba rulers by early 13th century (ibid.: 73–75). During the course of pilgrimage, these people not only donated and performed austerities and rituals, but also undertook vows (*vratas*). Thus, when the local ruler of Baijnath, in Kangra, undertook a pilgrimage to Kedaranatha around

1204, he vowed that he will thereafter not co-habit 'with the wives' of his subjects. The inscription compliments him that, 'if nevertheless his heart avoids the wives of others, what austerity is difficult to perform after that?'[5] Against these royal pilgrimages to the sub-continental centres, what has NP to offer? Absolution, boons, heaven, merits and redemption! Besides, it offers sacred banks for cremation, as doors to heaven; fearlessness from death; river-confluences to perform *tarpana* (libations) during eclipse and rites of passage (NP: 316–22; 501–3; 510). Finally, the tirthas releases one from the cycle of rebirths and provides *moksam* (salvation). With this regional perspective in mind, the NP univocally announces that: 'The Ganga does not excel Vitasta' (ibid.: 1428). Ganga only provides heaven while Vitasta grants salvation (ibid.: 322).

The sacred status of Vitasta was structured in a weeklong festival in the lunar month of *Sravana*. The ceremonies began with the propitiation of Varuna, the god of waters (*jalesvara*), on the fifth day, along with Uma (Vitasta is also Uma) and Dhanada, the god of wealth (ibid.: 784). On the sixth day, the 'virgins' (*kaumarih*), representing both the goddess and river, were purified by bathing and anointed to be decorated on the seventh (ibid.: 785). On the eighth day, people worshipped river Asokika, the one who brought merriment and cheers, after ritual cleansing by taking bath and anointing themselves with vermilion powder. They celebrated by organizing musicals (ibid.: 786–87). Free use of meat and wine (on occasion, sexual intercourse was also recommended)[6] was allowed in ceremonials, recommended particularly in some, though not in this case. On the ninth, people offered flowers, food, incense, 'bed' and 'seat' along with blanket. Only food mixed with sugar was consumed on this day, a way of purifying the body as a requirement for the next performance (ibid.: 788). On the 10th, Uma, the territorial goddess and the river, was worshipped as a bride, with incense, food, earthen lamps, garlands, curd, grain, sugar, safflowers, saffron, collyrium and bangles (ibid.: 789–90). On the 12th, the community leaders/priests (wise men) observed a fast and propitiated Hari (ibid.: 796). The ritual offerings made on this occasion consisted of sesame products (*tilavacca*) (ibid. NP: 526). On this day vocal musical performances were held and ceremonies related to touching auspicious things were performed (ibid.: 524). On the 13th, the birthday of Vitasta was observed (*Vitastajanamadivasam*), when people fasted (ibid.: 527, 791–92). The river was propitiated by offering perfumes, garlands, eatables, earthen-lamps, flags, red threads, bangles, various fruits, offering 'gratifying fires' (*yajnas*) and donations made to brahmanas. It was obligatory that people bathed in Vitasta for seven days, three days before and after the birthday. On the 14th, Mahesvara was propitiated by 'bathing the *linga* after removing its woollen covering' (*linga* was covered in wool). He was worshipped with scents, garlands, red-clothes, ointments, eatables, offerings of *yajna* and feasting the brahmanas. Night-long vigil (*bhaktyaratrautatahkaryamnrttagitaiehprajagaram*) was kept and people were engaged in listening to the stories of Siva and his incarnations (ibid.: 560). On the 15th, a mock sacrifice (sheep made of flour, a pointer to the brahmanic assertion) was made and meals consisting of ripe barley and cakes of sugar, cooked in/with sesame, were consumed (NP: 527–33). The post-birthday celebrations, however, revolved around dramatic performances, lasting further three days (ibid.: 791–95).

Similarly, in Chamba, an alternative cultural space was devised by Sanskritizing the local cultural ethos. Like Kashmir, linkages with the sub-continental cosmologies were appropriated – Sanskritizing the local or parochializing the Sanskritic. Cultural process became the legitimating tool and such symbols were also replicated/contested by the peripheral war lords. The process of creating consent to Chamba rule, particularly in periphery, was undertaken by the brahmans, who were sporadically settled in remote villages. Land grants played a major role in the brahmanic control over ideological sector by Sanskritizing the local cultural ethos, norms and values, dissemination of knowledge and thus creating a consent to rule. While brahmanic creation and mediation of the sacred domain firmed up the symbiotic relationship with kingship, they also created horizontal dominance by crystallizing the 'Puranic order'. A ritual space was, therefore, created by introducing and controlling pilgrimages, temple and everyday life rituals, rites of passage, calendared ceremonials and construction of Bhakti norms of vegetarianism, piety, *Ramayana* parental devotion, merits of donation (*dana-dharma*) and recitations of puranic texts as *Harivamsa* or *Bhagavata*. Cultural underpinnings, hence, sought to congeal the identity both of the territorial state and people. Linguistic hegemony was used as a unifying factor, a sense of Chambiali dominance and nationalism was enforced. Thus, disparate local communities acquired a larger social-cultural identity, a shared cultural pattern composing alternative worldviews, devised by common affiliations to the sacred domain (text, temple and ritual), kingship and language (Sharma 2009: Chapter I).

Figure 8.2 Watercolour painting by William Carpenter of a Varanasi ghat, ca 1885, V&A Museum London, South and Southeast Asian Collection. No. IS.107–1881 (2006AJ6676). Copyright: Trustees, V&A Museum London.

Both these examples, of Kashmir and Chamba, are rich in nuances – acculturation, assimilation, Sanskritization, parochialization, and such – whose significance becomes clear if we were to consider various explanatory models. In the following section, therefore, I will discuss rather than rearticulating various textual and anthropological models derived from the Indian society, which explain the subtleties in the above examples, which have contributed hugely to the shift in the present-day history writing.

Indic cultural models: methodological tools

When we think about 'culture' in the context of early Indian history, the nearest comparable term that comes to our mind is *Samskri (t-i/a)*: a base word that defines civilization (*Samskriti*). That civilization is not distinct from or is qualified by cultural nuances is evident from the further derivation of word *Samskara*, meaning to adorn, embellish, refine, elaborate or make perfect. That culture and civilization qualify each other is further evident from the word *Samskrit*, which represents language, an act of cultivating the mind and sound through training and education. Among all the meanings painstakingly culled from different canonical and literary sources by Sir Monier (particularly, the Vedic, Upanisadic, Epics and Early Medieval Dramas), the word *Samskrit/a/i* represents correctness and purity of speech; adornment, accomplishment and cleansing of the body, toilet, attire; dressing of food; refining, polishing and rearing; mental conformation or cultivation of the mind; the purification of mind, memory and mental recollection or impression (Monier-Williams 1983 [1899]: 1120b&c). *Samskriti* or Civilization is therefore only a socialization of the cultured people or the perfected body of or the cultivated body of the Cultured.

Even if both civilization and culture share the same roots in Indic texts, therefore complimenting each other, there are nevertheless subtle differences. When we think of civilization (*sabhyata* from *sabha* – the gathering), we are thinking of external markers – technology, production, territoriality, institutions; but when we think of culture (*sabhya* or those following the rules/etiquettes of the *sabha*) we are talking essentially of finesse that belongs to the category of 'inner' or internal – the spiritual quest to understand the 'beyond' and expressed through external symbols – the aesthetic representation of the dominant concerns. As Matthew Arnold (1963: 48–49) distinguished, the difference is between the moral and the material development. That culture builds upon and represents the civilizational is assumed. But there are certain cherished values, norms, which acquire dominance and therefore set in differentiation between people within the same civilization which we may understand as cultural. The culture-concept, thus, becomes a 'segregating' episteme as well.

Such a distinction between civilization and culture, may we remind, build upon the primary binary between the state of nature and humanization as well as the socialization of nature; the making of the early social ethical normative regulating human lives, refined over centuries into different systems of varied complexities and their defining achievements. Historically speaking, the articulation of civilization-cultural duo marks the transition from the lithic cultures to the early city-based complex or the coming of the historic civilization that supplanted the pre/proto-historic. This is, however, articulated as a cultural binary in all the early world-texts, differentiating between the civilized and barbarian, the literate (people with script) and the pre-literate. In most cases, this is the binary between the vanquished and the victor, the dominant and the subordinated. In the Indian context, this is the division that accentuates the divide between the Indo-Aryan speaking people and the indigenous populations, which were at the cross-roads of varied stages of historical development – like the city-based Indus Valley people and the Megalithic people as well.

If we were to continue with this understanding of interaction between the dominant and the subjugated, the Aryas and the indigenous, the Dasas of the Rik-Veda, the earliest interactions between the two civilizations are explained by the models of acculturation, whereby people were assimilated, segregated, integrated and marginalized into or by the physically dominant. As is evident from this model, the dominant civilization prevails upon and assimilates the larger subordinated people within its fold. The integration of the subordinated population is possible only by segregating some but marginalizing their dominant cultural values. This inherently means certain cultural appropriations of the marginal, borrowing particularly from their knowledge base and according significance, albeit insignificant, to their symbols of faith. New cultural symbols come out of this interaction, which are developed over centuries. We may think of the Atharva Veda, or the fourth Veda, as one such acquisition to the Indo-Aryan cultural heritage, which formed the knowledge base of the indigenous population. The other example may be of the introduction of sculpted images by the Greeks, which were adopted by the Buddhists and later the 'Hindus' and were to supplant the existing forms of ritual and worship. It may be noted that politically the Greek, Scythian, and Pahlava physical dominance was relatively small and they were assimilated over time into the larger social fabric of the sub-continent, yet their cultural influence was profound enough to bring about a major paradigmatic change during the last centuries of BCE–CE period: sculpture and drama, to name a couple of them.

Even if the acculturation model may be used to understand interactions between different civilizations, the Brahmanical textualists were also pondering on such questions. The most prominent articulation recognizing the cultural binary was recognized in the realm of music in the circa eighth-ninth-centuries treatise, *Brhad-desi* of Matanga, which distinguishes the 'music of the Way' to that of the provinces – Marga and Desi or the classical and the folk. This classification caught the imagination of the textualists, and the dichotomy was replicated thereafter, as in the 13th-century Sarangadeva's

Sangita-ratnakaram (Vatsyayan 1996: 118–19). Variously known, thereafter, as the canonical or classical (*Sastriyasangeeta*) and the folk or popular (*lokasangeeta*) or Marga–Vedic Sangeeta and Laukika Sangeeta. One way of sustaining this distinction in the Marga-Desi classification is in terms of time and authority. While the classical has the sanction of texts, a trajectory of evolution resting on the claims of authorship with an attempt to refine and develop, and is spread over larger tract – the nation or state – the folk-local is timeless, without any authority and text (see discussion by Babiarcki 1991a; 1991b: 69–90). It is 'popular' because it is sung by the masses, a culturally nuanced flavour of the community, locality or region. Sanyal (1984: 148–73) extended this classification to painting where *Marga* represented the classical as against *Jana*, literally, the people and therefore of indigenous derivation.[7] In such a classification, both categories are mutually exclusive, wherein Marga is considered pristine and therefore high.

There could be competing episteme even within the Classical or high culture. Romila Thapar (1978) enunciates this, taking the example of renouncers who constituted the counter-culture in the Early Medieval times. It must be noted that renunciation as a norm came to be expected as the last phase of aspirations – the spiritual quest leading to salvation (moksa) – among the four life-stations (asramas) in the Upanisadic literature. Later on, renunciation and asceticism became a sectarian affair, with people devoted solely to spiritual pursuits, distinct from the householders' quest for salvation. As they renounced the society and social, asceticism was understood as the social death of the person. The ascetic was no longer regulated by the rules and organization of the society. This, however, is incongruous. Ideally, the ascetics gave up the world and its ways in totality, abandoning the wherewithal of the social completely and dedicated themselves to the spiritual pursuits, without company and support. Yet, their repudiation of the social was not absolute. They sought the support of lay people to accomplish their mission. With the reinforcement of the monastic organization and the militarization of these 'orders', the renouncers sought the patronage of the society and state that they ostensibly served. Thus, while they maintained their opposition to the householders, they interacted with and lived off the society. In their own enclaves, that the monasteries were, they promulgated and followed certain binding rules, conformed to ecclesiastical hierarchy and acted towards the benefit of their order and monastery. These ascetics thus constituted a counter-culture, which was responsible for the revivalist (tradition enforcing, Sanskritic movements) as well as protest movements (parochializing movements) in the Early and Medieval India, thereby helping to develop and redefine the Sanskritic as well as the parallel regional cultures.

Similar to the Marga–Desi binary, Robert Redfield (1941; 1955; 1956), an anthropologist whose primary concern was to understand the peasant community, articulated an interdependent, yet independent of each other at the same time, the conception of Little Tradition and Great Tradition. As is evident from the typology itself, the 'Little' exemplifies the cultural traditions of the folk peasant communities, distinct from the Civilizational tradition or the Great Tradition. Having never visited India, Redfield located peasant local communities, which he understood as connected with other local communities through the intricate network of castes, marriages and kinship spread over generations. It is in this network of the 'self-contained community' that he searched for the structural unity of civilizational dimensions. He conceptualized 'rural India is [as] a primitive or a tribal society rearranged to fit a civilization'(Redfield 1955: 56–57). This peasant society comprised relatively stable 'local' and 'national' life consisting of the 'low' and 'high' cultural strata. He envisioned the local peasant cultural communities constantly communicating with the civilizational culture, particularly being shaped by its ideological sector, of worship, texts and rituals, and ceremonials. This would necessitate a formal interaction with the centres of civilization, and the local replication of such centres – as we discussed before in the case of Kashmir. Thus, the culture of peasants formed the numerous and fluid category of the Little Tradition, which interacted with and emulated the Great Tradition – of civilizational dimension (Chakrabarty 1992: 127–29).

What is significant from the viewpoint of Redfield (1955) is his conception of civilization as a construct consisting of both a social and a cultural system. If social system is characterized by people in relationships with one another, the cultural system similarly is constituted by differing ideas, patterns or symbols and their product interact with one another. Such interactive relationships provide conceptual unity within the civilization, attributing it with a distinct identity – which is cultural (succinct analysis of this model, see Chakrabarty 1992: 127–30).

The Little–Great Traditions binary was further elaborated by Milton Singer (1972). He conceived the Indian Civilization as evolved from the pre-existing folk and regional cultures and its Great Tradition was consequently derived from the continuity flowing from the multifarious Little cultures. This dynamic cultural continuity shared and produced a kind of collective cultural consciousness that was expressed in comparable mentalities and ethos. These attributes influenced the patterning of the constructs of Great Tradition – the text, literati, objects and aesthetics – leading to the self-conscious binary within one continuous Tradition. In this analysis, the Little Tradition images the cultural collectivity as it evolved naturally, while the Great Tradition articulates the self-image as more of an authorized ideological articulation. The Little Tradition is natural and elemental in its pattern, style and transmission where continuity is sustained by the process of natural-selection over time. The Great Tradition, in contrast, is a mental construct that is ideologically motivated, transmitted through self-conscious lineages using script (or mnemonics, as in *Vedic Sakha*s [lineages]), creating canonical texts, and finally bringing forth the notions of abstract and absolute. Both the Little and Great Traditions, however, are not mutually exclusive of each other, rather their interdependence is emphasized.

The assumption of a continuous interaction between the Little–Great Traditions resulting, therefore, in a dynamic cultural ethos is the novelty of this model. The interaction is multi-directional, as the influence are both ways, the folk-peasant influencing the Classical and in turn being influenced by the folk-peasant. Each therefore serves as a model for the other in as much represents the model of each other. This is much like the cultural model developed by Clifford Geertz (1976) in his account of Balinese society that how the cultural processes work and what they do. Geertz understood the term culture as public symbolic form that both expresses and shapes the meaning for all societal actors. He highlighted particularly the forms of subjectivity that cultural discourses and practices both reflect and organize. In other words, Geertz locates the culture concept in 'historically transmitted pattern of meanings embodied in symbols, a system of inherited conceptions expressed in symbolic forms by means of which men communicate, perpetuate, and develop their knowledge about and attitudes towards life' (Geertz 1976: 89). The symbols in turn are defined as 'tangible formulations of notions, abstractions from experience fixed in perceptible forms, concrete embodiments of ideas, attitudes, judgements, longings, or beliefs' (ibid.: 91). When we use religious 'symbols' to understand cultural patterns, i.e. 'systems or complexes of symbols', they are used both as 'models of' and 'for' to 'synthesise a people's ethos' and their world view. Such a synthesis confers both meaning (i.e. 'objective conceptual form') and an 'apprehension of reality' (i.e. organisation of cognitive and physical relationship) to religious symbols or cultural patterns (ibid.: 91–94). They have, thus, 'inter-transposability', as they pronounce conceptual form to social reality both by 'shaping themselves to it and by shaping it to themselves' (ibid.: 124) It is in this dual aspect of cultural pattern, both as the shaper and the shaped, that cultural dynamism may be located.

Much like Redfield's model, M. N. Srinivas (1952; 1980) developed the hypothesis of innate societal tendency to improve its status and ranking by emulating and appropriating the symbols of dominant high culture called Sanskritization. Though initially the dominant symbols and the dominant culture were perceived as brahmanical, it was later realized that each region had its own dominant culture and the sought after values were of the dominant caste rather than the abstract brahmanical values. Sanskritization has therefore come to be understood as a social process mapping social mobility and the consequent social change embedded in it. It may also be understood as a cultural process whereby various non-Sanskritic traits are radically altered and replaced by those of dominant culture by the mobile agents to narrow the boundaries of the 'low' and 'high' culture. However, in Srinivas's estimation the Sanskritic is a 'high' pristine cultural model – which is taken as given – that is so powerful that all 'low' cultural entities seek to imitate it and consequently, the status mobility is accomplished by fusing the 'low' with the 'high'. In this sense, Srinivas thought it to be unidirectional. For instance, the brahmanical norms of vegetarianism is used by all social-uplifting movements like Radha-Soamis, which envision a sort of 'liminal' community, transcending the barriers of caste, marriage, touch and commensality, to project itself as pure and therefore 'high'.

The concept of Sanskritization has been elaborated upon in different directions, determining the cultural flow based upon the conceptions of dominant caste and ranking in any given geographical area. It must be noted that Srinivas recognized caste as the structural basis of Hindu society; therefore he thought that it was 'not possible to understand Sanskritization without reference to the structural framework in which it occurs' (Srinivas 1952: 30). Accordingly, all analysis and criticism of the process of Sanskritization also revolve around the conceptions of dominant caste. For instance, Kulke (1976) formulates the model of Kshatriyaization based upon the concept of kingship as the most sought after norm and status as sustainer and upholder of the normative in the society. Similarly, there are instances of the cultural ethos of dominant trading community which are emulated by other communities as the dominant norm vital for social mobility (Chanana 1961: 409–14). The examples can be multiplied (Barnabas 1961; Sinha 1962; Sharma 1996). What these models, however, suggest is that there is not one universal 'high' culture, there are rather regional 'high' cultures which are unified by the caste normative – which vary – and influence the 'low' cultures that gravitate towards it as the cherished norm. Though still being one-dimensional, these elaborations, however, provide for a larger structural unity that accommodates the diversity and plurality within the larger conception of the high Sanskritic tradition. A reason that Sanskritization represented and sought out one-dimensional cultural flow, from 'high' to 'low', was due to the conception of Sanskritic as an abstract monolith representing all textual traditions as a large corporate body, the differences of time, sectarianism and place notwithstanding.

Such an understanding was however altered by Mckim Marriot (1955), who fused the Little and Great Traditions of Redfield with that of Sanskritization process. For him, the Sanskritic tradition was not a monolithic entity (also, Staal 1963). Rather, it was located in the symbiotic interplay with many local cultural traditions, such that Sanskritization was conceived as a complex two-directional process that ploughed into as well as drew out from the non-Sanskritic cultures. Marriot concluded his study of the annual festival cycle of village Kishan Garhi that while the upward process of universalization of the Little Tradition is demonstrated in the Sanskritization process, it does not account for the downward process of the Sanskritic which has become localized over time. This downward process constituted the reverse-Sanskritization or parochialization of the Sanskritic. For instance, the worship of Govardhan mount revisits the complex story of the fall of Indra (as the king among gods, the holder of thunderbolt and rains) and the subsequent elevation of cow-herd Krishna, the holder of the mount Govardhan, as the main deity of Vraja. In this myth one sees the upward mobility of the cow-herd deity which became a pan-Indian phenomenon. This is an example of reverse-Sanskritization whereby the cultural trait of the local community influences and becomes Sanskritic over time replacing the Sanskritic symbol. This does not constitute Sanskritization as the cultural trait is not conforming to the Sanskritic value; rather, it is becoming one. Thus three possibilities exist in this formulation: one, the cultural trait of the folk-peasant tradition emulates the high tradition and is elevated over time which is exemplified by the process of Sanskritization. Most of the local cults were thus assimilated into the sectarian folds in this way. Puranas, particularly the area-specific or Upapuranas, played a prominent role in providing such associations. Two, the local becomes the dominant cultural ethos. The example of Krishna, the cow-herd, who replaced Indra is of such genre. I would see this as reverse-Sanskritization, distinguishing it from parochialization. Three, the process of parochialization. In this process, the Sanskritic or the cultural trait of the Great Tradition is reduced to a local trait over time. The making of the regional language traditions competing with the Sanskritic from which they draw their lineages to completely replace it is one such example. For instance, the Bengali, Kashmiri or Mahrathi literary traditions became dominant textual traditions, particularly after the 13th century, replacing Sanskrit which was reduced to a minor literary language, relegated to a small ritual functional role.

The model of parochialization has recently been rearticulated by Sheldon Pollock (2006) who maps the evolution of competing literary cultures that legitimated the regional polity over a long-time period. Pollock locates himself in the Early Medieval period – after the collapse of the Gupta Empire – when there was a proliferation of small regional kingdoms, which were area-specific and clan dominated linguistic identities. In political terms, the difference between the metropole and periphery within the larger South Asia context was obliterated. The kingdoms coming up in the peripheral regions, like Kashmir, Assam, Bengal and the south Indian territorial kingdoms like, Coḷas, Ceras, etc., however, looked upon the Indo-Gangetic plain as the religio-cultural epicentre, which they either sought connections with or tried to replace by creative emulation, or replicating similar but competing symbols. Thus, two types of simultaneously competing processes are observed. One, the process of 'vernacularization', or leveraging of the regional culture represented ultimately in the development of regional language and literature, which competes with one another to assert a trans-regional identity whereby a particular hegemonic power emerges, such as Bengal and Bengali in eastern India; and two, associating with the Sanskrit cosmopolis that it seeks to replace in the first place, for instance, in Tamilnadu and Karnataka where Tamil and Kannada literature and regional 'etiquette' were developed, respectively, following a similar trajectory (Pollock 2006). This association is vital as it is by the carefully worked out symbols – of ideologues: the Brahmanas; the text: the *Puranas* or *Upa-Puranas*; and the dominant symbols of sectarian association: the temples and image – that the polity was legitimated. Yet, this period also witnessed prolific sectarian and secular literary productions. Taking a cue of the movement of production from the sacred to the secular, Pollock explicates the process of 'literization' and 'literarization' or the development of written language and the corresponding development of the 'imaginative or workly discourse.' It was with the Sanskrit in the regional courts to begin with that the impetus to literary discourse gathered momentum and it was soon supplanted by the corresponding development in the regional culture – the development of the literary language and the texts.

How conscious was the effort may be illustrated by the 1157 CE Stone inscription from Taldagudi. The grant was made to the school attached to the temple, the purpose of which was to support the temple rituals and for teaching the four *Veda-Khandikas* (the *Rik*, *Yajura*, *Sama* and *Kalpa*), as well as for the 'learned teachers of Kannada letters'. The establishment that had fifty residential students following strict Saiva regimen – prayers, liturgy and conduct – were also instructed in language and grammar; Sastras and *Puranas*; *Prabhakara Vedanata* and different schools of logic (Mysore Inscriptions: no. 102). Other grants, from Karnataka or Andhra make pronounced provisions to encourage the development of regional court-etiquettes and culture – a shift that is reflected in the growth of regional literature, particularly in Tamil. The peripatetic literati, the Brahmanas, played an important role in creating both the Sanskrit cosmopolis and the vernacularization of the court-etiquette leading to the competing regional identities reflected in the formation of linguistic cultural regions. This may also be seen as a process, where Sanskrit language in inscriptions gradually gives way to the bilingual and finally is totally replaced by the 'vernacular' inscriptions. A simultaneous development of the high regional literature is also witnessed, which complimented the oral tradition made popular by the poets and saints with radical outlook.

Some conclusions

Let us get back to our example of Kashmir to hypothecate and contemplate upon the Cultural concepts/contexts in Indian history. Certain conclusions can be safely drawn. One, unlike the earlier presumption that South Asia was largely considered as one Civilizational cultural area, at least from the perspective of Great Tradition, does not seem to be so. The devising of separate cultural area was a dynamic process that changed over time and continuously interacted with the dominant traditions of South Asia, either Sanskritizing itself or parochializing the dominant traditions. Moreover, the way the cultural space was devised in the Early-Medieval Kashmir text or in Chamba is indicative of how Little Traditions converged and were Sanskritized into regional traditions which in turn competed with the larger cultural ethos and space. This is what is also sometimes described as the 'ritual-model', where the local interacts and imitates the regional, which in turn interacts and emulates the 'national'. In such a schematic it is presumed that mentalities, perceptions and meanings of identity and community acquire a nuanced connotation in the sense of 'internal perception' of cultural identity – a common behaviour pattern and thinking process, the notions of Kashmiryat or Punjabiyat, for example. Thus, over time, the identities are reformulated and redefined, as are communities bound by the commonalities rather than divergence – Punjabi, irrespective of Hindus or Sikhs; Kashmiri, irrespective of Muslim or Pandits. Symbolism plays a significant role in containing divergence within cultural communities. Since symbol and symbolic are naturally multivalent and subjective, within their abstraction and ambiguities, the symbol/symbolic sheaths all divergences, hence providing a semblance of uniformity even when there is a creative interplay of variations that results in change and keeps the cultural space dynamic and vibrant.

Finally, we need to recognize that culture processes do not operate in isolation. The formulation of a cultural space, mentalities, identities, perceptions, experiences and along with them behaviour pattern, meanings, symbols, and other abstractions as thought and ways of thinking are conditioned by interactions taking place between different cultural entities that have a social function and responsibility. That there are fault-lines which keep on redefining the cultural processes should be recognized. If we recapitulate the models enumerated above, the differences are apparent. For instance, the *marga* and *desi* emphasize the binary by which the textual and popular are mapped, where the *desi* influences the *marga* (many *Raginis* are *desi*). This is unidirectional where the low is appropriated by the high; opposite to the working of the acculturation model whereby the dominant cultural ethos prevails upon the recessive, which is characterized as Classical. In this model the Classical is supposed as pristine and a monolith. Thapar, however, contests this and suggests that there are competing high-cultural episteme. By conceiving the alternative society of the renouncers, she brings to the cultural imaginary the notions of 'counter-culture,' which redefines and questions if there can be one dominant Classical tradition. Yet, in the Little and Great Traditions model, Redfield conceives the conceptual unity within civilization, achieved through cultural interaction between the two episteme, where again the Great Tradition is considered given. But, for Singer, the folk is the pre-existing and makes and shapes the Great Tradition, which borrows and refines the folk/popular episteme. Such continuous flow constructs the collective cultural consciousness. Srinivas, however, contextualizes the interactive flow in the inherent urge of cultural communities to improve upon their social status by imbibing the norms of Sanskritic, which is given. In his uni-dimensional model, the Little is always being Sanskritized. The process of Sanskritization, however, is defined by the regional conceptions of the dominant – which makes the dominant episteme that is sought after and acts as a transformative agency. Marriot delineates this uni-dimensional flow as a two-way process, whereby it is not only upward-mobile but moves down as well, what he calls parochialization. Similarly, Pollock considers the process by which 'literization' and 'literarization' are formed and how vernacularization of the Sanskrit-cosmopolitan culture is achieved, concretizing the competing regional identities. One would add to this the process of reverse-Sanskritization where the local cultural trait replaces the Sanskritic and in turn becomes the Great Tradition. What however is apparent is that not one model can explain the cultural dynamic satisfactorily. Each model is contextual and represents a particular time and space. In this sense, all the models articulated above, emerging from close observation – whether modern ethnographical or textual – should be harmonized. Like culture, there is not one dominant model; the novelty is in their creative usage as a methodological tool, in tandem or in isolation of each other.

Notes

1. This section draws upon ideas from the following: my earlier article (2008; for Kashmir), 'Puranic Texts from Kashmir: Vitasta and River Ceremonials in the Nilamata Purana', *South Asia Research*, 28(2) and Chapter I (2009), 'A Western Himalayan Kingdom', in my book *Western Himalayan Temple Records: State, Pilgrimage, Ritual and Legality* in Chamba, Leiden/Boston: Brill (Brill's Indological Library, 31).
2. *Nila* argues that how can he, who is known to be the lord of waters, fall in hell:*SnatamatramVitastayamjanatiVarunonaram/ Jaladhipenajnatsyanarkepatnamkutah//*(NP: 1437).
3. Dikshit (n.d.: 61–64) identifies it with what is mentioned in the *Rg Veda* as the 'healer' flowing to Paravata (IV.30.11). Following *Nirukta* (IX.25.3), he opines that it was earlier called *Arjikiya* and *Urunajira*. Both seem to be the Sanskritized names of the local.
4. This was a standard *Puranic* strategy. For instance, *Devi Bhagavata Purana* constructs such tirthas on the banks of Narmada, Ganga, Godavari, Gomati, Vetravati, Vipasa, Vitasta, Satadhrutira, Candrabhaga, and Iravati, among others (7.38.5–30). A similar strategy is adopted by *Skanda Purana*, mentioning Amoghaksi on Vipasa (5–3.198.66), Haṭakesvara on Devika (7–1.278.66–67), Mulasthana on Candrabhaga (6.76.2), among others. The cross-references legitimized the construction of regional sacred geography.
5. The inscription reads that after 'performing pilgrimage to Kedara, that cleanses from old sin, made this vow, "Henceforth shall all wives of others be sisters to me" . . . if nevertheless his heart avoids the wives of others, what austerity is difficult to perform after that?' The inscription further recounts ever since he 'has avoided the blameable pressing of the bosoms of the wives of others' (Buhler 1892: 110–11). Such instances can be multiplied.
6. For instance, Brahma was worshipped during sowing season in *Phalaguna* month 'with the flesh of water born (fish) animals' – *jalodbhavanammansenabhaksairuccavacaistatha* (NP: 571). Nikumbha was also worshipped by offering meat and other non-vegetarian food put in cow-pans and placed below trees, on crossings, rivers, mountain-tops, etc. 'the sporting men' passed night in courtesan's place listening to music, dancing, though vowed to celibacy. (147–48: 578–81) Similarly, on Nikumbha festivity, the atmosphere was quite carnivalesque, as demons 'enter all humans' who instigate sex; co-habit with women; licentious talk; followed by purification in the morning by worshipping brahmanas and lighting the fire in hearth to be kindled for six months (NP: 402–8, 544; *kriditavyamnarehsaha*). Drinking was common and allowed even in major festivities (NP: 542).
7. Sanyal elaborates: 'New idioms emerged in the process of cultural growth. These idioms . . . may be local in origin but they cut across the boundaries of localized ethnic group identities and spread over a larger territory with common cultural characteristics and aspirations, that is to say, des [desa] (in the traditional sense of the term, as against its modern meaning

of the nation state) . . . The growth of the intermediate level of culture is an effective force in consolidating the concept off as a cultural phenomenon, as also in defining the boundaries of the physical space covered by a desa' (1984: 168).

References

Arnold, Matthew. 1963. *Culture and Anarchy*. Cambridge: Cambridge University Press.

Babiarcki, Carol M. 1991a. *Musical and Cultural Interaction in Tribal India: The Karam Repertory of the Mundas of Chotanagpur*. Urbana: University of Illinois Press.

———. 1991b. 'Tribal Music in the Study of Great and Little Traditions of Indian Music', in Bruno Nettl and Philip V Bohlman (eds), *Comparative Musicology and Anthropology of Music: Essays on the History of Ethnomusicology*, pp. 69–90. Chicago: University of Chicago Press.

Barnabas, A.P. 1961. 'Sanskritization', *Economic Weekly*. 13(15): 613–18.

Buhler, G. 1892. 'The Two Prasastis of Baijnath', in Jas Burgess (ed.), *Epigraphia Indica*, pp. 97–118. Calcutta: Government Press.

Cabrera, Miguel A. 2001. 'On Language, Culture and Social Action', *History and Theory, Theme Issue*, 40(4): 82–100.

Chakrabarty, Kunal (2001) *Religious Process: The Puranas and the Making of a Regional Tradition*. Delhi: Oxford University Press.

———. 2000. 'Cult Region: The Puranas and the Making of the Cultural Territory of Bengal', *Studies and History*, 16(1): 1–16.

———. 1992. 'Anthropological Models of Cultural Interaction and the Study of Religious Process', *Studies and History*, 8(1): 123–49.

Chhabra, B.Ch. 1957. *Antiquities of Chamba State*. Part II, Memoirs of Archaeological Survey of India, No. 72. Delhi: Manager of Publications (Government of India Press).

Chanana, D.R. 1961. 'Sanskritization, Westernization and India's North-West', *Economic Weekly*, 13(9): 409–14.

Dikshit, S.K. n.d. *The Mother Goddess (A Study Regarding the Origin of Hinduism)*. Delhi: S.K. Dikshit.

Dubey, D.P. 2001. *Prayāga: The Site of Kumbha Melā*. New Delhi: Aryan.

Frecchia, Joseph and R.C. Lewontin.1999. 'Does Culture Evolve?', *History and Theory, Theme Issue*, 38: 52–78.

Geertz, Clifford. 1973. *The Interpretation of Cultures: Selected Essays*. New York: Basic Books Inc.

Kalhaṇa's Rajatarangini: A Chronicle of the Kings of Kashmir.(tr.) M.A. Stein (signed 1900). Vol. I, Delhi: Motilal Banarsidas Publishers, 1961 (reprint).

Kulke, *Hermann*. 1976. 'Kshatriyaization and Social Change: A Study in Orissa Setting', in S. Devadas Pillai (ed.), *Aspect on Changing India*, pp. 1–12. Bombay: Popular Prakashan.

Kumar, Savitri V. 1983. *The Puranic Lore of Holy Water – Places with Special Reference to Skanda Purāṇa*. Delhi: Munshiram Manoharlal Publishers.
Kumari, Ved (trans.). 1976. *The Nilamata Purana*. Delhi: Motilal Banarsidass.
Marriot, McKim. 1955. 'Little Communities in an Indigenous Civilization', in McKim Marriot and Alan R. Beals (eds), *Village India: Studies in the Little Community*, pp. 171–222. Chicago: The University of Chicago Press.
Monier-Williams, Sir Monier. 1983 [1899]. *A Sanskrit-English Dictionary*. Delhi: Motilal Banarsidass.
Pollock, Sheldon. 2006. *The Language of the Gods in the World of Men: Sanskrit, Culture, and Power in Premodern India*. Berkeley: University of California Press.
Redfield, Robert. 1956. *Peasant Society and Culture*. Chicago: The University of Chicago Press.
———. 1955. *Little Community: View Points for the Study of a Human Whole*. Chicago: The University of Chicago Press.
———. 1941. *The Folk Culture of Yucatan*. Chicago: The University of Chicago Press. Rice, Lewis (trans.). 1983 [1879]. *Mysore Inscriptions*. New Delhi: Navrang.
Sanyal, Hitesranjan. 1984. 'The Nature of Peasant Culture in India: A Study of the Pat Painting and Clay Sculpture in Bengal'. *Folk: Journal of the Royal Swedish Folklore Academy*, 26: 121–78.
Sartori, Andrew. 2005. 'The Resonance of "Culture:" Framing a Problem in the Global Concept-History'. *Comparative Study of Society and History*, 47 (4): 676–99.
Sharma, Mahesh. (1996) 'Brahmins, Jogis, and Sidh Shrines: Marginalisation and Appropriation', *The Indian Economic and Social History Review*, 33(I): 73–91.
Sharma, Mahesh. 1999. 'Dimensions of Pilgrimage: A Case Study of Jalandhara Pitha', in Joseph T. O'Connel (ed.), *Organisational and Institutional Aspects of Indian Religious Movements*, pp. 41–56. New Delhi: Manohar Publications.
———. 2001. *The Realm of Faith: Subversion, Appropriation and Dominance in the Western Himalaya*. Shimla: Indian Institute of Advanced Study.
———. 2008. 'Puranic Texts from Kashmir: Vitasta and River Ceremonials in the Nilamata Purana', *South Asia Research*, 28(2): 123–45.
———. 2009. *Western Himalayan Temple Records: State, Pilgrimage, Ritual and Legality in Chamba*. Leiden/Boston: Brill (Brill's Indological Library, 31).
Singer, Milton. 1972. *When a Great Tradition Modernizes: An Anthropological Approach to Indian Civilization*. Delhi: Vikas Publishing House.
Sinha, Surajit. 1962. 'State Formation and Rajput Myth in Tribal Central India', *Man In India*, 42(1): 35–80.
Srinivas, M. N. 1980 [1966]. *Social Change in Modern India*. New Delhi: Orient Longman.
Srinivas, M. N. 1952. *Religion and Society among the Coorgs of South India*. Oxford: Clarendon Press.

Staal, J.F. 1963. 'Sanskrit and Sanskritization'. *The Journal of Asian Studies*, 12(3): 261–75.

Thapar, Romila. 1978. 'Renunciation: The Making of a Counter-Culture?', in *Ancient Indian Social History: Some Interpretations*. Hyderabad: Orient Longman.

Vatsyayan, Kapila. 2007 [1996]. *Bharata: The Natyasastra*. Delhi: Sahitya Akademi.

Vogel, J. Ph. 1911. *Antiquities of Chamba State*. Part I, Memoirs of Archaeological Survey of India, No. 36. Calcutta: Manager of Publications (Government of India Press).

9
HISTORY, HISTORIOGRAPHY AND PUNJABI FOLK LITERATURE
Issues of canons and cultures

Ishwar Dayal Gaur

> They have read thousands of books, they have come to be known as great scholars, but the one word, 'love', they could not grasp — so helplessly they wander in delusion. — Sultan Bahu
> (Puri and Kirpal 2004: 63) [1]

The belief in *rational* understanding and employment of history has led many a mainstream historian to exclude folk and their voice from the craft of history writing. To them folk literature and folk culture or collective memory and lived experience of the folk are not genuine, true and pure (that is authentic) sources of history; rather in their opinion folk is contaminated by myths, beliefs and imagination (that is *ahistorical* consciousness). In the early 19th century, George Wilhelm Friedrich *Hegel* (1770–1831) excluded folklore from the discipline of history, disparaging it as 'dim and hazy forms of historical apprehension'. To him folklore belongs to 'nations whose intelligence is but half awakened' (Hegel 1956: 2).

Framing an argument: the statues of folklore

However, a folk community evolves and organizes its archives through various processes of socio-cultural and language contacts, displaying the characteristics of a syncretic ethos or cultural fusion (Khubchandani 1991: 81). It has its own authenticity claims and its lore constitutes an archive/discourse/text, different from the official or elite one.[2] Therefore, folk literature needs to be judged from the view point of its historical, cultural and social locations, functions and effects, rather than to be appreciated merely in terms of its aesthetic essence. Rooted in the cultural space of a specific folk community, it claims to be an original and spontaneous creation, organically associated with those who are its creators and carriers (i.e. folk community). Hence, folk archives are neither made nor manufactured.[3]

However, whether literature is merely a superstructural manifestation of a structure or it is autonomous, relatively autonomous, purely spontaneous, over-determined or counter-hegemonic is an issue of debate that one may locate in the writings of Karl Marx, Frederic Engels, Antonio Gramsci, Louis Althusser and Ranajit Guha. But it was Gramsci who directly dealt with folklore/literature in his *Prison Notebooks*, while suggesting that 'the official view' of life cannot be squared with their [peasants] lived experience (Gramsci 1996: 196–200, 323, 326 and 419). Gramsci validates the study of subaltern beliefs and consciousness (i.e. folklore), because they are the forms of expression of the life of the masses. Hence, to him no exponent of the philosophy of praxis can afford to ignore them. They have as much historical weight and energy as purely material forces (Arnold 1984: 158–59; Davidson 1984: 139–53). Nevertheless, Gramsci studies folklore from a class perspective and discerns through it the limitation of spontaneous philosophy of the masses (Gramsci 1983: 58).

But Ranajit Guha, the founder of *Subaltern Studies* in India underscores the importance of peasant insurgency independent of 'ism(s)': 'To acknowledge the peasant as the maker of his own rebellion is to attribute a consciousness to him' (Guha 1983: 3–4). In his *History at the Limit of World-History*, he foregrounds the significance of the autonomous 'repository of tales told by tradition' (i.e. *itihasa*). He describes in depth how this repository (folklore) was dislodged from civil society, and relocated in the state in the battle of paradigms of history. Eventually the battle was won for the West, when World-history triumphed over *itihasa* (Guha 2003: 61–72).

Though folklore/literature does not provide us with 'scientific knowledge', what it offers does necessarily maintain a certain specific relationship with knowledge. It makes us see, perceive, feel something which alludes to reality. If Reason invalidates folklore/literature, the latter also questions Reason that drains out concreteness that is, historicality, the true historical existence of man (ibid.: 2–3). Thus folklore illumines the deep but marginalized layers of history; it facilitates a fresh dialogue between historian and folk. Such an interaction calls into question a number of legitimized continuities; and de-monumentalizes the established archives or discourses. What is being suggested is that folk literature is capable of constructing an alternative or counter archaeology of knowledge.

HISTORY, HISTORIOGRAPHY AND PUNJABI FOLK LITERATURE

With reference to the advent of Islam and conversion in India, Richard Eaton in his writings underlines the significance of folklore and folk devotional spaces (shrines) of the different regions of Indian sub-continent (Eaton 1978: 135–74, 2007: 189–246). He deconstructs the popular historiographical discourse of 'Religious Sword' as a catalyst in converting the Indians to Islam (Eaton 1996: 113–34). Rather, he looks upon folk literature that played a historic role in getting the Indian masses attracted to sufis. He argues: 'One likely reason for the failure to explain the attraction of Hindu nonelites to Sufis has been the tendency among many scholars of Sufism to concentrate almost exclusively on the mystical literature, as opposed to the folk literature, as representing the sum and substance of the Sufi movement' (Eaton 2007: 190). In the 12th century Shaikh Farid (1175–265) and in the 15th century Guru Nanak (1469–1539) communicated their utmost concern for the sanctity of one's own soil and space and for dialogue with the 'other':

> Farid, do not abuse the earth, nothing is as great. It is under the feet of the living, above the dead. (*Salok*, 17, *Adi Granth*: 1378, Sagar 1999: 90)
> As long as we are in this world, O Nanak,
> We should speak and listen to others. (*Adi Granth*: 661, trans. mine)

Later on in the 16th, 17th and 18th centuries we find the above-mentioned message of Farid-Nanak primer transmitted through the different genres of Punjabi medieval poetry like the *kafis* of Shah Hussain (1539–99) and Bulleh Shah (1680–1758), and the *qissa* of Waris Shah (1720–80). Though these poets were well versed in Quran and Islamic Gnosticism, they were the first who documented and communicated the life and voice of the Punjab people. They were the *vernacular* poets of the Punjab, who expressed their concern for cultural specificity and sensitivity of an indigenous space and soil.

The first section broadly deals with the identity of the Muslims and the Sikhs as projected in historiography and folk literature. Section II presents Bhagat Singh in the cultural and folkloristic contexts of Punjab.

Post-Partition historiography

After the Partition of 1947, it took only less than one and a half decade for the communitarian and nationalist historians/writers to present their respective discourses on the east and west Punjabs, as well as on the history, language, literature and culture of India and Pakistan on the basis of what had been bequeathed to them by the colonial ethnography.

In 1960 Language Department (Bhasha Vibhag) Patiala of the Indian Punjab Government published a book in Gurmukhi, *Punjab: History, Art, Literature and Culture* (*Punjab: Itihas, Kala, Sahit Te Sabhiachar*) under the editorship of Mohinder Singh Randhawa (1909–88). It was an anthology of 21 essays written by Punjabi writers, artists and historians (*incidentally* non-Muslim). Telling about the said anthology, its editor writes in the Preface (*mukhbandh*) that the aim is to 'present a perfect and meticulous picture of Punjab history, art, literature and culture'.

One of the contributors, Ganda Singh, a historian, introduces the reader to the different nomenclatures of Punjab such as 'Sapt-Sandhu and Panchnada', which later on 'with the advent of the Muslims began to be called Punjab, the land of five rivers' (Singh 1960: 2) Betraying his Indian nationalist cum Sikh predilections, Ganda Singh informs that the earliest book of the Punjab/world is *Rig Veda*, and the history of Punjab, so far known, begins with the age of the Aryans who had two lineages: *Suryabansi* (Solar dynasty) and *Chanderbansi* (lunar dynasty). The great Lord Shri Ram Chandra was of a *Suryabansi* descent. His younger brother, Bharat, was a ruler of Kakaya Des, situated between the rivers, Jhelum and Chenab. North Sindh was also a part of his kingdom. Takash and Pushkar, the two sons of Bharat, laid the foundation of Takshasila (Taxila) and Pushkaravati, after having conquered Gandhara (a region on both sides of Indus and the districts of Rawalpindi and Peshawar) from Gandhravas (ibid.: 19–20). Ganda Singh further informs that the (Sikh) Gurus and the Mughal emperors ran parallel to each other: the Sikh gurus were building up a new nation in the Punjab when the Mughal rule was being established. The founder of Sikhism, Guru Nanak, was a contemporary of Babur, the founder of Mughal rule, and the last Sikh guru Gobind Singh was a contemporary of Emperor Aurangzeb (ibid.: 29).

At the time of its compilation in 1960 the anthology under reference was imagined as 'a watershed for the development of Punjabi [Gurmukhi] language' (Randhawa 1960: 'Mukhbandh' [Preface]). It introduces us to the 'modern' Punjabi artist only of eastern Punjab. There are about thirty pictures of 'Sikh' gurus, eleven pictures of Sikh Gurudwaras and five that of Hindu temples. Mainly, this 'perfect and meticulous' book is committed to Indian Punjab.

HISTORY, HISTORIOGRAPHY AND PUNJABI FOLK LITERATURE

Apart from the aforementioned discourse constructed in the post-Partition era, the protagonists of the two-nation theory do not look at the advent of Islam as an addition to Punjabi culture; rather they held Muslims responsible for causing cleavages in it. To these nationalist scholars the Muslims were conquerors, aliens who were not willing to get assimilated in the indigenous culture. These scholars identify medieval Punjabi poetry as a parameter for describing and sustaining religious group boundaries and in providing the cultural background against which a particular poet or poem found its place in history (Jaggi 2002: 176; Sekhon 1986; Singh 1976: 4–5, 1988: 20–23). This may be one of the reasons that medieval Punjabi poetry is trifurcated into 'Muslim' sufi-*kav*, 'Hindu' bhakti-*kav* and 'Sikh' gurmat-*kav*. Under such a scheme of division the major thematic equivalences between sufis, bhaktas, sants and gurus are pushed to the margins (for detail see Lawrence 1987: 359–73; Vaudeville 1987: 21–40).

The communitarian nuances in the historiography of Punjabi literature began to emerge in the colonial Punjab. For instance, the first history of Panjabi literature was written in English in 1933 (14 years before the partition of Punjab in 1947) by Mohan Singh Diwana who habilitated the first Punjabi saint-poet, Shaikh Farid, in 'Pre-Nanak Age'; and in the post-Partition historiographical texts of the East Punjab, Farid is registered as a Islamic missionary who converted many a Hindu to Islam. Farid's scholarly and philosophical vision is also judged as approximated to Sikhism (Ahluwalia 1982: 45; Diwana 1982: 151–60). Recently, a Punjab historian has argued that 'the origins of Shaikh Farid's Sufi ideology were outside the Indian subcontinent. He caught the popular imagination primarily because of his indigenous garb' (Grewal 2007: 58).

Like that of the historians of east (Indian) Punjab, a counter attempt was also made in Pakistan. In 1962 Ishtiaq Hussain Qureshi (1903–81) in his book *The Muslim Community of the Indo-Pakistan Subcontinent, 610–1947* set the tone and trend of Pakistan nationalist historiography. Qureshi argues that the Muslims of the Indian subcontinent have always been motivated by an intense love of Islam in their policies and movements. Disparaging the Turkish, Arabic and Iranian identities of Muslims, the historian under reference loves and likes to see the Pakistani Muslims 'only as Muslims'. Tracing the sentiments of pre-Partition Muslims, Qureshi informs that they seldom used the appellation 'Indian Muslims'; rather the expression of 'Muslims of India' was more common. At no time 'has their sense of belonging to the larger world of Islam been weak and often it has been stronger than the sense of belonging to their habitat' (Qureshi 2003: 93–94).

The basic thesis of monolithic Muslim community was further enriched to stand up to the Vedic/Aryan Indian discourse. Muhammad Yusuf Abbasi in his *Pakistani Culture: A Profile* argues: 'The highly developed Indus civilization symbolized by Mohenjodaro in Sind and Harrapa in the Punjab testifies to the hoary past of Pakistan'. The Civilization, in his view, 'had developed a Middle Eastern orientation due to its close commercial and maritime ties with the people of the Gulf', and it had 'developed a distinct cultural personality and political identity quite distinct from the rest of India'. Muhammad Yusuf Abbasi traces 'cultural continuity from the Indus Civilization to the cultural milieu of Pakistan'. He is critical of the progressive poets both of India and Pakistan who 'denounce Freedom and Creation of Pakistan, and mourn and bewail the artificial boundary which separated the two fraternal people' (Abbasi 1992: 2–4 and 70–77).

A liberal Pakistani nationalist discourse on Indus civilization is offered by Aitzaz Ahsan in his *The Indus Saga: From Patliputra to Partition*. He asserts that the Indian must not continue to deny the distinct and separate personality that Indus (Pakistan) has had over millennia, even during the period preceding the advent of Islam in South Asia. This distinct identity is primordial. During the last six thousand years Indus has, indeed, remained independent of and separate from India. Only the three 'Universal States' — Mauryans, the Mughals and the British — put these two regions together under a single empire. And the aggregate period of these States was not more than five hundred years. For the remainder, from prehistory to the 19th century, Indus has been Pakistan. Ahsan further argues that the year 1947 (that is the year of Partition) was only a reassertion of that reality. It was the reuniting of the various units – the Frontier, the Punjab, Sind, Baluchistan and Kashmir. Unlike Muhammad Yusuf Abbasi, Aitzaz Ahsan is of the view that the people of Pakistan do not share cultural commonality with the Arab [Middle East], though out of the entire Indus region, Sindh alone had direct political contact with the Arabs, and this contact was only of a short span of 144 years, that is, from 711 to 854 CE. Rather, the people of Pakistan racially, ethnically, linguistically and culturally are more closely associated with the peoples of Central Asia and Iran. But the Arabs provided, argues Ahsan, one significant insight into the distinctness of Indus from India. They always referred to Indus as 'al-Sindh' and to India as 'al-Hind'. Ahsan is also of the opinion that despite the best efforts made at the literary, linguistic, religious, social and political levels, Indus (Pakistan) and India remained distinctive and exclusive: 'neither Amir Khusrau's attempts to interconnect the two cultures by opting to write in the vernacular Hindi nor Kabir's rustic poetry could go very far. Nor, indeed, were Akbar's more authoritarian efforts to forge, by decree, a common religion, the *Din-e-Ilahi*, any more effective. Imperial marriages between Muslim emperors and Hindu princesses were also not sufficient to bridge the gap between the two cultures, two races and the people of the two regions. Deep down, the differences and dissimilarities remained' (Ahsan 2005: xiv, 11, 14–15, 179–81).

The aforementioned justificatory claims and the reductive religious and nationalist orientations, however, find no accommodation in the Punjab folk domain of literature, culture and religion. To veil the vernacular with the religious/nationalist meta-narrative means, what Karl Marx calls 'the act of superseding in which denial and preservation are bound together' (Marx 1977: 140). Let us discuss the identity of Punjabi Muslims of the medieval Punjab.

Punjab love legend of hir-ranjha and the muslim identity

Like Mir Muhammad Taqi 'Mir' (1723–1810) the great *ghazalgo* of the 18th-century Hindustan, Waris Shah (b. 1720) was an outstanding *qissakar* (poet-narrator) of the same period in Punjab. In 1767 he versified in length the legend of Hir and her lover Ranjha in 611 *bands* (stanzas). His versification is popularly known as *Hir Waris*. That Waris Shah was a folk poet who on the demand of the Punjab people picked up one of the legends from their repertoire draws a distinction between the *native* genre of narrative, that is, *qissa* (poetic narrative) and the Western one, that is, novel. The story (in history and novel) is the regime of personal experience, and is associated historically with the storyteller's initiative in the West (Guha 2003: 48–74).[4] But a *qissa/katha* owed its inauguration, as has been said, primarily to the listener's demand. This demand, for instance, is conspicuous by its presence in the *qissa* of *Hir* composed by Waris Shah in 1767:

> Friends came one day and made request
>
> > That the tale of Hir be told anew;
> > And bowing to friends' command
> > Did I this wondrous tale compose. (Sekhon 1978: 14)

Waris Shah's *Hir* is a writeable text, that is, a complex poetic text which records and narrates the cultural ethos of the Punjab people. The way the legend of Hir-Ranjha is versified in the *qissa* presents Waris Shah as (i) the skilled architect of the genre of *qissa*, (ii) an ethnographer and also (iii) a historian. He opens up the archives of the Punjab people interacting with sufism, Islam, the eroticism of bhakti, and with the Epics of the Great Indian Traditions. His *qissa* of *Hir* is a *history* of Punjabi society and culture in general and of Punjabi Muslims in particular. His narrative like that of a historian does not breathe in *facts*. But he infuses life into the legend: his narrative vouches for his ability to discern and document the cultural profile of the *oral* Punjabi Muslims. Waris Shah takes his reader to the local lanes of Islamic life and the indigenous culture of the Punjabi Muslims whose socio-cultural liminal space is not enlisted in the Islamic, Sikh and Hindu texts of history. Thus his description is different from the one which is theological and colonial, and which subscribes to fault-lines and documents/employs the diversities as differences.

With reference to *Hir Waris*' 'indigenous' narrative of the Punjab society, it is argued that monolithic historiographical discourses, as we know, are essentially rooted in a particular crisscross of power, and power habitually aims at domesticating and regulating a society. Historians engaged in exploring a cultural zeitgeist suggest protection of people from the enormous patronage of these elite discourses and their narratologies. Such a patronization does not let people's spontaneous and quotidian practices, and humble forms to acquire their due position and prominence in historiography (Burke 2009 [1978]: 23–48; Guha 1983: 4–5; Oberoi 2012: 163–88; Thompson 1980 [1963]: 11–12). Also under the dominant shadow of the said condescension are the issues such as how people's archives come into existence, what kind of potentials for meaning they contain, and what things they are capable of signifying and by what means they are suppressed. These issues constitute the poetics of people's archives (Mikko 2000: 89, 79 and 123–24). The poetics-oriented history writing is different from the one which is monolithic and linear, that is, prose-oriented. The latter longs for establishing finality and the former transcends such yearning for conclusiveness. Its truth is not single, but multi-layered. It searches for truths, not absolute truth. It does not merely reflect truth, but also digs up truth. It explores authenticities, instead of authenticity. To the 19th-century poet of England, P.B. Shelly (1792–1822), all high poetry is unfathomed. Veil after veil may be undrawn, but the innermost naked beauty of the meaning never gets exposed (LeBlanc 2000: 103–19). An age-old *saloka* of Sanskrit underscores the meaning potentials of poetics under our reference: 'Only that poetry is meritorious which like a gorgeous maiden of Maharashtra conceals as well as reveals its half meaning. It is not commendable to be too revelatory like a maiden of Andhra Pradesh, nor is it too well-mannered to be too veiled like a lassie of Gujarat' (trans. mine).

What is being suggested is that poetics offers a historian an alternative method and approach of conceptualizing and narrating history. A conventional-prose historian is prosaic, insensitive about the imperceptible and multiple layers of a society. He uses flat sources. His craft is scientific, singular, objective and dispassionate, whereas poetics of history resonates with multiple voices, multiple customs, multiple rituals, multiple celebrations so on and so forth. Its canvas is kaleidoscopic. So we need to identify: (i) what are the sources used for the making of a text of Punjab history, culture, society and literature, (ii) what kind of discourse this text propagates and (iii) how this discourse impacts reader/listener/spectator? A text is a semiotic being which does not have natural meanings, rather acquires them, depending on their contexts (Mikko 2000: 76). Thus a text is productivity; it is, as Roland Barthes says, 'the very theatre of a production where the producer and reader meet' (as quoted in ibid.). The tryst may be called a dialogical one.

The canvas of *Hir Waris* has been set on the three villages and three Muslim Jat (agriculturalist) communities: Siyals, Ranjhas and Kheras. The protagonist, Hir of the village Jhang is the daughter of Chuchak of the Siyal clan. He is a *sardar* of five villages. Dhido Ranjha, the lover of Hir, belongs to the village Takht Hazara. His father, Mauju, is its *chaudhari*. The third territory referred to in *Hir Waris* is Rangpur Khera, a village of the Khera clan whose chief is Ajju. These villages are situated on the banks of the river, Chenab.

The conversion of the fourteen clans of the Jats, including the Siyals, Ranjhas and Kheras, to Islam is said to have taken place during the time of Baba Farid in the 13th century (Eaton 2007: 215). However, the *qissa* of *Hir Waris* portrays a culture more ethnic (that is Punjabi) than 'Islamic'. Non-denominational names in the 18th-century *qissa* under reference such as Chuchak, Mauju, Ajju, Dhido, Hir, Kaido, Saida, Saihti and Malki do not reveal religious identity; rather they suggest that conversion does not mean sudden and self-conscious rupture or discontinuity from the pre-conversion life pattern, as the 'modern' nationalist and communitarian scholars (mis)perceive. For instance, Shaista Nuzhat in her monograph, *Sayad Waris Shah Da Samaj-Shastri Falsfa* (written in Shahmukhi Punjabi script), denominates Mauju as Mauzuddin or Maujudar Khan, Chuchak as Chuchak Khan, Malki as Malakia, Saihti as Shaista Bano and Kaidon as Qadir Khan (Nuzhat 2007: 14–15). There is obviously a distinction between conversion that is defined as a *rupture* and conversion that is *an addition* to the existing social life. One needs to know that dialectics of culture do not subscribe to the *total* negation of the previous cultural phase. This *previous*, putting in Raymond Williams' phrase, does not become *archaic*, but continues as *residual* (Williams 1978: 121–25).[5]

Waris Shah's was a period (18th century) when neither British officials nor zealous middle-class socio-religious reformers, nor the print media had intervened in public life. Punjab people visited the shrine of Shaikh Farid as his devotees and probably did not perceive themselves as staunch adherents of their 'new' religion, Islam. Rather they were *enrooted* Punjabi Muslims; and *Hir Waris* illustrates their lived life. In the *qissa* we come across a Brahman who is consulted for the date of the marriage of Saida with Hir (Sekhon 1978: 75). In Damodar's *Hir* (versified in 1600 CE), both a qazi and a Brahman perform the marriage rituals of the Punjabi Muslim family (Singh, ed., 2000: stanza nos. 10, 126, 435 and 637). The Islamic taboos regarding the use of alcohol and music do not intervene in the celebration of the marriage of Hir (Sekhon, trans., 1978: 76). The five sufi *pirs* grant Ranjha the love of Hir only after hearing the music he plays on his flute (ibid.: 52).

Thus we discover in the Punjab narratives such as *Hir Waris* that the exuberance and vibrancy of folk culture is retained in contrast to the puritanical concepts of Islam. The socio-cultural character of the Punjabi Muslims, as revealed by Waris Shah, is indicative of the steady and sustained impact of tribal and sufi-cum-bhakti traditions. References to a large number of Hindu and Islamic legends and myths in the *qissa* substantiate the existence of cultural fusion (ibid.: 145–46). The absence of reference to the basic Islamic practices, the profession of faith (*kalima*) and the five obligatory prayers (*namaz*) is significant. We do not find any reference to Muslim women folk veiling themselves. Rather a reader finds Waris Shah describing the beauty and frolics of the women who attend the marriage of Hir: 'They are all of fair figure and face. They sing, dance and scoff, and win applause. They open their shawls to show their breasts, and display their thinly veiled musk-pod navels' (ibid.: 163). Hir wears a partial veil (*ghund*) at her in-laws, but that is also condemned as an evil by her lover, Ranjha, who visits her in-laws in the guise of a yogi/jogi: 'The veil deserves to be put in fire. It is the cause of many ills. It blinds even those who have eyes' (ibid.). Waris Shah's contemporary Bulleh Shah in one of his *kafis* also takes the issue of veil: 'Lift your veil, my Beloved!/Why do you feel bashful now?/Your curly locks entwine my heart,/They bite me like the serpents' (Puri and Shingari 1986: 258).

Waris Shah also offers to his readers a kaleidoscopic canvas of the religious life of the Punjabi folk who worshipped a number of gods and pirs/sufis. Each god or *pir* is a patron of a certain occasion and of a certain group of people. Guru Nanak, Shah Madar, Kabir, Tehra, Shams, Nam Dev, Lukman, Khawaja Khizar, Raja Nal, Satan, Suleman Paras, Hazi Gilgo, Hassu, Farid and others were respectively the patrons of ascetics (*udasis*), jugglers (*madaris*), weavers (*julasis*), cobblers (*mochi*), goldsmiths (*suniars*), tailors (*chhimbas*), carpenters (*tarkhans*), blacksmiths (*lohars*), folk buffoons (*marasis*), barbers (*nais*), oilmen (*telis*), potters (*ghumiars*), Chishtis, sailors (*muhans*) and gamblers (Sekhon, trans., 1978: 138–39).

The religious mosaic of *Hir Waris* falsifies the idea of monolithic 'imagined' communities of Hindus and Muslims.[6] It reveals that the religious pattern of rural Punjabi Muslims was not a scriptural and codified religion. It was locally confined. Saints, pirs and gurus of different communities of a village had intimate relationships with their clients. No priestly ritual was required to invoke them, rather a rememberance or meditating on the divine name (*yaad or dhian* or *zikr*) being sufficient to seek their help and blessings. To be blessed with the love of Hir, Ranjha plays his flute to invoke the pirs, and they immediately appear. They get pleased with his melodies and grant him his desired love. The *ragas* and *ragnis* that Ranjha sings to appease the five pirs allude to the devotional songs of bhaktas or Shavite and *sirguna* bhakti traditions (Sital, ed., 1973: stanza no. 116). For example, Lalit, the name of a *ragni*, that the *Muslim* Ranjha sings, is pictorially described as a pretty young girl, with a radiant complexion. She holds a *vina*, and a cuckoo perches on her lotus-like hand. She is seated under the *kalpa-taru* (a tree which fulfils all wishes) with her breasts highly adorned. Another *rag*, that Ranjha sings, is Bhairon, a terrifying form of Shiva (Kaufmann 1968: 323; Kumar 1992: 61). Ranjha also sings the Vashnavite songs, called *bishanpatey* (*pad*/poetry of Lord Vishnu), and performs a sufic dance (*jalali*) for the pirs. Ranjha's total devotional absorption reminds us of synaesthesia: a personal experience of sensation emanating from the synthetic effect of music, dance, poetry, ritual and emotional religiosity.

In *Hir* Waris we find that Punjab folks' relationship to God is more a matter of faith and love than of doubt, fear and reason. Their universe is limited and simple to understand. Confronted with dangers to life and property from nature, and living in a constant fear of destruction, the peasant-tribal societies had developed the idea of God which happened to be close to the sufi and bhakti traditions, advocating direct association between devotee and the Almighty (*Rub*). Thus instead of looking at the institutional function of religion, the people of medieval Punjab looked on religion as something that helped them in their day-to-day life. Their belief in one God did not make them actually perceive any contradiction with their beliefs in many gods and pirs. The medieval agrarian Punjab society had developed a pragmatic approach to religion to meet the demands of their daily life. Such an approach would have cut across an imaginary boundary constructed in colonial and post-colonial Punjab. Ranjha invokes the five (Muslim) pirs, and visits the *tilla* (hillock) of Bal Nath jogi, because he desires to be blessed with the love of Hir, otherwise denied to him by the die-hard norms of the socio-religious patriarchs of his society. What is religiously and culturally important about pirs, jogis, gods and goddesses is that they deal with the pragmatic concerns of survival.[7]

Thus what has been suggested is that a monolithic and normative/canonical view of Islamic societies is not adequate in the study of folk Islam(s). Historians, who privilege the grand-route of Islam, overlook its local roots. In their studies biography of Islam prevails upon the autobiographies of folk Islams. They talk only of its *origins*, not of its *beginnings* in the diverse lands of Asia. This is the reason that Indian Muslims seem to them 'imperfect', 'half', 'partly converted' or 'census' Muslims who contaminated the purity of belief and practice in Islam in medieval India (Roy 1996: 11–12). Such a biographical view of 'pure' Muslims is not different from that of the medieval theologians. For instance, in *Hir Waris*, Dhido Ranjha of the Muslim Jat clan of Siyal visits a mosque, where he is rebuked by the *mullah* for his un-Islamic approach to coiffure and clothing. But the peasant youth, Dhido Ranjha snubs him.

The Mullah angrily says to Ranjha:

> A mosque is the house of God Himself,
> And the lawless have in it no place.
> Long locks like yours, long whiskers, too,
> Had best be singed, I must say.

And also a *lungi* that falls below
The ankle must be torn away.
A sinful friar, a prayerless man
And a fouling dog deserves no grace.
Ranjha mocks at the mullah:

'O tell me what your prayer is like,
And where indeed was she born and bred. . .
You shelter under the mask of law
The wicked, steeped in sin and crime.
Then when in the small hours of the night,
Hunger wakes you up, you crow for prayer. (Sekhon, trans., 1978: 22–24)

The Muslims of rural Punjab, as the folk legend of *Hir Waris* reveals, were nonchalant towards the rigidity prescribed by the ecclesiastical classes. When we study the expansion and existence of Islam within the local ambience or milieu of the rural Punjab, we find the discourse of 'impact/influence' of Hindu society on the Muslims and vice versa inaccurate and unsatisfactory. *Hir Waris* displays a historically evolved syncretic socio-cultural life pattern of the well-knit and integrated Punjabi Muslim society, and in no way can such a society be compared with that which is presented in the colonial and the Indian middle-class ethnography as segregated community. The Punjabi Muslims were not highly Islamic. At the core, as the legend reveals, they are a semi-tribal agrarian population; at the middle level, they are indigenously oriented with interaction between the Punjab 'roots' and Islamic 'routes', and on the surface they were Islamic. They were the members of Punjabi 'felt community' or a 'poetic community' which had/has common traditions, aspirations, emotions and interests, or immemorial continuities or a historically evolved rhythm, and hence, does not think of history as something past and gone.[8]

The legend of Hir-Ranjha is a valuable literary document which helps us not only to know the socio-cultural profile of the Punjabi Muslim, but also to perceive the nature and ethos of the Punjabi society of the medieval Punjab. The counter-hegemonic and counter-sectarian discourse of the Punjab folk as documented in *Hir Waris* needs to be contextualized and illumined vis-a-vis the communal discourse of Shah Waliullah (1703–62), a contemporary of Waris Shah. Shah Waliullah's *Wasiyat Nama* and *Hujjatt-Allah-il Baligha*, on the one hand, and Waris Shah's *Hir*, on the other, offer a contrast between a canonical text for the Muslims in general, and the cultural text of the lived experience of the Muslims of a 'particular' space. The decline of the Mughal Empire and the rise of regional forces like that of the Sikhs, Marathas and the Jats stirred many Islamic theologians like Shah Waliullah to correlate the political fall with the erosion of Islamic life among the Muslim masses. It was obvious for him to observe that the remedy lay in 'making concerted efforts to bring them [Muslims] closer to the true spirit of Islam. The fundamentals of the faith could be strengthened and the teachings of Islam made intelligible to the common man only if the message of the Holy Quran reached the votaries of Islam in word and spirit' (for details, see Waheed-uz-Zaman 1975). For that purpose Shah Waliullah rendered the Quran into Persian, which was then generally understood by the educated people. He exhorted Muslims to part with un-Islamic lifestyles, and disapproved of luxurious dowries, playing music, and wearing the bright and gaudy costumes at weddings – the pattern which we find in *Hir Waris*. Shah Waliullah writes in his *Wasiyat Nama* that the Muslims in India were like travellers because their ancestors came to this country as travellers. The Muslims should feel proud of both that they were Arabs by descent and their language was Arabic, and these two served as a source of access to the last Prophet (Muhammad). Shah Waliullah is said to have invited Ahmad Shah Abdali in 1759 to invade India for the sake of Islam: 'Certainly it is incumbent upon you to march to India, destroy Maratha domination and rescue weak and old Muslims from the clutches of non-Muslims. If Muslims would forget their religion . . . there will be nothing left to distinguish them from non-Muslims' (Nizami 1969: 83–98).[9]

Waris Shah and the Khalsa: discourse of Cunningham and McLeod

In the 18th century Waris Shah was waging a war on the literary front against the socio-religious patriarchs and the fanatics. On the other hand, his contemporary, the Khalsa-Singhs, were also engaged in a deadly battle against the Mughal oppression and Afghan invasions. But the century is (only half) emplotted, as it is characterized as a century of the Sikh struggle against the Muslim oppression, or 'the heroic period of the Sikh tradition' (McLeod 2000: 71). The genesis of such a procrustean presentation may be traced back to the tendency to eulogize a symbiotic relationship between history and state power. *History of the Sikhs* (1849), written by J.D. Cunningham, is a paradigmatic example of this perspective.

The establishment of the Khalsa Raj in 1799 by Ranjit Singh is preceded by its two phases – the first represented by Banda Bahadur (1708–16), and the second by Jassa Singh Ahluwalia. During the second phase (1765–85) the Khalsa-Singhs brought their nearly fifty years long relentless resistance and struggle against the Mughals and the Afghans to a successful conclusion, and embarked upon a career of conquest and consolidation of power. In the course of few years they became masters of the Punjab (Singh April 1977: 88–92). In 1783 they ravaged Delhi, the capital of the Mughal Empire, and for a short time also captured the Red Fort.

The increasing political Sikh influence at Delhi and the Ganga Doab caused anxiety to the British Governor-General, Warren Hastings (1773–85). He was keen to know about the Sikhs. For that purpose to achieve, he nominated James Browne as the British Agent and the Minister at the Court of Delhi on 20 August 1782. Browne left for Calcutta at the end of August 1782, and reached Delhi on 11 December 1783. He interviewed a number of Sikhs, collected information from them and then compiled his account under the title of *History of the Origin and Progress of the Sikhs* for the Governor-General, Warren Hastings, who was of the view: 'Every accumulation of knowledge and especially such as is obtained by social communication with people over whom we exercise dominion is useful to the state' (as quoted in Cohn 2002: 45).

After James Browne a number of Europeans like Antoine Louis Henri Polier, George Forster, John Malcolm, Henry T. Prinsep, Captain Murray, G. Carmichael Smyth, Steinback and W.L. M'Gregor wrote about the Sikhs. But the first *proper* history of the Sikhs was written by Joseph Davey Cunningham.[10] In 1844 he made up his mind to write about the Sikhs and completed it in two years (1846–48). It was published in 1849 under the title, *A History of the Sikhs from the Origin of the Nation to the Battle of Sutlej*.

Cunningham was a widely read person and had eclectic tastes in learning. He had keen interest in history, literature, philosophy and geography. In *History of the Sikhs*, his citations are important to be observed. He quotes Milton, Shakespeare, Homer, Dante, and Vigil, Plato, Herodotus, Tacitus, Gibbon. It was inevitable that while on the way to developing a philosophy on history, he should have made a critical study of Indian history. He made a thorough study of general Indian histories such as Elphinstone's *History of India*, James Mill's *History of British India*, Abuer's *Rise and Progress of British Power in India*, Thorton's *History of the Marathas* and Harlan's *India and Afghanistan*. He did a critical study of some Persian works in all probability both in that language and in translation. Among others these included *Debistan, Jahangir's Memoirs*, Shah Jahan's *Mirat-i-Aftab Nama*, and *Memoirs of Amir Khan*. He also read very carefully Malcolm's *Sketch of the Sikhs*, Lt. Colonel Lawrence's *Adventures in the Punjab*, Murray's *History of Ranjit Singh*, Colonel Steinback's *Punjab*, and Captain Osbourne's *Court and Camp of Ranjit Singh*. He also made himself familiar with *Adi Granth*, Guru Gobind Singh's *Gur Ratnavali* and one or the other *rehatnamas* (a recorded version of the Khalsa code of discipline) believed to be enjoined on the Sikhs by Guru Gobind Singh (Bal 1978: 85–133).

These Western writers and the colonialist British looked upon the Sikhs/Khalsa from the view point of their political ascendancy in the 18th century. Cunningham claims that his *History of the Sikhs* is popular and authentic because he was 'living among the Sikh people for a period of eight years [1837–45]' which was 'a very important portion of their history' (Cunningham 1956: xxiv). Earlier James Brown in the 18th century (1783/84), and later on W.H. MacLeod in the 20th century, also profess such claims. McLeod pays tributes to his predecessor, Joseph Davey Cunningham: 'the earliest generation of British observers were dependent on Sikh informants for much of their information, and with good reason to be impressed by the military skills of the Sikhs . . . Joseph Cunningham projects it clearly in *A History of the Sikhs*, thus supplying a major reason for the book's remarkably durable popularity' (McLeod 2000: 79–80).

These Western historians, or mainstream historiography, confine the Punjab history to Sikh politics, Sikh state, Sikh religion and Sikh life style. As a result, the ethnic profile of the *Punjabi* people remains relegated to the background. For example, Cunningham considers religion as the *only* basis for identifying and defining a nation. He also suggests that 'the Sikh people deserve the attention of the English, both as a civilized nation and as a paramount government' (Cunningham 1956: 12). He feels proud in writing that 'Sikhism has now come into contact with the civilization and Christianity of Europe, and the result can be known to a distant posterity' (ibid.: 80–81), though his contemporaries, like Murray and Steinbach, look down upon the Sikhs as 'uncivilized' and 'illiterate' ones who are averse to the 'acquisition of the Arabic and Persian languages, resulting chiefly from the ideas instilled, and prejudices imbibed in early age against everything, however, useful, and rational, that bears relation to, and is connected with, the religion and education of the Musalmans' (Steinbach 1970: 76). Perhaps Murray did not know or overlooked the fact that Guru Gobind Singh was a scholar of Persian language and the official language of the Khalsa Raj was Persian.[11]

Notwithstanding the low opinion about the Sikhs, Joseph Davey Cunningham did not want to alienate them, particularly when they were defeated in the First Anglo-Sikh War. Rather, he humours the Sikhs: the strength of 'Sikhs is not to be estimated by tens of thousands, but by the unity and energy of religious fervour and war like temperament. They will dare much, and they will endure much, for the mystic 'Khalsa' or commonwealth; they are not discouraged by defeat...' (Cunningham 1956: 12) Cunningham also laments that the Sikhs are regarded 'essentially as Hindus', though 'in religious faith and worldly aspirations, they are wholly different from other Indian'; a living 'spirit possesses the whole Sikh people, and the impress of Gobind Singh has not only elevated and altered the constitution of their minds, but has operated materially and given amplitude to their physical frames' (ibid.: 75–76). Cunningham does not seem to be acquainted with felt community of the Punjab; his language of narration is *sectarian*: 'Nanak *disengaged* his little society of worshippers from Hindu idolatry and Muhammadan superstition' (ibid.: 80, emphasis mine).

Thus in the Punjab itself, Cunningham characterized the Sikhs as a separate nation, whereas his contemporary Punjab poet, Shah Muhammad in his ballad, *Jang Hind-Punjab*, portrays a different picture. For Shah Muhammad the concept of the Khalsa is not narrow like that of Cunningham. He argues that it was Punjab (not only the Sikhs) at war with Hind or India which was under the East India Company. The title of the ballad itself underlines the point that it was a war between two sovereign countries, viz. India under the East India Company and Punjab as symbolized by the *Khalsa Darbar* (Nijhawan 2001: 42). Let us read two stanzas from Shah Muhammad's *Jang Hind-Punjab* wherein he recalls the communal harmony existing among the Hindus, the Muslims and the Sikh:

> Mahmud Ali marched out from his Majha country [central Punjab],
>   Taking awesome artillery pieces out of the city.
>   The brigade of Sultan Mahmud also came out,

With invincible Imam Shahi guns in row.
Elahi Baksh brought out his guns after polishing them,
And showing them worshipful burning incense sticks.
O Shah Muhammad! In such a way did the guns shine,
As if these were the flashes of lightning out to dispel darkness.
'The entire Punjab appeared to be on the offensive –
As no count was possible of those joining the action.
O Shah Muhammad! None could be stopped in that binding storm.
The Singhs now appeared determined to conquer Delhi.
(ibid.: stanzas nos 60 and 63)

Shah Muhammad's narrative is particularly relevant as a counter-discourse to the one like that of Cunningham who subscribed to the religion-centric trifurcation of the Punjab society and recalled the communal harmony existing among the Hindus, the Muslims and the Sikhs. Shah Mohammed was optimistic. He pronounces categorically: 'God willing, good things shall happen again \ What if the soldiers have lost the luster of their mien? \ Great commonality does exist between the Hindus and the Musalmans' (ibid.: 259, stanza no. 103). Joseph Davey Cunningham's fabrication of communal fault lines needs to be understood in the context of its ideological basis. Cunningham was a contemporary of James Mill (1773–1836) and W.H. Hegel (1770–1831) and was acquainted with the writings of the former. Both Mill and Hegel considered India as barbarous, stationary and stripped of rationality (Hegel 1956: 139; Philips 1961: 219). Hegel also suggested that one had to 'begin with the Oriental World, but not before the period in which we discover States in it' (Hegel 1956: 111). To him all the worth 'which the human being possesses, he possesses only through State. The State is the Divine Idea. The State is based on Religion. The former has proceeded from the latter. The form of Religion, therefore, decides that of the State and its constitution' (ibid.: 39 and 51).

One can now discern Hegelian streaks in Joseph Davey Cunningham's craft of writing the history of the Sikhs. His emplotment is solely concerned with the political rise of the Khalsa and the establishment of the Khalsa state. He is of view that in truth Ranjit Singh laboured hard to 'mould the increasing Sikh nation into well-ordered state or commonwealth, as [Guru] Gobind [Singh] had developed a sect into a people, and had given application and purpose to the general institutions of Nanak' (Cunningham 1956: 120). In such a state-/religion-oriented emplotment, the historically evolved text of the Punjabi community, its history and culture get marginalized, paving a way for the communitarian cleavages to appear prominently. For example, Cunningham's contemporary, Hegel wrote, 'the constitution of sect of the Sikhs is thoroughly democratic, and [they] have broken from the Indian as well from the Mohammedan religion, and acknowledge only one Supreme Being. They are a powerful nation' (Hegel 1956: 139).

After Cunningham, W.H. McLeod (1932–2009) is a celebrated historian of the Sikh history. Like Cunningham his 'primary objective has been to communicate an understanding of the Sikh people and their religion to educated *Western* readers'.[12] He believes that if Sikh history is to be the choice then with it goes Sikh religion, 'for it is altogether impossible to understand one without an intimate knowledge of the other' (McLeod 2004: 34 and 129). In his *Autobiography*, McLeod introduces a reader to his methods: 'I am a Western historian, trained in Western methods and adhering to Western notions of historiography... The attitude of the Western historian is firmly rooted in the Enlightenment, the essence being that all conclusions should be rational and all should be based on sources which are sound' (ibid.: 129 and 131).

Thus holding Enlightenment and the power of reason in high esteem, he constructs the universal and popular history of the Sikhs that 'includes the telling of stories from Sikh history in Punjabi homes'. Such a popular history 'pits truth and justice against treachery and cruel oppression' and it narrates 'heroes and martyrs on the one hand, and bigots and tyrants on the other' (McLeod 2000: 74 and 79). Since McLeod is a 'Sikh' historian, he explores popular *Sikh* history, instead of popular *Punjab* history, and eventually constructs an *oriental* emplotment of the 18th-century Punjab, and in the process traces the root cause of the partition of 1947 in this century. To him, the pronounced hostility between the Sikhs and the Muslims emerged in the beginning of the 18th century when 'Banda [Bahadur] was leading a rebellion against the rulers of the Punjab and there was no doubt that these rulers were Muslims'. McLeod further argues that 'feelings as deep as those which surfaced in the months following Partition cannot be explained simply by reference to the immediate past. They must have origins which lie further back in time. The eighteenth century was the period to which we must look when we seek an understanding of those attitudes' (McLeod 2006: 171, 174 and 179).

This account shows that the Western/colonial historians/philosophers like Hegel, Cunningham and McLeod converge together and present a picture of the Punjab which is different from the one we find in the vernacular literature like Waris Shah's *qissa* of *Hir* and Shah Muhammad's *Jang Hind-Punjab* and also in the devotional poetry of the saints and sufis of the medieval Punjab such as Shah Husain and Bulleh Shah.

Towards reformulating Punjabi identity

It would be interesting to add here that in the colonial Punjab *qissey* (plural of *qissa*) of *Hir Waris* began to be published in the last quarter of the 19th century both in Shahmukhi and Gurmukhi scripts concomitantly with the publication of the socio-religious tracts of the Punjab middle classes who aimed at reforming and reformulating the identity of the Punjab people as Hindus, Sikhs and Muslims (Jones 1999: 120–21; Mir 2010: 78–90). Bhai Kahn Singh Nabha's *Ham Hindu Nahin* ('We are not Hindus' 1899) and Lala Thakur Dass' *Sikh Hindu Hain* ('Sikhs are Hindus', 1899) are the prominent examples of such tracts (Sohal 2008: 164–5). Nevertheless, Punjabi *qissa* as a non-conformist and *secular* text continued to inspire the people and the freedom fighters. For example, after having killed Sir Michael O'Dwyer on 13 March 1940 in London, Udham Singh voluntarily surrendered. He confessed that he had avenged the massacre of the Punjab people in the Jallianwala Bagh, Amritsar.[13] A case was framed against him. To register his 'Punjabi' identity in the court, Udham Singh gave his name as 'Ram Mohammad Singh', and during his trial in London he demanded that he be allowed to take an oath on *Hir Waris*.

Qissa bhagat singh

In *Hir Waris*, the protagonist, Hir pronounces her agenda of crusade against the social patriarchs: 'The fruit of love will ripen on a severed head' (Sekhon, trans., 1978: 51). After a gap of about one and a half century the agenda of Hir reappeared, when on 22 March 1931, Bhagat Singh wrote:

> The desire to live is natural. It is also in me. I do not want to conceal it. But it is conditional. I do not want to live as a prisoner or under restrictions. My name has become a symbol of

Indian revolution. The ideal and sacrifices of the revolutionary party have elevated me to a height beyond which I will never be able to rise if I live. Today people do not know my weaknesses. If I escape gallows those weaknesses will come before them and the symbol of revolution will get tarnished or it may vanish altogether. On the other hand, if I mount the gallows boldly and with a smile, that will inspire Indian mothers and they will aspire that their children should become Bhagat Singh. Thus the number of persons ready to sacrifice their lives for the freedom of our country will increase enormously. It will then become impossible for imperialism to face the tide of the revolution. (Verma 1986: 157)

The ideal of Bhagat Singh and his struggle are emplotted in the genre of *qissa* which Waris Shah had adopted in the 18th for delineating the struggle of Hir. Didar Singh (1922–82)[14] penned the *Qissa Shaheed Bhagat Singh* (in Gurmukhi) in 1968 when Punjab was charged with the ultra Left ambience of Naxalism.[15] In the *Qissa* we find 'patriotic' form of love (*ishq*) and lover; and the medieval social patriarchs are replaced with the imperialist one (i.e. the British). Now patriotic love is the central issue of a narrative. We find in the *Qissa* the lover and the patriot fused together into a single identity of a revolutionary (Bhagat Singh). He is destined to be martyred like his 'medieval' predecessors, the lover-martyrs. In the *Qissa*, Bhagat Singh converses with his mother:

> Is it a sin / To die for the country / It is highest form of devotion. / O, mother, do not degrade my religion [patriotism] / By leading me away from death [martyrdom]. (Singh 2006: 84, trans. mine)

For the patriot-lovers, struggle for the liberation of the motherland is their *haj* (pilgrimage) which is performed only when martyrdom is achieved. Bhagat says: 'The court [British] has labeled us as prisoners of war. / Shoot us, and / Let our *haj* be performed' (ibid.: 96, trans. mine).

Qissakar, Didar Singh sets out to versify Bhagat Singh's patriotic traits. A sufic/bhakti motif of love and struggle against the social patriarchs in a medieval *qissa* now reappears against the imperialistic British patriarchs. Bhagat Singh is designated as a *surma* (brave) who fought with his head placed on his own palm, that is, he was engaged in an adventurous revolutionary praxis unto death. His journey on the road of patriotic love was bound to bring about a transformation – doing away with the exploiters. The *qissakar* eulogizes the revolutionary practice of Bhagat Singh. To him it is like a rise of the moon of immortal bravery in the atrocious and cruel dark night, illustrated by the British Raj. Bhagat Singh is portrayed as the one who sacrificed his life to awaken Punjab/India, that is, he laid the foundation of revolutionary consciousness (ibid.: 5–7).

Didar Singh is familiar with the nuances of the Punjab motif of love and sacrifice. It is evident from his repeated refrain: 'fought with his head placed on his own palm'. In the 14th–15th centuries, we find saint Kabir's (1398–1448) *saloka* (verse) proposing:

> The sky-resounding kettle-drum is beaten and the target has been hit. The warrior enters the battlefield. Now is the time to fight. He is recognized as a hero who fights for the sake of the wretched. Though cut limb from limb he may die, yet he does not flee the field of battle. (Fenech 2000: 101)

After Kabir, Guru Nanak (1469–1539) in the 15th century pronounces:

> If you want to play the game of love approach me with your head on the palm of your hand. Place your feet on this path and give your head without regard to the opinions of others. (ibid.: opening page)

In the 18th century Waris Shah's Hir declares before the assembly of her patriarchal family: 'The fruit of love will ripen on a severed head' (Sekhon, trans., 1978: 151). Bhagat Singh was also aware of this Punjab motif of love and sacrifice. He quoted the above verses of Kabir and Nanak in one of his essays.[16]

Didar Singh, the poet-narrator under reference, is well versed in the art of characterization of a hero as required by the genre of *qissa*. As Waris Shah presents the Amazonian and gorgeous image of his rebelling Hir, Didar Singh also portrays Bhagat Singh with the aid of a number of similes and metaphors. Bhagat Singh's youth is compared with the fore part of the foot that gambols in a folk dance; with a silver line that glitters in a dark cloud; with the moon that peeps through clouds in the dark night; with a blaze that emerges from a river; with a tufted turban standing aloft; with a fresh confidence floating in the eyes; with an adolescence that descends on a lion; with someone who gets engaged in contemplation; with someone who cracks jokes with death; with a tide that erupts from a sleeping ocean; with a bullet that crackles like a flash of lightening; with a blaze that emerges from a river; with a volcano that overflows; with the sun that tears a cloud; with an eagle that soars up into the sky; with a lover who defies death; with the Chenab river that overflows; with a rose that blooms; and with a youth who chants the ballad of Mirza, the Punjabi lover who was killed by the brothers of his beloved (Singh 2006: 10–12, trans. mine).

This exuberant image of Bhagat Singh, as narrated in the *Qissa Shaheed Bhagat Singh* is more revealing and multifaceted than the one which we find in the 'nationalist' and 'Marxist/Leftist' historiographical narrations. In the *Qissa* we find his multi-coloured collage of brain, brawn, beauty and bravery. The dialogical narration of Bhagat Singh's kinship relationship is the peculiar feature of the *Qissa*, when compared with the limited narrating capability, capacity and scope of non-literary sources. Bhagat Singh is shown in the condemned cell. His aunts, his sister, his mother and his younger brothers are shown sitting in front of the cell. The family members are emotionally stirred. The entire conversation boils down to the point that Bhagat Singh had 'fallen' in 'patriotic' love at an age when he was supposed to be enjoying his life and making merry (ibid.: 80–85). This family-segment of the *Qissa* alludes to the motif of marriage–martyrdom fusion. The *Qissa* ends with the description of a rebel. He is one who is a martyr. He is one who does not die even after his death. Longevity of his age does not depend upon years, that is, time. Death is his maidservant.

Ghori: a vernacular song of marriage–martyrdom fusion

The motif of marriage–martyrdom fusion, mentioned above, persuades us to study the popular image of Bhagat Singh as a 'martyr-bridegroom' or 'virgin-martyr'. Bhagat Singh's participation in India's struggle for freedom is culturalized when he is narrated, sung and portrayed as a *shaheed* (martyr), offering his head to Bharat Mata. His revolutionary militancy and non-conformism as described in the popular genres of Punjabi verses, like *tapey, bolian, ghori* and *qissa*, are not only simply of patriotic, nationalist or Leftist variety but are also projected as rooted in the heroic and chivalric traditions of Punjab. Bhagat Singh, the martyr, survives in the cultural cosmology of Punjab.

It is the peculiar characteristic of a folk society to satiate its aspirations and dreams with the help of its own constructed image of a hero. In other words, a person achieves the status of a hero and survives in popular cultural space only when he/she stirs the ethos of the people. A people's hero is born out of socio-cultural space and lives in a popular memory. This peculiar phenomenon questions the proposition that heroes are constructed from 'above' and then through ascendant ideology they descend down into the people's space.

The people of Punjab, as the history of their traditions and literature informs us, have been responding enthusiastically to those who were non-conformist, counter-hegemonic, non-sectarian and rebellious, whether they were kings like Poros[17], the 'Muslim' sufis like Baba Farid, Shah Hussain and Bulleh Shah, the 'Sikh' gurus like Baba Nanak, Arjan Dev and Gobind Singh, the 'outlaws' like Dulla Bhatti, or the 'lovers' like Hir-Ranjha. Another interesting feature of the society of Punjab is that it has been a frontier society. From the outset it has experienced the trauma of repeated invasions and destructions. Emotionally it cannot afford to see its young virgins killed at an age which is fit or appropriate for marriage. Therefore, whenever a young virgin dies during his/her struggle against oppression, he/she is perceived as a martyr. In the case of a male virgin, he is said to have wedded 'death'. Such a 'marriage' may be considered as a way to assuage the pain (of departure) through strong emotional ties. The prominent image of Bhagat Singh as a bridegroom-martyr hero in Punjabi literature illustrates this perception of the 'felt community' of Punjab. In its cultural space, the virgin-martyr like the four sons of Guru Gobind Singh and Bhagat Singh are remembered through the folk genre of *ghori*.

Ghori is a song which is sung by womenfolk a few days before and during the celebrations of the marriage ceremony of a boy. The people of Punjab, as has been said, conceive the virgin young martyrs as bridegrooms and pay their tributes to them in the form of marriage songs or in the ceremonial language. The following *ghori* was sung by a poet, named Tair on 23 March 1932 to commemorate the first death anniversary of Bhagat Singh who was executed in the Central Jail, Lahore, on 23 March 1931. The text of the *ghori* rendered into English is given below:

> Come on sisters / Let us sing together the songs of marriage, the *ghorian*, / The wedding procession, *janj*, has got ready. /

> Sardar Bhagat Singh, the patriot is about to repair / To marry Death, the maiden. / For a solemn bath / Bhagat Singh, you turned gallows into a wicker-mat, *khara* / And, like a bridegroom, you have seated yourself cross-legged on it. / Have a bath with a pitcher brimful of tears. / And put on a solemn red thread, *mohli*, dyed in blood. / Fashioning the cap/hood of execution into a crown / Bhagat Singh, you have sported a frilled chaplet. / O bridegroom, / With a sword of patience / You have slashed the *jand*-tree of tyranny. / Flanked by your best-men, the *sarbalas*, Rajguru and Sukhdev / You have mounted at the centre of the gallows. / Sisters are to take solemn money / For holding the bridle of your wedding-mare, the *vagh pharai* ceremony / And you owe your sisters that token-amount. / Hari Krishan is your brother-in-law, the *sandu* / You together have arrived at your in-laws' house for marriage. / O bridegroom, / Thirty five crore people / Join your wedding procession / Many are mounted / Many are on foot. / Attired in the black / The wedding procession has proceeded / 'Tair' is too ready for the same (trans. mine).

The *ghori* describes the martyr, Bhagat Singh, as a bridegroom. To eulogize his chivalry and execution, the ceremonies of marriage are invoked as metaphors. He is visualized as the celebrated one who is going to wed a girl, named Death. The death penalty and its perpetrators are defied and belittled. The *ghori* transfigures the hard wooden gallows into a solemn bathing square mat (made of reeds), that is, *khara*. It is used by the 'bridegroom', Bhagat Singh, for taking a ceremonial bath before mounting a 'mare' (scaffold) that would carry him to his 'bride's house' (death). The terrifying and imposing grandeur of the imperial gallows is reduced to the level of a bathing mat. The gallows, which illustrate the termination of life, are also envisaged as a 'mare' that would initiate a new phase in Bhagat Singh's life, as it would carry him (the bridegroom) to his fiancée (Death). A black hood of execution, meant for the condemned, has been metamorphosed into a crown and chaplet of Bhagat Singh, the bridegroom-martyr.

Conclusion

The accounts of Hir and Bhagat Singh suggest that contextualization is not only a profession of history; folk poetry (literature) also contextualizes history by asserting its merit as *poetry of history* (LeBlanc

2000: 103–19). Hence, it stands critically parallel to the conventional *history* of poetry. What I wish to submit is that contexts are not simply backgrounds, some kind of static assemblies of ideas and values, passively waiting to be received and greeted (Mikko 2000: 110–32). They are also site of conflicts, assertions and discourse. A task of a historian and a literary critic is not only confined to search for *formulaic* contexts, but to create *fresh* contexts from the domain of history, literature and culture. Understanding of a relationship between vernacularity and its literature can defy the constructed identities.

Are we interested in searching out the causes of the emergence and preaching of dominant 'isms'? Are we aware that why, how and for what purpose we practise these 'isms'? Representation of a vernacular culture/literature as an autonomous 'text' can rescue it from being marginalized. Discovery of such a culture/text has little to do with the literacy, writing and print culture of its *author*. People of the Punjab and their organic leaders (saints, sufis and bhaktas) in the pre-colonial times were well aware of the significance of their literary heritage as catalyst in the fight against the hegemonic and dominant. Now there is a need to consolidate this counter-hegemonic discourse, instead of consolidating and justifying the hegemonic ideologies with people's culture and literature.

Notes

1. Sultan Bahu (1629–91) was a Punjabi sufi poet. He adopted the genre of *siharfi* to communicate his mysticism (for details, see Krishna 1973: 47–59).
2. For the elite origin of archives and the hermeneutic right of the elites to interpret the archival documents, see Derrida, Summer1995. It also needs to be noticed that a document 'has a history which charts a turn-around in meaning and application. Its root (French), docere, meaning to teach, determined its early usage to mean 'a lesson, an admonition, a warning' (Barber and Corinna 2009: 1).
3. Edward Young in his *Conjectures on Original Composition* (1759) writes: 'An Original may be said to be of a vegetable nature; it rises spontaneously from the vital root of genius; it grows, it is not made. . .' (as quoted in Williams 1960: 37).
4. In the colonial era there was a conscious effort to replace the listener's or collective demand with the *subjective* class-demand of the colonial masters. Henry Schwarz calls it 'The Ruse of Progress'. He informs us that John Stuart Mill, the great English theorist of individual liberty, was of the view that 'to achieve success within the English-run administration, English-educated Indians would indeed be required to reproduce English form, not through English language alone but in the guise of vernacular

literatures explicitly tailored after English model. This internalized reproduction of English knowledge in the vernacular would guarantee the true assimilation of European ideas; it would determine equally the condition of native promotion and the sign of trustworthiness' (Schwarz 1977: 11–12).
5. With reference to denominational identity under our discussion, an information supplied by R.C. Temple, a Cantonment Magistrate at Ambala (1883), is worth considering: 'In India, where surnames are practically unknown, names of men and women so conspicuously fail to finally distinguish them, that it is necessary to add the parental and caste names, and even then, until the age is superadded, only doubtful success is attained ... A little careful attention to what is said in a case will show that a prisoner Ali Nawaz Khan of the police report is the Alia of the evidence, and that the Witnesses Govardhan Das and Durga Parkash are known as Gobra and Durga to their friends, and I would remark that Ali, Gobra and Durga are the real names of these worthies, the grander ones being used merely for the occasion' (Temple 1883: 5 and 15).
6. Besides the legend under reference, a number of Punjabi folk songs apprise us of a syncretic space where 'Hindu' gods and goddesses and Muslim pirs and fakirs plus jogis and Sikh gurus meet together (for folk songs see Randhawa and Sityarthi 2002: 160–65).
7. Harjot Oberoi's explanation of the Sikh participation in popular devotion at the shrine of Sakhi Sarwar, Gugga Pir, goddess Devi (worshipped under numerous names like Stla Devi, Mansa Devi and Naina Devi) may further enrich our understanding of the syncretic culture and religious boundaries (Oberoi 1997: 139–203).
8. For the concept of 'felt community' see Ray 2007: 3–15 and 172; and for that of 'poetic community' see Jacobitti 2000: 4–5.
9. The Pakistani Islamic nationalist historian, Ishtiaq Husain Qureshi writes: 'The rescue [by Shah Waliullah] of the [Muslim] community's conscience, its beliefs, and its faith in its moral purpose from the debris of the 18th century was no mean achievement in itself. Shah Waliullah, however, achieved even more; through his works he made lasting contributions to so many fields of Muslim thought' (Qureshi 2003: 217).
10. H.L.O Garrett (1881–1941), Professor of History, Government College, Lahore, in his 'Introduction' to Cunningham's book under reference writes: 'The whole book bears evidence of most meticulous care, and the voluminous footnotes show the breadth and variety of the author's study' (Cunningham 1956: iv).
11. Bhai Nand Lal (1633–1713) was a 17th-century Persian and Arabic poet in the Punjab region. He was one of the fifty-two poets of Guru Gobind Singh's Darbar (court).
12. Cunningham also claimed in 1849 that he wished to 'make known the history of a new and peculiar nation of the Sikhs' (Cunningham 1956: xxi).
13. In the massacre that took place on the day of *Baisakhi*, 13 April 1919, a large number of Punjabis – Hindus, Sikhs, and Muslims – were fired upon by General Dyer and his troops.
14. Didar Singh was a professor of English in Government College, Ropar (now Roopnagar, Punjab).

15. *Qissa Shaheed Bhagat Singh* was published by the Yuvak Kendar, Jalandhar in 1968. In this paper, I have used the 2006 edition.
16. The Punjab Hindi Sahitya Sammelan organized an essay competition on the problem of Punjab's Language and Script in 1923. It was for that competition that Bhagat Singh wrote this article. The General Secretary of Sahitya Sammelan, Shri Bhim Sen Vidyalankar, liked the article much and preserved it. Bhagat Singh got a prize of Rs. 50 for this article. Subsequently, it was published in Hindi Sandesh on 28 February 1933 (Singh 2000a: 20).
17. Poros ruled over the territory between the rivers Jhelum and Chenab and valiantly confronted Alexander the Great.

References

Abbasi, Muhammad Yusuf. 1992. *Pakistani Culture: A Profile*. Islamabad: National Institute of Historical and Cultural Research.

Ahluwalia, Jasbir Singh. 1982. 'Shaikh Farid Di Rachna Vich Darshnki Ansh', in Pritam Singh (ed.), *Shakarganj* (in Gurmukhi). Amritsar: Guru Nanak Dev University.

Ahsan, Aitzaz. 2005. *The Indus Saga: From Patliputra to Partition*. New Delhi: Roli Books.

Arnold, David. 1984. 'Gramsci and Peasant Subalternity in India', *The Journal of Peasant Studies*, 2(4).

Bal, S.S. 1978. 'Joseph Davey Cunningham', in Fauja Singh (ed.), *Historians and Historiography of the Sikhs*. New Delhi: Oriental Publishers and Distributors.

Barber, Sarah and Corinna M. Peniston-Bird. 2009. 'Introduction', in *History Beyond the Text: A Student's Guide to Approaching Alternative Sources*. London: Routledge.

Burke, Peter. 2009 [1978]. *Popular Culture in Early Modern Euope*. London: Ashgate Publishing Limited.

Cohn, Bernard S. 2002. *Colonialism and its Forms of Knowledge: The British in India*. New Delhi: Oxford University Press.

Cunningham, Joseph Davey. 1956. *A History of the Sikhs from the Origin of the Nation to the Battle of Sutlej*. New Delhi: S. Chand and Co.

Davidson, Alastair. 1984. 'Gramsci, the Peasantry and Popular Culture', *The Journal of Peasant Studies*, 2(4).

Derrida, Jacques. 'Archive Fever: A Freudian Impression', *Diacritics*, 25(2).

Diwana, Mohan Singh. 1982. 'Shaikh Farid Vich Lok Ate Akil Latif', in Pritam Singh (ed.), *Shakarganj* (in Gurmukhi). Amritsar: Guru Nanak Dev University.

Eaton, Richard. 1978. *Sufis of Bijapur, 1300–1700: Social Roles of Sufis in Medieval India*. Princeton: Princeton University Press.

———. 1996 [1993]. *The Rise of Islam and the Bengal Frontier, 1206–1760*. Berkley: University of California Press.

———. 2007. *Essays on Islam and Indian History*. New Delhi: Oxford University Press.
Fenech, Louis E. 2000. *Martyrdom in the Sikh Tradition: Playing the 'Game of Love'*. New Delhi: Oxford University Press.
Gramsci, Antonio. 1983. *The Modern Prince and other Writings*. New York: International Publishers.
———. 1996. *Selection from the Prison Notebooks*. Quintin Hoare and Geoffrey Nowell Smith (trans. and eds). Hyderabad: Orient Longman Limited.
Grewal, J.S. 2007. *Lectures on History, Society and Culture of the Punjab*. Patiala: Punjabi University.
Guha, Ranajit. 1983. *Elementary Aspects of Peasant Insurgency in Colonial India*. New Delhi: Oxford University Press.
———. 2003. *History at the Limit of World-History*. New Delhi: Oxford University Press.
Hegel, G.W.F. 1956. *The Philosophy of History*, Sibree, J. (trans). New York: Dover Publications.
Jacobitti, Edmund E. 2000. 'The Role of the Past in Contemporary Political Life', in *Composing Useful Pasts: History as Contemporary Politics*. Albany: State University of New York Press.
Jaggi, Rattan Singh. 2002. *Punjabi Sahit Da Srot-Moolak Itihas*, Part-V (in Gurmukhi). Patiala: Punjabi University.
Jones, Kenneth W. 1999. *Socio-Religious Reform Movements in British India*, in The New Cambridge History of India, III: I. New Delhi: Cambridge University Press.
Kaufmann, Walter. 1968. *The Ragas of North India*. Calcutta: IBH.
Khubchandani, Lachman M. 1991. *Language, Culture and Nation-Building: Challenges of Modernization*. New Delhi: Manohar Publications.
Krishna, Rama Lajwanti. 1973. *Panjabi Sufi Poets: A.D. 1460–1900*. New Delhi: Ashajanak Publications.
Kumar, Narendra. 1992. *An Encyclopaedic Dictionary of Indian Culture*. New Delhi: Agam Kala Prakashan.
Lawrence, Bruce B. 1987. 'The Sant Movement and North Indian Sufis', in KArine Schomer and W.H. McLeod (eds), *The Sants: Studies in a Devotional Tradition of India*. New Delhi: Motilal Banarsidass.
LeBlanc, Jacqueline. 2000. 'Gigantic Shadows of Futurity', in Edmund E. Jacobitti (ed.), *Composing Useful Pasts: History as Contemporary Politics*. Albany: State University of New York Press.
Marx, Karl. 1977. *Economic and Philosophical Manuscripts of 1844*. Moscow: Progress Publishers.
McLeod, W.H. 2000. *Exploring Sikhism: Aspects of Sikh Identity, Culture, and Thought*. New Delhi: Oxford University Press.
———. 2004. *Discovering the Sikhs: Autobiography of a Historian*. New Delhi: Permanent Black.

———. 2006. 'Sikhs and Muslims in the Punjab', in Asim Roy (ed.), *Islam in History and Politics: Perspectives from South Asia*. New Delhi: Oxford University Press.

Mikko, Lehtonen. 2000. *Cultural Analysis of Texts*, Aija-Leena Ahonen and Kris Clarke (trans.). New Delhi: Sage Publications.

Mir, Farina. 2010. *The Social Space of Language: Vernacular Culture in British Colonial Punjab*. New Delhi: Permanent Black.

Nijhawan, P.K. (ed. and trans). 2001. *The First Punjab War: Shah Mohammed's Jangnamah*. Amritsar: Singh Brothers.

Nizami, Khaliq Ahmad (ed.). 1969. *Shah Wali Ullah Ke Siyasi Maktubat* (in Urdu). Delhi: Nudwat-ul-Musannifin.

Nuzhat, Shaista. 2007. *Sayad Waris Shah Da Samaj-Shastri Falsfa* (trans., Iqbal Deep). New Delhi: Punjab Akademi.

Oberoi, Harjot. 1997. *The Construction of Religious Boundaries: Culture, Identity and Diversity in the Sikh Tradition*. New Delhi: Oxford University Press.

———. 2012. 'Brotherhood of the Pure: The Poetics and Politics of Cultura; Transgression', in Anshu Malhotra and Farina Mir (eds), *Punjab Reconsidered: History, Culture and Practice*. New Delhi: Oxford University Press.

Philips, C.H. 1961. 'James Mill, Mountstuart Elphinstine, the History of India', in *Historians of India, Pakistan and Ceylon*. London: Oxford University Press.

Puri, J.R. and T.R. Shangari. 1986. *Bulleh Shah: The Love-Intoxicated Iconoclast*. Beas: Radha Soami Satsang.

Qureshi, Ishtiaq Husain. 2003. *The Muslim Community of the Indo-Pakistan Subcontinent*. Karachi: University of Karachi.

Randhawa, Mohinder Singh (ed.). 1960. *Punjab: Itihas, Kala Ate Sabhiachar*. Patiala: Bhasha Vibhag.

Randhawa, Mohinder Singh and Sithyarthi (eds). 2002. *Punjabi Lok Geet* (in Gurmukhi). New Delhi: Sahitya Akademi.

Ray, Rajat Kanta. 2007. *The Felt Community: Commonality and Mentality before the Emergence of Indian Nationalism*. New Delhi: Oxford University Press.

Roy, Asim. 1996. *Islam in South Asia: A Regional Perspective*. New Delhi: South Asian Publishers.

Sagar, Brij Mohan (trans). 1999. *Hymns of Sheikh Farid*. Amritsar: Guru Nanak Dev University.

Schwarz, Henry. 1977. *Writing Cultural History in Colonial and Postcolonial India*. Philadelphia: University of Pennsylvania Press.

Sekhon, Sant Singh (trans.).1978. *The Love of Hir and Ranjha*. Ludhiana: Punjab Agricultural University.

———. 1986. 'Punjabi Sabhiachar: Ik Sanvad', in Harmandar Singh Deol and Kulbir Singh Kaang (eds), *Punjabi Sabhiachar* ((in Gurmukhi). Faridkot: Baba Farid Sahit Samelan.

Singh, Attar. 1988. *Secularization of Modern Punjabi Poetry*. Chandigarh: Punjab Prakashan.

———. 1976. 'Sheikh Farid and Punjabi Poetic Tradition', in *Socio-Cultural Impact of Islam on India*. Chandiagarh: Panjab University

Singh, Didar. 2006. *Qissa Shaheed Bhagat Singh* (in Gurmukhi), Malwainder Singh (ed.). Barnala: Vishwbharti Prakashan.

Singh, Fauja. 1977. 'The Mizaldari Period of Sikh History', *The Punjab Past and Present*, 11(1/21).

Singh, Ganda. 1960. 'Sapt-Sandhu – Punjab: Bhugol Ate Itihas', in Mohinder Singh Randhawa (ed.), *Punjab: Itihas, Kala, Sahit Ate Sabhiachar*.

Singh, Jagmohan (ed.). 2000. *Shaheed Bhagat Singh Ate Unha De Sathian Dian Likhtan* (in Gurmukhi). Ludhiana: Chetna Prakashan.

Singh, Jagtar (ed.). 2000. *Heer Damodar* (in Gurmukhi). Patiala: Punjabi University.

Sital, Jit Singh (ed.). 1973, *Hir Waris* (in Gurmukhi). Delhi: Navyug Publishers.

Sohal, Sukhdev Singh. 2008. *The Making of the Middle Classes in the Punjab (1849–1947)*. Jalandhar: ABS Publisher.

Steinbach. 1970. *The Punjab: A Brief Account of the Country of the Sikhs*. Patiala: Language Department.

Temple, R.C. 1883. *A Dissertation on the Proper Names of Punjabis with Special reference to the Proper Names of Villagers in the Eastern Punjab*. London: Trubner and Co.

Thompson, E.P. 1980 [1968]. *The Making of the English Working Class*. London: Penguin Book Ltd.

Vaudeville, Charlotte. 1987. 'Sant Mat: Santism as the Universal Path to Sanctity', in Karine Schomer and W.H. McLeod (eds), *The Sants: Studies in a Devotional Tradition of India*. Delhi: Motilal Banarsidass.

Verma, Shiv (ed). 1986, *Selected Writing of Shaheed Bhagat Singh*. New Delhi: National Book Centre.

Waheed-uz-Zaman. 1975. 'Shah Wali Ullah and His Times', in Ahmad Hasan Dani (ed.), *Proceedings of the First Congress of Pakistan History and Culture*, Vol. I. Islamabad: University Islamabad Press.

Williams, Raymond. 1960. *Culture and Society, 1780–1950*. London: Chatto and Windus.

———. 1978. *Marxism and Literature*. Oxford: Oxford University Press.

10

USES OF THE FOLK

Cultural historical practice and the Guga tradition[1]

Anne Murphy

The multiple lives of a folk tradition

How do we write a cultural history of the 'folk' as an integrated cultural field? The immediate context for this question is the epic and worship tradition of Guga Pir, a hero-deity popular across northern India for protection against snake bites, and as a part of a broader devotional landscape animated by local heroic/martial and saintly figures (Harlan 2003). Is this tradition found at the intersection of the 'great' and 'little' traditions conceptualized by Robert Redfield and Milton Singer; or, in more recent terms, is it an expression of larger institutional or cultural forms, as Dominique Sila-Khan has suggested in her effort to create an overarching Nizari Ismaili history for traditions across northern India that might include Guga (2003 (1997): 232–3)? Or, is it a form of subaltern religious experience – perhaps akin to the subaltern religious experience of the Dalit adherents of Kabir, for whom, according to Milind Wakankar, the intersection of the divine and violence produced a 'singular' and immanent mystical truth unavailable in existing institutional religious forms (2010: 8)? If it is 'the popular' or the 'folk', then how can we adequately express and appreciate its relationship with cultural production in courtly or other elite quarters, without making it subservient to/derivative of such traditions? (Hiltebeitel 1999: 16 ff.)

The answers to some of these broad questions may seem self-evident: the cult or worship of Guga Pir might easily be seen as a quintessential expression of a subaltern, folk tradition, outside the realms that we understand as elite or literate. There are compelling reasons for this: it is indeed most commonly found as a rural oral tradition, and worship of Guga takes places for the most part in informal and/or transient settings. It also sits uneasily with the defined religious identities that we are comfortable with in our historical moment, containing as it does a narrative of conversion and a history of practice that spans religious boundaries. It is most strongly associated with lower caste cultural performance and worship, perhaps indicative of a larger independent martial tradition that can at times act as a resource in contemporary Dalit assertion (Gooptu 2001: 201). At the same time, this tradition also exists in multiple guises, in elite or quasi-elite forms of cultural production both pre-modern and modern that, at times, embrace all or part of these aspects of the tradition. These 'uses of the folk', as we might call them, in elite terms, occupy a dynamic relationship with the more 'popular' tradition of Guga. What would it mean, then, to write a cultural history of the Guga tradition, folk and elite, folk-in-use and folk-as-popular, contributing to the production of our present – a present that includes the ongoing unfolding of the Guga tradition?

This chapter represents a move toward such an emergent cultural history and of the many forms and uses of the 'folk' that the case of Guga reveals. We can begin with one example: the work of Neelam Man-Singh, a recipient of the Padma Sri and prominent theatre professional ('A Prized Performer' 2011). 'Tradition', as a category, figures heavily in her work, though she sees herself not as using 'tradition as tradition... but tradition as transformation' (Group Discussion 1998). She has described her art as that of taking traditional narratives from Punjabi folk culture, as well as 'world classics' and classics from other parts of India, and transforming them into 'indigenous' theatre. She described herself in 1998 as working with a group of low-caste actors, whom she portrayed as worshipping a Muslim Pir (whom she named as Guga Chauhan), having Hindu names, and enacting Sikh rituals, 'representing the best of us', she said, before religion got 'messed up' with politics (Group Discussion 1998). Like many other modern directors and playwrights of the last century, she commonly draws on folk themes in her work, which in Punjab include the figure of Luna from Puran Bhagat, and the Hir-Ranjha story cycle; she is also influenced by Western forms. She noted that she was interested in the story of Guga Pir, for its sense of 'drama'. She told me that her actors would not perform his story, however, because they worshipped Guga and believed that to perform his epic as 'theatre' would cause them to go blind.

Man-Singh's musings on a folk tradition shared by all take place within a broader engagement of the folk and of 'tradition' in the articulation of an artistic vision for modern Indian creative work. The use of the folk in theatre was a staple of the Indian People's Theatre Association or IPTA, which represents in Rustom Bharucha's words an 'indispensable point of reference for almost any discussion on cultural politics in India' and a 'utopic moment' in Indian cultural history that is 'an integral element of a secular imaginary that has yet to be realized' (1998: 50–51). Such moves towards the folk took place in conversation with parallel moves elsewhere; thus art critic and theorist Geeta Kapur has called attention to the 'pastoral nostalgia' of 19th-century Bengal, reminiscent of a broader alliance of 'the progressive gentry with the folk in matters of culture' that characterized European romanticism in parallel terms (2000: 270). Such interests continued and intensified in the 20th century. There are many cloths in modern theatre, art and literature woven from the thread of the folk; as Kapur notes, we might see 'the appropriation of the folk as an indigenist project. . . [as] a way of deferring the drive for a westernizing modernism until it can be handled by a more independent, properly middle-class intelligentsia' (2000: 271–72). In this way this interest is a pause, on a path to another place, within the hands of elites. Such texts produced from the folk have acted as a form of negotiation with the national, and in this way 'fashion the cultural self-image of a new nation declaring its resistance towards imperialism through a homogenizing representational schema of their own' (Kapur 2000: 273). As Kapur notes, this functions on some levels as a kind of 'plunder' (2000: 273). On other levels, it is meant to destabilize otherwise hegemonic cultural forms associated with Western cultural production and force a new way of understanding Indian subjectivity as simultaneously modern and Indian – and not Western. Yet, at the same time, such engagements with the folk as a category have strong affinities with cultural movements in the West and elsewhere, so strong international impulses accompany those that are self-consciously local in their gambit (Bharucha 1998: 29). As Marilyn Ivy has observed in her discussion of a similar Japanese interest in folk traditions, the search for 'true' non-Western Japan is itself also a modern endeavor 'essentially enfolded within the historical condition that it would seek to escape' (1995: 241).

In general, the formation of the 'folk' in elite cultural production has posited such forms in the arena of 'tradition', with widely divergent senses of what this means. For contemporary cultural production, as we will see, this is 'tradition-in-use', as Kapur calls it (2000: 280). For others, a more nostalgic perspective is visible. Man-Singh, like other artists and scholars, has resorted to folk narrative and epic traditions to articulate a hybrid identity that all can participate in, to reconceptualize 'hardened' community definitions and create an option for 'religion' that does not get caught in communal divides and loyalties. As will be discussed, she is not alone in this. Yet, there is danger in such idealized visions of the folk. As Partha Chatterjee has pointed out, the 'popular' has been problematically mobilized in both the colonial and post-colonial periods as what he calls the 'repository of natural truth, naturally self-sustaining and therefore timeless' (1993: 73). This has for instance commonly been the only means through which Islam has been integrated into the 'national culture in the doubly sanitized form of syncretism' (Chatterjee 1993: 74). We must take care, therefore, with the nuances of 'the popular': the political and cultural work that it enables and the forms of difference it both allows and erases.

As we explore the formations of the 'folk' in the context of the Guga tradition, and their relationship to different kinds of postcolonial Punjabi and national cultural discourses, we must therefore do so with attention both to Chatterjee's words of warning and to the transformative potential of the folk, in a way that embraces both such uses of the folk, and the ways of being in these life-worlds themselves (Wakankar 2010). The 'popular' in such uses may be fundamentally modern, but in this it is not any less so than the so-called 'traditional' forms of cultural and religious production referred to by Man-Singh's actors. This is the continuum between the Guga of folk actors and Guga in elite cultural and scholarly production, the dynamic production of a 'tradition'. It is one however that is shot through with contradictions and inequities. The representation of the folk is always, as Rustom Bharucha has argued, 'fragmented, dispersed, and ruptured through the mediations of "national culture", festivals, intercultural exchange and cultural tourism' (1998: 38) – the forms of cultural production that now reproduce 'the folk' on international stages. All too often these reproductions/transformations replicate the power differentials that are found in local contexts. In this way, in keeping with broader cultural and political closures associated with our current moment, we see how, in the words of Jean and John Comaroff, 'the politics of consumerism, human rights, and entitlement have been shown to coincide with puzzling new patterns of exclusion, [but also] patterns that inflect older lines of gender, sexuality, race and class in ways both strange and familiar' (2001: 2); here, we must add 'caste' to this list of older and reinscribed patterns of exclusion. This essay explores some aspects of how this continuum is articulated and how debates about the folk – as well as 'culture' and 'tradition' themselves – must be considered in a critical cultural historical practice on a tradition like Guga's. The essay is thus exploratory in nature, an initial foray into modern Punjabi literature *itself* as a form of such a practice.

The guga tradition

The historical figure, Guga Chauhan, is said to have hailed from Rajasthan and is thought to have been active in the 11th century, but little concrete sense of the historicity of the figure exists (Hiltebeitel 1999: 14; Murphy 1995). Whatever the uncertainties as to the identity of the historical Guga, however – and we would do well not to focus too much on them – there is no shortage of evidence regarding his cultural and ritual importance in Rajasthan and other parts of North India (Malik 2005: 68 ff.). Guga is worshipped as a hero-saint and protector against snake bites, and his life story and the tale of his miraculous deeds are recited in an oral epic tradition that spans Rajasthan, Uttar Pradesh, Punjab, Haryana and Himachal Pradesh (as well as contiguous areas in Pakistan). His worship in Punjab is, for example, described in some detail in the rich account of Punjabi village life by Giani Gurdit Singh, *Merā Piṇḍ* (2003). Guga is portrayed in his epic as a Rajput hero of Chauhan descent confronting multiple familial and martial opponents, with strong affiliations with the cult of snakes and the Nath yogi tradition. 'Guga' is one of his many names – others include Zahir/Jahir Pir, Zahir/Jahir Diwan, Gugga or Goga. The epic associated with the Guga tradition is transmitted orally and sung primarily on and around 'Guga Naumi', Guga's holy day in the late monsoon season (on the ninth day of the dark half of Bhadon) (Murphy 1995). Still worshipped throughout North India, Guga is known both as '*vīr*' and '*pīr*', reflecting a hybrid tradition, as is clear from the content of the epic associated with him, described below. In some versions of his epic, he converts to Islam at the end of his life – thus becoming 'Guga Pir'. In India today he is increasingly portrayed as '*vir*', however, and the Muslim associations of '*pir*' are effaced. The contestation over the religious definition of the Guga cult is not only recent: as I'll discuss, Giani Ditt Singh of the Lahore Singh Sabha wrote a tract against Guga worship in 1902, and in the 1950s, the right of a

Muslim family to control a *Goga Meṛi* (near Suratgarh, Rajasthan) was contested in court (Sarkar 1984: 48).

The worship of Guga is not a thing of the past; it persists today. This is so even in the Indian Punjab, where Sikh and other reform movements in the early 20th century condemned the practice. The Guga epic tradition has been seen as representative of a cross-religious cultural and regional set of alliances, alliances which have been perceived in Punjab in different registers: in the form of threat, in the writings of those opposed to 'folk practice' and in the form of promise, exhibiting a regional expression of identity and cultural practice that exceeds religious affiliation and purports to create a possible shared tradition – in religious terms – *across* religious traditions. What is striking about both of these orientations towards the folk, in celebration or censure, is that they share basic assumptions about the nature of this folk tradition as 'other', as outside. This is a discourse overall, therefore, that is framed within the cultural politics of the modern. Such a convergence therefore should not surprise us.

Most of the texts of the Guga tradition (oral and written) follow a core narrative. Guga is born to a woman named Bachal, who has been barren for many years and whose dedication to Gorakhnath has earned her the boon of a son. This boon is not easily received, however, Before Bachal is able to receive it, her sister Kachal goes to Gorakhnath disguised as Bachal and receives the boon of twin sons. Later, Bachal goes to the Guru to receive her boon, only to be told that it has already been granted. Guru Gorakhnath ultimately gives her the boon that brings about the birth of Guga, but Bachal's visits to him have made her marital family suspicious. She is sent away, only to be later restored to her marital home by the power of her son and Gorakhnath. As a young adult, Guga desires to be married but his marriage choice does not find favor, in turn, with his mother and the bride's family. Through Guga's power over snakes and the intercession of Gorakhnath, the marriage does take place. The Gods are in attendance at his wedding and there is great celebration. At the death of his father, Guga ascends the throne as is his right and responsibility. Guga's twin cousins, however, desire a share of the kingdom. Guga refuses to accommodate them. They then leave to enlist the help of an outside force (which varies in the different versions) to help them gain control of the kingdom. With the help of this foreign power, the twins attack Guga. Guga prevails and the twin cousins are killed, allowing Guga to retain his kingdom. Bachal, his mother, is however displeased that her nephews have been killed. She banishes Guga from the kingdom as punishment. He leaves, only to return at night to appease his pining young wife. Bachal suspects that Guga has returned and asks his wife about his visits. Against Guga's wishes, the young bride reveals to her mother-in-law that Guga returns to her. The next time Guga visits, his mother appears and taunts him. In anger and dismay, he asks the earth to take him in (*samādhi*), but she refuses, claiming that she can only take in a Muslim. Guga converts, and then enters the earth as a Muslim mounted on his great horse.

Versions of the Guga epic represent a cross-section of status levels, genres and periods. The oral epic is the primary expression of the tradition and is a part of a larger oral epic genre in north India, through which, according to Janet Kamphorst, poets gave voice to 'distinctive interpretations of what it means to be a warrior, sometimes in accord with but at times also in contradiction to [a] dominant martial ethos' (2008: 11, see also: Blackburn et al. 1989; Gold 1992; Gooptu 2001: 201; Malik 2005; Pandey 1995; Smith 1991). Outside the folk epic genre, the tale of Guga is also performed in more formal folk theatre traditions and expressed in writing in historical and courtly bardic traditions, as well as in a range of popular vernacular texts, primarily in Hindi and Rajasthani. Each has its own set of priorities and approaches to the form and meaning of the narrative. In certain contexts, Guga is presented decisively as a martial hero; in others, he is seen in connection with a set of ritual and religious concerns related to snake worship and Nath traditions. In some, he is portrayed as a part of a more local tradition; in others, connections are made to pan-Indian traditions. No one text holds the definitive version. The narrative's different forms thus reveal a diverse array of social and literary contexts where the Guga tradition has found expression, connected to each other and to other epic performance and ritual texts through a rich set of intertextual relations (Malik 2005: 73 ff.).

As Komal Kothari has pointed out, in order to understand the place and meaning of epics like Pabuji (another hero figure prominent in Rajasthan, where Guga is prominent) and Guga, we must understand their performance context and 'the Rajasthani cultural ethos in which concerns for propitiating the powerful spirits of those who died untimely deaths continually feeds the epic traditions of the area' (1989: 102; on Pabuji see Smith 1991; Hiltebeitel 1999, ch. 4). This cultural ethos of memorialization is pursued on a variety of levels in Rajasthan, with varied categories of spirits who are worshipped after death. As Stuart Blackburn and Joyce Flueckiger have argued in their discussion of the oral epic in India overall, epic heroes in India are a part of a ritual complex which explores the relationships of the world of human activity with that of the divine (in Blackburn et al. 1989: 4; for more on the articulation of this relationship, see Kamphorst 2008: 20).

The role of Guga as hero changes in the different textual forms of the narrative. In some versions, the heroic nature of Guga is the central, if not the only, concern. In others, his role as hero is subsumed among ritual and religious concerns. Blackburn and Flueckiger (1989) have described three categories of Indian oral epic, which they refer to as the martial, sacrificial and romantic (in Blackburn et al. eds. 1989: 5). Blackburn has had trouble identifying Guga within his tripartite classification scheme, however, mainly due to the enigmatic ending of the epic, in which Guga meets his demise willingly and does not die in battle. This and other elements of the narrative distinguish Guga's epic from other martial epics. The enigmatic ending of this epic and its focus on renunciation and snake propitiation instead tie it to a broad spectrum of texts related to Naths yogis who have a prominent place in folk and oral culture in India. Gorakhnath, the prototypical Nath yogi, figures prominently in the narrative, and the renunciation expressed in Guga's demise relates strongly to Nath lore. With its unusual conversion episode, the narrative also reflects a world of Hindu and Muslim religious and cultural synthesis (the exact contours of which are open to some debate; see Khan 2003 (1997)). These religious issues are an important part of the 'life' of the text, which takes place within a ritual context associated with snakes and cross-religious practice. The oral and performed nature of the epic texts thus directly connects them to this world of religious and social praxis.

As Blackburn has noted in his examination of the Bow Song Tradition in Tamil Nadu, there is often a tendency to overemphasize the 'oral' in current discourse on epic and performance over a more textured understanding of the ways oral and literate worlds interact (1988, xvii–xviii). An earlier 'allergy' to texts took place within a broader theoretical debate that sought to distinguish between two seemingly absolutely distinct spheres of cultural and literary production, the oral and the written. This debate gave rise to a theory of orality and literacy that posited fundamental differences between oral and literate societies (Goody and Watt 1968: 27–68; Halverson 1991: 301–17; Ong 1982). Such an attempt to understand 'essential' differences between oral and literate cultures was a problematic undertaking at best, and most proponents of the theory have backed away from its grander, insupportable conclusions. This was particularly the case because many of the 'ideal' cases for the great divide reflected the intervention of colonial power into a given social context; a 'great divide' between the oral and literary, thus, was often not just observed by actors during and immediately after colonial rule, but in some cases was caused by it. In India the interaction between the oral and literate has always been more complicated, but it is not alone in this (Finnegan 1988: 77; Novetzke 2008: 100–101, 122–31; Pollock 2006: 78, 83, 86, 304–6). Not only is there no set of characteristics that ultimately defines something as oral or not, there is in fact a large degree of overlap between these domains. This does not negate the power of the oral-formulaic theory, which has proved a powerful model of oral (and particularly epic) composition. John Foley, who has written extensively on oral literature, has conceded this overlap between oral and written, emphasizing the importance of exploring the interactions between the literate and the oral and the different genres and methods of oral composition (1991, xiv).

The Guga tradition stands at the cross-roads of the oral and the written, the elite and the popular. The earliest mention of Guga in Western scholarship is in the Annals and Antiquities of Rajasthan of Lieutenant Colonel James Tod, political agent to the Western Rajput States, which describes Guga as having 47 sons and dying fighting on the banks of the Sutlej (1971: 841). Later British colonial scholars also collected and explored his epic, as well as Svang (later known as Nautanki) theatrical versions (Crooke 1895: 49–56; Cunningham 1970 [1882]; Dalmia 2006: 155; Elliot 1978 [1869]; Rose 1911–1919 [1893]; Steele 1882: 32–39; Temple 1963 [1884]); Kathryn Hansen has noted, however, that ritual associations of the Guga tradition did not find a place in the Nautanki theatrical context (1992: 39). Versions were collected by later Western anthropologists as well as by later South Asian folklore collectors and anthropologists; several modern publications in Braj Hindi, Punjabi, Rajasthani and Himachali contain or summarize versions collected orally (Caran 1962; Lapoint 1978; Satyendra 1956, 1974; Sharma 1974; Shastri and Dipa. eds. 1981). In recent years, the epic has been studied by various scholars, including most recently (in the context of Punjab) by Harvinder Bhatti of Punjabi University (2000) and Virinder Kalra and Navtej

Purewal of the University of Manchester (see also Wadley 1967). Ajay Bhardwaj's film *Milāṅge Bābe Ratan de mele te*/Let's meet at Baba Ratan's Fair' (2012) demonstrates the living dimensions of the tradition in Punjab today. The most ubiquitous written form of the epic today is in the vibrant world of vernacular publishing, where versions exhibit hybrid forms characteristic of oral and written literature – for example, the use of simple and repetitive poetic forms as well as simple prose – and the association of the epic with broader pan-Indian literary forms and religious traditions, such as in the transformation of Guga's *gāthā* into a *Mahāpurāṇ*, in 100 parts (Prithvirajji n.d. a and b; Kucaman Nivasi n.d.).

The Guga tradition is also found within literate and elite traditions in the pre-modern period: several 18th- and 19th-centuries indigenous bardic historians of Rajasthan mention the tale. These poet-historians known as *caraṇ* (and conventionally described in English as 'bards') were employed by local rulers in Rajasthan and other parts of northern and western South Asia and produced an extensive poetic literature in which heroic ideals played an important role (Kamphorst 2008, ch. 8; Thompson 1991). Poems about Guga have been attributed to two *caran* poets in Rajasthan: Barhat Asa (1493–1593) and Meha Vithu, who is believed to have lived in the latter half of the 16th century (Kamphorst 2008: 45; Maheshwari 1980: 57–59). The poems by these authors describe individual episodes within the Guga narrative and do not express the breadth of the narrative found in most of the other texts (Murphy 1995). In Suryamall Mishran's *Vaṁs Bhāskar*, a history of the Bundi court, begun in 1841 and published in 1902, Guga is placed within the lineage of the Chauhan ancestors of the kings of Bundi. Mishran (1815/6–68) was a *caran* by birth and lived at the time Colonel Tod was compiling his Annals of Rajasthan, and served as 'poet laureate' in the court of Maharao Ram Singh of Bundi (1811–89) (Qanungo 1960: 103). His *Vaṁs Bhāskar* was styled to compete with the Mahabharat. In it, Guga is an incarnation of Airavat, Indra's elephant (Murphy 1995: 15–16). This connection with the 'great tradition' is striking: in oral versions, connections with pan-Indian and supra-local traditions are few. Two figures with the name of Guga or Goga are mentioned in the historical and genealogical works by Muhnot Nainasi (b. 1611), whose family held high offices in Jodhpur and was appointed Diwan by Maharaja

Jaswant Singh in 1658 CE: one Guga is mentioned in connection to Pabuji and the other, a Rajput named Gogade, seems unrelated (Murphy 1995). The most commonly found forms of the Guga narrative today, however, are its oral epic form, performed in ritual contexts, and the popular published versions mentioned earlier. In the past as well, we can assume, the oral epic would have been ubiquitous. That form of the text however is unrecoverable now. The Guga tradition in its premodern form thus reflects a variety of relationships between the 'folk' and the 'elite', the oral and literate; the same is true in the present. The contextual factors which effect the construction of the Guga narrative as a 'text' in the modern period are complex: they relate to the process of collection of an 'oral tradition' by anthropologists, both Western and Indian, who have influenced the text through this process of collection and the fixation of a changing text into a definitive version. They also reflect the process of adaptation of religious stories for secular plays, in the Svang Theater, or in the adaptation of what seems to be a regional story into a supra-regional one. The latter is particularly visible in many popular print versions of the epic today, where connections to pan-Indian traditions are emphasized. All of these constructions of the narrative, premodern and modern, are built upon, it might be said, the common base of the Guga epic. Yet, the common base is not a single text, but instead a kind of proto-narrative from which narratives grow and develop in different contexts. Whether he be a hero, God, or an ancestral icon, the figure at the centre of these stories is brought to textual life in different forms, with different meanings, and for different purposes, so that, as Foley argues, 'the necessarily partial reflection of the larger story is actually never complete' and 'any single performance merely instances an unexpressed, and inexpressible, whole, a larger story that will forever remain beyond the reach of acoustically rendered, oral-dictated, or even written textualization' (1991, xv). This idea of not performing the 'whole' has been shown elsewhere, as in the case of similar epics such as Pabuji, Dhola and Gopichand, which, although often memorized and not composed extemporaneously, are almost never performed in their entirety. The audience plays an important part in determining which parts will be compressed or omitted and which parts should be included and expanded (Gold 1991: 104; Smith 1977: 144). Each instance of the Guga tradition, written or oral, similarly draws upon a larger tradition (Smith 1991: 72).

Valorization and censure: representations of Guga in modern culture-work

As Ivy describes, the condition of 'modernity-in-common' – that is, our common experience of modernity in its diverse forms – is characterized by 'national culturalism and its relationship to the uncanny . . . The contradictory longing for superseded forms of being – the pre-modern, the 'traditional', the irrational – and the recurrence of these forms in commodified guises; the desire for origins and for unmediated practices of the voice' (1995: 241). Nostalgia and vilification both are paired, constructing the folk in the imaginary of modernity as that which it is not, what it needs not to be and what it desires. This constitutes another evolving aspect of the formation of the Guga tradition.

The cultural politics of the folk has received significant attention in the past in scholarly circles, as it has in literary and artistic ones. Harjot Oberoi's early work focused on the ways in which traditions like Guga's expressed a pre-modern hybrid religious universe, one that was deemed unacceptable to the modernist politics of religious identity in Punjab in the early 20th century (1994: 4). In characterizing pre-modern Sikhism, Oberoi argued that 'most Sikhs moved in and out of multiple identities grounded in local, regional, religious, and secular realities. Consequently, the boundaries between what could be seen as the Sikh "great" and "little" traditions were highly blurred: several competing definitions of who constituted a Sikh were possible' (ibid.: 24–25). This 'older pluralist paradigm of Sikh faith', he argued, 'was displaced forever and replaced by a highly uniform Sikh identity, the one we know today as modern Sikhism' (ibid.: 25), while in a prior period, contemporary vehicles of knowledge – myths, texts, narratives, folklore and plays produced by non-Sikh authors – were accorded a firm place within Sikh cosmology (ibid.: 422). Farina Mir has more recently argued for a field of shared religious practice in late 19th-century Punjab in similar terms. Mir's conclusions rely upon her reading of *qissā* (story) literature of late 19- and early 20th-centuries Punjab, which she rightly argues were 'remarkably different from the tracts, treatises, newspapers, and modern genres of literature, most of which were produced by religious reformers, that have been important for scholarly studies of the period' (2006: 729). She argues that the *qisse* reveal that 'an ethos of piety continued to be both salient to and shared by Punjabis, despite the political context' (ibid.: 730). Pir veneration, Mir finds, is the core location of this shared religious space, for all Punjabis (ibid.: 747). This is the space in which the worship of Guga can be seen to reside as well.

The worship of Guga has been appealing in aesthetic and intellectual terms to Man-Singh, Oberoi and others because of its boundary-crossing potential: this mirrors more general orientations to the folk as a discourse of the modern, in the hands of both nationalists and cultural producers since the beginning decades of the 20th century. As Wakankar has argued: 'What drew indigenous scholars and thinkers to the inexhaustible archive of popular religion was the idea that had begun to establish itself of the nation as an age-old community of many faiths and creeds' (2010: 40). The Guga tradition has also however been the subject of censure: this censure was highlighted by Oberoi as an aspect of the rupture in the definition of what it meant to be Sikh in the late 19th century. One example of this is found in the novel *Sundarī* – the first modern Punjabi novel – published in 1898 by Bhai Vir Singh, a major Sikh reformer and leader of the Singh Sabha movement (Murphy 2012, ch. 4). This novel provides a useful example of a larger discourse on the problem of the folk that has accompanied the valorization of the folk in Punjabi cultural production in the colonial and post-colonial periods. While the ethical value of the folk is construed in radically different ways in these two perspectives, both share a particular characterization of the folk as a discourse of hybridity. They agree, therefore, in their construal of the *nature* of the folk as 'outside' and hybrid.

Sundarī portrays the struggle of the Sikhs in the first half of the 18th century through the figure of a woman, Sundari, who dedicates her life to that of the *paṅth*. Towards the end of the work, Bhai Vir Singh censures folk traditions (cited, in part, in Oberoi 1994); for example, he admonishes women for engaging in folk practices, arguing in the first-person voice of the narrator (violating the otherwise third-person narrative structure of the work):

> Look at yourself, and see how the decline of the Sikh nation is happening at your own hands. Having abandoned your God and the Gurus, you worship stones, trees, gods, and funeral sites. You have become neglectful of the Dharm of the Singhs, and are lost in other religions. Having turned away from the Gurus you teach your children about other religions. Your children will be as ill-trained as you, Sikh in their heads, Brahmans around the neck, and Muslim from the waist. . . .

Having abandoned the living God you feed sweet breads to snakes and . . . having abandoned God, you set your feet on the road to hell and bring your husbands and sons along with you (2003 [1898], 84). (All translations mine.)

This section of the novel is striking in stylistic terms in multiple ways; it is the only point in the novel where the narrator takes a harsh and direct, admonitory tone. He also, it should be noted, directly references practices related to the Guga tradition. Here we see a censure of religious practices that are seen to undermine Sikh identity, as Oberoi indicated in his reading of the work. This is not, however, the only attitude towards religious and cultural difference in the novel: there are other *accommodations* of difference in the novel that must be accounted for alongside such criticism. For example, Bhai Vir Singh portrays the oppression of both the common people (mostly Hindus) and the *Khālsā* at the hands of the Mughals and their functionaries, but he is careful for the most part not to equate Muslims with Mughals, and he carefully positions the *Khalsa* as the defender and guarantor of the rights of both Hindus and Muslims. In an important speech, Sham Singh (the leader of the *Khalsa* militia that Sundari is associated with through her brother) maintains the position of the *Khalsa* as follows:

Our home is not prejudiced, nor do we have any enmity with anyone, our Gurus had no enmity with Hindus or Muslims, neither. All of creation is one to us. We have come to destroy injustice, to weigh it and make it whole. This time those Hakams who are oppressive, we have come to correct them, we correct injustice. (ibid.: 33)

The Sikh leader Sham Singh, who speaks these lines, is further questioned by a Brahmin character regarding this stance towards the Turks: why do the Sikhs not just make alliances with the Turks, if they have no special enmity for them? Sham Singh further elaborates his position:

We do not have any enmity with the Pathans and Turks as Muslims, nor do we have a problem with their rule, per se. The meaning of our destruction of the rule of the Mughals is that they are the emperors, and they give grief to the people. They are unjust and kill the innocent and blameless. They take tax, but do not protect the people. They interfere with religion, and by force cause people to abandon their religions. These are sins, and this not the *dharm* of rule. Because of this we destroy their rule of cruelty. We have no enmity with any caste or creed, our Gurus came to spread *dharm*, so we destroy those people who perform *adharm* and give grief to the people (*prajā*). See here, the Hakam [whom the militia had deposed] was cruel and violent, he had no fear of God; nor was there any power in Delhi [to stop him] (ibid.: 33–34).

Generosity and coexistence are emphasized in these passages and must be understood in relation to a notion of 'good governance' in relation to the 'people' or *prajā* that Bhai Vir Singh develops through the novel (Murphy 2012, ch. 4). In his novel *Sundarī*, Bhai Vir Singh is thus not only interested in Sikh religious reform and the expression of a Sikh identity above all others, although this is how his work is generally read and was a preoccupation in general terms in his career. It is a highly complex book, reflecting sometimes contradictory currents in Sikh and Singh Sabha reform, nationalist mobilization and religious revivalism. Religious difference in general terms is not simply construed in the novel, as these brief examples show.

Why, then, does the folk represent such a problem for Bhai Vir Singh in this work, when he is able to accommodate other forms of difference? Anshu Malhotra has brilliantly shown how discourses over caste and gender were intimately tied in late 19th-century and early 20th-century Punjab (2002: 116–63); danger was perceived in the affinities of certain practices by upper caste women with those of lower castes. The admonition for women against participating in the folk cult of Guga (and similar practices) therefore may be more related to caste concerns than to issues around religious identity. At the very least, the two are tied. Bhai Vir Singh's concern for folk practices stems from the problem of caste mixing and the association of women in the *panth* with lower caste practices. Indeed, at one point, Bhai Vir Singh admonishes women that their practices will 'make them like Shudras' (*jadoṅ hor pūjā te nem dhāre, tadoṅ hī shudrāṅ vaṅṅgū ho jāogīāṅ* (Bhai Vir Singh 2003 [1898]: 95). The problem of mixing that Bhai Vir Singh vilifies, therefore, is fundamentally marked by caste. These issues emerge in the work of the Dalit Sikh reformer Ditt Singh as well, writing in the beginning of the 20th century. The sense that the worship of Guga is a problem is a sentiment that persists among many; Gurdit Singh opened his introduction to Ditt Singh's *Guggā Gapaurā* with a comment regarding how the people of Punjab have suffered under the force of superstition (1976, 'Introduction'). In the

USES OF THE FOLK

work itself, the author bemoans how Sikhs who might wear a proper turban, know Gurmukhi, and keep their *kesh* still engage in the worship of Guga (Giani Ditt Singh 1976: 9). One of the main narrators of the text, who argues against Guga worship, claims that those who worship him have lost their senses (Giani Ditt Singh 1976: 16).

Yet, despite such opposition, the worship of Guga has persisted in Punjab. It is an aspect of *Punjabiyat* or Punjabiness – as such, it is present in the *virāsat* or 'heritage' portion of the *Khalsa Virāsat Kendra* in Anandpur, where a small worship site for Guga is portrayed. And while the caste dimensions of the Guga tradition may have brought it scrutiny, it is perhaps the importance of caste – rather than religion – in the Guga tradition that accounts in many ways for the continuing presence of Guga in the Punjabi cultural landscape. Thus, the Chappar mela associated with the major Guga shrine in Ludhiana is attended by all major politicians, Akali Dal and Congress, in the current day (Web.). The politics of caste mobilization in Punjab more recently demand such political attention. The 'work' of the folk in the formation of religious and literary sensibilities in the colonial period therefore expresses multiple formulations of difference and inclusion, in relation to both religion and caste. We would do well to note the observation of Tony Ballantyne that the Singh Sabha period – so often characterized as the time of the rigid definition of what a Sikh is and so closely tied to Bhai Vir Singh's work – was also the time of the proliferation of multiple Sikh subjectivities within India and in an increasingly accessible diaspora, such that, in Tony Ballantyne's view, 'these visions of the encounter of Punjabis with modernity and the fashioning of clear Sikh identities can only stand if we consciously exclude . . . stories of mobility, cultural loss, creative adaptation, and passionate yet flexible anti-imperial resistance' (2006: 83). In the same way, the censure and valorization of the folk have coexisted and been co-produced.

Theatrical renditions

The concerns of some religious and social reformers about folk practices in the colonial period are parallel to the treatment of these practices and cultural traditions by some literary and cultural reformers. In that context as well there was concern for the relationship between the popular and the classical, the low and the high. As Vasudha Dalmia has described, the nineteenth 19th-century Hindi critic, author and publicist Bharatendu Harishchandra (parallel in many ways to Bhai Vir Singh in terms of his role and stature) took great pains to establish a modern Hindi theatrical realm that would be classical in its orientations and untainted by the messy forms of popular theatre in the 19th century (2006: 153). Critique of the folk as 'low', as we saw in Bhai Vir Singh's *Sundarī*, thus can be placed within a wider discourse of the attempt to define 'high culture'. The definition of 'the folk' was indeed central to these efforts, as Dalmia notes: 'this interest in folk culture, as well as the category 'folk' came into currency at the same time as the 'high' literature in the modern Indian print languages began to take shape and set up a canon for itself' (ibid.: 155). Cultural reformers sought to establish the credentials of modern Indian languages through claims to a classical past and elite modern present.

Other artists and cultural producers welcomed the meaning and significance of folk traditions in the formation of Indian literary and performance traditions in the context of colonial rule. The valorization of the folk in this context also reflected broader discourses of the day: the idea of the 'folk' in Europe represented the search for 'essential' cultural sources for emerging European 'nations'. Popular and folk traditions served a similar role in South Asia. Interest in folklore studies grew among South Asian intellectuals in the late 19th century into the beginning of the 20th century as a part of the nationalist project that had as its goal, Wakankar tells us, ' to derive from the popular in its many practices, precepts and doctrines, that primitive accord between subaltern and elite . . . that would hold Indian society together' (2010: 41). Folk traditions provided fertile ground in particular for the turn to the representation of the interests and the experience of common people that inspired and animated the Progressive Writers Movement from the 1930s on, which itself had strong international affiliations as a part of a global anti-fascist and leftist movement in the arts (Gopal 2005). The Indian People's Theatre Association or IPTA grew out of this context in the early 1940s, with, as Vasudha Dalmia describes, a 'new emphasis on Indianness, a new enthusiasm for the culture of the people coupled with a fervent post-1942 patriotism that condemned alien rule in its entirety' (2006: 153). This formulation dismissed differentiation between Indian elite and popular cultural production (ibid.: 161) This, Dalmia notes, was one of the problems of the IPTA, its tendency to 'melt difference by extracting some exotic features and integrating them into a totalizing metanarrative' (ibid.: 162). The remolding of traditional or folk theatre forms for contemporary purposes was one aspect of the IPTA's approach, and accompanied experimentation with European theatrical forms and 'realism' in urban contexts, pushing work produced in this vein out of a dogmatic and patronizing 'use of tradition' into something more experimental. After 1947, the IPTA itself came into conflict with the post-colonial state and did not remain the locus of theatrical activity after the late 1950s, when organizations like the Sangeet Natak Akademi were formed. In this context, we see a reversal again: folk traditions were configured as 'rural derivations of and deviations from the all-encompassing Sanskritic tradition, from which they had emanated and into which they could, under the new dispensation, flow again' (ibid.: 170). Well-known theatre director and critic Balwant Gargi produced the first book on Indian folk theatre in English in 1966, in which he articulated a vision of the folk's direct relationship to Sanskrit theatre. Such efforts were however accompanied by those that emphasized the importance of the folk on its own terms, and the need to coin 'a modern urban idiom, using the vocabulary of the 'folk'' (ibid.: 177). As Dalmia points out, the approach of Bertolt Brecht became an important means for the achievement of this goal.

In the 1960s and 1970s, folk theatre was influential in several respects. Plays were taken from the folk context in both form and content and molded for a more formal theatrical context; folk forms were utilized for Western and classical plays; folk forms were utilized on their own terms to produce a political or social message; and in some, folk themes and elements were borrowed and integrated into urban theatrical productions (ibid.: 1933–94). After the devastating effect of the Emergency – which sought to quell dissent and threatened any kind of creative and political expression – the uses of folk theatre changed again, producing in Dalmia's words 'a kind of inner Orientalism' that used folk art and performance as 'export items that backdated culture in a move that was as anachronistic as unscrupulous' (ibid.: 200). Here we can refer to Kapur's discussion of the uses of tradition in contemporary art – it is only vibrant in so far as it engages modernity fully, not as a holdover or remnant.

Progressive interpretation and creative engagement with folk tradition therefore has valorized the folk; it has also sought to classicize it. On one hand is the sense of 'plunder', the 'internal orientalism' that produces the folk as both a contributor to and an effect of the national. On the other is the reliance of this discourse on the folk as 'other'. The valorization of the folk as hybrid has thus again mimicked its censure.

The construction of folk traditions in these terms, as Ivy (1995) has argued, in fact positions the folk at the centre of the modern, not at its periphery, as the 'other' that constitutes it within. A similar position is staked out with respect to the religious. As Rustom Bharucha has pointed out, progressive formulations of the folk have exhibited an overt allergy to the religious, a refusal 'to acknowledge the liberatory possibilities of religion, or more specifically, of religious material transformed into another kind of cultural discourse through oral narrative or performance, which functions with its own norms, quirks, grammar, levels of interruption and inscriptions of the worldly and the political' (1998: 37). As Christian Novetzke has shown, the religious also occupies an ambivalent location in the work of the subaltern studies collective, which has under-theorized religion even as it has 'made religion central to its understanding of 'peasant consciousness' and the motivations for "counterinsurgency"' (2006: 101). In this context, religion is portrayed as the non-modern, outside the rational and the contained; this also makes it a possible location for the possibility of insurrection and subaltern aspiration. Milind Wakankar's recent work on Kabir proceeds from such a coalescence of religious experience and subaltern subjectivity, towards an embrace, ultimately, of the primacy of a 'pre-religious' mystical and singular experience (vii). The religious and the folk are parallel: problematic and valorized alike, outside and inside at the same time.

Another modern Guga

Punjabi theatre has been fundamentally shaped by these cultural forces and the legacy of IPTA. Balwant Gargi is only the most famous example of Punjabi theatre directors and playwrights who helped to shape modern Indian literary theatre with a commitment to the portrayal of village life and to political uplift. Theatre served as a vehicle for social change perhaps most famously in the hands of Gursharan Singh, the master and champion of street theatre. It is thus to a play by Charan Das Sidhu – another leading director and playwright – that I would like to now turn to examine yet another dimension of the production of the Guga tradition. This expression of Guga's epic is fraught with materialist concerns, keen awareness of caste structures of power and a complex understanding of human relationships. Inversion and boundary crossing are central to the play. Here in the hands of Sidhu, Guga comes alive in socially activist theatre. C.D. Sidhu was active until his death in 2013 and takes as his topical inspiration a range of material – his play on Ghalib was staged in 2010 – and retains his commitment to speaking in the voice of the 'common man' (Bajeli 2012). The folk here is explicitly political and is mobilized to call into question the social hierarchies that structure life today. At the same time that we can see this as a 'use' of the folk, it is imperative that we not simply dismiss this as 'appropriation'; this play too partakes of the Guga tradition in the complex ways identified for an earlier period. Indeed, to dismiss this engagement with the tradition would be to invoke the discourses of authenticity and the 'otherness' of popular and folk traditions that are just as much a part of the modern as is modern theatre. The newness and modernity of experimental vernacular theatre do not make it 'less' of the Guga tradition.

Baba Bantu was first produced in 1982. It portrays the life and trials of a devotee of Guga, and healer in his name, Bantu. Bantu is heavily in debt to a local landowner, Sarban, as a result of his daughter's wedding. As we discover as the play unfolds, this wedding itself was forced upon the family, because of the lecherous designs of this landowner on Bantu's daughter, Satti. Bihari, Bantu's son, is very unhappy with the situation of his family, and his own and his father's powerlessness: he calls his father a slug, a bug who crawls in mud (Sidhu 1984: 27–38). When another landowner's child is bitten by a snake, we begin the process by which the epic of Guga is brought into the present debacle, through its performance in the play, and also through the transformation of Bantu, as the wrath of the God takes shape. Bantu sings of the birth of Guga, through the intervention of Gorakhnath, following the trajectory described earlier for the epic: his mother's service, his aunt's trickery. Meanwhile, in the main story line of the play, Bihari, Bantu's son, accepts the advances of Sarban's wife, Mindo, as a form of revenge for her husband's designs on Bihari's sister.

The epic recitation continues, describing Guga's quest to marry and the conflict that ensues as his twin cousins challenge his right to his inheritance. Parallel to the inversions in the epic, we see a set of inversions regarding power in the world of Bantu – the advances of the landowner's wife, Bihari's intention to overcome his father's powerlessness and his rejection of *izzat* in these terms (ibid.: 34). Bihari has embraced transgression: he dances, engages in what his father calls a profession of prostitutes (ibid.: 33); his involvement with the landowner's wife promises an opportunity for revenge (and perhaps for fulfilling the family's debt) (ibid.: 48–50). The father has the ability to harness the power of Guga but is unable to protect his family. Such inversions are only furthered in the tale when we see Sarban interact with Satti (Bantu's daughter), who returns home for a visit, revealing a kind of intimacy between them that cannot be entirely subsumed within feudal inequities of power – the playwright gives a sense of Sarban's humanity, even as he overpowers and uses those around him (ibid.: 63). Indeed, it is Satti who reveals to Sarban the possibility of a liaison between her brother and Mindo, Sarban's wife, which results in Sarban's murder of Bihari. With this, the tension in the play begins to build feverishly, as Bantu faces the reality of his son's death at the hands of the powerful landlord to whom he is indebted. This is when Bantu recites the end of the epic, when Guga kills his cousins and then disappears into the earth, leaving his wife behind.

The power of the figure of Guga reverberates through the play, with the epic narrated in juxtaposition to the events taking place in the story. At the beginning of the play, when Bihari taunts his father Bantu about his powerlessness – his inability to benefit from his medicinal/spiritual power, and his inability to seek revenge – Bantu retorts that 'the Sants gave me a boon. Is there anything more a sin than killing someone?' (ibid.: 35). He is powerful but does not want to use this power; he warns of the landlord's power. These are the two forms of power that run through the play, in constant contest. The powerful hand of Guga and his epic run parallel to the events in the play, as the evils of Guga's twin cousins are juxtaposed with the actions of Sarban and his wife, who from Bantu's point of view leads Bantu's son astray. This is yet another inversion of the play – she describes herself as the true *mālak* of the family (ibid.: 46). When Bihari, Bantu's son, is killed, Bantu sings of Guga's cruelty (ibid.: 75). Gorakhnath, in the epic of Guga, kills the father of Guga; in the play, Bantu's son is killed. Guga comes into conflict with his cousins, and Bantu must confront the killer of his son.

The climax of the play is centered around Bantu's response. His daughter has been the object of the lecherous gaze of the landlord; his son has been killed by him. All of this is in addition to the economic exploitation that does not allow Bantu ever to repay his debt. Bantu defers within the play, when others in the village praise his power, to argue that all the power is Guga's (ibid.: 45). In the end, however, it seems that he takes on the power of Guga himself, and the landlord Sarban is bitten by a snake. Rather than cure Sarban – as he must, as a healer, but cannot, as the father of a murdered son and a threatened daughter – Bantu allows himself to be bitten, punished for appropriating the power of the deity, but extracting revenge in the end. Just as Guga's wife is left at the end of Guga's epic, Bantu's wife is left, alone and bereft of husband as well as son (ibid.: 94). She continues to lead the Guga epic narrative, without her Guga. As in the epic, the wife is left alone.

Sidhu uses the Guga tradition to protest material circumstances and seek their redress. His play is about the crossing of all kinds of boundaries, but not specifically *religious* ones. The play demonstrates the productive possibilities of such a tradition in modern literature, not as 'other' or as 'authentic' – which are common but less interesting uses of the trope – but as productive engagement in political and materialist terms. Guga provides the means for boundary crossing in this play: discourses of alternative forms of subjectivity are narrated through the epic and the worship associated with it. In some senses this was as true in existing late medieval and folk forms of the epic tradition, as in modern theatre. In this way, the play expresses concerns that Chatterjee identified for popular religion as an expression of subaltern consciousness, whereby new religions and movements are formed in the process of struggle between dominant and subordinate groups (1989: 192). For Chatterjee, such practices express 'the common understanding of the members of a subaltern group engaged in the practical activity of transforming the world through their own labor, often at the behest and certainly under the domination of the ruling groups' (1989: 171). Thus, the adherent of popular religion bears the marks of domination, as well as dissent. Popular religion does not provide a simple 'other' to elite religion, nor to subaltern insurgency, as elements of both are contained within it.

C. D. Sidhu's play denies simple designations of alterity, because his characters are so deeply implicated in personal relationships that themselves are shot through with hierarchies of power. Sidhu's work suggests boundary crossings personal and class- and caste-based, in some ways making irrelevant the question of religion and impossible the designation of comfortably distant bodies marked by clear difference. In a way, the post-colonial state itself produced the conditions possibility of the Sidhu–Guga story in the late 1970s and early 1980s: perhaps the failure of the state to protect subalterns adequately lends a certain mythic proportion to subaltern struggle, as expressed in the play. In this tale, power is uneven and unruly, and death alone awaits. The power of Guga, however, still operates.

A cultural history of the folk and the modern

Geeta Kapur suggested in 1989 that 'if the third-world intelligentsia, among them artists, perform a task, it is to bring existential urgency to questions of contemporaneity... [where] tradition is turned into a critique, modernity into lived experience, and both into a revised civilizational discourse that goes beyond nation-state and third-worldist dogmas, beyond also the divisive bigotries of the present world, so as to gain a utopian dimension' (2000: 282). In this she also asserted the allied aims of artists in the non-third world. We see *līla* or play in the Guga tradition, from its lived dimension as an oral tradition to its presence in courtly literature, from its life in modern theatre to that found in scholarly argument. This is a 'play' that speaks to Kapur's imperative, and to the problematic place of both religion and caste in the writing of cultural history. Karin Zitzewitz has argued that the utilization of religious forms within the modern artistic canon is an aspect of secularist practice – 'the content of religion is encircled by the secular, and through that process, it is transformed into an inclusive ethics' (2008: 24). We have seen that this aspect of folk traditions – its operation as the religious and as that outside of 'the religious' in conventional forms – has been asserted by both critics and those who praise these traditions; Guga's world is thus transformed into another kind of secularist practice, a counter-narrative to the formation of 'religion' as a historical, nationalist, and bounded product (Wakankar 2010; Mandair 2009). At the same time, it is that which is problematic about the 'folk' that gives it cultural power, both within its lived, performative ritual contexts and performances such as those staged by Sidhu. The folk, one might say, is the spectre of critique, always already present, always prior and after at the same time, always modern and that which is not. It is its absence that might constitute the desire for its instantiation in the modern, but in South Asia it is also always present-in-its-absence as well. This may be what is distinctive – and most interesting – about the South Asian 'use' of the folk. Marilyn Ivy has noted, in her discussion of the place of 'tradition' and the 'folk' in the constitution of Japanese modernity, that 'modernist nostalgia must preserve, in many senses, the sense of absence that motivates its desires' (1995: 10). The folk therefore must remain as such, at the same time that attempts are made to contain it and use it, sometimes in the guise of political action, and at others through the commodification process of the 'folklorization' of the rural, by the urban (Niranjan et al. 1993; Hacker 2000: 164).

The modern requires this double movement. Critical cultural historical practice must somehow account for this presence-in-absence and outside-that-is-inside, for popular practice and literary production, oral and written tradition and for the complexity of the exclusions and inclusions that constitute each. This too is where Guga's power operates.

Note

1. In memory of Alan Entwistle of the Department of Asian Languages and Literature at the University of Washington, accomplished scholar and guide (1949–96). This essay reflects in part work completed under his supervision.

References

'A Prized Performer'. 2011. Indian Express. Web. 28 January. http://www.indianexpress.com/news/a-prized-performer/742855/.

Ballantyne, Tony. 2006. *Between Colonialism and Diaspora: Sikh Cultural Formations in an Imperial World*. Durham, NC: Duke University Press. Print.

Bajeli, Diwan Singh. 2012. 'In Ghalib's Skin'. *The Hindu*. 7 May 2010. Web. 18 February. http://www.hindu.com/fr/2010/05/07/stories/2010050750200300.html.

Bhardwaj, Ajay. 2012. *Milānge Bābe Ratan De Mele Te*/Let's Meet at Baba Ratan's Fair. Film, 95 minutes. Language: Punjabi with English Subtitles.

Bharucha, Rustom. 1998. *In the Name of the Secular: Contemporary Cultural Activism in India*. New York: Oxford University Press. Print.

Bhatti, H.S. 2000. *Folk Religion: Change and Continuity*. Jaipur: Rawat Publications. Print.

Blackburn, Stuart H. 1988. *Singing of Birth and Death: Texts in Performance*. Philadelphia: University of Pennsylvania Press. Print.

Blackburn, Stuart. H., Peter J. Claus, Joyce B. Flueckiger and Susan S. Wadley. Ed. 1989. *Oral Epics in India*. Los Angeles: University of California Press. Print.

Caran, Candradan. 1962. *Gogājī Cauhān rī Rājasthānī Gāthā*. Bikaner, Rajasthan: Bharatiya Vidya Mandir. Print.

Chatterjee, Partha. 1993. *The Nation and Its Fragments*. Delhi: Oxford University Press. Print.

———. 1989. 'Caste and Subaltern Consciousness'. In *Subaltern Studies VI: Writings on South Asian History and Society*. Delhi: Oxford University Press. 169–209. Print.

Comaroff, Jean and John Comaroff. 2001. *Millennial Capitalism and the Culture of Neoliberalism*. Durham: Duke University Press. Print.

Crooke, W. 1895. 'A Version of the Guga Legend' *Indian Antiquary* 23 (February): 49–56. Print.
Cunningham, A. 1970 [1882]. *Archaeological Survey of India: Report of a Tour in the Punjab in 1878–79.* Varanasi: Indological Book House. Print.
Dalmia, Vasudha. 2006. *Poetics, Plays and Performances: The Politics of Modern Indian Theatre.* Delhi: Oxford University Press. Print.
Elliot, H.M. 1978 [1869]. *History, Folk-lore and Culture of the Races of North Western Provinces of India.* Edited by John Beames. Vol I. Delhi: Sumit Publications. Print.
Finnegan, Ruth. 1988. *Literacy and Orality: Studies in the Technology of Communication.* Oxford: Basil Blackwell, 1988. Print.
Foley, John Miles. 1991. *Immanent Art: From Structure to Meaning in Traditional Oral Epic.* Bloomington: Indiana University Press. Print.
Gold, Ann. 1992. *A Carnival of Parting: The Talkes of King Bharthari and King Gopi Chand as Sung by Madhu Natisar Nath of Ghatiyali Rajasthan.* 1992. Berkeley: University of California Press. Print.
———. 1991. 'Gender and Illusion in a Rajasthani Yogic Tradition'. Ed. Arjun Appadurai, Frank J. Korom and Margaret A. Mills. *Gender, Genre, and Power in South Asian Expressive Traditions.* Philadelphia: University of Pennsylvania Press, 1991. 102–35. Print.
Goody. J and Ian Watt. 1968. 'The Consequences of Literacy'. *Literacy in Traditional Societies* Ed. J. Goody. Cambridge: Cambridge University Press. 27–68. Print.
Gooptu, Nandini. 2001. *Studies in Indian History and Society, Volume 8: Politics of the Urban Poor in Early Twentieth-Century India.* Cambridge: Cambridge University Press.
Gopal, Priyamvada. 2005. *Literary Radicalism in India: Gender, Nation and the Transition to Independence.* London/New York: Routledge, 2005. Print.
Group Discussion. 1998. Neelam Man-Singh, with Punjabi Studies Summer Program (Columbia University). Chandigarh.
Hacker, Katherine. 2000. 'Traveling Objects: Brass Images, Artisans and Audiences'. *Res: Anthropology and Aesthetics.* 37 (Spring): 147–65. Print.
Halverson, J. 1991. 'Goody and the Implosion of the Literacy Thesis'. *Man* (NS) 27: 301–17. Print.
Hansen, Kathryn. 1992. *Grounds for Play: The Nautanki Theatre of North India.* Berkeley: University of California Press. Print.
———. 2010. 'Who wants to be a cosmopolitan? Readings from the composite culture'. *The Indian Economic and Social History Review.* 47, 3: 291–308. Print.
Harlan, Lindsey. 2003. *The Goddesses' Henchmen: Gender in Indian Hero Worship.* New York: Oxford University Press.
Hiltebeitel, Alf. 1999. *Rethinking India's Oral and Classical Epics : Draupadi among Rajputs, Muslims, and Dalits.* Chicago: University of Chicago Press.

Ivy, Marilyn. 1995. *Discourses of the Vanishing: Modernity, Phantasm, Japan.* Chicago: University of Chicago Press. Print.

Kamphorst, Janet. 2008. *In Praise of Death: History and Poetry in Medieval Marwar (South Asia).* Amsterdam: Amsterdam University Press. Print.

Kapur, Geeta. 2000. *When Was Modernism? Essays on Contemporary Cultural Practice in India.* New Delhi: Tulika. Print.

Khan, Dominique-Sila. 2003 (1997). *Conversions and Shifting Identities: Ramdev Pir and the Ismailis of Rajasthan.* New Delhi: Manohar.

Kothari, Komal. 1989. 'Performers, Gods, and Heroes in the Oral Epics of Rajasthan' *Oral Epics in India.* Ed. Blackburn et al., 102–17. Berkeley: University of California Press. Print.

Kucaman Nivasi, Lacchirama. n.d. *Goga Chuhāṁ kā Mārvāṛī Khyāl.* Ajmer: Phulchand Bookseller. Print.

LaPoint, Elwyn. 1978. 'The Epic of Guga: A North Indian Oral Tradition' In *American Studies in the Anthropology of India*, 281–308. New Delhi: American Institute of Indian Studies. Print.

Maheshwari, Hiralal. 1980. *History of Rajasthani Literature.* Delhi: Sahitya Akademi. Print.

Malik, Aditya. 2005. *Nectar Gaze and Poison Breath: An Analysis and Translation of the Rajasthani Oral Narrative of Devnarayan.* New York: Oxford University Press. Print.

Malhotra, Anshu. 2002. *Gender, Caste, and Religious Identities: Restructuring Class in Colonial Punjab.* New Delhi: Oxford University Press. Print.

Mandair, Arvind-pal Singh. 2009. *Religion and the Specter of the West: Sikhism, India, Postcoloniality, and the Politics of Translation.* New York: Columbia University Press.

Mir, Farina. 2006. 'Genre and Devotion in Punjabi Popular Narratives: Rethinking Cultural and Religious Syncretism' *Comparative Studies in Society and History.* 48, 3: 727–58. Print.

Murphy, Anne. 2012. *The Materiality of the Past: History and Representation in the Sikh Tradition.* New York: Oxford University Press. Print.

———. 1995. 'Texts of the Guga Tradition: Diversity and Continuity in Changing Contexts'. M.A. thesis. University of Washington. Print.

Niranjan, Tejaswini., P. Sudhir, and Vivek Dhareshwar. Eds. 1993. *Interrogating Modernity: Culture and Colonialism in India.* Calcutta: Seagull Press. Print.

Novetzke, Christian. 2006. 'The Subaltern Numen: Making History in the Name of God'. *History of Religions.* 46, 2: 99–126. Print.

———. *Religion and Public Memory: A Cultural History of Sant Namdev in India.* 2008. New York: Columbia University Press.

Oberoi, Harjot. 1992. 'Popular Saints, Goddesses, and Village Sacred Sites: Rereading Sikh experience in the Nineteenth Century' *History of Religions.* 31, 4: 363–84.

———. *The Construction of Religious Boundaries*. 1994. Delhi: Oxford University Press. Print.
Ong, Walter J. 1982. *Orality and Literacy: The Technologizing of the Word*. New York: Routledge. Print.
Pandey, Shyam Manohar. 1995. *Lorikāyana: The Hindi Oral Epic Tradition*. Allahabad: Sahitya Bhawan. Print.
Pollock, Sheldon. 2006. *Language of the Gods in the World of Men: Sanskrit, Culture and Power in Premodern India*. Berkeley: University of California Press. Print.
Prithvirajji, Srī *Gogā Mahāpurāṇ*. Delhi: Merath Pustak Bhandar, n.d. Print.
———. *Gogā Caritra*. Delhi: Merath Pustak Bhandar, n.d. Print.
Qanungo, Kalika Ranjan. 1960. *Studies in Rajput History*. Delhi: S. Chand & Co. Print.
Rose, H.A. 1911–1919 (1893]. A *Glossary of the Tribes and Castes of the Punjab and North-West Frontier Provinces*. Lahore: Printed by the Superintendent, Govt. Printing.
Sarkar, J.N. 1984. *Thoughts on Trends of Cultural Contacts in Medieval India*. Calcutta: OPS Publishers Pvt. Ltd., 1984. Print.
Satyendra. 1974. *Lokvārtā kī Pagadandīya*. Udayapur: Bharatiya Lok-Kala Mandal, 1974. Print.
Satyendra, ed. 1956. *Jāharpīr: Guru Guggā*. Agra: Hindi Vidyapith. Print.
Sharma, Devaraj. 1974. *Gugā jāhar pīr*. Bilaspur: Navin Printing Press. Print.
Shastri, Ramanatha. and Sivarama Dipa. Eds. 1981. *Guggā-gāthā: Himāchalī Rūp*. Jammu: Dogari Samstha. Print.
Sidhu, C.D. 1984?. *Bābā Baṅtū*. Delhi: National Book Shop.
Singh, Bhai Vir. 2003 [1898]. *Sundarī*. New Delhi: Bhai Vir Singh Sahit Sadan.
Singh, Giani Ditt. 1976. *Guggā Gapauṛā te Sultān Puāṛā* Ed. Giani Gurdit Singh. Amritsar: Prabhjot Printing Press/Jaspaal Printing Press. Print.
Singh, Gurdit. 1976. 'Introduction' ('*Arāṁbhak Shabd*') In *Guggā Gapauṛā te Sultān Puāṛā*. Ed. Giani Gurdit Singh. Amritsar: Prabhjot Printing Press/ Jaspaal Printing Press. Print.
Singh Gurdit. 2003. *Merā Piṅḍ*. Chandigarh: Sahit Prakashan.
Smith, John D. 1991. *The Epic of Pabuji: A Study, Transcription, and Translation*. New York: Cambridge University Press, 1991. Print.
Smith, John. 1977. 'The Singer or the Song? A Reassessment of Lord's Oral Theory'. Man (NS). 12, 1 (April): 141–53. Print.
Steele, F.A. 1882. 'Folklore in the Panjab' *The Indian Antiquary*. 11 (February): 32–39. Print.
Temple, R.C. 1963 [1884]. *Legends of the Punjab*. London: Turner & Co. Print.
Thompson, Gordon R. 1991. 'The Cārans of Gujarat: Caste Identity, Music, and Cultural Change'. *Ethnomusicology*. 35, 3 (Autumn): 381–91. Print.
Tod, James. 1971. *The Annals and Antiquities of Rajasthan (1829–32)*. Vol.2. Delhi: Motilal Banarsidass. Print.

Wadley, Susan. 1967. ''Fate' and the Gods in the Panjabi Cult of Gugga: A Structural Semantic Analysis'. M.A. thesis. University of Chicago. Print.
Wakankar, Milind. 2010. *Subalternity and Religion: The Prehistory of Dalit Empowerment in South Asia*. New York and London: Routledge, 2010. Print.
Web. 15 Feb. 2012. http://www.ludhianadistrict.com/mela.php.
Web. 15 Feb. 2012. http://www.festivalsofindia.in/chappar-mela/.
Web. 15 Feb. 2012. http://www.tribuneindia.com/2005/20050918/ldh1.htm#3.
Zitzewitz, Karin. 2008. 'The Secular Icon: Secularist Practice and Indian Visual Culture'. *Visual Anthropology Review*. 24, 1: 12–28. Print.

Part IV

CULTURAL POLITICS AND MASS MEDIA

11

(IN)VISIBLE PUBLICS

Television and participatory culture in India

Abhijit Roy

A rubber stamp with the name and address of a person must be very common. But what were uncommon in this little black-ink stamp I discovered sometime in the early 1990s were the two Bengali words of designation: *Betar Srota* ('Radio Listener'). Proudly displayed by the rightful user, a *paan*-shop owner in the southern fringe of Calcutta, this text used to appear below his signature in every letter he wrote to All India Radio's Calcutta station, particularly to Vividh Bharati. Apart from being an indicator of popularity of radio in the heydays of public television in India, this is also an amazing testimony of how the subject interacting with media constitutes its identity. Such personalization may be rare but it hints towards the myriad histories of participatory culture in India and their various relations with the personal, the private and the public. In this essay I seek to understand some of them with a view to roughly propose a critical agenda for studies in Indian participatory cultures.

Indian television has achieved a certain height of interactivity, participation and mobilization through the genres of Reality TV and news. I focus in this essay on the many legacies of the current phase of participatory culture around Reality TV launched with *Kaun Banega Crorepati* (KBC) in 2000. More than 'public opinion' that is primarily associated with news television, important in our discussion are 'participatory culture' and broadly forms of publicness and collectivity around mass media, radio and television to be precise, from the 1950s to the 1990s. Such distinction between Reality TV and News (and for that matter any generic distinction) is a contingent discursive necessity to understand the complex of generic confluences and overlaps that characterize our times. The questions I am asking are: Can we now reflect back and think of a 'pre-history' of the current form of participatory culture around Indian television? If yes, what continuities and ruptures enable us to historicize forms of publicness in the 21st century?

The first in this project is possibly the task of probing into the under-researched forms of participation in the era of exclusive dominance of state-controlled radio and TV. While print media's forte in this regard had mainly been deliberation on civic issues through 'letters to the editor' (and occasionally participation in 'contests'), the radio used to primarily invite participation through song-request programmes. Television, on the other hand, was to be understood by what James W. Carey once called 'transmission view of communication', being an apparatus that either discouraged or tried to control participation (1989: 14–23).[1] The Indian state's scepticism about the legitimacy of the cinematic public in the project of nation-building extended to radio, as radio became a major site for the transmission of Indian popular film songs. In 1952, B.V. Keskar, the then Minister for Cultural Affairs banned film songs from radio on the charge of vulgarity but had to lift the ban because, according to a press release, 'it cost the broadcasting organization too much in popularity' (Chatterjee 1992: 36).[2] The broadcast public, directly under the aegis of post-colonial State pedagogy, could never be the libidinal 'vulgar' public of popular cinema, the constituency of capitalism's enchantment with the erotic, the vestige of colonial expansion worldwide of 'entertainment'. One can in fact go to the extent of suggesting that the kind of public the State-controlled Media tried to create till the 1980s, though largely in vain, was in many ways opposite to the public of popular cinema in India. While the popular cinematic public was conceived as one associated primarily with the streets and lumpen public spaces, the territory of the broadcast public was essentially the home and the family, the sanctity of which, it was thought, could better sustain a citizenship premised upon the patriarchal order of the nation-family bondage.

Microcosms of the public manifest in small physical assemblies have always been created around portable media like the transistor and the newspaper. The home-centric sets like the electric radio, the 'record player' and, later, the television, also, had the capability of bringing the neighbourhood and acquaintances together, especially when the access to such media was not widespread. This surely was not a 'participatory' public but definitely one that was, at least partly, *mobilized* by a particular medium, in the form of small listening/viewing/reading and discussing communities. One of my vivid childhood memories of a railway township in eastern India in the 1970s and 1980s is of women enjoying a sunny winter afternoon sitting around a radio set, listening and chatting while knitting sweaters. Another image is of young boys and men assembled in the corner of a field listening to the live commentary of a Mohun Bagan–East Bengal football match or a cricket match from Calcutta's Eden Gardens. Yet another memory is of *Mahisasurmardini*, a programme designed by 'Akashbani Kolkata' narrating Goddess Durga's triumph over the evil Mahisasur with songs and parts read from *Chandi*, the Sanskrit script on Durga's deeds. This programme, since 1931, has woken up millions of radio-possessing Bengali families at 4 o'clock in the morning on the last day of the Hindu practice of paying the fortnight-long tribute to forefathers on the eve of Durga Puja. Associated tales range from compulsory bathing before the programme to people listening with flowers in their folded hands in the mode of a mass prayer. Such was the popular appeal of this programme that we took long to realize that the day had any other significance than the 4 o'clock broadcast. The association of this radio programme with a contingent community or the act of 'coming together' still continues as many local clubs transmit the programme every year through loudspeakers in sync with the early morning broadcast.

We also heard from elders how Akashbani Kolkata's news broadcast on East Pakistan's war of liberation, read by Debdulal Bandyoadhyay (whose voice had a peculiar mélange of romance with an imminent sovereign Bangla nation and the determination of *muktijoddha*s, soldiers fighting for liberation), also drew people around the radio set. The indifference in this popular tale towards the relative silence of Calcutta radio about the brutal repression of the Naxalites in West Bengal around the same time needs to be further investigated. The structure of civility and citizenship within which the collective engagement of the educated middle class with media and news grew was always unstable, as the mainstream public was eerily discomforted by, but couldn't address, the other form of collective engagement based on disavowal of the codes of such civility and citizenship, and questioning of mainstream media's politics. Since a large part of the leadership in the 'other' form of mobilization emerged from the same 'bhadralok' section, the mainstream could never rid itself from the uneasiness of a blurred boundary between the sensibilities of civility and that of delinquency constructed under repressive state regimes.

How do we understand such publics? Is there any need to begin to historicize participatory culture from such a vantage point? In case of early television, one can remember the days of popularization of live cricket when people from non-television homes would go to a neighbour's place to watch the matches. The funeral of Indira Gandhi televised live in colour on Doordarshan[3] comes also to mind as a media event that made large number of people gather in homes having colour television. Whatever may be the reason, problem of access or the pleasure of collective reception (an overlap of the two possibly describes the phenomenon best), these contingent little communities had radio or television at their centre. These little popular assemblies, I suggest, cannot merely be understood as a public that were forcefully brought together by a 'lack' and that gradually dispersed as demands for access were met. I would rather like to explore what correspondence these gatherings had to structures of already existing communities. One corresponding frame of such collective reception beyond the familial space was the 'modern' culture of discussing topical issues around the day's newspaper. The centrality of newspaper (and broadly of the print) in nationalisms across the world has been amply historicized and theorized. The degree of mobilization of reading publics however has not been examined in terms of the ways information proliferated, networks crisscrossed and territorialities precipitated into gatherings, groups and forums. The energy and vibrancy in such places of exchange of various interpretations of information come from specific histories of crowds and publics bearing the legacy of a colonial modern. The rather weak distinction between the private and the public in the colonial context, unlike Western modernity, lent a special charge to communitarian engagement and forms of publicness. What makes the little assemblies interesting is that they exhibit various orders of public intrusion into the private and vice versa, bringing into the fore the porosity of the two categories in our modernity. While the newspaper's usual constituency was the public space where strangers could (and continue to) easily come in close contact with each other, radio tended to draw a community of acquaintance around, with lesser chance of encountering a stranger, be the gathering at home or outside. The 'passerby' however was always a possibility. Television-at-home was distinct from newspaper and radio in largely preventing the possibility of accommodating strangers or passerby.

Radio and television were unique in relegating the erstwhile primacy of communitarian reception of popular entertainment to privatized consumption. They remain primarily responsible for expanding the semantics of community/public leisure in which, the element of 'going out for the speciality of a spectacle' constantly negotiates the new lexicon of 'entertainment', the ever-presence of a domestic flow of sound and images. The larger community of the nationwide watching public, however, always intrudes as a rule through the apparatus itself, generating a peculiar space of 'privatized public'. Television particularly has given rise to a new home, a site that is torn between a sense of threat to its property and peace, and a sense of security, an intensification of the boundary of home underlined by the 'distance' of reception. The impression that is created in any act of watching TV is not exactly of 'being at home' but possibly of 'being in one of the homes'. The home and the familial space here harbour a certain order of porosity and ephemerality. The order of communitarian engagement, hence, is not completely lost from television. In a way the gatherings around media, in its early form and present incarnations (for instance, collective watching of a high-power football or cricket match in spaces from malls, multiplexes and restaurants to local clubs) bear with them a concoction of the traditional communitarian assemblies and the nation-wide 'coming together' of people across a live network. The rise of participatory culture and the power of the network have not weakened the corporeal experience of the territorial community but may have subjected the local physical assemblies to enter into an inter-constitutive relationship with the emerging virtualities shaping the public.

It was through the Satellite Instructional Television Experiment (SITE) that the state in 1975–76 tried to involve residents of nearly 2,500 villages in North India, giving each village a television set around which the villagers were expected to assemble. But it was not 'participation' per se since the villagers were conceived merely as viewers with no active role to play in this grand design of the state. SITE couldn't excite much the villagers who were groomed for ages with communitarian engagement around local 'entertaining' performances, an audiovisual configuration of a different order. Public television in this era tried to align itself to a realist–developmentalist aesthetic concomitant with a state-sponsored cinema.[4] The rural addressee could never be much attracted to what was a relatively new audio-visual regime for them, the modern realist codes of documentary-style representation. It's significant that we keep alive the point of association of participatory culture with issues of form and style, largely of the 'screen', the area much demonized in Media Studies. Extending this argument, I have suggested on another occasion (Roy 2014) that the demise of the form of 'discrete programming' (the modern realist mode I have referred above) and the simultaneous rise of the flow form on Indian television, a process gaining impetus between 1982 and 1991, did create a space for mass *identification* with television and therefore participatory culture around it. The argument basically suggests that the form of 'flow' (originally proposed by Raymond Williams) that was discontinuous, rupturous and open-ended, also inseparably connected to consumerism, could generate tropes of identification in the relatively non-modern subject because of the form's correspondence with the popular performative traditions in India.

The first major instance of a 'network' of participation emerged around *Binaca Geetmala*, a radio programme and 'Vividh Bharati', the radio station. *Binaca Geetmala* started airing on Radio Ceylon in 1952, shifted to Vividh Bharati in 1989 and continued till 1994, having taken various names in its career, *Cibaca Sangeetmala*, *Cibaca Geetmala* and *Colgate Cibaca Sangeetmala*. Aswin Punathambekar (2010: 191) has chronicled the wonderful journey of Radio Ceylon and Binaca Geetmala through an interview of Ameen Sayani, the legendary announcer of *Binaca Geetmala*. Sayani offers an amazing account of participatory culture around radio, compelling us to compare the details with our times. American entrepreneur (Dan Molina), cross cultural broadcast signal (Beamed from Ceylon), commercial multinational sponsors (Swiss companies from CIBA to Ovaltine), competition and 'hit parade' formats – all of Radio Ceylon seem to be resonating with the consumerist televisual culture in post-Liberalization India. A certain form of simple comprehensible Hindi on television that has helped create a pan-Indian audience post-1982 may also have been popularized for the first time by Hindi film songs in the 1950s. Sayani refers to the role of Hindi film songs in popularizing 'Hindustani' that was 'open, colloquial' and also 'not sanskritized, nor does it have too many difficult Persian or Arabic words' (ibid.: 193–94). The nature and the extent of audience participation in our times also remind us without fail of audience participation in programmes like Binaca Geetmala. Sayani (ibid.: 195) says: 'The very first program, broadcast on December 3, 1952, brought in a mail of 9,000 letters and within a year, the mail shot up to 65,000 a week'. Along with this, 400 radio clubs and arrangement with 40 record stores across India, colossal influence over film industry and record sales, controversy regarding the ranking system in the 'hit parade', alleged manipulations in making song-requests – make radio in India an indispensable referent in the genealogy of the televisual national culture of our times. Punathambekar (2009) looks at such role of radio as facilitating Bombay film industry's drives to create a national culture:

> What I am arguing for is a consideration of radio's role in making the films, songs, and stars of Bombay cinema a part of the daily life of listeners across India, creating a shared space for listeners in locations as diverse as the southern metropolis of Madras and a small mining town like Jhumri Tilaiya in the northern state of Bihar, binding together the nation-as-audience, and enabling the Bombay film industry to imagine a 'national audience'.

The film song genre emerged as the iconic signifier of popularity and participation in All India Radio, though other minor forms of participation were also selectively invited from common people (farmers and children). Keskar not only had to quickly revoke his decision of banning film songs from the AIR in 1952 (*Binaca Geetmala* started airing on Radio Ceylon in the same year), but he had to address the growing popularity of Radio Ceylon to which people started to tune in due to AIR's moralist search for pure Indian music. Keskar announced the launch of Vividh Bharati devoted to 'popular music and other light items' in 1957, as a response to the immense popularity that Radio Ceylon and particularly its programme *Binaca Geetmala* had achieved by that time (Punathambekar 2010: 191). But, more importantly, it showed the growing anxiety of the Indian state over the appropriation of a nationwide participatory culture by agencies other than the Indian state. That Vividh Bharati's mode of broadcasting and the corresponding 'commercial' participatory culture (of the *Binaca Geetmala* model) had a future became apparent when the government, while announcing Vividh Bharati in 1957, declared that the duration of such programmes 'may be increased according to necessity and the listeners' interest'. Special arrangements were made to transmit the programmes from two powerful transmitters simultaneously from Madras and Bombay to ensure that 'the programmes would be heard in any part of India without the necessity of relaying it', signalling that such programming was gaining a significant autonomy in Indian state broadcasting (ibid.). The connection between the nationwide network that television has made possible after the 1990s and the early 'national' networks of interactivity conjured by Radio Ceylon and Vividh Bharati is not merely of interesting parallels, but of a certain history of tastes, habits and ways of engaging with media that, along with ruptures, exhibits trajectories of *continuity*. This continuity doesn't refer to consistency of any trait but to the sustenance of certain conditions that have made possible transition from one kind of participatory culture to another. The moments of rupture like the 1952 ban on broadcasting film songs or the repressive control over mass media during the 1975 emergency have not been able to tear apart the thread of participatory networks.

Despite inhibitions, state television had to include popular film and film-song-based programmes like *Chitrahaar* very early, not only considering the popularity of Hindi films, but also taking into account the low-cost availability of films and pressure from the Bombay film lobby. *Chitrahaar* became a key conduit for the making of a 'national audience'. The film-based popular (programmes like *Show Theme* on Doordarshan) found a major currency post-1982, but audience participation around film-based programmes didn't start on Doordarshan until *Superhit Muqabla* in 1992. The 'National Network' (every evening 8: 40 pm onwards and Sundays also during the daytime, starting in 1982) that became the signpost of an emergent consumer culture and interactivity also inaugurated the other two popular television genres of the 1980s: the progressive melodrama and the mythological, both greatly helping the formation of a 'national audience'. While the former got considerably 'frontal' in its mode-of-address (Ashok Kumar's speeches at the end of each episode of *Humlog*) and treatment of topical issues (*Rajani*, for instance), the latter resonated with contemporary politics and seduced a nationwide audience into a mishmash of golden past and futuristic dream. A 'national' televisual popular seemed to be emerging for the first time, in the context of fast expansion of television's audience-base in the 1980s primarily through the Low Power Transmitters (LPTs). Sayani reflects back:

> Just like how the streets would be empty when B.R. Chopra's Mahabharat or Ramanand Sagar's Ramayan would be on television, the same thing happened to Geet Mala. It was on Wednesdays, 8–9 p.m. Wednesdays came to be known as Geet Mala day. (ibid.: 196)

One of the reasons for diffusion of the exclusive role of Hindi film music in conjuring a national audience was largely the rise of commercial television that popularized many other genres. Television at one level is an extension of radio, but at another level, due to its ability to 'show', is more capable of satisfying popular curiosity and the general urge for authenticity in representation. Televisual audio-vision, bearing in it legacies of primacy of aurality in colonial modern and also of the ocular-centric modernity of the West where the visual is privileged, would be much more capable of bringing together split publics, to use a category used by Arvind Rajagopal (2001: 151–211).[5]

The continuities and ruptures therefore are to be sought in a larger history of the audience that has moved from one register to another at various levels: space (from territorial gatherings to networks), identity (from tactile acquaintances to anonymity), geography (from local to the national and the global), medium (from radio to television and the internet), behaviour (from consumption to participation), technology (from terrestrial transmission and single medium to satellite communication and convergence), genre (from music to Reality TV and news) and of course the larger social registers (from state controlled to privately owned media, for instance) difficult to exhaustively list here. Crucial is to remember that none of these paradigms of audience engagement has disappeared, nor the 'shift' here means a linear temporality where a new tendency or development necessarily abolishes the old. While the relationship between the dominant, residual and the emergent keeps changing in this history, almost everything, from the local tactile assembly to the *geetmala* format, stays and incessantly undergoes redefinition.

Participation on doordarshan

Doordarshan never tried to invite much audience participation through the 1960s and the 1970s. All it tried to create at most was a 'national audience' through either development programming or its idea of 'entertainment' later through programmes like *Chitrahaar*.

Doordarshan drastically re-fashioned itself to fit into the post-1991 environment of competition and entertainment-programming marked by the presence of a number of privately owned satellite channels. Sevanti Ninan argues that in the 1990s,

> perhaps the most remarkable turnaround for Doordarshan was the change its image was undergoing in popular perception.

The perennial whipping boy of the press, parliamentarians and public was increasingly selling itself successfully as the only viable network for the sub-continent, backed strongly by an array of indigenous Indian satellites with plenty of future transponder capacity. (1996: 39)

The greatest instance of Doordarshan's commercial reach-out drive was DD-Metro (introduced in 1984 as DD 2 and changed to DD Metro in 1993), focusing on greater number of Hindi Films, advertisement and entertainment. It was on DD Metro that *Superhit Muqabla*, a countdown show of popular Hindi film numbers based on audience poll like *Binaca Geetmala*, generated a significant amount of audience participation. Hindi film once again came to play the role of a crucial unifying force behind participatory culture. *Superhit Muqabla* presented top 10 songs of the week based on audience response that came in huge numbers in the form of postcards. Many such countdown shows, though none becoming as popular as *Superhit Muqabla*, appeared on television subsequently.

The flagship 'interactive' show of Doordarshan, recording the highest audience participation on Indian television for quite some time was *Surabhi* (1993–2001). The show reportedly received over 1.4 million postcards in a single week for the programme's weekly quiz open for participation (Ayyagari 2006). A special category called 'Competition Postcard' was devised by the Indian postal department for writing to the programme. The many gazes of the different classes, cultures and identities, from which the abstraction of 'Indian culture' could be looked at and negotiated, were now consolidated into a grand *representable* level of 'Indian public'. This was not similar to (though homologous with) the institutional drives of creating a homogeneous citizenship. This rather made the idea of public figurable and measurable in some apparently concrete sense. The pile of postcards and other empirical representations amounted to a sort of *statisticization* of publicness, capable of producing a convincing sense of 'Indian public' and 'Indian culture' through the responses from a sample section of the public. It is interesting to note that such samples, in their many incarnations, were largely occupied by the emergent middle class of the country. Varied territorialized gazes were now appropriated by the gaze of an emergent new middle class, which enjoyed certain privilege of being not only the voice of the nation but also possibly the only class that could imagine *itself* as a community of consumers. The Indian state possibly acknowledged the exclusivity of this community by making the price of the 'competition postcard' INR 2, as opposed to 15 paisa, the price of the usual postcard. *Surabhi* presented little communities and cultures, through its very own rhetoric of tourism, ethnography, adventure, art appreciation, leisure and lifestyle. The idea of 'media' as staging people's interest and participation still needed public enterprises like *Doordarshan* and the Indian postal department, but notably couldn't surface at all without the agents of emerging commercialization (private producer, corporate sponsors).

A key constituency of the urban middle class ideas of civility, aesthetics and patriotism that *Surabhi* propagated was formal education, which till then could not be aligned to consumerist reception through Doordarshan slots like the 'Countrywide Classroom'. Attaching the values of education to consumer culture in fact started a bit earlier, in the phase of Doordarshan's new-found commercialism after the 1982 Asian Games, through particularly quiz programmes like *Quiz Time*. Starting in 1985, this English-language programme was pioneer in giving a new lease of life to quizzing as a culture in India from the mid-1980s with quiz competitions becoming popular in schools, colleges and almost every street corner functions. More than the quiz programmes per se, 'quiz' as an easy way to *involve* people by offering reward for answering questions became the most common way for getting the audience to interact, write letters, come to studio and grow as consumers with the growing business of Bournvita 'growth' drink or Cadbury chocolates. This was true for many other kinds of programmes, from what was to soon emerge as Reality TV like *Kaun Banega Crorepati* (produced notably by the same Siddharth Basu, the host and maker of *Quiz time*) to numerous game shows, talk shows and even soaps. It was common practice in the serials of the 1990s to ask questions at the end of episodes and offer prizes for the right answer. Questions asked in the conventional quizzing mode of 'which' 'when' and 'who' fitted well into the emerging structure of segmentation on television. Increase in segmentation had a toll both on the length of argumentation and hence argumentation itself, and the attention span of the television viewer itself got considerably short simultaneously. In general, television content started to get *informatized* from this point of time, with 'knowledge' becoming synonymous with 'information', street-smartness and the promise of inclusion into the world of new consumption.

Participation on private channels

It is precisely from such vantage points of statisticization, informatization, consumption and participation that we can start exploring some major trends of participatory culture on private television. The same trends also continued on Doordarshan but it was the private channels that primarily emitted the appeals of new relationship between participation and consumerism. Participatory culture requiring the intervention of state agencies had to decline after a point of time, as the values of the state, public good and welfare were to a large extent appropriated by the emergent forms of private media. A great example of such appropriation was the legal-juridical acknowledgement of dissolution of the state's right to be the exclusive custodian of public good and of 'public property' like the airwaves.[6]

Carrying the legacy of *Quiz Time* in many ways, *Cadbury Bournvita Quiz Contest* (CBQC), a quiz contest for school students, started in 1994 on Zee TV. Originally held live in cities across the country since 1972, CBQC became a radio show and then shifted to television in 1994. The show shifted from Zee to Sony Entertainment Television in 2001, continued till 2005 and came back on the Colours channel in 2011. CBQC's comeback in 2011, due to a huge campaign of its fans on social media, has made it the most popular and the longest running quiz show on Indian television. The show reportedly reached over 11,25,000 students in 4,000 schools across 66 cities in the country by 2005 when it closed (Hemrajani 2011). Reaching beyond India (the UAE, Kuwait, Qatar, Bahrain, Oman, Nepal and Sri Lanka) and in numerous quiz events at schools and companies, the show, hosted by Derek O'Brien, has been synonymous with popular quizzing in India in the post-Liberalization India.[7] The career of this programme could be an important testimony of how popular quizzing, brand promotion around 'education' and knowledge, and a corresponding participatory culture dominated by the young consumers have evolved from the early days of liberalization to the present.

The historical role of Hindi film songs in emitting a sense of nationwide connectedness found a major place in private channels as well. Singing competition programmes like *Close-Up Antakshari* (CUA) were full of nostalgic numbers evoking the memory of 1950–70s. Starting in 1993 on Zee TV, CUA was somewhat symptomatic of the new-age television's compulsive drive worldwide towards subsuming age-old traditions into structures of informatization and consumption. *Antakshari* is a traditional game played at homes and on social occasions in the Indian sub-continent in which each contestant sings the first verse of a song that begins with the letter on which the previous contestant's song ended. But more than rendering a whole song, the competence demanded by this game is sharp memory of the first few lines of a song. The song-as-information was a perfect fit into a popular culture that celebrated informatization, consumerism and of course film songs.

The new entertainment was a peculiar mélange of work and 'time pass', a phrase that is often used by local train hawkers selling peanuts to passengers. While 'work' involves cerebral investment required for answering questions and earning 'fabulous gifts', *time pass* refers to enjoyment of idleness, either as choice or under compulsion. The title song of CUA had these lines *Baithe, baithe, kya karein? Karna hai kuch kaam/Shuru karo antakshri, leke prabhu ka naam*, meaning 'What do we do sitting idle? We need to do some work/Let's start playing Antakshari, with blessings of the Almighty'. The two categories also operate in the very act of watching television. We are referring to an era when time pass is no more voluntary or optional; it rather is a compulsive drive, a *work* without which one cannot keep updated and socialize, one cannot live, so to say. We are looking into 'informatization' as a symptom of such convergence of work and leisure, information and entertainment. Notably, the 1990s was undergoing an 'information revolution' and was at the doorstep of an imminent boom in the information technology, a sector that embodied the promise of a new India. CUA had participants from all walks of life. A list provided by a fan goes like this: Navy, Army, Air force, postmen, engineers, doctors, firemen, singers, cricketers, film and TV actors and disabled people. Shows were held in Dubai, Sharjah, London, New York, Pakistan. As a whole CUA from 1993 signalled every single feature of what was to be Reality TV proper in the next decade: Huge audience participation from India and the diasporic community, continuing currency of the film song, appropriation of tradition into contemporary frameworks of consumption and informatics, convergence of leisure and work, and as a whole signalled the coming into being of what Gupta calls 'a television society'. Gupta, after completing a massive sample survey of the television audience in West Bengal in 1998, commented:

> From the results of the survey, one of the general observations that may be offered is that the entire phenomenon of watching television is ultimately linked to the social aspirations and changes that modernity is bringing into Indian

society. While there is a sense of guilt associated with the act of watching television, the viewers seem to be using television programmes to redefine their lifestyles in various ways. Indian society is becoming a television society in more than one sense. (1998: 136)

Informatization, as a process of creating a set of simple challenges for getting the audience to participate, proliferated out of quiz programmes to suffuse into almost every televisual genre. A good example where consumerism and informatization were almost graphically realized to attract considerable audience participation was a programme called *Tol Mol Ke Bol* ('Tell Us The Right Price', Zee TV). *Tol Mol Ke Bol* had a studio audience tightly packed into rows of seats waiting for the host to enter. The host enters, runs up to the stage and calls for some names, which are written on small pieces of paper kept in a bowl. He picks two chits up and calls those selected from the audience. The participants have to guess the exact price of a product. In *Double Trouble* (Zee TV), if one could not answer a question, one had to go for a physical round ('climb up the rope-ladder and come back within 20 seconds') and was eliminated in case of a failure (see Roy 1999: 17–18).

Game shows testing the individual's grasp of information and physical ability had markedly increased in the immediate aftermath of the 1991 liberalization. Corresponding focus on the psychological interiority of the participants started generating a great degree of affect in these programmes. Stories of individual virtues and vices, moral integrity and turpitude, competence of the body and the mind lent certain elements of melodrama to all that was shown on TV. The social, in this scheme of things, appeared to be an effect of the personal and the moral. Beyond the capitalist trait of portraying the individual as the driver of the grand narrative of history, what television of the new era demonstrated was a playful engagement with life and world in general. And such playfulness had mainly to do with one's luck. Capability alone doesn't bring one success; one has to be 'lucky' enough to be the winner of prizes in the lucky draws. Betting was found in programmes like *Double-O-Slip* (Sony TV), *Joh Winner Wohi Sikander* ('Whoever Wins is the King', Sony TV) and the 'Surf Wheel of Fortune' (Sony TV). The neo-liberal undermining of social construction and historical agency of the individual in the times immediately after the liberalization may also be taken as neo-conservative reactions to the radical 1960s and the 1970s. Astrology, vaastu, feng shui and other such vocations in the 'luck industry' seemed to get a new lease of life due to liberalization's opening up of new technologies of circulation like internet, mobile convergence and interactive promotional TV. As a whole, television in the 1990s became the most significant demonstrator of the discourses of personal ability and luck, two ideas key to the sustenance of the 'world view' that drives consumer culture.

There were some programmes like *Purush Kshetra* ('The Male World', Zee TV) with a fair degree of what is popularly known as 'social' content, involving the common people and presenting starkly 'real' problems and unpleasant issues. Patriarchy was the key object of critique here, with strong focus on personal agonies and struggle. Popular factual entertainment in the form of talk shows started occupying a large space in Indian television from this time where many issues not brought to the domain of popular culture till then, were discussed openly. While one should definitely look at these programmes as exploring the new found possibilities of spreading awareness about certain social issues and questioning traditional social outlook, one shouldn't ignore in analysis a certain economy of such exploration. Not all issues can be touched; the foundational class-questions can never be addressed in the manner practices like dowry or even patriarchy can be subjected to critique; the boundary of activism seems to be greatly defined by only those issues that the state considers as 'problems'. Popular activist television has always focused on issues about which there is a fair degree of consensus between a majority and the state. This is precisely the reason why a *Satyamev Jayate* can never accommodate a discussion on the Armed Forces Special Powers Act (AFSPA), 1958, that empowers the state to violate human rights in places like Manipur. It is right to acknowledge the contribution of such programmes towards spreading awareness. But wrong would be *not to* analyse the ways such programmes work within a horizon of possibility that the mainstream culture offers as natural, given and irreversible. It would also be wrong not to assume that 'spreading awareness' that such programmes are worth for can only happen under the condition of a perfect liaison between the media, the state and the corporate India, a liaison that promotes 'silence' about many non-mainstream issues.

Indigenization of the global: a key condition for participatory culture

A major condition of possibility for Reality TV and participatory culture in India was the transnational character of channels, programming and formats, and certain practice of 'indigenization' (crucial for 'identification' to generate) that flourished in the 1990s. The process of indigenization was first signalled when the STAR started to produce programmes in India and transformed STAR Plus to a Hindi-language channel. Prasad aptly summarized the connection established in the 1990s between indigenization and globalization:

> The 'indigenisation' of transnational channels . . . provides an interesting instance of the dialectic of globalization versus national identity . . . Given the way it is developing STAR is definitely a candidate for the kind of quasi-state television status that the networks (ABC, NBC and CBS) enjoy in America. Other channels that cannot indigenize content, like Discovery, are offering their programs in Hindi. MTV, following Channel V's example, is airing more Indian Music Shows and looking for local VJ talent. It would seem from all this instances that indigenization is the only path to globalisation. (1999: 126)

But if we look at indigenization as a broader category beyond language, as a process of re-fashioning the emergent global *values* to appeal to national, regional and local identities, examples could be drawn from many trends in the 1990s, the most significant was the TV commercial. It is important to remember that 'indigenization' could not be a simple process of merely 'fitting into' any stable and straight-jacketed notion of 'India', but had to assume an 'Indianness' that was always multiple and in flux. Along with adopting wholeheartedly the global consumerist tenor, the new commercials made it a point to project a successful and self-sufficient India. BPL-Sanyo commercials, which counted on the celebrity status of the film star-turned-entrepreneur Amitabh Bachchan, tried to counter the effect of the entry of the transnational brands like Sony, Akai and Panasonic in the Indian market by posing Amitabh Bachchan in front of international landmarks in London and Paris. Bachchan said in one of the commercials 'kahte hain international naam ho to sab chalta hain' ('people say any "international" name sells') and the commercial ended with BPL's logo and the catch line 'Believe in yourself'. This was clearly an indication of a double take on 'international' brands that the Indian entrepreneur harboured at this point of time in the face of global challenges. The statement made by Bachchan may mean that the international brands have earned a name because of their quality or it may also mean that they are mere *names*, without much substance for us, to be transformed into something substantially Indian. Whatever may be the case here (I think both of these levels simultaneously play here), the key point at both of these levels is that the consumer wants something of international quality or name. But this was not enough. Time had come to 'believe' that an Indian brand could achieve such international standard and infuse Indian quality in international names. In both of these cases, trying to innovate the distinctly Indian or an Indian product of international standard, the Indian and the international seem to be located at a distance from each other, each struggling to fit into the other's context. I wish to argue that if we look at the history of participatory entertainment programming on Indian television, the former tendency (effort to present the 'truly Indian') flourished in the early period of India's liberalization, but largely waned in the new millennium to pave the way for indigenization. The preponderance of indigenous formats from the cultural magazine programme *Surabhi* to singing competitions like *Close Up Antakshari* and *TVS Saregama* to dance competitions like *Boogie* Woogie, all signalled in the 1990s certain effort to locate 'India' amidst a popular notion of globalization that largely meant 'Westernization'. Something like a 'global standard' was always working as an aspiration at the back of each of such programmes. Such 'Indian' drives to engage with the global is what I suggest acted as a major condition for the 'indigenization' that we are witnessing in an *Indian Idol* or KBC where the global and the local don't show distinct signs of struggle but have achieved a relatively coherent bond. This is not to suggest that the commonsensical Indian–Western distinction has completely disappeared from popular perception. I am conjecturing that such distinction may not be fashionable for any brand or Reality Show to encourage any more. The popular sense of the 'Indian' now seems to have greatly appropriated the global as a condition and a value.

In both of these forms of negotiation – engaging the familiar signifiers of 'Indian popular' to take lead in hybrid formations (being the major trend in the 1990s) or transforming this hybridity into a sense of wholeness where the Indian and the Global become inter-constitutive – the idea of what constitutes the 'Indian' (way of living, values, morality) continues to be hegemonic in many senses. Stark display of ethnicity started looking unfashionable in the new terrain of national identity already in the 1990s. In one of the Ortem fan commercials, men from different states in India (Bengal, Punjab and many others) pronounced 'ortem' in the accent of their respective provincial vernaculars. A teenaged girl, who looked Indian but whose ethnic identity was not made discernible, appeared every time to say 'no' to them. At last a handsome, jeans-clad young man, whose provincial origin could not be figured as well, appeared with what was the familiar Indian way of sophisticated English pronunciation and then the girl said 'yes'. The commercial suggested that in order to be an 'Indian' one had to amply conceal one's ethnic identity. This may not have been the notion of Indianness in all spheres, but in the sphere of the consumerist popular which the average Indian aspired to be part of in the 1990s, globally conditioned nationality and citizenship started emerging as a new value. Without the history of such indigenization where the global remained a condition, Reality TV formats wouldn't have been successful in India and anywhere in the world. Such a popular took some time to move from the abstraction of a 'national popular' to the many ethnicities and localities that too, after a point of time, started emitting the charge of the global. The exploration of small towns and remote corners of India by capital and media would be much more evident in the programming of the new millennium.

It is all very well that we look at participatory programming typified by post-2000 Reality TV as a break from televisual traditions in India, since a great deal of innovations and novelty can be marked at the turn of the century in efforts to involve the audience. But not locating such programming within a larger historical context would give us a truncated view of conditions that made possible the 21st century brand of participatory culture, marked by certain capability of a network of consumer-audience to *mobilize* itself as a public. If television was the most significant agent behind the creation of a pan-Indian network in the 1980s and 1990s, by the turn of the century it was convergence of a host of networking technologies from television and the internet to mobile phones and social media that helped reconfiguration of such network. Such developments have not essentially marked the dissolution of the agency of the state but the rise of Media, in the singularized popular sense of a super-visioning, 'never-to-be-objectified' and benevolent institution, that claims to represent the ideals of both the state and market and thus to represent the public at large more aptly than any other institution. The public in turn, using the media and the networking technologies, tends to emerge as a relatively autonomous institution, representing the 'collective conscience of the society'.[8]

(IN)VISIBLE PUBLICS

Notes

1. Carey suggests that the 'transmission view of communication' looks at communication as a tool for controlling space and people through one-way traffic of messages from the sender to the receiver. This view defines communication by words like 'sending', 'imparting' and 'transmitting' as opposed to a 'ritual view of communication' in which, terms like 'sharing', 'exchange' and 'interaction' become important. The development-communication model of Nehruvian socialism is largely explainable by the 'transmission view of communication'. (See Carey, pp. 14–23).
2. Lelyveld reads this as an effort of the 'subdominant' groups of colonial India, Brahmins in this case, to restore their ideological authority over the post-Independence Indian society at large by trying to popularize Sanskrit-oriented Indian classical music on state-controlled radio (1994: 111–27). According to him, 'The damage done to Indian music, Keskar believed, was not only the result of British imperial neglect and the wandering attention of maharajahs. More fundamentally Keskar placed the blame upon the shoulders of North Indian Muslims, both the rulers of earlier centuries and the Muslim musicians who, in Keskar's view, had appropriated and distorted the ancient art, turning it into the secret craft of exclusive lineages, the gharanas, and, ignorant of Sanskrit, divorced it from the religious context of Hindu civilization' (ibid.: 117). He further suggests, '. . . cinema offered an opposing style of music that challenged the aims of the national cultural policy. The lyrics, aside from being in Urdu, were generally 'erotic', and since the late 1940s there were noticeable infusions in orchestration and to some extent rhythm and melody from Western popular music, which Keskar identified with a lower stage of human evolution' (ibid.: 120).
3. Doordarshan is India's public service television. Starting as a wing of All India Radio (AIR) in 1959, India's state-controlled television was separated from AIR and was named Doordarshan in 1976.
4. Ashish Rajadhyaksha (1990: 41–42) rightly recalls the connection between the progressivist series like *Humlog* and *Buniyad* with the project of New Indian Cinema of the 1970s.
5. In a section called 'A "split public" in the making and unmaking of the Ram Janmabhoomi movement', Rajagopal talks about the 'boundary-piercing character of television' (2001: 152) while referring to television's capability of enacting the conflict between the erstwhile split publics. I would suggest that more than staging the antagonism, television can create a broader formal level of semiotic exchange between and co-existence of various subjectivities and identities and thus become a quasi-nation, quasi-globe space. And precisely because identities tend to increasingly collate, chances of extra-televisionic conflicts escalate, drawing our attention to the peculiar relation of popular television to the intensification of identity politics in India.
6. In 1995, the Supreme Court of India, critiquing the idea of any kind of monopolistic intrusion into the freedom of expression of a newly

conceivable 'public', declared that 'the airwaves or frequencies are a public property'. While such an ideal manifest largely in the proposed Broadcast Bill has not been realized so far by an Act of Parliament, privately controlled media, particularly satellite television, has grown big to claim to *represent* the public more than any other institution in democracy. See Supreme Court of India (1995: 50).
7. For details of the show, its history and the activities of Derek O'Brien Associates, http://derek.in/pages/in_schools_students_02tvshows.aspx (accessed on 14 July 2012).
8. The famous judgement by the Supreme Court (4 August 2005) which found Mohammad Afzal Guru guilty of conspiring the 2001 attack on the Indian Parliament and sentenced him with capital punishment, did say in so many words that the judgement was to satisfy the 'the collective conscience of the society'. NDTV aired Afzal's video confession on 20 October 2006, without mentioning that this was by then a five-year-old footage discredited in a court of law. Most of the SMS texts shown on the show called for hanging Afzal. The death sentence was upheld by the Supreme Court on 12 January 2007. For an analysis of the role of media and public opinion in the Afzal case, see Hutnyk (2014).

References

Ayyagari, Yamini. 2006. 'Surabhi Ke Sunehre Pal', http://www.boloji.com/index.cfm?md=Content&sd=Articles&ArticleID=3447 (accessed on 19 September 2012).

Carey, James W. 1989. *Communication as Culture: Essays on Media and Society*. New York: Unwin Hyman.

Chatterjee, P. C. 1992. *Broadcasting in India*. New Delhi: Sage.

Gupta, Nilanjana. 1998. *Switching Channels: Ideologies of Television in India*, New Delhi: Oxford University Press.

Hemrajani, Nikhil. 2011. 'Bournvita Quiz Contest back on TV', *Hindustan Times*, http://www.hindustantimes.com/Entertainment/Television/Bournvita-Quiz-Contest-back-on-TV/Article1-713123.aspx#sthash.RQIuNakO.dpuf (accessed on 17 August 2012).

Hutnyk, John. 2014. 'NDTV 24X7 Remix: Mohammad Afzal Guru Frame by Frame', in Abhijit Roy and Biswarup Sen (eds), *Channeling Cultures: Television Studies from India*. New Delhi: Oxford University Press.

Lelyveld, David. 1994. 'Upon the Subdominant: Administering Music on All-India Radio', *Social Text*, no. 39: 111–27.

Ninan, Sevanti. 1996. *Through the Magic Window: Television and Change in India*. New Delhi: Penguin.

Prasad, M. Madhava. 1999. 'Television and National Culture', *Journal of Arts and Ideas*, no. 32–33: 119–29.

Punathambekar, Aswin. 2010. 'Ameen Sayani and Radio Ceylon: Notes towards a History of Broadcasting and Bombay Cinema', *BioScope: South Asian Screen Studies*, 1(2): 189–97.

———. 2009. 'Colombo Calling: Radio Ceylon and Bombay cinema's 'national audience'', *Flow*, http://flowtv.org/2009/09/colombo-calling-radio-ceylon-and-bombay-cinema%E2%80%99s-%E2%80%9Cnational-audience%E2%80%9D-aswin-punathambekar-the-university-of-michigan/ (accessed on 21 April 2013).

Rajadhyaksha, Ashish. May 1990. 'Beaming Messages to the Nation', *Journal of Arts and Ideas*, no. 19: 33–52.

Rajagopal, Arvind. 2001. *Politics after Television: Hindu Nationalism and the Reshaping of the Public in India*. Cambridge: Cambridge University Press.

Roy, Abhijit. 2014. 'TV after Television Studies: Recasting Questions of Audiovisual Form' in Biswarup Sen and Abhijit Roy (eds), *Channeling Cultures: Television Studies from India*, pp.17–40. Delhi: Oxford University Press.

———. 1999. 'Television: The Indian Experience'. Study material exclusively for the participants of the online 'Eurinfilm Screenwriting Workshop', conducted by the European Union–India Cross-Cultural Programme, http://www.academia.edu/1337370/Television_The_Indian_Experience (accessed on 12 November 2014).

Supreme Court of India. 1995. 'Airwaves judgment'. The Secretary, Ministry of Information and Broadcasting vs. Cricket Association of Bengal. http://indiankanoon.org/doc/539407/ (accessed on 18 March2011)

12

TRANSFORMATIVE ENERGY OF PERFORMANCE

'Budhan Theatre' as case study

Tutun Mukherjee

> *Theatre is our way of saying we are alive. It's a way of telling our people, we count; even if we are poor or illiterate, we have a voice.*
> – Dakxin Bajrange Chhara (personal interaction, Nov 2009)

> *Theatre remains any society's sharpest way to hold a live debate with itself. . . . If it doesn't challenge, provoke or illuminate, it is not fulfilling its function.*
> – Peter Hall (*The Necessary Theatre* 5)

The term 'political theatre' conjures up many images: comedies of Aristophanes, Plautus-Terence; Shakespeare's history plays; Ibsen's realist plays; Brecht's epic theatre; the Living Theatre's 'rehearsing the revolution'; Dario Fo's satires; Augusto Boal's Forum Theatre; the IPTA movement in India; Utpal Dutt's agitprop plays; Badal Sircar's Third Theatre; Safdar Hashmi's 'Jana Natya Manch'; different forms of Protest and Street Theatre and so on.[1]

As is true of many different forms of artistic expression, theatre and politics are deeply connected. Politics is ingrained in theatre. History documents strict vigilance, censorship and even prohibition of theatre performances from earliest times to suppress or restrict its political influence. Some performances are covertly political while others are overtly ideological if not propagandist. This chapter looks at theatre as an instrument of social revolution, upliftment and change.

Rooted in the specific and very challenging environment and milieu of Gujarat's tribal belt, the work of Budhan Theatre from Tejgarh, Gujarat, demonstrates many different concepts of political theatre as political act, from representation of life to protest to social teaching to the wider dissemination of tribal culture and heritage. As Budhan Theatre is the expressive medium of the Chhara tribe, it is important to know who the Chharas are. According to a website description:

> Entering Chharanagar always felt like crossing an invisible border into another world. Located beyond the Naroda railway crossing on the eastern periphery of Ahmedabad, the streets are narrower and dirtier, sandwiched between a warren of houses and small shops set out like weekly market stalls. The area is crowded and noisy — roughly three square miles teeming with 20,000 human souls. The only open spaces are pools of stagnant water overrun by pigs feeding on the abundant refuse. The sharp stink of illicit liquor emanates from the muddle of dilapidated, dark dwellings whose occupants eye strangers with suspicion and fear. No auto or taxi operator would drive here . . . (Malekar n.p.)

As also described in the 'Hole in the Wall' educational blog 'Who are the Chharas', the tribe traces its origins from the nomads of Punjab who transported commodities like salt and honey from the forests to the coasts. Through the eighteenth and nineteenth centuries, the East India Company and later the British colonial masters used the tribes' help in procuring forest resources and their knowledge of the country to guide their armies through unknown territories and to establish trading relationships. However, the building of railways and roadways made the tribals dispensable and post-1857 they began to be seen by the colonial masters as unruly and dangerous elements. Soon they were dubbed 'thugs' and in 1871 an Act was passed for 'the notification of criminal tribes'.[2] This was the direct consequence of the unfortunate tendency to associate the tribal with the dreaded Thuggee Cult of robbers/murderers that menaced travellers through the nineteenth century. Saurabh Mishra writes that in 1835 Major-General W. H. Sleeman concluded that the thugs and the tribes were the same people and this linkage was confirmed by in 1852 by H. Bereton, the superintendent of Thuggee Investigation Punjab (7), although there were obviously many loopholes in such conclusions. But overnight, hundreds of tribes were no longer identified as *Vanavasis* or forest-dwellers but as criminals and could even be shot at sight.[3] Historian David Arnold suggests the possible reason for this could be that the small communities of nomadic people living on the fringes of the society as petty pastoralists and traders eking out a rudimentary existence were not considered 'civilized' as per the British colonial idea. Arnold explains that problem began when the European idea of 'peripatetic lifestyles as social menace' permeated into British colonial thinking and dictated that such 'dangerous classes' are best kept under surveillance. The problem escalated when criminality or professional criminal behaviour was taken to be hereditary rather than habitual, and as Arnold says, that is when crime became ethnic and what was social determinism till then became biological determinism.

After Independence, the tribes were formally denotified in 1952, but were reclassified as 'habitual offenders' in 1959. Even now there are laws and regulations in various states that prohibit certain communities of people from travelling while others must register at police stations in the districts they pass through. However, sensitivity to their exploitation has increased although much more needs to be done to address their many problems and issues.[4] The Chharas believe they were notified and settled as agricultural and industrial workers by the colonial masters at Chharanagar in the 1930s where they continue to stay having no other resources or other means of livelihood and no useful skills. Dakxin Bajrange Chhara vouches for the innate and extraordinary acting talent among Chharas. In the 1990s, they began by participating in city theatre groups when called, before building their own performance group.

Budhan Theatre, named after Budhan of Kheria Sabar community in West Bengal's Purulia district who died in police custody, was started in the manner of a community development project with the purpose of creating awareness among the tribals about their rights and among the general people about the neglect suffered by and the continuing oppression and exploitation of the tribal/subaltern people. The theatre group has about a dozen senior actors and nearly thirty adolescent and child actors. Dakxin's theatre is inspired and urged by the untiring activism of Mahasweta Devi and G.N. Devy to obtain dignity, livelihood and other rights of citizenship for the nomadic *adivasi* or the tribal indigenous peoples of India who are still listed as 'Denotified Tribes' and treated in a neo-colonial manner. They still carry the stigma of being regarded as 'born criminals'.[5]

In his forceful book *Budhan Bolta Hai* (Budhan Speaks) (2010), Dakxin details incidents from his life which interweaves the experiences of his community, their collective memory of the past, the deprivation, pain and suffering in the present, the terrible atrocities committed on them when taken forcibly to police stations. The question that must be raised is: Aren't Chharas citizens of a free country with equal civic rights? Dakxin also traces the beginning of his endeavour towards building a performance group. In his insightful book on the subject titled *A Nomad Called Thief: Reflections on Adivasi Silence* (2006), Devy offers 'a random list' of what the mainstream Indian society has given the adivasis through centuries and more relevantly, through the sixty-seven years of Independence:

> Forest Acts depriving them of their livelihood; a Criminal Tribes Act and a Habitual Offenders Act; . . . existence as bonded labour; forest guards and private moneylenders; mosquitoes and malaria; naxalites and ideological war-groups; . . . a schedule of their identity defined from outside and perpetual contempt. (2006: 6–7)

Using street theatre idiom to create a participatory and intimate theatrical space, Budhan Theatre dramatises 'lived-history' or the real situations in a tribal's life like police oppression, encounter killings, rape and cruelty that tribals experience daily. It is a theatre with a purpose and commitment, and the performances illustrate passionate experiential urgency to mobilise popular support or sensitise the audience to social and political atrocities being committed in front of their eyes. Their theatre is not for entertainment alone but is intended to question political and social 'truths'. According to Dakxin, 'acting' comes 'naturally' to the adivasis. They are born performers (rather than 'born criminals'!) as they must rely on their skills to earn their living. Denied the means of ordinary livelihood, they hone their performing skills like acrobatics, mime, singing and dancing (displaced tribals use them as tricks to beg at city crossroads too). Often, in earlier times, their performative skills were used as distraction to enable their team members to steal or pick pockets (an interesting picturisation of this was through the song 'jhumka gira re' in the Hindi film *Mera Saaya* – a strong reminder of their association with criminal activities). Chharas face considerable disadvantage in terms of jobs and education due to their history of nomadism and forced sedentarisation. They encounter social stigma and are often the usual suspects for police and are victimised. They are also forced into illegal trade such as brewing country liquor. This places the Chharas in an ambivalent relationship with the authorities and has often resulted in a high rate of incarceration, recounted graphically in *Budhan Bolta Hai*. The young Chharas find it very difficult to acquire and retain employment. Yet given the opportunity, they exhibit high motivation to excel at education.

From 1998 onwards, Budhan Theatre has tried to raise the awareness of the nation to the long history of the suffering, neglect and the 'deliberate criminalization' of the tribals, their forced dependence, their experience of denial and deprivation, underdevelopment, physical and economic exploitation and oppression and their present condition of severe material and social poverty. Viewing theatre as a mirror to the world, their theatre is the dramatisation of their actual living condition and experience vis-à-vis the mainstream society. The dramatic efforts are derived from their belief that when one watches the enactment of the socio-economic reality of their world embedded in recognisable symbols and experiences, one is better equipped to understand that reality along with its social construction of meaning. The driving force behind Budhan Theatre is Dakxin Bajrange Chhara, himself an actor, scriptwriter and director. Budhan Theatre's evolution offers insight into the very slow change in the general attitude of the people in the mainstream to tribal issues in India. This chapter examines the subject matter of these dramatic presentations in an effort to: (1) understand the motivation for the performances, (2) uncover memories or feelings associated with the theatre and (3) highlight the way the design features of the theatrical interior correspond to its oppressive and hierarchical surroundings.

Elizabeth Fine distinguishes two types of performances – primary and secondary. She defines 'primary performance' as behaviour, that is, the performance of social roles and interactions based upon norms or rules learned through socialisation or psychological conditioning. She describes 'secondary performance' to comprise verbal art, folklore, literature and drama as these imitate and in the process often comment upon primary forms. Consequently, secondary performances become ways of learning, teaching and, in some cases, changing primary performances. It would then appear that secondary performances derive their energy from primary performances and through a reversal process are capable of transforming primary performances (1994: 3–20).

It is noteworthy that Richard Schechner nuances 'performance' in particular and maintains that more than other art forms such as painting, sculpture or even writing, performance re-presents actual behaviour 'as it is behaved'. Therefore, for the performer, the process of embodiment of ordinary behaviour framed within the particularity of 'a performance' often arouses ineffable dimensions of experience which augment expression (1988: see Introduction xvii–xix). The tribal seems to possess not only natural grace and suppleness especially suited for performance but also certain honour in the way they regard the human body, which gives special cadence to their performative acts. G. N. Devy writes that this attitude is intrinsic to their nature and emanates from the way they regard the human body:

> When one looks at the adivasis, what stands out most is the powerful presence of the adivasi body. There is something fascinating about it. It is not just the absence of obesity, or the natural grace and charm with which an adivasi man or woman conducts himself or herself. There is something more to it, and it the adivasi attitude to the human body. They do not look at the human body as cursed with mortality. They look to it as made of imperishable material towards which they have a great responsibility. (2006: 5)

The performance by the Tejgarh tribals, led by Dakxin Bajrange Chhara, exemplifies this complex process of moving from the primary realisation to the secondary stage of expressivity that lends transformative energy to their performance. However, the process of structuring a performance as emerging in the form of 'secondary formulation' that can comment on the 'primary process' of representing existential angst by reflecting upon significant experiences through performance is not always easy. By not just intellectually but viscerally reflecting upon experience through performance, the actors must discover and communicate latent meaning from their own lives. The theatrical even draws upon the performative embodiment of oppression. The examination of this process of reciprocity and the resulting impaction is the focus of this chapter.

On 6 January 2009, at Nizam College, Hyderabad, Budhan Theatre performed their Hindi play *Choli Ke Pichchey Kya Hai* (*What Is beneath the Blouse*) which was inspired by Mahasweta Devi's outstanding short-story 'Stanadayini'. This play combines historical reality of oppressed tribals as subalterns who want to provoke resistance to the repression, exploitation and violence of the exploitative instruments of the state apparatus with Mahasweta Devi's story. In Dakxin's words (during a personal interaction), the play's relevance is in replaying history to illuminate the characteristic conflicts in the contemporary society in terms of law and civic justice.[6]

Through his experiments with the People's Theatre in Peru and the Arena Theatre in Brazil, director Augusto Boal argued that performance is a potent forum for the oppressed to address problems, explore solutions and create change. While describing these experiments in *Theatre of the Oppressed*, he demonstrates the way previous theatrical models have actually contributed to what he calls the poetics of oppression by relegating these people to passive roles as spectators. With Aristotle's theatre, for example, 'the world is known, perfect or about to be perfected and its values are imposed upon spectators who delegate power to think and act to the characters' (Boal 1979: 9). Boal cites the example of Brecht's theatre which he says shows the world in transition and demands that spectators think, but characters still take responsibility for action. In Boal's *Theatre of the Oppressed* everyone is expected to think and act. Because the oppressed do not yet know what their world will be, theirs is a theatre of rehearsal showing images in transition rather than a finished spectacle reflecting the system's made world. Through their performance experiments people begin to discover their power to create change. This discovery often produces the sense of motivating and transformative mission as is reflected in the theatre of Utpal Dutt and Badal Sircar. Boal says that theatre itself may not on all occasions be revolutionary, but without a doubt theatrical forms provide the rehearsal of revolution. While Boal, Dutt and Sircar seek to highlight the condition of the oppressed, their approaches are slightly different in their individualistic ways. Boal's Forum Theatre, Image Theatre and Invisible Theatre use psycho-dramatic role-playing aimed at problem-solving and are activist and participatory; Sircar's technique is similar and provides more opportunity for improvisation of situational and extempore kind. Dutt's theatre reflects more aesthetic concern. Rather than using the direct engagement methods of Boal, Sircar or Dutt, Budhan Theatre *at this instance* opts for a scripted text and weaves contemporary situations into it. It may be relevant to recollect and adopt Turner's explanation (inspired by Dilthey) to describe the Budhan Theatre experiment as significant experiences, or *erlebnis*, that unfold in 'moments' of (1) a perceptual core where sensations are more intense than in ordinary experience, (2) vivid recall of images from past experience, (3) renewal of feelings from past experience, (4) emergence of meaning from 'feelingly thinking' about the relationship between past and present experiences and (5) communication of meaning to others. Most of the actors belong to a social group where there are few to speak or act on their behalf, living a kind of life where the readymade images of social systems do not make sense. Through performance these actors try to discover their own power, the power to find meaning and reshape their world.

TRANSFORMATIVE ENERGY OF PERFORMANCE

Since Budhan Theatre's play *Choli Ke Pichchey Kya Hai* was to be performed on the stage, Budhan's planned presentation was perhaps slightly stylised in setting than their usual street-theatre mode, though with minimal setting and props. Moreover, along with the percussion beats of the 'dhol' which is the usual and only accompaniment in their street performances, recorded music was used to open the performance. The song that blared was the popular raunchy number from the Hindi film *Khalnayak* from which the play took its title. Along the walls near the entrance to the sitting area for the audience, strings of garish cinema posters were hung showing female actors alternating with pictures of goddesses. The stage was set showing at the background a small temple-like structure with the picture of Goddess Durga being worshipped by a priest with a lot of fanfare and burning of incense. A well-dressed bejewelled lady, representing the rich man's wife who would offer Jashoda the job of a wet nurse, circumambulated the stage chewing *paan* and looking arrogant. In the foreground sat two lanky emaciated figures facing each other like mirror images. The actors playing Jashoda were male and the reason for this becomes clear in a highly dramatic scene towards the end when unable to bear the pain of cancer Jashoda tears apart her blouse (*choli*) to exhibit her mangled breasts. A tiered effect is achieved through the placing of props at different levels and the positioning of the actors. For instance, the small temple is at a higher level to the rich lady who walks around, and Jashoda, her husband and the many dolls representing babies sit or lie around on the floor. The tiered arrangement also suggests the class hierarchy – from the upper to the lower. It also serves to contrast stasis with movement. There is a lot of energy in the performance and passion; more action and less dialogue; perhaps aiming more at the 'spectacular'.

The two figures sitting in the foreground facing each other as in a mirror image enact the character of Jashoda. As the director Alok Gagdekar explained, the experimental technique of 'doubling' is used for emphasis, taking a cue from Peter Brook's theory of experimental theatre expounded in his book *The Empty Space* (of course, an unforgettable example of 'doubling' or 'parallelism' is *Waiting for Godot*). The idea the director tries to convey through the mirroring is the layered concept of human life. It also serves to depict at once the two aspects of Jashoda's life, in her own home and in the house of the rich woman. Throughout the entire performance, Jashoda does not move from her place. The poignant and sordid tale of Jashoda unfolds, recounted from the perspective that of the disprivileged subaltern. Such occurrences are not unusual in the lives of the tribal people also.

Figure 12.1 Budhan Theatre, 'Choli ke Peechhey kya hai', 6th Jan 2009 at Nizam College, Hyderabad.

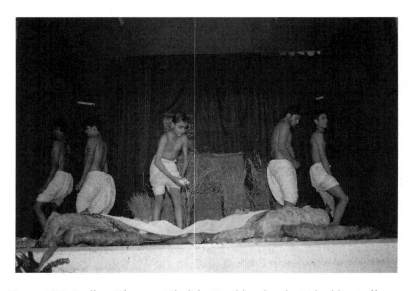

Figure 12.2 Budhan Theatre, 'Choli ke Peechhey kya hai' 'doubling' effect.

Exploitation and injustice are inevitable experiences in their 'abject' lives. Jashoda submits to the lust of her crippled husband who wants to keep her producing babies so that she could breastfeed the rich men's babies with her surplus milk. She is also the object of lust of the priest. Dolls representing babies lie strewn about on the floor as Jashoda struggles to feed them. Her breasts are gradually wrung dry and it seems it is the blood of her arteries that she converts into milk. She is inflicted by cancer and when the pain of cancer grows, she is alone with her suffering. No longer of any use, Jashoda is left to die. Her corpse is dragged away like that of a decaying animal by the sweepers who come to clean the road.

Related in an ambivalent way with theatre studies and drama studies, performance studies now trace the horizon of an energetically expanding field characterised by a range of aims, methods and objects of inquiry. Performance studies have developed in a number of trajectories: – (a) 'ethnographies of performance' (Conquergood 1992); (b) psychoanalytic and postcolonial models of representation; (c) institutional and/or street performance studies; (d) performance as art and in everyday life; (e) embodiment of the theatrical act and (f) theoretical investigations of identity, gender and performance. The focus of performance studies is especially on the non-dramatic, non-theatrical, ceremonial and usually non-scripted everyday-life performances – that appear, and indeed make a concerted effort – to depart from the 'authority' of texts. One can argue, but isn't this what drama always does? Performance studies hold drama as a type of performance derived from and driven by texts, although it may not always be that the text prescribes or restricts the meanings of the performance. Performing reconstitutes the text but it need not necessarily echo, give voice to, or translate the text. As Dwight Conquergood points out, while performance may share the rhetoric and the general tendency of 'opposition to foundationalist thought' (1992: 80), to consider 'performance' as a mode of resistance to textual authority would mean mistaking the instrumental for the essential. While writing is sometimes associated with colonial hegemony (in some situations, at least), complicity with authority is hardly foundational to textual practices. The authority of writing and other performances as modes of cultural production is determined within an elaborate, historically contingent, dynamic network of referential possibilities like any speech act. Conquergood is alert to this point and with reference to performances as forms of cultural production and asks the pertinent question: 'How does performance reproduce, enable, sustain, challenge, subvert, critique, and naturalize ideology?' (1992: 190). For example, Shakespearean drama may now be regarded as part of textual culture, even as part of an avowedly imperial educational project, but in Shakespeare's own time his plays contained subversive politics. Therefore, distinct boundaries cannot be drawn between theatre, drama and performance studies. It may perhaps be maintained that the purview of the performance studies is more inclusive of genres, forms and types than the former two.

Using the stimulating theoretical framework of performance studies one can proceed to examine the construction of the performative text within the specific context that generates its performative force and the way the dramatic enactment deploys the reiteration of a specific vision of social order and processes of socialisation which determines the 'materiality and historical density of the performance' (Diamond 2003: 66). In this case, the process of embodiment through performance, and not the text, becomes central to the theatrical experience. Moreover, this embodiment has to be empathised with by other bodies of the *sahridaya* or the spectator. Watching a play can deeply disturb the audience instead of providing just pleasurable experience. Traditionally, the theatre-goer is defined as that of either an observer or spectator who watches the plot unfold on stage, possibly with strong feelings of empathy, but must refrain from interfering. Even if a character on the stage (e.g. Othello) sets out to kill another (Desdemona), the audience knows that the murder is but pretence and that the actress playing Desdemona and the actor playing Othello will soon join for the final curtain call because theatre is specifically process-oriented – through the actions of the actors, aimed at creating specific relations with the audience, and through the reactions of audience members, which either endorses the actors' proposed relationship, modifies or seeks to undo it. Therefore, to negotiate the relationship between stage and the audience in order to constitute the reality of the performing body and theatre is of crucial importance. First and foremost, the actions of the actors and spectators are signified only by what they accomplish. They are self-referential as well as constitutive of reality and hence comprise what can be called 'performative' as described by J.L. Austin (as explained in his classic study 'How to Do Things with Words' 1955/1976]. The dissolution of boundaries in the arts, repeatedly proclaimed and observed by artists, scholars and critics and philosophers, is increasingly defined as the performative turn.

Be it art, music, literature or theatre, the creative process is best realised in and as performance. Instead of creating works of art, artists increasingly produce events which involve not just themselves but also the observers, listeners and spectators in 'interactive workshop sessions'. The concept of the 'performative' has been used extensively in Judith Butler's theorisation of the body. The basic difference in the way Austin and Butler use the word is that while Austin emphasises the criteria of success/failure, especially the functional conditions for success, Butler examines the phenomenal conditions for embodiment as per Merleau-Ponty's views of not regarding the body merely as a historical idea but as a repertoire of infinite possibilities and symbolising the process of embodying certain cultural and historical possibilities (1988: 520–3). According to Butler, the stylised that repetition of performative acts embodies certain cultural and historical possibilities and the performative acts in turn generate the culturally and historically marked body as well as its identity. Butler takes the example of embodiment in a theatrical performance and argues that the acts that generate and perform specific roles (especially gender) are 'clearly not one's act alone' but constitute a 'shared experience' and 'collective action' because they have always already begun before 'one arrived on the scene'.

Contemporary theorisations on the body, time and space as conditions governing art production and reception have changed and continue to do so in crucial ways. The pivotal point of these processes is no longer the work of art, detached from and independent of its creator and recipient, but which arises as an object from the activities of the creator-subject and is entrusted to the perception and interpretation of the recipient-subject. Instead, one is dealing with an event, set in motion and terminated by the actions of all the subjects involved – the artists and the spectators.

What are the ethical stakes of seeking out, encountering and writing about people's lives through the intimate frame of experience? As Michael Jackson puts it, 'Understanding others requires more than an intellectual movement from one's own position to theirs; it involves physical upheaval, psychological turmoil, and moral confusion' (2009: 239). An outstanding performance event can collapse layers of liminality to enjoin aesthetics and social, art and politics. As Erika Fischer-Lichte writes in her analytical study on *The Transformative Power of Performance*, 'Performance allows entirely ordinary bodies, actions, movements, things, sounds, or odors to be perceived and has them appear as extra-ordinary and transfigured. Performance makes the ordinary conspicuous' (2008: 179–80). Budhan Theatre group explains what they do:

> We, at Budhan Theatre do not hide reality in our work. Rather, we perform hard truths and real facts, no matter how disturbing, because it is in this way we connect with our history. It is in this way that we use theater to show our people that we need to change our future. It is in this way the many people of India, from common people to mainstream society members, to policymakers, to educators/intellectuals, to government officials and beyond, may finally recognize the human needs of the Chhara community. It is in this way that we fight for dignity and social justice for all De-notified tribes of India. (Budhan Theatre)

Budhan Theatre's *Choli Ke Pichchey Kya Hai* can thus be described as activist theatre/performance as a process to make the 'ordinary' not just conspicuous but extraordinary. It transcends the 'authority' of the written text to encompass 'lived experience' of a kind the audience can relate to. What it presents is the performative realisation of 'experience as narrated' as 'experience as lived' and explores the multi-layered structuring of experience in terms of the temporal organisation of 'meaning', 'values' and 'ends'. Within the hegemonic social–political–economic matrix of our society, Budhan Theatre may not be able to immediately overthrow the system or radically alter the landscape of their material poverty, but they have with their persistent effort made theatre the instrument of change and transformation. And in that process they are on their way to achieving their goal of spurring in the spectators what Dewey calls 'the inclusive integrity of experience' (1925: 9) through understanding and empathy.

Notes

1. 'Political theatre' is a term that has been used to refer to three different things: theatre that comments on political issues, political action or protest that has a theatrical quality to it and any action by politicians that is intended to make a point rather than accomplish something substantive. (See Wikipedia https://en.wikipedia.org/wiki/Political_theatre.)
2. For further information on the subject, see Y.C. Simhadri's *Denotified Tribes: A Sociological Analysis*, relevant excerpt available at http://ccnmtl.columbia.edu/projects/mmt/ambedkar/web/readings/Simhadri.pdf; also, wikipedia.org/wiki/Criminal_Tribes_Act; and G.N.Devy's (2006)

A Nomad Called Thief: Reflections on Adivasi Silence. Hyderabad: Orient Longman, especially pp. 20–22.
3. See poignantly written 'The Year of Birth -1871: Mahasweta Devi on India's Denotified Tribes' by Mahasweta Devi, available at http://indiatogether. org/bhasha/budhan/birth1871.htm
4. See 'National Commission for denotified, Nomadic & Semi-nomadic Tribes' Official website of the *Ministry of Social Justice and Empowerment*.
5. See for detailed discussion, Meena Radhakrishna (2001) *Dishonoured by History: 'Criminal Tribes' and British Colonial Policy.* Orient Blackswan and Henry Schwarz (2010) *Constructing the Criminal Tribe in Colonial India : Acting Like a Thief.* New York: Wiley-Blackwell.
6. 'Stanadayini' translated by Ella Dutt as 'Wet Nurse' and by Gayatri Chakravorty Spivak as 'Breastgiver' is the story told in flashback of a cancer-ridden corpse of a woman left unclaimed in the morgue, later dragged away by scavengers. The woman was Jashoda engaged to breast-feed infants of a rich family. She did this to sustain her family after her husband was crippled by an accident. She bore children herself to be in milk. Finally ill with breast cancer, there was no succour from all the infants she fed, and none to claim her body. Spivak presents her as victim in an exploitative system, as most subalterns are.

References

Arnold, David. 1985. 'Crime and Crime Control in Madras 1859–1957', in Anand A. Yang (ed.), *Crime and Criminality in British India*, pp. 62–88. Tucson: University of Arizona Press.

Austin, J.L. 1962. *How to Do Things with Words: The William James Lectures delivered in Harvard University in 1955*, edited by J.O. Urmson and Marina Sbisà. Oxford Paperbacks. Oxford: Oxford University Press, 1962.

Boal, Augusto. 2000[1979]. *Theatre of the Oppressed*, trans. by Charles A. Leal McBride and Maria-Odilia Leal McBride and Emily Fryer. London: Pluto Press.

Budhan Theatre, available at http://www.budhantheatre.org/#!what-we-do/c24qo.

Butler, Judith. 1988. 'Performative Acts and Gender Constitution: An Essay in Phenomenology and Feminist Theory', *Theatre Journal*, 40(4) (Dec.): 519–31.

Conquergood, Dwight. 1992. 'Ethnography, Rhetoric, and Performance', *Quarterly Journal of Speech*, 78: 80–123.

Devi, Mahasweta. 1987. 'Stanadayini or the Breastgiver' in Gayatri Chakraborty Spivak (ed. and trans.), *In Other Worlds: Essays in Cultural Politics*, pp. 222–40.. New York: Methuen.

Devy, G.N. 2006. *A Nomad Called Thief: Reflections on Adivasi Silence.* Hyderabad: Orient Longman.

Dewey, John. 1925. *Art and Experience.* New York: Minton, Balch & Co.

Diamond, Elin. 2003. 'Performance and Cultural Politics', in L. Goodman and J. De Gay (eds), *The Routledge Reader in Politics and Performance*, pp. 66–70. London: Routledge.

Fine, Elizabeth C. 1994. *The Folklore Text: From Performance to Print*. Bloomington: Indiana University Press.

Fischer-Lichte, Erika. 2008. *The Transformative Power of Performance: A New Aesthetics*, trans. by Saskya Jain. Oxon and New York: Routledge.

Gamson, William A. 1992. 'The Social Psychology of Collective Action', in Aldon D. Morris and Carol McClurg Mueller (eds), *Frontiers in Social Movement Theory*. pp. 53–76. New Haven: Yale University Press.

Hall, Peter. 1999. *The Necessary Theatre*. London: N.Nick Hern Books.

'Hole in the Wall' education blog 'Who Are the Chharas', available at http://www.hole-in-the-wall.com/News09.html, 2011.

Jackson, Michael. 2009. 'Where Thought Belongs', *Anthropological Theory* 9(3): 235–51.

Malekar, Anosh. 'Budhan Bolta Hai', available at http://infochangeindia.org/agenda/intercultural-dialogue/budhan-bolta-hai.html (accessed on March 2012).

Mishra, Saurabh. 'A Study of Criminal Tribes in India', available at https://www.academia.edu/8014667/A_STUDY_OF_CRIMINAL_TRIBES_IN_INDIA.

Radhakrishna, Meena. 2001. *Dishonoured by History: 'Criminal Tribes' and British Colonial Policy*. New Delhi: Orient Blackswan.

Schechner, Richard. 1988. *Performance Theory*. London, New York: Routledge Classics.

Simhadri, Y.C. 'Denotified Tribes: A Sociological Analysis', available at http://ccnmtl.columbia.edu/projects/mmt/ambedkar/web/readings/simhadri.pdf.

Turner, Victor and Edward Bruner (eds) *The Anthropology of Experience*. Urbana: University of Illinois Press, 1986.

13

REINVENTION AND APPROPRIATION OF THE FOLK IN DALER MEHNDI'S POP VIDEOS

Pushpinder Syal

An exploration of the formation of cultural iconographies is generally regarded as being a valid area of concern in cultural studies. Some may still argue that these phenomena, that are so transitory and part of the apparently frivolous activities associated with everyday entertainment, are hardly the subject of serious consideration, and even if such consideration is undertaken, may not yield much of interest. But if we accept one of the basic tenets of cultural studies that entertainment is one of those significant activities in cultures in which much energy and much economic value is invested and that modes of entertainment as well as the people who are created as focal figures or 'icons' are evidence of the construction of cultural identities as well as repositories of emotion that people imbue them with, the effort may prove worthwhile. The concentration of the attention of a large number on a particular object, even if it is for a short period of time (Andy Warhol's 'in the future, everyone will be famous – for fifteen minutes'[1]) is a construct made out of the instruments and agents of mass media, very much tied to specific circumstances and events taking place at a particular time, and voices the prevalent concerns and interests of groups of people. It can be an instrument of cohesion among groups that are not otherwise connected; it can tie together participants in cultural events in an experience of pleasure, which is not insignificant in its effects. In fact, the cultural icon, whether a film or pop star, or fashion model or sports idol, becomes a factor in forming or changing the constitution of a group or community; effectively, it is the locus of power.

In the Indian context, where the folk and folk traditions are still prevalent, current cultural iconographies have the power to rework and reinvent existing forms. The present discussion hinges on changes that seem to have occurred in the notion of 'folk' in both production and reception through the emergence of new forms of entertainment. The 'folk' used to be seen as a community in local terms, a localized, homogenized entity, but in the course of changes such as migration, economic liberalization and the growth of global consumerism, it has become scattered in location and diverse in composition and modes of experiencing. In this process, the sense of a community bound to its land, perpetuating its common, received wisdom through its folk traditions, many of them esoteric and unavailable to people outside of them, and of these traditions themselves becoming a record of shared community experience, is constantly being reinvented. Since the community now has a disparate identity or identities, it is the hybrid cultural forms that begin to speak for it – through the more accessible mediations of music, television video and film. The nature of hybridity can be understood as being such that while some clear distinctions/disjunctions, for instance those between the rural and urban experiences, the affluent and the lower economic groups, the literate and non-literate sections of society, continue to be maintained, other specificities are elided or levelled out to draw a sort of lowest common denominator meant to be comprehensible and acceptable to those both within the tradition and outside it. Thus, while there is some sense of discordance, it does not achieve the level of discomfort, and a part of this is due to the sliding of some forms, styles and expressions under others, so that voices and traces from all these emerge and submerge in an ever-changing pattern. This has long been understood and practiced in the cinematic forms that we have come to label as 'Bollywood', itself a word reflecting the same process. Classical dance forms and *ragas* are made accessible in Hindi films through some sorts of rhythmic combinations and expressive gimmickry so that viewers can take in the grace and the glamour of a dancer without being bothered about the grammar of the form. Equally, the more esoteric and localized elements in folk dance and music are elided under some relatively straightforward rhythms and beats synthesized to blend into each other. What Ila Arun did with regard to Rajasthani folk music in some Hindi films, Daler Mehndi, the Panjabi singer and performer, does to Panjabi folk, that is, he helps it transcend the rural–urban, traditional–modern divides, glamorizes it (a necessary condition for the television age), but in the process, changes its original sentiments, its connection with the emotive bedrock that supported its earlier existence. It may be emphasized here that Daler Mehndi is not to be regarded as a *person*, but is a composite construction, with features and dimensions at once fictional and symbolic, as much as they are real and concrete in their visual form.

Whether the forms generate the folk or the folk generates the forms may not always be distinguishable, but it can be said that in each emerging form, there is a redefining or reinvention of whatever is to be understood as 'folk'. Often, scholars of folklore have been hesitant to agree to this kind of formulation, because for them, folk is an essence, whether of wisdom or traditional practice, expressed in some long-lasting immutable structure, such as, for instance, a narrative, poetic, musical, dance or theatre convention, or craft, or medicine, among others. They do acknowledge that these forms change from one place to another, thereby becoming constitutive of the cultural identity of their practitioners, and the region to which they belong, and by that very token, closely and irrevocably bound together. However, the emergence of cinema and television (*door-darshan* is indeed *door*, seeing at a distance) and of synthesization and digitization of music has provided a medium for reinvention of folk, through it, the very notion of what constitutes it. How this reinvention takes place is a matter of historicity, ideology and power, the outcome of which is that the folk begins to see themselves in the images presented by the forms. A manner of recreation, so to speak, becomes the *re-creation* of the community.

And what is the constitution of this community? As mentioned earlier, it is not a homogenous and single group. Panjab, landlocked, and subjected, in its entire history, to constant invasions from the north and west, evolved a sense of its 'folk' within the geographical boundaries of the land of the five rivers. Post-partition, it was not invasions, but internal division and strife within the Indian state that began to form a substantive influence in the re-constitution of Panjabi sense of community. People who had travelled from West Panjab at the time of partition found a place to establish themselves in the 'dil' of Hindustan, Delhi. A community came into being, which could now be characterized as the 'Delhi Panjabi', the inflections of its everyday life and language, different from the Panjab of the towns of Jalandhar, Ludhiana and Amritsar, both still different from the villages, hamlets and *kasba*s and the little satellite townships away from the GT road. One point of difference was that the Delhi Panjabi could afford a somewhat grander lifestyle than the village or small town Panjabis, with Karol Bagh being a centre of trade, business and fashion, to be replaced later by the more upscale Rajaouri Garden and Panjabi Bagh areas (but this too is not a picture of uniformity; less affluent Delhi Panjabis from Tilak Nagar, like similar communities everywhere, suffered the most during the anti-Sikh pogrom of 1984). The religious divide that sharpened and reached unimagined heights during the eighties cut into the Delhi Panjabi communities in ways that are yet to be reconciled fully. Further, the large-scale migration to Western countries from the heart of Panjab resulted in the formation of the ex-patriate Panjabi community, a complete newly constituted 'folk' in itself. Given the diversity of experience of all these communities, (the ex-patriate, for instance, saw the horror of 1984 as *door-darshan*, seeing-from-a-distance, except for some who survived it, and migrated later), it is perhaps inevitable that the sense of 'folk' would become, if not fragmented, then at least diversified, because memory would not any longer be able to construct a unity of experience.

In some sense, it is all these communities, each of whom finds some aspects of themselves reflected in the emergence of Panjabi popular music in general. It is in this context that Daler Mehndi's emergence as a pop musician in the early 1990s and the popularity of his songs and videos as a reinvention of the folk idiom is to be seen. The phenomenon has to be seen against the backdrop of the tumultuous events of the 1980s in Panjab. At that time, Panjab was limping back to a semblance of normalcy, after massacres, bus killings, vicious police encounters and curfews, due to which the land of the *bhangra* had fallen into a sullen and terrified silence. Meanwhile, Panjabi music had grown its roots in the soil of UK and Canada, and experimentation, such as that of Bally Sagoo, Apache Indian and various groups, was rife, and it had already created a base for further development of the genre. The 1980s in the West was also the decade of the pop video, the promotional videos brought out by pop singers and groups, which sprang visual interest and narrative into the accompaniment of song, of which one of the leading examples was Michael Jackson's *Thriller* (1983). This, of course, introduced a whole new visuality vis–a-vis the appearance of the pop star, spawning new styles and fashion as never before (for example Madonna, Culture Club, Queen, Prince and many more). In India, however, this took off later, as even until the mid-1980s, colour television was not available everywhere (though it had been introduced in 1982), and cable television came in towards the end of the decade, bringing in MTV – and then the world changed forever. The 1990s ushered in a relative calm and the liberalization of the Indian economy began to take place, the stage was set for the new televised music video, and people were in a mood to celebrate. Not that there was anything in particular to celebrate – the horror experienced in Panjab was of the kind in which there are no winners – but the pendulum had swung away from the problems that were – and still are – enormous and unresolved. As culture is part of the overall enterprise of a society to embody its felt experience, those forms are generated and accepted which support that enterprise, while other, sub-cultural ones may integrate into or begin to resist. A part of the symbolism of Daler Mehndi as a cavorting figure on the television or stage was related to the re-establishment of the image of the 'jolly Sardar' as a replacement of the figure of the 'terrorist', or Khalistani militant of the 1980s. It was the image that the nationalist culture would want to see – the well-fed and happy-go-lucky figure that stood for a Panjab that was affluent, problem-free, supplying the nation with grain and demanding nothing but belonging to the national community. That this sense of belonging had been severely tested did not seem to matter anymore. The public imagination had already instituted the image of the Sardar as the soldier, one of the stock characters that are often appropriated as representations of a community. It was an attempt to resolve the ambiguities regarding the Sardar which were always resident in the construction of Indian nationhood through that crucible of modern Indian culture – the Hindi film – that created the image of the soldier and the pleasant buffoon. The fear that had crept in, of the incendiary figure of the Sikh militant, that threatened to unsettle the stable idea of the Sikh as a loyal servant of the Republic, was sought to be replaced by a new image, partly a reiteration of the old jovial, harmless and neutral person and partly an invention comprising colourful, celebratory and magical elements. The popularity of this image showed a strategy for forgetfulness was in operation, its repeated impingement on the popular imagination making it appear more 'real' than the image of the subversive, who appeared to recede like an uncomfortable dream. The hypertext of Mehndi's videos picturing the Sardar cavorting with assorted females repeated itself time and again, and with it, the viewers began to believe in its reality. Any number of weddings in the 1990s had Mehndi's songs playing to similar enactments by the revellers of the actions of his dances, and they captured their imitation of his dances in their own wedding videos, the latter becoming an essential record of the wedding celebrations. The folk, whether in Delhi, Jalandhar or Toronto, was reinventing itself in the form of a happy dancer.

Dance had of course been popular before too, but *bhangra* was arguably in danger of becoming a fossilized show-piece kind of folk art before it was rejuvenated by the new artists. Mehndi was instrumental in devising variations in the dance. The new *bhangra* was, for one, being revisualized by the expatriate Panjabi singers as a form hybridized with rap and western rhythms and almost seemed unrecognizable as compared to the traditional form. Secondly, the choreography of dance in Hindi films was influential in creating Mehndi's dance. It incorporated both these influences, but was yet different. Not only is it the case that the dance movements that constitute Mehndi's performance were taken from indigenous *bhangra* movements, but also that the variations he effects in them are his own, and the total personality of Mehndi himself contributes to the establishment of this in no small measure.

There is, first, the turban. Expatriate singers, the 'cut Surds' (sardars who cut their hair), did not wear it. Even Gurdas Mann, whose work had already been much acclaimed, did not flaunt it. Mehndi not only wore it as a prominent part of his costume, but chose bright colours and strung it with jewels. It must be pointed out that the colours of the turbans were not the dark saffron (*kesri*) or the dark blue worn by religious Sikhs. This casual inclusion of the turban as part of his dress as a performer was a token of belonging to the Sikh community, without making too much of it as a religious sign, and Mehndi wore it framing his smiling, chubby face and with an aplomb that not only endeared him to his audience but set a style trend that was followed by others (such as Malkiat Singh and Surjit Bindrakhia). The other distinguishing characteristic of his costume was the long *zari* (embroidered) coat which he wore over his shirt and trousers, even when picturized dancing in the streets. It added to his comfortable frame, amazingly agile even if a bit bulky. (One cannot say for sure whether he took a cue from the Sikh designer of Delhi, J.J. Vallaya, who popularized shiny embroidered coats for men, a reinvention of the formal *sherwani*.) This, along with a certain set of gestures, seemed to create the picture of a smiling magician, an energetic showman. The costume is a hybrid mix of the indigenous and the western, evoking both familiarity and strangeness at the same time. The long coat is a formal dress, but Mehndi chose to dance wearing just such a coat instead of the traditional *kurta-laacha* of a bhangra dancer or the jacket and jeans worn by the expatriate pop musicians. This created a defamilarizing effect, foregrounding Mehndi as an unusually eye-catching figure on the television screen.

In contrast, the troupe of women dancers accompanying him in the videos are dressed in modern clothes – pantsuits, halters, shorts and minis. The Panjabi woman is represented here as streetsmart, an energetic dancer, and more often than not, unfaithful in love. If we consider one of the popular videos, the picturization of the song *dardi rab rab kardi*, we see images of a woman in a red miniskirt atop a straw-filled cart, amalgamating westernized and rural Panjabi images. These were the first appearances of something that became the staple format of Panjabi pop videos, women in skimpy Western dresses accompanying the male singer who is usually in more traditional or somber garments. In the case of this song, the lyrics talk about the shyness and diffidence of the Panjabi woman, the *chui-muyi*, but the costumes and gestures and come-hither looks of the female cast contradict the traditional lyrics. The contradiction is not lost on any viewer but is one to be enjoyed rather than resented. It is in keeping with a tradition in which the woman affects coyness while flirting or being courted or praised, while being otherwise 'modern' in her gestures and dance movements. In these picturizations, Mehndi usually occupies centre stage, in the midst of the dancers, yet distanced from them. He is shown as not looking at them or touching them (except in one video where he takes a ride on a roller coaster with the object of his rhapsody), and instead looks straight at the viewer with a twinkle in his eye and carefully choreographed dance movements.

There is an attitude of in-your-face insouciance being projected by the characters, even when the narrative in the video involves lovers breaking up or walking off with other partners. *Ho jayegi balle balle* is one such short narrative. 'Balle balle' is a kind of celebratory cheer, with which the sequence of a folk *boli* often starts. Here, it becomes a mocking comment on a failed love affair, when the woman goes off with another man. The nature of the lover is spoken of thus:

> mil jaye dooja yaar
>   Tey phir nahi puchde
> Ho jayegi balle balle, ho gayi teri balle balle.[2]

> they find another lover, they forget about you,
>   and that will be the end for you. (translation mine)

While the music is upbeat, preventing the sentiment of failure and loss of love from being taken too seriously, there are residual traces of the voice of the doomed lover which came out so strongly in the traditional romantic legends of Panjab, in a slowing of tempo in this song and a plaintive *toombi*-like acoustic. Mehndi uses traditional instruments in which he had been trained. These are, however, subsumed within the techno rhythm and flowing beat of the electronic synthesizer and, in the video, in the pattern of the dance. The woman, instead of being identified as the tragic beloved of a traditional tale, such as Heer, is here anonymous, reduced in the video to a dancing shape among other similar dancing shapes. It is the singer Mehndi alone who is definable, the singing, commenting male voice at the centre, the gesturer, the magician who has conjured up these shapes and conjures them away again. The irony of modern-day love, which makes lovers able to meet and celebrate love more freely than the heterosexual couples of the folk legends whose love was conscribed within the network of community relations, but at the same time, makes that availability itself a source of anxiety and uncertainty, is an undercurrent in these videos of dance and celebration.

Here, it may be observed, there is a change in the functionality of the lyrics. In the older folk lyrics, a commentary was usually embedded in the form of some utterances of a proverbial nature, which conveyed some of the perceptions and word view of the community. In his lyrics, however, Mehndi has appropriated this space and this role, bringing in ironic commentary and a deflatory attitude towards any such notion as romantic love or doomed attachment. This comes out strongly in the picturization of the videos, which convey that while tradition is fine, laughing at it is also fine. A break with tradition, a forgetting of emotional and societal linkages, is indicated. Mehndi's gestural language, with the shrugging of the shoulders and twisting of wrists in a don't-care manner, expresses his stance as someone uninvolved in conveying traditional beliefs. Even the comments made, such as the one in the song discussed earlier, are interspersed with a repetitive nonsense chorus, for example 'aaha, chiknaa, chiknaa, chiknaa', or as in another song 'bolo, ta-ra-ra-ra', or even with a sprinkling of English 'hi, hi, hello, hello, see you, see you, *munde karde*'. There is no content, and the implication is that there is not much need for it either.

It is not as though there is always a concerted effort by a definable agency to deliberately install particular images for public consumption. Yet ideological forces are operative precisely where agencies may not be clearly defined, and the popularity of Daler Mehndi shows how the emergence of certain forms is a locus, a coming together of a number of processes and circumstances, that define a moment in a

THE FOLK IN DALER MEHNDI'S POP VIDEOS

culture. Mehndi's popularity shows how artists cannot but be products of their age, in this case, their very emergence being dependent on television and recording machines. One may speculate whether the dreamy flow and melodious strains of Asa Singh Mastana's *Peke jaan waliye* or *Gori diya chanjaran* would have been experienced differently if they had been picturised in a television video, but it is clear that the impact of Daler Mehndi would not be what it has been without the videos. The promotional and glamorizing power of the videos which sold millions of audio cassettes also brought in a change in the way in which the lyrics were received, even if they had their origin, or part origin, in folk songs and sayings. It is also the case that the invention and fusion of new rhythms and catchy beats also made lyrics less relevant for a dispersed public while extending the reach of the music to them, resulting in more commercial profit. Mehndi opened the floodgates for more and more singer-performers, and a boom occurred in the music scene, even as employment opportunities for Sikh youths shrank, the green revolution faded, education took a back seat in government policy and the menace of drugs stalked Panjab. Music and television have provided outlets for some, but overall, they only cover up the situation and build a false sense of euphoria, the uses of which the vested interests in the ruling dispensation are well aware.

In so doing, the sense of 'folk' in a community is transformed. The community reinvents itself through the medium of television, utilizing tradition only in so far as it is a source of playfulness and utilizing the cultural icon as source of pleasure. But this reinvention is itself an illusion, as sections of the community and the central icon itself has already been appropriated as a necessary part of the process of manufacturing and disseminating the cultural objects, that is the music videos. The rapidly changing trends in the music industry bring in new players, who often ride over the 'original' creators of the music, whether the compositions or the lyrics (Mehndi himself has been controversial in this regard). With regard to folk forms, ownership has always been a matter of contestation and these issues are further complicated by the commercial interests that dominate music production. Thus, however playful and inconsequential Mehndi's music may seem to be, political and economic forces are integral in its production and reception and in the reforming of cultural communities which perhaps can no longer be called the 'folk' in the sense it was previously understood.

Notes

1. Andy Warhol made this statement on television in 1968.
2. Daler Mehndi's songs and videos can easily be found and downloaded from *www.youtube.com*. and *his* own website *www.dalermehndi.com*. The particular songs that have been mentioned are:

   'Bolo tara ra ra ra', 1995 (accessed on 5 April 2012).
   'Dardi rab rab kardi', 1996 (accessed on 5 April 2012).
   'Ho jayegi balle Balle', 1997 (accessed on 5 April 2012).

14

SUBVERTING THE MALE GAZE
A case study of *Zindagi Na Milegi Dobara*

Vivek Sachdeva

Gaze is neither natural nor apolitical. The way one looks and what one looks at carries high cultural and political dimensions. Be it all seeing eye of God, or of Big B or Foucault's Panopticon, one who enjoys power in any social or political system also has the power to 'see' or 'look at'. In patriarchy, men have always been enjoying the privilege of 'seeing' and 'looking at' their counterpart – women. Speech and Sight had been two instruments through which men have created and exercised their hegemony. Speech gave men the freedom of expression both in personal as well as public sphere, and Sight gave them the power to see. With men, the power to see also became an instrument of subjugation of women. Men were looking at and women were always being looked at. Different societies developed their own ways to circumscribe females' domain such as the veil, *parda* and *zenana*. to subjugate them. Women were constantly kept under check by not allowing them to go beyond the dominating sight of the male eye.

Men's privilege to look at women and 'see' them also gave them the opportunity to look at female body as they desired and the freedom of Speech (expression) gave men the privilege to portray women as they wanted to see women. In every art form – be it literature, painting, sculpting or films–female body has been fetishized to provide visual pleasure to men. Dominance of male viewpoint also played an important role while crystallizing notions about beauty as well. In case of films, male directors have been using camera to portray female body in such a fashion as to provide visual pleasure to the male audience. The way shots are taken and films are structured, it can be assumed that directors also assumed audience to be only male. Camera was not only expressing director's fantasy, but also catering to the fantasy of the male audience. Thus camera, in the hands of male filmmakers, became a tool to fetishize female body and, by using female body for his gratification, also an instrument to exercise men's dominance over women. Since 'every image embodies a way of seeing' (Berger 10), in the present chapter, the attempt shall be to explore what changes can be there in a cinematic narrative if the person behind the camera is a female. The hypothetical position is to study if a female director can use camera as a tool of subversion while working in a male-dominated system. To hypothesize my study, I propose to do a detailed analysis of *Zindagi Na Milegi Dobara* (Akhtar 2011), a film directed by a young female director, Zoya Akhtar. The study shall allow me to explore the following – first, if there can be a female gaze in cinema; second, can female gaze function independently of the influence of the dominant male gaze in cinema; third, can this film be taken as a denominator of changing paradigm in Hindi cinema; fourth, this chapter shall also allow me to touch upon the changing contours of female subjectivity in Hindi cinema. The attempt is to make a point that Zoya Akhtar has also made an attempt to subvert the male–female power equations through the portrayal of male and female characters. The filmmaker has made a conscious choice of not using female body as a spectacle for the consumption of male viewers. I shall bank upon Laura Mulvey's path-breaking essay titled 'Visual Pleasure and Narrative Cinema'. However, in the chapter, the gaze shall not be seen only in relation with identification and subjectivity. I look at the concept of gaze beyond psychoanalysis and see it in relation to power equations in society, as hinted in the beginning of this chapter as well.

Images have always surrounded human eye or, to be politically more correct, the male eye. Starting from cave paintings, sculpture, paintings, literature, cinema and advertisements, in almost every art form, images of women have been presented as a spectacle for the male voyeuristic gaze. John Berger wrote that in the history of art men do the act of seeing and women had been appearing before men's gaze. This reflects the stereotypical role that the male artists in different art forms have been assigning to men and women. In the politics of gender power, men have always been the 'bearer of the look' (Mulvey 837) as suggested by Mulvey, and women had been looked at. Laura Mulvey, British filmmaker and film theorist, appropriates psychoanalytic theory 'as a political weapon, demonstrating the way the unconscious of patriarchal society has structured film form' (Mulvey 833). Laura Mulvey in the essay *Visual Pleasures and Narrative Cinema* 'draws on

Freudian and Lacanian psychoanalyses to examine the pleasures of scopophilia and narcissistic identification that the classic Hollywood cinema offers' (Kazmi 92). She asserts that male viewers in the patriarchal society have the power to see, gaze and desire. The gaze in cinema is identified with the camera. In the dark cinema hall, where no viewer has the fear of being looked at while he is looking at the images on the screen, by controlling camera position and composition of the cinematic frames, women's body is offered as spectacle for visual pleasure of male audience.

Psychoanalysis gives us an insight into the human consciousness, the relationship between an individual's subjectivity and society. From Freud's conflicts between id and super-ego to archetypes to Lacanian stages of identity formation, psychoanalysis has shown us that human consciousness is not a stable plane; rather human consciousness is the site where politics of sexuality, subjectivity, identity and also gender is played. In the anxiety ridden arena, men and women have different roles to play, according to earlier psychoanalysis. What interests me in this chapter is how psychoanalysis from a theory to understand human psyche became a tool of socio-cultural politics either in the hands of theoreticians or creative minds – in this case a film maker.

The relationship between psychoanalysis and films goes back to the last decade of the 19th century. Both, psychoanalysis and films, were said to be born together. The relation between them grew little later. Both, films and psychoanalysis grew independently of each other, though psychoanalysis in its own way has contributed a lot to make people accept film as an art form. Sigmund Freud published his essays in 1890s and it was the later part of the same decade that witnessed screenings of films made by Lumiere brothers. It was only after the First World War that two groups within film criticism could be identified. The first group was that of Eisenstein, whose film making and theoretical essays established film as an art form. After the Second World War, emerged Andre Bazin on the scene of film theory, and a new style of filmmaking and film criticism emerged. Both the schools were linked with formalistic analysis of film as well as theory of film making.

The influence of Bazin was short lived and after the wildcat strike of 1968 in France, every text became political as nothing was believed to exist outside or above politics. Camera, which earlier was an objective instrument of recording reality, became a tool or instrument for recording 'unformulated, unauthorized, unthought-out world of the dominant ideology' (Jean-Louis Comolli and Jean Narboni as quoted by Murphy in Psychoanalysis and Film Theory Part 1:'A New Kind of Mirror')[1]. In the hands of filmmakers that have strong ideological commitments, camera began to be identified with the eye of the filmmaker. Althusser blended Marxism with psychoanalysis, Robert Lapsley and Michael Westlake were using Lacanian theory in film studies. Semioticians were also trying to study films from a linguistic or semiotic point of view. In this context, Metz's work the Imaginary Signifier was a path-breaking thesis which looked at the screen–spectator relationship. Metz writings have gone a long way in defining the nature of the film art. He proposes that unique feature about film is that in cinema signifier is present through its absence. Film perception takes place in real time, but what is perceived is not real – as it is only image. 'Cinema involves us in imaginary' (Metz 802), he said. On the other hand, according to Metz, literature operates with the help of 'presence in absence' and theatre, where actors perform in flesh and blood, on the contrary operates on the principle of 'agreed absence of reality'. But films seem to offer real objects, real bodies and landscapes to the gaze of the viewers. It is with images that a spectator identifies, a position which stands very close to Lacanian imaginary.

Laura Mulvey blended Althusserean ideas, feminist film theory and psychoanalysis to give insight into how gaze operates in cinema. Laura Mulvey's essay 'describes a psychic context in which voyeurism, fetishism and narcissism all structure film viewing' (Humm 14). Mulvey gives us the insight how 'fascination of film is reinforced by pre-existing patterns of fascination' (Mulvey 833). The pre-existing patterns also structure the unconscious of individuals and also reflect the structural patterns of a society. Cinema, according to her, is structured like unconscious of the patriarchal system. Thus, cinema, by reducing female subjectivity to a commodity, provides its viewers the scopophilic pleasure. She has given three ways through which gaze operates in cinema: first, the camera operated by men looks at the body of women as objects; second, the gaze of the male actors within the film and third, the gaze of the male spectators on the female who identifies with the gaze of the camera/actor. According to Mulvey, male viewer can indulge in visual pleasure in number of ways. It can be his voyeuristic gaze without the knowledge of the subject/object (woman) or by fetishizing her body and can be the narcissistic identification with the male protagonist, which Mulvey found on the insights of Lacanian psychoanalysis. During the process of narcissistic identification, male viewer identifying himself with the male protagonist participates in male protagonist's sexual adventures. Thus, in the process, the viewer also participates in making the women an 'object' of visual pleasure and desire. Mulvey's reservations are that cinema, even though it operates in viewing conditions in which every viewer is separated by dark, exists in an isolated space and has no fear of being seen, and thus encourages the voyeuristic gaze of the male viewers. While commenting on Hollywood classical films, she says that films mainly focus only on the male actors, who are participants in the narrative and female characters are subservient to their male counterparts. Women in cinema are meant to be loved by male actors in the narrative and desired by male viewers in the audience. Cinema fetishizes the female body and provides scopophilic pleasure to the male eye. In such a scheme, women are only images and men are the 'bearer of the look'. While watching a film, the spectator identifies himself with the images on the screen. Paula Murphy in the essay 'Psychoanalysis and Film Theory' says:

> Identification is with the projector, the camera and the screen of the cinematic apparatus. The projector duplicates the act of perception by originating from the back of the subject's head and presenting a visual image in from of the subject. The various shots of the camera are akin to the movement of the head. As vision is both projective and introjective, the subject projects his/her gaze and simultaneously introjects the information received from the gaze.

However, the images on the screen cannot be compared with the mirror image. The basic ontological difference between them is that mirror 'reflects' back the real, whereas cinema-screen 'projects' the pre-recorded image. Despite the difference, what is said in the above quote is the supremacy of imaginary over the symbolic, the idea Christian Metz has also stated in The Imaginary Signifier. Since, the viewer in this theoretical frame is supposedly male, the cinematic apparatus has been an instrument of male gaze, producing representation of women. Laura Mulvey's essay 'Visual Pleasure and Narrative Cinema' is seen as reaction to the dominance of male gaze and the use of Lacanian psychoanalysis in film studies. Second, the position taken vis-à-vis the male gaze in the essay is that the role of male gaze cannot be limited to the portrayal of women as an object to provide visual pleasure to men. The male gaze, as a cultural phenomenon, also determines the roles that are assigned to women either in society or in narratives – cinematic or literary. The male gaze also determines how men want to see the women and what role men want women to perform. Thus, women are seen either as goddesses or the fallen women. Those who do not conform to the norms of the society are labeled as witches and whores.

What Mulvey has suggested in relation to Hollywood popular cinema stands equally relevant for Hindi popular cinema too. The way women subject is captured with certain camera positions and angles to highlight certain parts of the female body and the role that is assigned to women in cinematic narratives justify the male gaze operating in Hindi cinema as well. In early popular Hindi cinema, women were supposed to play the archetypal role of Sati Savitri and Sati Sita[2]. Their characterization was less human and more linear in nature. But even while portraying the pure woman, their sensuality was explored and shown by the film maker. The camera angle and lighting are used in such a manner so as to enhance sexuality of female actors; or the woman was portraying the figure of suffering woman who does not compromise on her purity even in testing circumstances. Radha (Nargis) in *Mother India* (Mehboob Khan 1957), a remake of his own earlier film titled *Aurat* (1940), who raises her two sons despite all odds, trials and tribulations, Bharat's (Manoj Kumar) mother (Kamini Kaushal) in *Upkaar* (Manoj Kumar 1967) and Bharat's (Manoj Kumar) mother (Nirupa Roy) in *Kranti* (Manoj Kumar 1981) are a few to mention among a long list of the archetypal images of the suffering Indian mother who stands for values of sacrifice, struggle and chastity. In films like *Naya Daur* (B.R. Chopra 1957), there is a woman who works along with men on the road; but she does not disturb the apple cart. She works within the prevailing patriarchal social structure and is no threat to the established order. Another dimension of women that is generally portrayed in popular Hindi films is that of the 'vamp' – the fallen woman.

Despite dominance of voyeurism in Hindi cinema as well, there had been some moments in the history of Indian cinema when either the female body was not overly sexualized or the male gaze was inverted. To quote Gokulsing and Dissanayake:

> In artistic cinema, directors associated with the New Cinema sought to present a very different image of women – women

not as objects of male desire, but as products of diverse social formations and seeking to transcend their sordid circumstances. The directors are interested in capturing the plight of women as they are caught in the contradictory pulls of tradition and modernity, past and present, and individuality and community (80).

Parallel Cinema filmmakers Satyajit Ray, Shyam Benegal, Mrinal Sen, Ritwik Ghatak, Mani Kaul, Kumar Shahani, Adoor Gopalakrishnan have been interested in dealing with social political issues in their film than mere commodification of female body for providing scopophilic pleasure to the audience. Shyam Benegal's first feature film *Ankur* (1974) is known for its 'frank and incisive social criticism in its concern with inequity and injustice' (Hood 197). The film deals with the issues pertaining to women's condition in feudal social structure of Indian rural society, and so does *Nishant* (Shyam Benegal 1975) and *Mirch Masala* (Ketan Mehta 1987). Along with male directors there had been some female filmmakers in Indian parallel cinema such as Aparna Sen, Sai Paranjpaye, Kalpana Lajmi, and later Deepa Mehta and Meera Nair, the diaspora filmmakers, who have made women oriented films. Women filmmakers, especially from the Indian New Wave, were less interested in fetishizing female body for male voyeuristic pleasure; they were rather more interested in exploring areas pertaining to growth of woman's self, her gaining an identity or, sometimes, woman's status in Indian society. Sai Paranjpye's *Saaz* (1998) deals with two famous female singers of Bollywood, Lata Mangeshkar and Asha Bhonsle. Aparna Sen's *36 Chaowrangi Lane* (1981) deals with loneliness of Anglo-Indian school teacher; Vijaya Mehta's *Rao Sahib* (1986) explores the condition of women caught between tradition and modernity and Kalpana Lajmi's *Rudaali* (1992) focuses on the life and sufferings of a low-caste woman. Women filmmakers in these films are not interested in displaying female bodies as sexualized objects but are trying to explore socio-psycho dynamics of female subjectivity.

Deepa Mehta and Meera Nair are two filmmakers who have used sexuality as a tool to subvert the male gaze through their cinema. Deepa Mehta in *Fire* (1996) explores female sexuality as an assertion against patriarchal structure, which gives stereotypical functions and scope to male and female sexuality. In a social order that expects them to be silent recipients of love and sexuality, through their lesbian relationship, the narrative gives them a personal space against the male-dominated public space. By entering into a relationship, these two women gather strength to throw men out of their extremely personal space of sexuality. 'Fire explores ways out of the male gaze as the act of surveillance limits truth to the exclusion of the other. Multiform and reflexive ways of gazing structure the film, certain key moments represent a female-female gaze which challenges the look of surveillance' (Datta 81). Similarly, Meera Nair's *Kamasutra* (1996) explores the areas of sexuality both in men and women. Sangeeta Datta is of the opinion that Meera Nair in this film exoticises female sexuality to transform it into a consumable commodity in the cultural market of the West. On the contrary, in my opinion, Meera Nair has tried to make a point how female sexuality need not be subservient to men, a notion propagated by patriarchy; rather, women in the film are trained by a woman teacher (Rekha) on how to use their sexuality to rule over their men physically, sexually and emotionally, and subvert man's position of dominance through sexuality. Besides women filmmakers in the Indian New Wave and diaspora filmmakers, there is a long list of contemporary women filmmakers in India such as Anjali Menon, Nandita Dass, Shonali Bose, Preeti Aneja, Farah Khan, Pooja Bhatt, Zoya Akhtar and Meghna Gulzar.

Using journey as a motif, Zoya Akhtar's *Zindagi Na Milegi Dobara* (2011) deals with the growth and self discovery of three male characters – Kabir (Abhay Deol), Arjun (Hritik Roshan) and Imraan (Farhan Akhtar). On their bachelor trip to Spain, they encounter certain situations which help each one of them: first, to overcome their personal fears through sports; second, they discover themselves and understand each other through relationships. The rough corners between Arjun and Imraan are ironed out; they understand each other better and are able to forgive each other for something done in the past. Kabir, who is engaged to Natasha (Kalki Koechlin), discovers that he is not ready to marry Natasha as the bond between them was based on other than love; and third, Arjun discovers the value of love and how to seize the day through Laila. This film can be read in different ways. Through the theme of carpe-diem, this film makes a strong statement against increasing materialism in our present times. Laila reminds Arjun of transience of human life and teaches him the lesson to catch the present moment 'when the world is too much with us'[3] and suggests a way of life contrary to present-day increasing materialism[4].

If camera had earlier been identified with the male gaze, here the attempt is to explore if the present narrative offers us the female gaze. Though central to the narrative are three male characters, what deserves to be observed and studied is how these male characters have been portrayed. As mentioned earlier, the gaze is not limited to scopophilic pleasure, rather it also determines the role one is assigned in the society. The gaze is not meant to be understood only in terms of voyeurism. Voyeurism is central to it, but gaze has more cultural insinuations too. It also assigns the role that individuals play in the narrative or even in the society.

With this position, if the narrative of the film is studied, it is found that through characterization and portrayal of male and female bodies in the film, the presence of female gaze cannot be denied. It cannot be said with a certainty whether it was a deliberate choice on the part of the film maker or it was her instinctive choice. Whatever the case may be, psychoanalysis allows us to study both the slip of the tongue and consciously made statements, as the interplay between the latent content and the dormant content in any kind of discourse. If the choice is deliberate, it invites a political reading of the text; and in case it is instinctively done, it cannot escape the political reading. In both the cases, the presence of a female eye behind the camera makes a major shift in the narrative, which deserves to be taken a cognizance of.

The film begins with engagement party of Kabir and Natasha, which is actually his mother's birthday party but accidently turns into his engagement party too. In next two sequences, problems in the personal lives of other two male characters are introduced. Arjun has strained relationship with his ex-girlfriend, who is getting married to someone else. He is an ambitious man, who wants to earn money so that he can live comfortably after 40. Imraan's mother can read his intentions behind going to Spain as there lives his biological father. Imraan wants to meet him, which his mother is not comfortable with.

The presence of female gaze can be felt the way three male characters have been portrayed. Behind the seemingly realistic portrayal of young men's world and their fascination for certain things, the tone of each scene is ironic and critical of the things that men value and appreciate in their lives. While proposing marriage to Natasha, Kabir gave her every reason but for love. Arjun's relationship with his girlfriend gets strained because he gives more value to money than his relationship. He is working successfully with stock exchange in London and has bought a big spacious flat for himself, which he brags about in front of his friends in Spain. However, mise-en-scene, when Arjun comes to his flat, and listening to his friend's call on speaker, tells a different perspective. The room of the successful, rich young man is shown in different shades of black. He is wearing black and is surrounded by black leather furniture; even windows are also given the black frames. The world outside his room is bright, but inside it symbolizes gloom. In the scene, the space without seems to reflect the space within the character. Whenever Arjun is shot in close-ups, he is never shown happy. Intense gloom is always lurking large on his face. While his friends can enjoy themselves, he is wearing melancholic looks. During his stay in Spain, however, he reflects back on the circumstances that threw his relationship out of rhythm.

In the male-dominated cinema, women have rarely been given the role of an agency of change. In most of the narratives, women are recipient of the action. Frequent portrayal of women as mother or the next-door girl has denied women their own identity and status. They have always been shown subservient to men and recipient of men's acts of love, violence or hatred. But in the present film, the character of Laila is central to the narrative. Critically speaking, she becomes the most important character in the narrative, in spite of the fact, she does not occupy as much of the screen space as three male characters. Laila is a working and independent woman, who not only acts as their diving instructor, but also initiates Arjun to the path of how to live life. It is under her supervision that he graduates as a lover and acquires strength even to lose his job for the sake of love. In most of popular fairy tale like Hindi films, male character is shown to be 'superman'. In his larger than life portrayal, he not only performs extraordinary exploits but also has the strength to overcome all odds. But in this film, all the three male characters have their own fear rooted in their minds that they need to grow out of. They are shown in their natural human self with their idiosyncratic weaknesses. Arjun also needs help to overcome his fear of water. In his case, it is once again a woman who helps him overcome his fear and when it comes to expressing love, it is Laila who follows Arjun and kisses him first. Of all the characters, Laila has been shown as a composed and clear sighted person. She knows what she wants from life. She has the emotional stability and maturity not only to handle any situation, but also to guide others. She always seems to be on perfect terms with herself and understands psychology and problems of other male characters. She understands life so well that she becomes Arjun's *guru* to guide him on the path of life.

Another area where the presence of female gaze can be easily felt is the manner in which male and female 'bodies' have been shown on the screen. Laila (Katrina Kaif) is introduced at a beach where people have gathered to enjoy the sun. Imraan and Kabir decide to have a swim and Arjun, as usual, works on his laptop. People in the background are shown with fewer clothes, as expected on a beach; but Laila, who is enjoying herself all alone, is in full dress. When Laila is introduced, she just appears like an ordinary woman. There is no attempt to highlight her physical charms with the help of camera angles or lighting; nor does she emerge out of sea wearing a swimsuit and water dripping from body to make her look more attractive and suitable commodity for male voyeuristic gaze. Malvikka Sanghavvi is of the opinion that *Zindagi Na Milegi Dobara* 'is a textbook example of the female gaze: a big female star like Katrina's entrance, for instance, is not objectified in the way that we would have expected, with the camera clinging lasciviously to her curve'. The conscious choice by the filmmaker (a woman) not to show off female flesh on the screen, which had always been a practice with the male filmmakers, seems to be a plausible argument. On the contrary, on various occasions, male bodies have been offered as a spectacle for the female audience. Whether it is immediately after the deep sea diving sequence, Imraan's poetry is heard as voice over or it is tomatina festival, male well-shaped muscular bodies have been commodified and presented as spectacle for visual pleasure of the female audience. During the festival, when they were splashing tomatoes on each other and having a public shower in the open to wash themselves, not even a single attempt has been made to show female flesh. In the next scene, when Laila's friend is followed by Imraan in the bath room, the camera does not follow Imraan in the bathroom or when they are together or when Arjun and Laila are in the bed together. The filmmaker has, it seems, deliberately chosen not to display female bodies on any occasion. The male fantasy has been ruled out of the film by excluding prospective love making scene on this occasion. On the contrary, the film seems to encourage female audience identification with other female characters.

Laura Mulvey in the beginning of the essay wrote that she is making political use of psychoanalysis, her essay has been widely quoted and referred to in film studies. Laura also stated in the same essay that the female gaze is not possible in cinema. The mainstream cinema, whether Hollywood or Bollywood, has always portrayed stereotypical images of women. Going by the argument, if the entire institution of cinema is dominated by men, the question that bothers all critics is that – Is it possible to have a female's point of view in cinema? Is female gaze possible? Can there be a female auteur making cinematic statements from a female's position to subvert or invert patriarchy? Does a feminist film or film made by a female filmmaker have a different language from that of the male filmmakers? These questions sound very similar to the one that were once raised for female authors/writers as well. If the language (verbal language) is primarily phallagocentric, can we say that the language of cinema is phallgocentric too? Camera may not be a vertical object to become a crude and direct phallus symbol according to Freudian symbology; but, at the same time, camera can be seen as akin to a pen, a tool of asserting one's dominance in a society. Alexander Astruc, who in his essay 'the Birth of a New Avant-Garde: *la Caméra-stylo*' identified the camera with writer's pen, the metaphorical penis, said that it is through camera that directors inscribe their ideas into their films. If this be the case, then camera is not merely a mechanical instrument through which images are recorded. Camera signifies the director's vantage point that he/she takes while shooting film. Hypothetically speaking, if camera has been used to encourage voyeuristic gaze in the hands of male filmmakers, in the hands of female filmmakers or even male filmmakers, it can also become a tool to subvert the structured way of looking at reality. As discussed earlier in this chapter, this is what some female filmmakers and male filmmakers from Indian New Wave Cinema did.

'I want to paint with my phallus, too' says Van Gough to Gauguin in *The Way to Paradise* by Mario Vargas Llosa. The statement itself reflects a lot about the process that goes when a male artist expresses himself. To paint with phallus on the one hand expresses the passion with which an artist works; on the other hand, reference to phallus and its becoming central metaphor in creative expression also reflects that male artists have been expressing the domains of their sub-conscious through their art and writings, the phenomenon is also central to the voyeuristic gaze in art and literature. Can it be said that the most of the filmmaker shoot films with the phallus? If this be the case, is it possible for a female filmmaker to come out of the dominance of phallagocentric camera while shooting her film. Eve-Maria Jacobsson while discussing *Fatal Attraction* (Adrian Lyne 1987) tries to put forward the same issue. She argues that though the film seems to present before us the male gaze, but since the film was operating in a male dominated system, the filmmaker had to bring in certain changes so that the film could be accepted by a patriarchal society.

Even though in *Zindagi Da Milegi Dobara* male bodies have commodified the way female bodies were earlier commodified in other films, the echoes of patriarchy can be heard in the narrative. Though Laila is a central character and plays a very important role in the narrative, the narrative revolves around three male characters. It is the male characters who change, learn and grow. Two important female characters in the film – Laila and Natasha – have been given linear personalities. Laila's role is to help Arjun graduate as a lover and teach him the basic lesson of life, and Natasha, irrespective of earlier dreams, behaves like a conventional 'Indian woman', who is jealous and ready to sacrifice her personal ambitions for the sake of marriage. If Laila has been portrayed as the *guru* and as one who knows what she wants from her life and if she is a confident, perceptive and astute, what becomes important to note here is that Laila is not an Indian woman in the film. She is only half Indian. She lives in Europe and works independently. The values and worldview that she represents in the narrative cannot be called the world view of Indian woman in the film. Natasha, on the contrary, is portrayed as typical conventional Indian woman, though her characterization also suffers from the defect of linear and stereotypical characterization. Despite her modern outlook, high education and being a working woman, she portrays a stereotype of Indian woman. Two important female characters of the film have been perceived in a stereotypical manner and given almost linear characters. Both Natasha and Laila have fallen a prey to the sharp stereotypes of East and West. Despite being made by a female director, it is not a woman-centric film, the kind of centrality to women-oriented issues has been given by filmmakers like Aparna Sen, Deepa Mehta and Meera Nair. It seems Zoya Akhtar could only win one battle, but not the entire war. Keeping these ideas in mind, it would be interesting to relook at *Zindagi Na Milegi Dobara* from another critical vantage point to study what are the other elements in the narrative that ensure that phallagocentic camera asserts itself, with or without the knowledge of the filmmaker.

However, it cannot be denied that Mulvey's essay does give us insight into the 'male structure of looking' (Humm 14). The 'gaze' is the result of interaction between film language, spectatorship and viewing pleasure in a male-dominated system. There is a long list of critics who have tried to study the representation of women, identification, subjectivity in relation to film. What makes this long tradition of feminist theory, psychoanalysis and film studies important is the critical insight that critics have developed to study the hidden layers of a film text and also the social and cultural patterns that structure the film form as well.

Another dimension that was critically added to this study was to discuss the representation of lesbian and black women on screen. Laura Mulvey has been criticized on the grounds of having missed the perspective of lesbian and black women. E. Kaplan raised a pertinent question in relation to Mulvey's thesis in her essay that 'Is the gaze male?' Kaplan's further opens a train of questions pertaining to other possible positions or possible 'gazes'. Kaplan and Silverman both argued against Mulvey's essay saying that it is not necessary that male is always active and female is always passive. All such critical view points are well taken, but what goes to Mulvey's credit is the insight that she has provided regarding the cultural-political dimensions of cinema. Images are not innocent and apolitical. They are signifiers of the social, political and cultural milieu in which art is produced. Laura Mulvey's essay threw light on the issue that how patriarchy functions while any art form is being created. Even if voices against patriarchy were being raised when Mulvey published her essay, it cannot be said that the movement of feminism was able to obliterate patriarchy completely from the world. Patriarchy is still asserting itself in different ways. The difference that has been made is that women have also become or are becoming open about their sexuality. Deepa Mehta's *Fire* (1996) gave a very strong portrayal of female sexuality and lesbianism; something which was perhaps not possible in Indian cinema twenty years before the film was made. Though there was a suggestive lesbian scene in Kamal Amrohi's film *Razia Sultan* (1983), that is one of the few exceptions. At the same time, the song sequence is more suggestive than being open and bold. Deepa Mehta's film overtly challenged patriarchy. While speaking on the political and cultural potency of images, Spence, the British feminist photographer, asserts that photographic images should be 'studied as personification of a singular and individual eye but as a diversity of practices, institution and historical conjunctures in which the photographic text is produced and deployed' (Spence and Holland as quoted by Humm 9). Moreover, when Laura Mulvey's essay was published, it was rare that male body was commodified for providing scopophilic pleasure to the female maze. It does not mean that females were passive, but the system was so strongly male dominated that the female perspective was not included within the purview of artistic imagination. Media was largely catering to the fantasy of the male viewer. It is in recent times, in Indian context, that male bodies are being used in advertisements and films as commodity.

It is difficult to say if Zoya Akhtar has been able to subvert the patriarchal structures of mainstream Indian cinema. It would be too ambitious a claim to make. What cannot be denied is that she has successfully made an attempt to make a difference in the narrative. It would be too early and naïve to establish her as a feminist Auteur of Indian cinema, especially when the nature of Indian cinema has changed so radically in the last two decades. Moreover, it would not be theoretically appropriate to talk about auteur in the contemporary context, ever since Lacan and Discourse Studies in poststructuralist world auteurism has lost theoretical leverage it used to enjoy once. In her very short career of filmmaking, Zoya Akhtar has made only two films. In both the films, she has shown her penchant to look at the existing system with a keen critical eye. If images are signifiers of the social and cultural system which they originate from, *Zindagi Na Milegi Dobara* does hint towards the changing paradigm in Indian society and cinema. To justify this statement there is a long list of unconventional portrayal of women characters in recently made films such as *Ishqiya* (Abhiskhek Chaubey 2010), *7 Khoon Maaf* (Vishal Bhardwaj 2011), *Kahani* (Sujoy Ghosh 2012), *Dirty Picture* (Milan Luthria 2011) and so many others films that portray a very unconventional image of Indian woman, which should be studied after having removed the spectacles of narrow morality. On the other hand, it should also be noticed how in other films and also in advertisements, the muscular male bodies are being offered as a spectacle. The three Khans of Hindi cinema flaunting their six pack abs, fashion shows in which men walk on the ramp without vests and the use of well-shaped male bodies in advertisements all hint towards the shifting paradigm in Indian society too. Zoya Akhtar's film *Zindagi Na Milegi Dobara* deserves to be seen in this perspective.

Notes

1. For details, kindly see the works cited at the end.
2. The story of Sati Savitri is told in the Mahabharta. She was married to Satyavan. Owing to her dedication and devotion, she successfully snatches the life of her husband from the jaws of Yama, the god of death. Sati Sita

refers to the protagonist of the Ramayana, who was married to Lord Rama. Both epitomize the archetypal image of devoted and dedicated wife in Hindu mythology and epics.
3. The phrase has been borrowed from a poem by William Wordsworth with the same title.
4. The author is aware that looking at the frame of globalization, tourism and consumerism in which this film operates, it is difficult to make this claim that film makes an overt statement against materialism. In spite of such inherent paradoxes, the filmmaker has tried to make a statement against materialism, which does invite another reading of the film.

References

Berger, John. *Ways of Seeing*. London: BBC, 1972. Accessed at http://engl101-f12-lombardy.wikispaces.umb.edu/file/view/BergerWaysOfSeeing.pdf (accessed on 26 July 2012).

Datta, Sangeeta. 2000. 'Globalization and Representations of Women in Indian Cinema', *Social Scientist*, 28 (3/4): 71–82.

Gokulsing, K. Moti and Wimal Dissanayke. 1998. *Indian Popular Cinema- A Narrative of Cultural Change*. Hyderabad: Orient Longman.

Hood, John W. 2009.*The Essential Mystery*. Hyderabad: Orient BlackSwan.

Humm, Maggie. 1997. *Feminism and Film*. Edinburgh: Edinburgh University Press.

Kazmi, Fareed. 2010. *Sex in Cinema: A History of Female Sexuality in Indian Films*. New Delhi: Rupa Publications Pvt. Ltd.

Llosa, Vargas Mario. 2004.*The Way to Paradise*. (Trans. Natasha Wimmer). London: Faber and Faber.

Metz, Christian. 1999. 'From the Imaginary Signifier', in Leo Braudy and Marshall Cohen (eds), *Film Theory and Criticism: Introductory Readings*, pp. 800–17. New York: Oxford University Press.

Mulvey, Laura. 1999. 'Visual Pleasure and Narrative Cinema', in Leo Braudy and Marshall Cohen (eds), *Film Theory and Criticism: Introductory Readings*, pp. 833–44. New York: Oxford University Press.

Murphy, Paula. Psychoanalysis and Film Theory Part 1:'A New Kind of Mirror'. *Kritikos: an International and Interdisciplinary Journal of Postmodern Cultural Sound Text and Image* (vol. 2), 2005. Available at http://intertheory.org/psychoanalysis.htm (accessed on 26 July 2012).

Sangghavi, Malvika. 2011. 'No Sex Please'. *Business Standard*. http://www.business-standard.com/india/news/no-sex-please/444965/ (accessed on 26 July 2012).

Part V

CULTURAL IMAGINATION AND NEW IDENTITIES

15

NEW CULTURES OF REMEMBERING

The Indian memory project

Pramod K. Nayar

In 2010, Anusha Yadav, a photographer, book designer and archivist trained at the National Institute of Design, Ahmedabad, founded the Indian Memory Project, or IMP, an 'online, curated, visual and oral-history based archive that traces the personal history of the Indian Subcontinent, its people, cultures, professions, cities, development, traditions, circumstances and their consequences'.[1] It archives family and school photographs, letters, records and such, donated by individuals and families. The works are available in open access. The archives contain fascinating material of public personalities as well as complete unknowns. Thus, we have a portrait, by a family member, of Gyan Singh, the first Indian to lead an expedition to Mount Everest, or personal recollections from individuals such as Radha Nair's account of her parents. There are photographs of the pre-Independence era, from families now in Pakistan. There are of course other such archives. One of the best known is SPARROW (acronym for Sound and Picture Archives for Research on Women), run by the Mumbai-based Tamizh short story writer, C. S. Lakshmi (pen-name: Ambai), and which documents women's history in India.[2] Sparrow's motto is 'different ways of seeing, different ways of remembering, different ways of writing history'. So how does digitization of old family photographs, letters and voices contribute to 'our' history? What does Yadav mean when she proposes a 'personal history of the Indian Subcontinent'? What, in any case, is personal history of a country or culture? What does SPARROW mean when it calls for 'different' ways of remembering and writing history? This essay examines new cultures of memory that have been enabled as a result of the digital. It argues that IMP's digitization and collation of private memory produces a whole new way of thinking about citizenship and national/community identity itself. Acts of private remembering that 'go public', so to speak, in the form of IMP's public-private archives generate a 'memory citizenship'.

Digitization and private memory

The digital is not, it must be noted, a radical change in memory-making. Memory has always been mediated. There have been, since the prehistoric era, forms of memory-recording, and recall, such as artwork, textile weaves, photographs, letters, diaries, audio records, catalogues, songs, portraits and paintings, artefacts (material culture), motion pictures, monuments, inscriptions and now digital archives. Memory is therefore mediated through technologies of remembering. The digital is one more mnemonic medium, with a greater reach and a greater degree of access possible. But the IMP does something more with mediated memory, as I shall demonstrate.

Digitization and Open Source in IMP together constitute the publicness of private memory. As David Simpson (2006) and Andreas Huyssen (2003) have demonstrated in the case of post-9/11 USA, private grief gets subsumed into a national narrative of mourning, and indeed mourning or collective grief (where mourning is the *performance* of grief) becomes a marker of national identity, patriotism and even ethnicity.

Family albums, letters, love poems, and such constitute private memories of/for individuals and families. When these go online they suddenly acquire a public visibility. The fact that both Sparrow and IMP allow feedback and people generously post comments and responses (not just 'like' in the Facebook mode) means that private memory has been the cornerstone of a significant exercise: in sharing and networking of hitherto private memories. What used to be a technology of private viewing and recollection – the photograph – is now morphed as a technology of sharing when the same photograph gets uploaded into the digital medium.

What is also important to note in these new cultures of memory is that the digital domain allows a whole new shareable and transmissible *materiality* to memories. Family photographs, facsimiles of historical records, but also oral traditions and stories that IMP archives constitute a process of mobile memories where the digital format enables materiality to be shared and transmitted across zones, people and national borders. This suggests a transcultural memory itself, made possible by the digital domain. Memory theorist Astrid Erll (2011) has proposed that such a wandering of carriers, media, contents, forms and practices of memory constitutes a transcultural memory but one that is made possible through the *travels* of memory across spaces. Individuals who possess these memories in the IMP constitute embodiments of memories. When they move into the digital domain in the form of 'my grandfather's photograph' or 'our family's home', we can treat the individuals or families as carriers of memory, where the carrying is *not* restricted to a corporeality to IMP's digitization. In other words, I am proposing here that the carriers of memory that Erll sees as central to memory work are not only corporeal entities but also *virtual*.

Travelling memories involve the use of multiple media formats in the digital domain. Sound and visual texts remain the cornerstone of the IMP archives. Without the provision of transcoding (the process of shifting data from one form into another, such as the analog to the digital), carriers of memory would not acquire the reach we see here. Yet, what is interesting in these new cultures of memory is that digitization calls attention to the materiality of memories when the IMP archive shows us scanned originals of letters, passports, photographs, and such. It is brought home to us in the virtual that somewhere the fragile, musty and brittle material paper actually exists. I, therefore, do not see the new cultures of memory exemplified in IMP as doing away with the material but rather as emphasizing the materiality, especially the mortality of materiality. It is in the interstices of the faded, dog-eared, blurred, and yellowed photographs or papers that I recognize the mortality of both the people therein 'captured' and the material that seeks to immortalize them.

From personal to cultural memory

The visuals and voices not only become 'public', but it transforms the way we as individuals come to our 'own' family or personal history when we see these responses. People writing in with more photographs and links, information and recollections that link with our own, means that we view our grandparents' photographs and lives differently – not simply as 'my' grandparents alone but as people who shared lives, spaces and belief systems with several *others*. It suddenly strikes me that the person I saw only in terms of 'my' or at the most 'my family' is one of the many, located amongst others. This shifts, I propose, the very nature of our perceptions of these individuals. The multiple formats of the digital domain mediate my experience of these people in the archive. To phrase it differently, our minds actualize the memories we see on IMP.

Mnemonic forms – symbols, icons – that enable repetition across contexts constitute an important aspect of travelling memory (Erll 2011). What IMP does is to offer the space of the digital as the space of such repetition across multiple contexts. With no border restrictions, passports or territoriality, the digital archive of memories is at once untethered and local, global and personal. Icons such as the freedom movement or school buildings (which seem to be a particular favourite among IMP contributors) are repeated from Old Delhi to 19th-century Madras, from pre-Independence days to the present. Ferguson College, Madras Christian College, Victoria Terminus and other such icons serve as mnemonic forms for digital recall on the IMP. But this is not all.

All personal memory morphs into cultural memory. Cultural memory, as Marita Sturken defines it, is a

> [f]ield of cultural negotiation through which different stories vie for a place in history . . . a field of contested meanings in which [people] interact with cultural elements to produce concepts of the nation, particularly in events of trauma, where both the structures and the fractures of a culture are exposed.
> (1997: 1–3)

Cultural memory is usually associated with cultural objects that exist outside formal – official, governmental, corporatized – historical accounts and histories, mainly within private collections and objects. Experiences of schooling, growing up, clothing trends that we see shared in the IMP collections means that these experiences, although not always the same or even remembered the same way, now contribute to our overall sense of a period, fashion, belief, practice, or custom. This is the intertwining of individual and collective memory that we see in IMP's archives. We imagine eras and belief systems that exist outside our immediate perceptions or practices through these collections, drawing links, noting parallels and forging alliances.

This argument would immediately encounter the opposing one that such individual or familial memories do not constitute History (the upper case is important, for it signifies official history). However, there is no one way of 'doing' history. History often consists of conflicted stories about the same event. Personal and cultural memories constitute two such modes of remembering the events that might support or subvert the officially sanctioned memory of the same. For families from the pre-Independence days, the Raj meant something very different, and these memories (which we can see in several photographs from IMP) might be at odds with the official narrative of racial suppression and subjugation. What an online archive like IMP does is to make these conflicting narratives part of a wide open database of possible interpretations. History after SPARROW and IMP must always be seen as a set of contested and multiple interpretations to which – and this is important – all of us can contribute minus official sanction. A miniscule amount of agency and freedom, thus, comes to the common reader through such digital projects as IMP. I see IMP and its contributors as people who are not mere consumers of knowledge handed down but as producers of knowledge. They contribute to a more open, less censored, knowledge base. In the new cultures of memory this act of archiving memories produces a whole new ethos, belonging and identity, to which I now turn.

Memory citizenship

Michael Rothberg and Yasmin Yildiz (2011) propose that memory has often functioned as 'ethnic property'. Migrant archives of memory, argue Rothberg and Yildiz, are multidirectional, where the migrants engage with the past and with a history and memory of which they are ostensibly not a part of. The archive of trauma is read from different vantage points, especially by those who are 'migrants', such as second-generation family members but also general visitors to the IMP website such as myself, to that archive. IMP makes it possible for all and sundry to become migrants to the memories of, say, pre-Independence India.

To participate in a memory project such as the IMP from different corners of the world is to affect a community belonging. Thus, Radha Nair's account of her family is situated, in this digital space, alongside that of Laxmi Murty, Anupam Mukerji, Sawant Singh, Raj Rajendra Singh, Paritosh Pathak and others. These contributors are geographically diffused in terms of current location: Pune, Bengaluru, Mumbai, and the USA, among others. It is in the space of the digital archive that a new geography of affinity is forged, linked by the theme of 'education' (this is the tag for a whole bunch of photographic records in this database). IMP pulls individuals into the archive and we can, if we wish, become cultural insiders, because we are contributors, to local, community or national history. Since much of the online world of this kind (Flickr, for example) thrives on non-commercial sharing and participation we can envisage an entire community of 'Indian historians' represented in IMP. Communities of interest, such as those represented in IMP, are built through a sharing of virtual territory (recalling the territorial roots of community) but also through the cultural *work* we see embodied in the amount of information people collate and put online. What I am suggesting as 'cultural work' is the leisurely, non-commercial and participatory 'work' of compilation and uploading enabled by digital technologies. It is labour, but of the 'immaterial' kind (that is, wageless), founded on a belief in sharing and networking. Payment is not expected except in terms of 'likes' and feedback. Communities of interest that we see in the huge responses and participation in IMP and SPARROW constitute a 'fun-way' of doing history where my grandpa's photograph connects me to your family and, in incremental fashion, enables both me and you to come to a shared understanding of the times they lived in. Take a look at how this cultural work is described in the IMP:

> Please do ensure you know of the people in the photograph, their professions, about their lives, the location, the approximate year, even if not exact. Asking around with relatives and friends can always offer up new information. Photographs could be of your parents, relatives, friends, associates, extended family, grandparents and/or higher in ancestry . . .

For Photographs Names, Approximate/Exact year the image was taken, location in picture, profession, alternate professions, religion (if not obvious) and whatever other history/and details of their lives you'd like to add.

These suggestions tell us not only about how the cultural work is to be undertaken but also about the making of histories. First, these do not seek or claim verifiable, exact historical details. Like memory, which is notoriously selective and random, the chronicles we see on IMP are approximate, inexact and often random. Second, these do not ask for extensive research or definite connections. All the IMP expects is that the contributor should see *some* significance. The onus here is on the significance of the particular letter or visual to the family and by extension to other participants in the project. Thus, the IMP shifts the writing of history *away* from the historically significant incident or event to personally significant events and people. 'Small histories', as we can think of these materials on the IMP database, is the historicizing of local and personal stories. Third, many of the materials are accompanied by emotional and personal write-ups, a far cry, as we know, from the dry-as-dust History we read in books and official records. This, I suggest, is a major shift in the conceptualization of history itself: history is made of emotionally significant events and people who, perhaps, do not contribute to or appear in 'national histories', but have informed lives somewhere. Fourth, IMP does not suggest this writing of emotionally relevant histories that then accrete into a larger history as work. Cultural work is the participatory work performed by those who find meaning outside the frames of reference of standard history writing (which involves research, peer review, acceptance, publication and the like).

The cultural insiderness that this sharing produces offers a whole new way of perceiving each other and ourselves. Cultural insiderness is the making of a contributory history of ourselves, sharing borders, lives and belief systems with a larger community of interest. When IMP places a condition for the selection of contributions it gestures at precisely this cultural insiderness – 'The Photographs/Letters can be from anywhere in the world, as long as it has a connection to the people and/or places in South Asian Indian Subcontinent.'

This tenuous linkage to the South Asian Indian Subcontinent offers us a map of connections outside the national histories of people, families and communities. The connection itself is often nebulous, vague and primarily personal since the materials, as noted earlier, are sent in because they hold emotional significance for the contributors. Cultural insiderness is the forging of such connections of memory work.

I want to conclude by proposing something even more radical. With the cultural insiderness of the participants as they bring to IMP their personal records and data, there is a whole new sense of belonging that develops. I have already suggested that communities of interest constitute a new geography. I now want to propose that participants in the IMP are engaged in 'memory citizenship' (Rothberg and Yildiz 2011). Performances of memory are also acts of citizenship, acts that are beyond the norms of citizenship and regardless of formal citizenship status. They define new ways of belonging. In a globalized world, to participate in a project, such as the IMP, is to simultaneously be disaggregated from roots and origins in the physical sense but belong in the affective, mnemomic and virtual sense. Memory citizenship is the sense of belonging emerging from this sense of emotional recall of, and emotional response to, such materials as we have discussed above. The memory citizenship of the IMP is not merely tokenist or nominal. The memories produce emotions, as we can see from the responses on the website, and these make memories *material*. Memory citizenship undeniably offers a sense of belonging and attachment. Whether these are Non-Resident Indians or resident ones, it is memory citizenship that brings them together in their very acts of remembering. Acts of remembering, in my reading, transform into acts of solidarity.

The Indian Memory Project is a radical decentering of history where remembering constitutes acts of history-writing. In the age of globalization, the digital is what facilitates the memory citizenship of people. Remembering, mediated thus, is no less real. When we share personal memories we create cultural memory. And when we engage with the distant, unknown others in the space of the other, we produce a post-national, a geographical memory citizenship. New cultures of memory are new ways of belonging.

Notes

1. For more details, see http://www.indianmemoryproject.com/about/, accessed on 14 November 2014.
2. For more details, see http://www.sparrowonline.org/, accessed on 14 November 2014.

References

Erll, Astrid. 2011. 'Whither Memory Studies', *Parallax*, 17(4): 4–18.

Huyssens, Andreas. 2003. *Present Pasts: Urban Palimpsests and the Politics of Memory*. Stanford: Stanford UniversityPress.

Rothberg, Michael and Yasmin Yildiz. 2011. 'Memory Citizenship: Migrant Archives of Holocaust Remembrance in Contemporary Germany', *Parallax*, 17(4): 32–48.

Simpson, David. 2006. *9/11: The Culture of Commemoration*. Chicago and London: Chicago University Press.

Sturken, Marita. 1997. *Tangled Memories: The Vietnam War, the AIDS Epidemic, and the Politics of Remembering*. Berkeley: University of California Press.

16

ROMANTIC IMAGINATION
Science and empire in the works of Amitav Ghosh

Sakoon N. Singh

J. P. S. Uberoi in *The Other Mind of Europe: Goethe as a Scientist* (1984) begins with the contention that we must recognize non-standard methods of the organization of knowledge 'in the sciences and the arts, within and without the university, and other principles of the relation of knowledge to life whether European or non- European'. He further elaborates that 'this in turn requires independent studies of the development of modern European culture, not only in its relation to India and Asia during the modern colonial periods but also in relation to itself'. (Uberoi 1984: 9) It seems Ghosh had similar perceptiveness while working on the two titles of his Ibis trilogy. Exuding much more than a simple postcolonial anxiety to prove the damages of import of Western science to India, these two books of the proposed trilogy can only be understood if they are placed in the larger culture of scientific knowledge existing in Europe at this time. It is important to problematize the culture of knowledge that was coming to India here with the arrival of the Western powers. This phase of colonial expansion was coinciding with the progress of science both as technology and discipline in fascinating ways. Ghosh shows us through these works, layers of differing approaches to Western science and knowledge as it came to the Indian shores.

Through his two books of the Ibis trilogy, *Sea of Poppies* (2008) and *River of Smoke* (2011), he builds up situations and characters that suggest the existence of two strains in the building up of science as a discipline in those times. The Utilitarian tendencies were pushing scientific knowledge in the direction of empire building, whereas a more subtle but equally important Romantic strain was defining science in the sense of demystifying nature without compromising the essential connect between nature and man. Its view of nature as a seamless flow of energy that conjoins man, flora and fauna became critical of the mechanistic worldview being promulgated by the ascending Newtonian brand of science. The Romantics felt that the Enlightenment emphasis on rational thought through deductive reasoning and mathematization of natural philosophy had created an approach to science that attempted to control rather than to peacefully co-exist with nature. According to the philosophies of Enlightenment, the path to complete knowledge required a dissection of information on any given subject and a division of knowledge into categories and sub-categories, known as reductionism. There was a sanguine belief in man's intellectual prowess that could understand every aspect of nature. The Romantics, on the other hand, focused on processes rather than functions, whole rather than parts. The Romantic Movement, which was initially a reaction to the devastation that Industrial Revolution had incurred on the fabric of the British society, was thus a critique of the use of science in a way that had allowed for glaring inequities, child labour, poverty and squalor.

According to Pratik Chakarvarty, it was industrialization in the 19th century which actively polarized the intelligentsia of Europe into scientific technical rationalists and cultural romanticists or *geistewissenschaften* (2004: 205) He further points out that Romanticism as a philosophy was emancipatory, non-conformist, individualistic as well as essentialist. It insisted on the centrality of agency, human research for individual and cultural originality, imagination and spirit. He adds that there remained in Europe a group of philosophers and scientists who did not believe in the mechanistic view of science. In the decades preceding and following 1800, there existed in Germany a science related to Romanticism called *Naturphilosophie* that

> did not reject empiricism but sought to integrate the details contained in eighteenth century encyclopaedias of natural history into a larger whole, reflecting the unity of nature. Practitioners of this new kind of science refused to submit to the mechanistic interpretation of the world and saw the order of nature as related to the hierarchy and wholeness characterizing traditional cosmology. (ibid.)

Goethe (1749–1832),[1] the German poet-philosopher and scientist, endorsed the Romantic worldview and like Uberoi contends, he felt that 'Science is not only a model of reality but simultaneously also a model of our human knowledge of it.' (Uberoi 1984: 23) Goethe in his scientific methods went neither by induction nor by deduction but by what is now referred to as participant-observer method '. . . i.e. regarding himself and nature as forming a single whole, whose two parts can enjoy a semiological reciprocity of perspective' (ibid.). In his study of Botany, Goethe insisted on the use of the system of metamorphosis, which he felt was the key to the whole alphabet of nature. He preferred *Bildung* in the sense to build and change versus *Gestalt*, to set, to place or put, since this assumes that whatever forms a whole is made of is cut off and fixed in character (ibid.: 30). In the following lines, his philosophy on nature becomes clear:

> Nature! . . . she is creating new forms eternally.
> Life is her finest invention,. . . her masterstroke, death.
> She has separated her creations by cleavages, yet in them is the urge to
> draw close . . . She is complete, yet ever unfinished (ibid.)

This conflict between the two 'schools' of science in Europe is captured in Amitav Ghosh's *Sea of Poppies* and *River of Smoke*, with characters drawn on either side of the divide. His attempt in problematizing Western science is not merely to sensitize us to the existing varieties of science but also to show that science was a powerful influence in the 19th Century imperial politics. Since science was not a phenomenon limited to the confines of a laboratory, but had implications on the culture and vision of the ordinary people, it becomes imperative that we go back to the details of what this culture meant for the colonial project.

The history of the Romantic Movement is canonical enough for any student of English Literature; however, what is lesser known is the nature of what has been previously mentioned as 'creative production.' This category included not only Romantic poetry which hit a high point with the influence of the high priests of Romanticism but permeated into nature study, astronomy, chemistry, all of which were fast evolving into the form we know them today. The terms science and poetry were not as mutually exclusive as we know them today and as Richard Holmes says in his fascinating study of Romantic science *The Age of Wonder: How the Romantic Generation Discovered the Beauty and Terror of Science* (2008): 'In effect, there was Romantic science in the same sense that there is Romantic poetry and often for the same enduring reasons' (Holmes 2008: xvi). While nature was at the very heart of the Romantic poetic imagination, it was no less so for the men and women of science at this time. There was a lively inspirational exchange between poetry and science, the two fields traversing each other rather unapologetically. Sherwood elaborates about this tendency in the context of Wordsworth and elaborates thus:

> twin birth of nature and human soul, the Divine expressing alike in the beauty of natural things and in the instinct in man that apprehends this beauty; hence the hidden correspondence, the inner sympathies, the mystical meanings of natural things. These ideas come to exquisite flower in Wordsworth, who had a living perception of corresponding life in primrose and daffodil, linnet, glow-worm and overshadowing tree. (1934: 169)

'Wordsworth was passionately absorbed in nature. It has been said of Spinoza, that he was drunk with God. It is equally true of Wordsworth that he was drunk with nature' (Whitehead 1928: 103). According to Whitehead, Wordsworth did not hide his dislike of mechanistic science which was ascending at this time. His phrase 'We murder to dissect' succinctly sums up his broader attitude towards science divorced from nature. He felt that science imposes a fairly strained and paradoxical view of nature on our thoughts. His own philosophy towards nature was one that embodied divine energy which was not only to be observed but felt and also partaken of. The *Hand of God* was the dominant metaphor of the times, Nature was its manifestation and its close observation was the calling of both poetry and science. William Paley's *Natural Theology* (1802) was a strong argument in favour of design in nature as 'evidence of God's direct intervention in earthly affairs.' Works such as these marvelled upon the detailed care bestowed by the creator on the most minute of creatures and the 'manifold ways in which the organisms were adapted to their environment' (Jones and Cohen 1963: 15). These arguments reached their height with the publication of Bridgewater Treatises of the 1830s, commissioned by Francis Henry, the Earl of Bridgewater, who directed the Royal Society to publish works on the

> power, wisdom, goodness of God, as manifested in the creation: illustrating such works by all reasonable arguments, as for instance the variety and formation of God's creatures

in the animal, vegetable and mineral kingdoms, the effect of digestion and thereby conversion: the construction of the hand of man and the infinite variety of other arguments: as also by discoveries ancient and modern in arts, sciences and the whole extent of literature. (ibid.: 37)

Yet another dimension to this reigning sentiment was duly added with the arrival of exploratory voyages and colonization. In this context, Holmes argues that 'the idea of an exploratory voyage, often lonely and perilous is in one form or the other a defining metaphor of Romantic science' (2008: xvi). The realm of literature too was mirroring these voyages being undertaken on the strength of improving seafaring and navigational skills and the quest for discovering far flung lands. *The Rime of the Ancient Mariner* (1834), with the sea voyage over perilous seas and the mariner's fear of creatures known and unknown, natural and supernatural, quite captures the spirit of these times. In the poem, the mariner kills an albatross and invites a curse to fall upon his mates and vessel. The mariner lives to see the frightening consequences of this curse, and one by one, his mates die. At this point, he sees a pale woman '. . . her lips were red, her looks were free, her locks were yellow as gold . . . the night-mare Life-in-Death was she . . .' (Coleridge 1834: 190–93) who is death herself and feels exhausted and beaten. He unwittingly blesses the sea creatures that he sees shining in the moonlight... 'a spring of love gushed from my heart and I blessed them unaware' (ibid.: 284–85). Before he knows it, the curse of the dead albatross is reversed owing to his praise of nature and his crew members come back to life again. The turning point in his journey is his unwitting blessing of sea animals and thus his voyage comes to a successful end. The poem is told as a story by the presently old mariner, much in the vein of the yarn spun by sailors for the benefit of listeners in a wayside inn. There is a 'moral' to the story too, which is stated by the mariner as follows:

> He Prayeth well, who loveth well
> Both man and bird and beast.
>
> He prayeth best, who loveth best
> All things both great and small;
> For the dear God who loveth us,
> He made and loveth all. (ibid.: 612–17)

The poem brings together two powerful tropes of the Romantic imagination: the exploratory voyage to unknown lands and second, the acknowledgement of nature's superior power over man. The poem further highlights the manifestation of the spirit of God through the most infinitesimal creature, the careful observation of which will help us get closer to God. The poem, which is considered one of the greatest by Coleridge, is very useful in discussing the nature of Romantic imagination as it touched all spheres of existence and became a link between science and poetry. The exploratory voyages of this time had both imperial as well as scientific purposes. These naval expeditions from Europe in the search of unexplored lands, therefore, invariably began with the convention of having botanists and zoologists on board. So whether it was Joseph Banks on board the *Endeavour* or Darwin on board the *Beagle*, they were all willy-nilly part of the imperial expeditions in search for new lands.

By the middle of the 19th century, however, romantic science was dubbed as mere metaphysics and left there. This time combined with the coming of Darwin's *The Origins of Species* (1859), the fierce economics of laissez-faire, and aggressive imperialistic activity which changed the tenor of these times from cooperation to one of competition. With discoveries in Geology and Darwin's evolutionary thesis, the Biblical account of genesis of man began to be discredited. The idea of God's design in nature came to be replaced by the concept of evolution. This was the deep religious dilemma in Victorian times, where science in its ascending march was beginning to call into question the very fundamentals society had hitherto clung to. Darwin's book was preceded by discoveries in geology where the idea of 'deep space and time' was beginning to replace the Biblical accounts of time. Writing almost thirty years before the momentous publication of Darwin's thesis, in the spring of 1829 Thomas Carlyle in his influential tract *Sign of the Times* claimed the demise of Romanticism and the beginning of the 'Age of Machinery.' In this essay he attacked the dehumanizing effects of utilitarianism, statistics and the science of mechanics and opposed the world of sciences to that of art, poetry and religion. The chasm between the 'two worlds' was beginning to be felt. He claimed that the contemporary scientists were fast losing touch with nature and were practicing a more derivative science: 'Scientists now stand behind whole batteries of retorts, digestives and galvanic piles and interrogate nature, who shows no haste to answer' (Holmes 2003: 436).

By the turn of the century, the aim of biological sciences was not to catalogue dead animals and plants but to understand the inner workings of living, breathing bodies. This break from the past symbolized a major move away from observational natural history towards a more experimental, laboratory-based form of investigation. What earlier went under the nomenclature of natural history branched out into more specialized fields and most of these fields came to be practiced indoors under controlled laboratory conditions. Romanticism became 'the other mind of Europe' then on; however, it kept coming back as a strain in the history of the world every now and then. It is also useful to talk about Romanticism as perhaps the first organized reaction from within the European society towards the ills of using science to create sweeping inequalities. Europe was set to perpetuate these inequalities in the lands it annexed.

Empire and the march of botany

All thy works praise thee, O Lord!
— Inscription on the title page of Roxburgh's
Flora Indica (1832)

In Ghosh's *Ibis trilogy* the tension between these two tendencies is well illustrated through the fledgling science of botany. According to Janet Browne, 'much neglected by historians, botany during the 19th century was the most significant science of the day, creating and destroying colonial cash crops according to Government policy and building the economic prosperity of a nation' (2006: 91–92). The discipline had undergone many changes in its growth and outlook in the early part of the 19th century and the brush with the imperial enterprise changed its very nature. From the Romantic worldview which ascribed to botany the pietism required in unveiling the mysteries of nature representing the 'hand of God', it had travelled to unknown lands where nature became an exploitable entity in search for greater profits. While for the Romantics, botany was a way of unveiling the hidden secrets of nature as manifested in the awe-inspiring bounty of plants, for the Utilitarians, with the ascending needs of colonialism and trade, it was plants which would be source of wealth and riches to the country who would first unlock the potential hidden within the secrets of plant life.

In this context, *Sea of Poppies* highlights the immoral propagation of opium in India and its sale in Chinese markets. As far as trade with China was concerned, the British were losing out because of an imbalance; China was remitting consignment after consignment of Chinese tea, silk and porcelain and draining the British of their bullion. In the latter half of the 18th century, Britain was importing large quantities of tea from China that was to be paid for in bullion. The British are known to have imported expertise for the purpose by bringing in several Chinese farmers in order to grow tea successfully in India. Eventually they identified a patch of land between Bengal and Bhutan where they successfully propagated many varieties of tea.

However, with the production of opium, the trade tilted in the favour of the British and the ordinary Chinese were in grips of a debased addiction to opium. The Indian angle in this tripartite model of trade was the forced cultivation of poppy on Indian farmers and then their subsequent role as labourers in the *carcannas*[2] set up for opium refinement. Ghosh highlights this practice extensively in *Sea of Poppies*. While tea, indigo, jute and other items were used profitably by the British, Ghosh's choice of the opium plant symbolizes the worst of this utilitarian tendency that accompanied the *Laissez-Faire* at this point.

According to David Arnold, botany was a discipline in which the gulf between Western science and Indian knowledge can be found. With the introduction of Linnaean taxonomy, the field had 'left Europe drowning in plant novelties. . .trying to keep track of different species and to establish a common system of plant identification' (Arnold 2000: 38). Carl Linnaeus (1707–78), a Swedish naturalist, had earlier introduced the binomial nomenclature, a taxonomic system whereby every known species in the plant and animal world would be recorded under a binomial system, identifying them according to their reproductive system and re-cataloguing them according to genus, species and family. These two facts together, first, the availability of a boundless 'brave new world' and, second, the race to get the distinct flora and fauna of these lands catalogued, sparked off a competition amongst the continental biologists to source every known plant and animal and to get it catalogued as per Linnaean taxonomy. Pierre Lambert, in *Sea of Poppies*, the Assistant Superintendent of the Calcutta Botanical Gardens, importantly is also a man who is considered by the British society in Calcutta as being a bit of an eccentric and really outside the circles of the European gentry. He is in India to taxonomically arrange the flora of India according to the Linnaean system; however, he is equally keen on retaining the indigenous Bengali as well as Sanskrit names.[3] For this purpose, he duly engages the services of a learned *munshi* to help him curate the collection. His insistence on using the Indian appellations is in the Romantic tradition which believed in the idea of cultural knowledge. His daughter, Paulette, under his tutelage is helping him combine his book *Materia Medica*. He provides her a rigorous grounding in the fundamentals of the science giving her hands on experience. She acquires an intimate understanding of plants over time and ultimately steers into the direction of following a vocation of botany. When she is offered a job on board *The Redruth* by her father's friend Fitcher, she closely examines the architecture of the vessel. Since it is mainly fitted to transport Fitcher's collection of plants in Wardian cases[4] to be traded and exchanged across continents, all its functions are well suited to ensure minimum damage to the collection. Also Fitcher's handiwork had been driven by motives of thrift and profit. Her consignments required no 'outlay of capital, no tying up of finances and yet the returns they offered were potentially astronomical. . . at the same time her goods were such as to be proof against both pilferage and piracy, their true value being unknown to but a few' (Ghosh 2011: 77) . . . (*The Redruth*) was something much plainer: the handiwork of a diligent nurseryman – not a man who was a speculative thinker but rather a practical solver of problems, someone who looked upon nature as an assortment of puzzles, many of which, if properly solved, could provide rich sources of profit.' (ibid.: 78). Fitcher belonged to a milieu wherein Botany as a science and as a commercially viable enterprise was ascending in Europe.

As a young man, Fitcher had enjoyed the patronage of none other than Joseph Banks himself, who had by this time become something of an institution. He had risen as the President of the Royal Society, a coveted post which Newton had held in the past, and became the Director of the Kew Gardens. These Botanical Gardens in London were in their infancy at this time and Banks extended his unflinching patronage towards their growth. Banks ably discharged this mission he was entrusted with and established his reputation amongst the leading horticulturists and botanists. In so doing Kew became a living tribute to the increasing navigational skills of Britain. These plants were a proof of the expeditions that were yielding enormous wealth. Banks interviews young Fitcher for the job of accompanying an expedition to China in search of some elusive varieties as the region was poorly represented 'a country singularly blessed in its botanical riches being endowed not only with some of the most beautiful and medicinally useful plants in existence but also with many that were of immense commercial value' (Ghosh 2011: 101). Paulette, however, has been reared on very different ideas about nature:

> This cast of mind was totally novel to Paulette. To her father, who had taught her what she knew of Botany, the love of nature had been a kind of religion, a form of spiritual striving: he had believed that in trying to comprehend the inner vitality of each species human beings could transcend the mundane and its artificial divisions. If Botany was the scripture of this religion, then horticulture was its form of worship: tending a garden was for Pierre Lambert, no mere matter of planting seeds and pruning branches-it was a spiritual discipline, a means of communicating with forms of life that are essentially mute and could be understood only through a careful study of their own modes of expression- the language of efflorescence, growth and decay: only thus he had taught Paulette, could human beings apprehend the vital energies that constitute the spirit of the earth. (ibid.: 78–79)

Pierre Lambert is certainly a Romantic and in his attitude poles apart from the other European figures in the trilogy. Evocative of the Romantic tradition, he embraces a 'theory of education' which he uses to rear his daughter, Paulette:

> Paulette heard his words as though they were spoken by her father in French . . . a child of nature, that is what she is, my daughter Paulette. As you know I have educated her myself, in the innocent tranquility of the Botanical Gardens. She has had no teacher other than myself, and has never worshipped at any altar except that of Nature; the trees have been her Scripture and the Earth, her Revelation. She has not known anything but Love, Equality and Freedom: I have raised her to revel in that state of liberty that is Nature itself. If she remains here, in the colonies, most particularly in the city like this, where Europe hides its shame and greed, all that awaits her is degradation: the whites of this town will tear her apart, like vultures and foxes, fighting over a corpse. She will be an innocent thrown before the money-changers who pass them off like men of God. (ibid.: 137)

In addition to this, she was an assistant to her father in labelling his collection of plants at the Botanical Garden. To discharge her duties well she was made to learn not only Latin and French but also Sanskrit and Bengali from the *munshis* employed by her father.

In this is apparent the two attitudes prevalent in these times towards the study of Botany. Whereas Paulette represents the best of Romantic tradition which her father has bequeathed to her, Fitcher represents the new fangled utilitarian creed which is asserting itself in these times. Son of a green grocer hawker, he had been pushed into earning for himself as a young boy. He had come to the attention of the parish doctor, who introduced him to 'botanizing' which improved as time went by. He rose in this profession and established the Penrose Nurseries as a major force in the world of British horticulture. He had come at a level when he was financing many exploratory voyages of many collectors. He eventually commissioned the making of the *Redruth*, named after her wife's birthplace, to be able to personally navigate to China in search of plants.

Through these books Ghosh has tried to retrieve the voice of the Romantics as they tried to influence the direction of science as it was developing in these times. Their influence gradually declined but in them one can see the critique of the mechanistic progress that Europe first began to see in its own lands and then propagated in lands overseas.

Notes

1. Another famous work by Goethe is *Treatise on Colour* (1810). This work, considered an important text for German *Naturphilosophie*, is conceived on very different lines from the principles of mechanistic science. According to him, perception of colour is a complex phenomenon involving the physical as well as psychological aspects. The Newtonian science, on the other hand, considered colour to be a phenomenon based on wavelength alone.
2. Ghosh's portrayal of the opium factory in *The Sea of Poppies* was based on a detailed account of an opium factory written by a Scotsman who was the head of one such factory and curiously the account was meant to be used as a tourist guide. Ghosh sets this factory as a grand structure and in its impermeability, almost like a fort. The grandness of colonial structures has a lot to do with power projection and it was precisely this purpose to which it was put. The awe-inspiring *carcanna* had many levels like concentric circles, the innermost circle preserving the end product in specially designed vaults. The shadowy presence of the waif thin, dark labourers going about their work in a mechanical fashion is a foil to the severe portly white superintendents lording them over (Interview with Sheela Reddy. 2008. 'The Ghazipur and Patna opium factories together produced the wealth of Britain', *The Outlook*. 26 May).

3. William Jones, the founder of the Asiatic Society, was of the opinion that the classical language Sanskrit should be used for a deeper understanding of the medicinal value of plants inscribed in the ancient texts. It is romantic essentialism that posits a great deal of importance in specific languages as being repositories of cultural knowledge. For Sanskrit would be of help to botanists to not only cull out the hidden knowledge from the ancient Sanskrit texts but also because the romantics believed in original essence of cultural knowledge. Jones believed in the essentialist spirit of ancient India which could only be approached through its own languages. He lamented the fact that many continental botanists like Van Rheede and William Roxburgh had not bothered to go back to the Indian languages to ground their knowledge of Indian flora. Pierre Lambert, by employing the services of a munshi is trying to catalogue Indian plants according to the Ancient Indian texts, in the tradition set by Jones rather than other continental scientists. This aspect of Jone's orientation is discussed by Zaheer Baber in *The Science of Empire: Scientific Knowledge, Civilization and Colonial Rule in India*. Albany: State University of New York Press, 1996.
4. Wardian Cases, 'these were new inventions: glass-fronted boxes with adjustable sides, they were in effect miniature glass houses. They had revolutionized the business of transporting plants across the seas, making it much easier and safer; the Redruth had scores of them on board, securely tied down with cables and ropes' (Ghosh 2011: 76).

References

Ghosh, Amitav. 2011. *The River of Smoke*. New Delhi: Penguin.
———. 2008. *Sea of Poppies*. New Delhi: Penguin.
Andrew C.F. David, 'Cook, James (1728–1779)', Oxford Dictionary of National Biography, Oxford University Press, 2004; first published 2004; online edition, Jan 2008. http://dx.doi.org/10.1093/ref:odnb/6140
Adas, Michael.1989. *Machines as the Measure of Man: Science, Technology and Ideology of Western Dominance*. Ithaca: Cornell University Press.
Arnold, David. 2000. *The New Cambridge History of India- Science, Technology and Medicine in Colonial India*. Cambridge: Cambridge University Press.
Baber, Zaheer. 1996. *The Science of Empire: Scientific Knowledge, Civilization and Colonial Rule in India*. Albany: State University of New York Press.
Beck, William S. 1958. *Modern Science and the Nature of Life*. London: Macmillan.
Bowra, C.M. 1950. *The Romantic Imagination*. London: Oxford University Press.
Browne, Janet. 2008. *Darwin's Origin of Species: A Biography*. Bhopal: Manjul.
Butterfield, H. 1960. *The Origins of Modern Science 1300–1800*. New York: The Macmillan Company.
Chakarvarty, Pratik. 2004. *Western Science in Modern India: Metropolitan Methods, Colonial Practices*. Ranikhet: Permanent Black.

Cohn, Bernard. 1997. *Colonialism and Its Forms of Knowledge: The British in India*. New Delhi: Oxford.

Coleridge, S.T. 1834 'The Rime of the Ancient Mariner.' *The Poetical Works of S.T. Coleridge*. ed. Henry Nelson Coleridge. London : W. Pickering, http://rpo.library.utoronto.ca/poems/rime-ancient-mariner-text-1834

Headrick, Daniel R. 1981. *The Tools of Empire*. New York: Oxford.

Holmes, Richard. 2008. *The Age of Wonder: How the Romantic Generation discovered the Beauty and Terror of Science*. London: Harper Press.

Jones, Howard Mumford and Cohen I. Bernard. 1963. *Science Before Darwin*. London: Andre Deutsch.

Kuhn, Thomas S. 1962. *The Structure of Scientific Revolutions*. Chicago: The University of Chicago Press.

Kumar, Deepak. 1995. *Science and the Raj 1857–1905*, New Delhi: Oxford.

Makdisi, Saree. 1998. *Romantic Imperialism*. Cambridge: Cambridge University Press.

Mendelssohn, Kurt. 1976. *Science and Western Domination*. London: Thames and Hudson.

Morrell, Jack and Arnold Thackeray. 1984. *Gentlemen of Science: Early Correspondence of the British Association for the Advancement of Science*. London: Royal Historical Society.

Murray, Robert H. 1925. *Science and Scientists in the Nineteenth Century*. London: The Sheldon Press.

Prakah, Gyan. 1999. *Another Reason: Science and Imagination in Modern India*. New Delhi: Oxford.

Scott, Patrick. 1971. *Victorian Poetry: 1830–1870*. London: Longman.

Sherwood, Margaret. 1934. *Undercurrents of Influence in English Romantic Poetry*.Cambridge, Massachusetts: Harvard University Press.

Stimson, Dorothy. 1949. *Scientists and Amateurs: A History of Royal Society*. London: Sigma Books.

Uberoi, J.P.S. 1984. *The Other Mind of Europe: Goethe as a Scientist*. Delhi: Oxford University Press.

Vickziany, Marika. 1986. Imperialism, Botany and Statistics in early Nineteenth- Century India: The Surveys of Francis Buchanan (1762–1829)' *Modern Asian Studies*. 20(4): 625–60.

Whitehead, Alfred North. 1928. *Science and the Modern World: Lowell Lectures*. London: Cambridge University Press.

Willey, Basil. 1955. *Nineteenth Century Studies: Coleridge to Matthew Arnold*. London: Chatto and Windus.

17

CULTURAL ECONOMY OF LEISURE AND THE INDIAN PREMIER LEAGUE

Raj Thakur

April certainly is not the cruellest of months when it comes to modern-day leisure and the Indian Premier League (IPL), the natural bed fellows of late capitalist society. In the post-industrial society, there occurs a convention of projecting 'free time' with leisure experience, but the theoretical close reading suggests that the concept of free time has no intrinsic meaning; rather, its meaning always depends on the social context in which it occurs. 'Leisure shapes and is shaped by history and the interplay of social interests' (Roberts 1978: 47). One of the potent catalysts behind this process is the mass production of packaged sports in the likes of Champions Leagues and Premier Leagues, Grand Prix, Entertainment Wrestling and Extreme Sports–X Games. The growing popularity of sports-entertainment culture reflects emergent media and leisure economies, combining global cosmopolitanism with local cultural identities and histories. The institution of leisure has extended the power of discipline throughout the leisure activities, oozing out as an unreflected type of excitement.

Deconstructing the neoliberal confluence of corporate sport, the IPL in particular, and mass culture in general reveals that it is consumed within the realm of leisure economy as a popular culture sport. Modern competitive sports have developed in line with the logic of late capitalist modernity. The development is towards faster spectacular events through the packaging and presentation of events for audiences with short attention span. Hence, there has been a creation of new forms of 'express sport' (Rowe 2004: 19), most spectacularly, cricket in the form of IPL.

CULTURAL ECONOMY OF LEISURE

Neo-Marxists depict how the role of capital is theorized as aiming to run leisure activities on strict commercial lines by commodifying leisure pursuits wherever possible:

> Corporate institutions have transformed every means of entertainment and 'sport' in to a production process for the enlargement of the capital . . . So enterprising is capital that even where the effort is made by one or another section of population to find a way to nature, sport or art through personal activity and amateur or 'underground' innovation, these activities are easily incorporated in to the market as far as it is possible. (Braverman 1974: 279)

The classical view saw leisure as the basis for culture. Aristotle in the *Politics* says a curious thing — that the Spartans remained secure as long as they were at war; they collapsed as soon as they acquired an empire (58). The leisurely hours prepared the Spartans for war. For Aristotle, the words peace and leisure came together very often. The Western concept of leisure traces its origin to the Greek society and to the Greek word *schole*, 'a state of being free from the necessity to labor' (Murphy 1974: 67) corresponding to *ananda* in the Vedic age. The concept of contemplation in the Greek sense is close to leisure. Plato equates the notion of gazing at the stars to pure leisurely contemplation, a form of a 'blessed solitude' (ibid.). Leisure evolved in ancient Greece with the 'cultivation of self' (ibid.). This traditional or classical view of leisure emphasizes contemplation, enjoyment of self in search of knowledge, debate, politics and cultural enlightenment. Philosophers advocate leisure as a 'condition or state of being, a condition of the soul, which is divorced from time' (ibid.). The Industrial Revolution changed the concept of time, including free time; the gate way of leisure. 'Time became industrialized' (Roberts 1978: 34). Leisure-sport practices are, thus, deftly located within the cultural economy of *spare time spectrum* (emphasis added).

The shift from pre-industrial to post-industrial society had facilitated pitching in of 'game' as 'sport', a shift from ritual to record and from artefact to performance. Archery, once a military necessity, became a popular sport. Polo, which for many years had been popular with the Indian army made its debut in England as sport. Take the case of fencing, a subject on which a number of treatises were written in the 16th century. For us it may be a sport, but for the gentlemen of the Renaissance it was serious art.

Cricket was first played in India in the late 18th century, imported by British sailors and soldiers as a derivative sport. It was creatively adopted to fulfil political imperatives and to satisfy economic aspirations. In Pierre Bourdieu's terms, cricket, as a game, provided class fractions, in terms of symbolic capital-'prestige' and cultural capital-'tastes', leading to formation of individual 'habitus' (1993: 339). History draws inspiration from C. L. R. James' epigram, 'What do they know of cricket who only cricket know' (2005: 308). With wrestling and body-building proving inadequate to counter the colonial stereotype of Bengali effeminacy, the *bhadralok* resorted to European sports like cricket and soccer. Parsis and feudal Gujaratis used cricket to climb up the social ladder. Bombay Pentangular tournament was based on communal lines and Palwankar Baloo was among the first Dalit cricketers of colonial India. Princes like the Maharaja of Vizianagaram and Maharaja of Patiala saw cricket as a means of self-aggrandizement. Cricket in today's global environment has been altered a great deal by new technologies and revised geopolitical landscapes. Ashis Nandy traverses this path by exploring the shifting dynamics of cricket and examines how, with the advent of free-market economy, the game has softened as a cultural form and has culminated into a 'mediagenic and business friendly . . . showing a growing tolerance for nationalism as the new past time for its atomized, uprooted, urban spectators' (2000: 74).

In reference to Walter Benjamin's remark in *The Work of Art in the Age of Mechanical Reproduction*, there is an overt shift in telegenic sport from 'cult value' to 'exhibition value', 1992: (219). Cricket had a special place within the idea of the Empire, 'encompassing notions of muscular Christianity, gentlemanliness and what was later called the games ethic' (Nandy 2000: 121). James in *Beyond A Boundary* depicts a cult value of a sport; equanimous to art, an emancipatory force, absorbed a moral code, where 'A straight bat' and 'It isn't cricket' became the watch words of moral and virtue (2005: 217). The exhibition value of the sport set in with the growing marketing and ensuing neoliberal trends in cricket. The trajectory of which can be traced right from Kerry Packer's[1] World Series Cricket down to T20[2] cricket and the Indian Cricket League (ICL)[3] and the IPL[4].

The genesis of Indian cricket's financial pre-eminence since 1980s is inextricably linked with the deregulation of the Indian media market and a confluence of other factors: economic liberalization, the creation of large middle class and broader trends in globalization. Ramachandra Guha is of the opinion that the live coverage of cricket, as well as India's success, broadened the sport's 'catchment area' and 'it got more housewives involved in watching cricket, as well as more people outside the big cities' (2004: 76–77). At a time when other Indian sports were languishing, television made cricket central to the Indian sports fan's imagination. The creation of a national network became a magnet for advertisers because it opened up the possibility of constructing a *commodified public sphere* (emphasis mine). The focus of this advertising was on the 'exploding new middle classes' and television in the eyes of the advertisers enabled their transformation into consumers (Majumdar 2004: 405). Boria Majumdar depicts that cricket's fluidity in to the realm of mass culture was in a way fostered by

> [n]ewly structured hours of work with increased leisure opportunity for workers, the emergence of salaried middle class professionals with a conscious investment in leisure and the growth of commercial culture in colonial India shaped the fortunes of what is de facto India's national sport. (ibid.: 231)

This omnibus account of the game within the Indian psyche makes Asish Nandy say that 'Cricket is an Indian game accidentally discovered by the British' (2000: 1). Thus, the development of sport in the 21st century and its relationship to mass media can be perceived in the context of the general industrialization of culture, promoted and packaged by interested parties as a consumable leisure competing in a market against similar leisure pursuits. As in the case of IPL, it was created as the BCCI response to the rebel ICL of television mogul Subhash Chandra. Mass media broadcast added the touch of simulation, the verbal commentary was augmented by appropriate sound effects of crowd noises and bat striking the ball to provide the more 'convincing sense of reality' (Cashman 1980: 101). In a similar context, Richard Cashman says:

> Synthetic cricket distorted the game in number of ways. Not only were fictitious happenings invented to cover a break in the cables, the commentary even falsified the game itself on some occasions ... Radio also made cricket appear to be faster moving, more exciting game than it actually was. (ibid.: 102)

The striking innovation involving the IPL is the structure of the game itself. The code of cricket used in the IPL is Twenty20, a recent English invention shortening the austere format of long-form Test match cricket, and even more abbreviated than the one-day game as a more convenient and lively spectacular experience. While Test matches run for five days, Twenty20 cricket lasts for approximately three hours after the conventional working day has ended and is, thus, constructed to fit more easily into leisure time patterns and primetime television schedules. This truncated format of televisual nature is also evident in the spectacularized version of cricket that its rules stimulate.

The IPL schedule is organized along the lines of the US sports entertainment model, with matches played on a nightly basis throughout the season in order to provide maximum primetime content for its television partners. Teams are based in major urban centres, such as New Delhi and Mumbai, rather than in the more traditional regions. In addition, the IPL is structured according to the US-based sports franchise system, with team names such as Delhi Daredevils and Kolkata Knight Riders. Cheerleaders are imported and franchises are awarded to the highest bidders (in a number of cases, actors from the Hindi film industry) in a highly publicized and lucrative team auction run by the BCCI.

In the light of this discussion, the mass consumption of sports today (for example, the IPL) fits closely under the clutches of the apparent late capitalist gush of quickies in the likes of fastfood chains and virtual tourism, and leisure is becoming increasingly packaged. The new emerging cultural attitude towards leisure was given intellectual justification by Huizinga (1949), who argued in his treatise *Homo Ludens* that 'play' was a type of an activity that met basic human needs and was, therefore, an indispensable element in all human civilizations. Today such cultural attitudes toward 'play and leisure have been firmly institutionalized' (ibid.: 56).

In the Indian subcontinent sports is synonymous with cricket. Cricket in the subcontinent first subbed traditional sports like hockey and football. Gradually it predated weekends, with traditional weekends with family being taken over by one-day Internationals. Finally, it has taken over entertainment with Twenty20 cricket, which preyed on the leisure time which would ordinarily have gone to hobbies but more likely to TV serials or movies. Much like Marx's idea of religion as an opiate for the masses, cricket's truncated form, IPL, thrives on as the happy by-product of sports-industrial complex. As an insatiable opiate for masses it provides the basis for spectacular shows and circuses that narcotize large segment of the population. IPL as a leisurely spectacle may offer mass gratification and instant sugar hits via its performative codes and the grammar of spare time, but on the flip side it carries the imprint of values consistent with existing economic and political practices wherein functions of leisure are manifestations of an oppressive capitalist infrastructure together with its state apparatuses of social control.

Cultural consumption is viewed as centring on fascination with the spectacular surfaces of media forms, the play of ever proliferating and intermingling signs and images. This symbiotic relation between leisure industry and media–sports complex serves as an extension of the culture industry, where mass culture takes IPL into custody. The culture industry is the 'societal realization of the defeat of reflection' (Adorno 2001: 13). The effect of late capitalism has further weakened old power structures of sports. The discourse of sport was once 'descriptive' (*emphasis added*) and had its own pace much like test cricket. Nevile Cardus, one of the earliest legendary cricket writers would portray cricketing stroke as 'poetry in action' (2008: 67). On the contrary, hyper competition is the dominant culture of modern-day cricket. Ashis Nandy says that 'Victorian cricket as a cultural artefact was masculine, having connotations parallel to Brahmnic concept of mind, reflecting form over substance and mind over body'(2000: 37); IPL, on the contrary, reflects a new masculinity of cricket, built purely on raw performances, which doesn't go much beyond the commentators melodramatic punch, offering leisure-centric bites in terms of 'Volkswagen Super Six', 'DLF maximum' or 'Karbonn Kamaal Catch' or 'Maxx Mobile Strategic Time out', integrating cricket in terms of mass culture and entertainment.

It becomes a ' "perfect spectacle linear to Indian commercial films concept of dedetailing" (please note that both the references have been quoted from Nandy's The Tao of Cricket) owing to image bombardment which stands in stark contrast to "classical" relying on particulars and details' (Nandy 2000: 142). IPL as a 'sportainment' is construed to its potential to provide exciting and titillating space, whether through the cheerleaders or through its '30 Seconds Dugout Interviews' in between the play sessions – blurring the line between leisure, sport and entertainment. Similarly, matches under the floodlights create the simulacra of the day. To quote Guy Debord, from the *Society of the Spectacle*, the reality of time has been replaced by creating 'pseudo-spectacular time' (1983: 157). This packaged form of cricket and its politics of spectacle imply the coercion of visual freedom. Projecting the 'occularcentric politics' (of IPL's sporty décor, mediated sport constantly devises narrative strategies of overt spectacle and display, where ' "scopophilia" or scopic drives (pleasure of looking) takes priority over "epistemophilia" (desire to know)' (Dyer & Pinney 2001: 34–35). Debord puts forward the idea in close proximity to corporate sport, where 'the economy transforms the world but transforms it only in to the world of economy' (1983: 154).

Watching the IPL is like encountering one of those post-modern narratives that seek to satirize consumerism. Player outfits look like a collage of flyers, heavily loaded with sponsorship tags. The beautiful baize of the field is defaced by anywhere between five and eight giant logos, one or two on the straights, and the remaining square. Inside the advertising boundary boards, the boundary triangles carry branding, as do the sightscreens and stumps. The fibreglass of the dugouts is tattooed in logos. There is an MRF blimp in the sky. A giant screen constantly fizzes with advertisements. Even the banners in the crowd can be sponsored as 'Cheer your City'. The flashy advertisement boards, colourful and gaudy team attires and the glitzy show under the floodlights offer a mix visual delight. The normative form of the game is packaged through the element of pastiche and parody where the accessories and spinoffs take the mainstage. Statistical bombardment regarding the vital statistics of the player mediates the ultra-competitiveness, which is at the heart of this over-organized, sports-packaged sporting spectacle. Vital stats of the players include the number of 20s and 30s (runs) scored and catches taken to the existing norms of half centuries and centuries scored, strike rate and batting average. Analysing the performance principle of sport, Ashis Nandy cites that in the new mass culture of sport, statistics is not used as partial description of good or bad play rather the game is played to pile up the statistics: 'Individuals reside not in the game, but in the measure of performance' (2000: 118). Similarly, purely market-driven auction is based on *cost per run* and *cost per wicket* (emphasis added), franchise owners react to the basic laws of demand and supply and this is the reason why Ravinder Jadeja and Robin Uthappa overshadow batsmen like VVS Laxman and Ricky Ponting. This goes by the ethics of consumable sport under market economy.

The culture industry exploits the individual's leisure time; it functions to induce the uncritical mass. Adorno asserts, 'The power of culture industries ideology is such that conformity has replaced consciousness' (2001: 64). IPL, in its very sporting/spectacle form is *staged* (emphasis added). Salvo of action on and off the field constitutes what Baudrillard considers as 'spirals in the simulacrum of popular culture' (1998: 245). The greatest criticism of the culture industry relates to its claim to keep the customer amused. Its allotment of 'administrated pleasures and calculated distraction' is condemned by Adorno and Horkheimer for its 'minimalist aspirations' (1979: 124). Its mediation through mass media speak through frame and here frame is the picture, McLuhan's 'medium is the message' (1993: 8) speaks through frames (media/TV) which penetrate the sport. The paralysis of critical thought, they argue, is the price exacted for the mere amusement of the individual and leisure here is mass deception. Raymond Williams' 'flow' (1974: 75) is quite apparent in IPL's televisual manoeuvres, where the goal is not to get viewers to watch the game carefully but to keep them from turning it off. IPL, therefore, feeds less on cricketing logic than television logic.

While the IPL is reflective of contemporary Western sports frameworks, it incorporates the highly stylized visual aesthetic and potent celebrity cachet of Indian cinema culture, with its match entertainment and team branding. This *Bollywoodization* (emphasis added) of cricket, involving the merger of Indian sport with the entertainment values of its film industry, has diversified the traditional cricket audience, drawing more female and family-oriented spectators and diluting the traditional partisanship associated with Indian cricket crowds. The Kolkata fans, in the streets, flaunt replica shirts stamped with 'Khan-11' – representative of the most popular actor and the owner of the Kolkata Knight Riders (KKR). The Shah Rukh Khan shirt, spotted in other Indian cities as well, says a lot about the new breed of fans watching the IPL games. Kolkata's sports fans are supposed to be the most passionate in the country, yet the manner in which they chose Shah Rukh Khan over Sourav Ganguly suggests that the hard-core sports-lover is staying away.

The lopsided allocation of IPL teams is insensitive to democracy and demography. One of cricket's historical peculiarities is that its competitive units have been based on counties, provinces and states rather than cities. But the new franchises, unlike the English football clubs on which they're modelled, are not the creations of history and community; they do not belong to the fans the way Manchester United or Liverpool do. They have been created from the top-down and sold as a finished but ephemeral item to a passive audience, making the IPL a characteristic product of the 21st century corporate culture, advocating free-market forces disregarding national boundaries. It depicts the pre-Independence cricketing phenomenon when the affluent Parsi merchants and the crème de la crème from other denominations dominated the scene.

Uttar Pradesh (UP), the most densely populated state in India, two-time winners of the Ranji Trophy (2005–6), has no team representation in the IPL. Maharashtra, in comparison, has a population of little more than half of UP, but two of its cities, Mumbai Indians and Pune Warriors form IPL's so called *clubs* (emphasis added). It is hard to justify Pune having an IPL team over cities like Kanpur, Lucknow, Agra, Banaras and Allahabad. On the other hand, Kerala, Tamil Nadu, Karnataka and Andhra Pradesh together account for less than one-fourth of the country's population. There is not one IPL team from those three larger states in North India, whereas as IPL 2011 came up with Kochi Tuskers[5] and Pune Warriors[6] from the southern region. But the choice of new franchises cannot be justified in terms of cricketing logic either. Kochi has a weaker case as franchises could have gone for Madhya Pradesh, the state of Holkar, which dominated the Ranji Trophy, prior to Mumbai, and has a far better record in comparison to Kerala, which has the lowest record in the tournament. Apart from the urban industrial populace of Pune and Kochi, its active night life in contrast to the northern cities makes it the first choice for the 'sportainment'. Considerations such as these, and not the pure competence at cricket, are what the new entrants share with existing franchisees, such as Bangalore, Delhi, Hyderabad and Mumbai. Consequently, the Indian Premier League (IPL) may be more appropriately renamed the League of Privileged Indians.

Notes

1. Kerry Packer Series/World Series Cricket was professional cricket administered by Australian media tycoon Kerry Packer's Channel Nine in 1977. It was in response to Australian Cricket Boards refusal to accept Channel Nine's bid to gain exclusive television rights to Australia's Test matches in 1976. The modern-day rise of one-day cricket (50 over each team) is an offshoot of Packer's revolution.
2. Twenty20 is the Truncated form of one-day cricket (50 over per side) often abbreviated to T20. Eponymously it comprises 20 over a side contest. It was originally introduced by the English and Wales Cricket Board (ECB) in 2003 for professional inter-county competition in England and Wales.

3. Much like Packer's cricket revolution, Indian Cricket League, ICL, came about when Indian cable network Zee TV made a bid for the Indian domestic cricket TV rights. A deal was struck that awarded Sony the rights. Angered and frustrated, Zee TV founder Subhash Chandra decided to produce his own cricket league, the ICL, based on Twenty20 format (20 over each team). It operated between 2007 and 2009 in India.
4. Indian Premier League was launched in 2008 as the Indian professional Twenty20 league cricket. It is based on major city-based franchises. As the brainchild of the Board of Control for Cricket in India (BCCI), IPL has developed into the most popular and lucrative sports leagues in India currently.
5. Kochi Tuskers Kerala was a franchise cricket team that played in the Indian Premier League representing the city of Kochi, Kerala. The team was one of two new franchisees added to the Indian Premier League (IPL) for the 2011 season alongside the Pune Warriors India. Failing to meet the financial obligations, Kochi Tuskers Kerala was expelled from the league in 2011.
6. Sahara Pune Warriors franchise met the same fate in 2013 when BCCI decided to terminate its agreement on the account of failing to provide the necessary bank guarantee as directed by the Bombay High Court. Antecedently, Hyderabad Deccan Chargers, one of the eight founding members of the IPL in 2008, owned by Deccan Chronicle Holdings Ltd., has been shut down since 2012 failing to comply with deadline to pay overdue player fees.

References

Aristotle. 1946. *Politics*. Trans. E Barker. London: Oxford University Press.

Adorno, Theodor. 2001. *The Cultural Industry: Selected Essays on Mass Culture*, ed. by J. M. Bernstien. London: Routledge Classics.

Adorno, Theodor and Marx Horkheimer. 1979. *Dialectic of Enlightenment*. London: Verso.

Baudrillard, Jean. 1998. 'The Gulf War Did Not Take Place', in Mark Poster (ed.), *Jean Baudrillard: Selected Writings*, pp. 231–53. Cambridge and Oxford: Polity.

Benjamin, Walter. 1992. 'The Work of Art in the Age of Mechanical Reproduction', in Hannah Arendt (ed.), *Illuminations: Essays and Reflections*, pp. 211–44. Trans. Harry Zohn. London: Fontana Press.

Bourdieu, Pierre. 1993. 'How Can One Be A Sports Fan?', in Simon During (ed.), *The Cultural Studies Reader*, pp. 339–55. London: Routledge.

Braverman, Harry. 1974. *Labour and Monopoly Capital*. New York: Monthly Review Press.

Cardus, Neville. 2008. *Cardus on Cricket*. New Delhi: Rupa & Co.

Cashman, Richard. 1980. *Patrons, Players and the Crowd: The Phenomenon of Indian Cricket*. New Delhi: Orient Longman.

Debord, Guy. 1983. *Society of the Spectacle*. Detroit: Black and Red.

Dyer, Rachel and Christopher Pinney (eds). 2001. *Pleasure and the Nation: The History, Politics and Consumption of Public Culture in India*. New Delhi: Oxford University Press.

Guha, Ramchandra. 2004. *A Corner of a Foreign Field: The Indian History of a British Sport*. New Delhi: Picador India.

Huizinga, Johan. 1949. *Homo Ludens*. London: Routledge.

James, C.L.R. 2005. *Beyond A Boundary*. London: Yellow Jersey Press.

Karl, Marx and Friedrich Engels. 1965. *The German Ideology*. London: Lawrence & Wishart.

Majumdar, Boria. 2004. *Twenty Two Yards to Freedom: A Social History of Indian Cricket*. New Delhi: Penguin.

McLuhan, Marshall. 1993. 'The Medium is the Message', in *Understanding Media*, pp. 7–23. London and New York: Routledge.

Murphy, James F. 1974. *Concepts of Leisure: Philosophical Implications*. London: Prentice Hall.

Nandy, Ashish. 2000. *The Tao of Cricket: On Games of Destiny and Destiny of Games*. New Delhi: Oxford University Press.

Roberts, Kenneth. 1978. *Contemporary Society and the Growth of Leisure*. New York: Longman.

Rowe, David (ed.). 2004. *Critical Readings: Sport, Culture and Media*. Maidenhead: Open University Press. (error regretted: the one which I mentioned happens to be the printed ref. not the published one.) UK: Bell & Bain Ltd.

Srinivas, Alam and T.R. Vivek. 2009. *IPL, Cricket & Commerce: An Inside Story*. New Delhi: Roli Books.

Williams, Raymond. 1974. *Television: Technology and Cultural Form*. London: Fontana Press.

INDEX

Abbasi, Muhammad Yusuf 144
Abhinavagupta 40
Ad-dharm movement 67
adivasis 20, 22–7, 224–5, 227
Adorno, T. 291–3
The Age of Wonder: How the Romantic Generation Discovered the Beauty and Terror of Science (2008) 275
ahimsa 9
Ahsan, Aitzaz 144
AIR *see* All India Radio
Akhtar, Zoya 248, 254, 259, 261
Akida, Gurnam 66, 68, 69, 71, 72, 77, 79–82, 84
Akkarmashi (1984) 69, 83
Akk da Dudh (Atarjeet) 66, 75, 84
Alam, Gurdas Ram 66
All India Radio (AIR) 201, 207
Alma Kabutri 26
Amrohi, Kamal 260
Ankur (1974) 253
anthology 26, 29, 142
aphasia 21–2
Arif, Sadhu Daya Singh 66
Armand, Jorge 10
Arnold, David 280
Arnold, Matthew 4, 124
art 30, 36–42, 46, 142, 160, 171–2, 186, 211, 231–2, 248, 258, 260, 273, 277–8, 287–8; work of 37–8, 40, 42, 231, 288

Asian Drama (Myrdal) 102
Astruc, Alexander 258
Atarjeet 68–9, 72–3, 75, 77–81, 88
authorly aesthetics 82–92
authorship 67–8, 70, 89, 126
autobiographers 68–9, 84, 86–7, 89
autobiographies 65, 68–71, 78, 83–5, 87–8, 90, 150, 157
awareness 66, 215, 224, 226

Baba Bantu 189
Bahujan Samaj movement 66
Bajarange, Daxin 26
Baluta (Pawar) 69
Banjaras 25
bathing 71, 119, 121–2
Baudrillard, Jean 49
beauty 15, 147–8, 161, 247, 275–6
Benegal, Shyam 253
Benjamin, Walter 288
Berlin, Isaiah 112
Bhabha, Homi 53
Bhagavad Gita 12
Bhakhda Patal (Madhopuri) 68
Bhoomikar, Santosh 83
Bhutto, Benazir 69
'the Birth of a New Avant-Garde: *la Caméra-stylo*' (Astruc) 258
Blackburn, Stuart 177
botany 279–82
Bourdieu, Pierre 48, 288
Brihad-deshi 20
Brook, Peter 229

INDEX

Buddhism 9
Budhan Theatre 30, 222–9, 234

Carlyle, Thomas 278
Carvakas 13
Cashman, Richard 289
Celtic race 4
censure 181–5
Chakarvarty, Pratik 274
Chakrabarty, Dipesh 114
chamars 74–5, 80–1, 91
Chamba 117–20, 122–3, 133
Changiya Rukh (Madhopuri) 66, 70, 73–4, 81, 90
Chatak, Govind 26
Chattisgarhi Lokakshar 26
Chharas 29, 222–7, 238
Christian culture 9
cinema 239, 248–51, 253, 257–8, 260–1
civilization 18–19, 43, 100, 105, 107, 123–5, 127, 134, 144, 154
classical Indian aesthetics 35–43
classical Indian tradition 35–6, 39, 41
Close-Up Antakshari (CUA) 212–13
cognitive project 107–10
Colonial India 288–9
colonial modernity 47–50
colonial taxonomies 19–20
commitment 58–9, 107–8, 188–9, 225
Communist culture 86
communities 4, 6, 21–3, 25, 27–30, 130, 133, 147, 149, 202, 204, 211, 237–41, 244–5, 269–71; cultural 127, 133–4, 245; de-intellectualized 3, 8; indigenous 21–2; of interest 270–1; nomadic 20–1, 23–5, 27
comrades 77–8, 86, 88
conceptions 99–100, 118–19, 127, 129–30
connections 35–6, 59–60, 131, 176, 179–80, 207, 216, 239, 271
contemporary culture studies 35–6, 40–3
contention 273
continuity 82, 128, 202, 208–9

conversion 86–7, 141, 147–8, 171, 277
counter-culture 126, 134
Cratylus 12
cricket 286, 288–94
Criminal Tribes Act (CTA) 23, 27, 225
cultural studies: future of 30; Indian aesthetics for 35–43; issues and problems 45–50; theoretical approaches and practical realities 52–61
culture 4, 31, 36, 38–40, 42, 50; contemporary popular 35–6, 38–9; discipline of 35, 42, 47; diversity 31; dominant 129, 291; economy 286–94; history 26, 170–2, 192–3; iconographies 237–8; identity 133, 237, 239; imaginary 134; industry 47–8, 291–93; insiderness 271; memory 267–9; modern 7–9, 204; national 173, 207; ontology of 36–7; patterns 128–9, 260; people's 164; production 23, 170–3, 182, 231; reformers 185–6; regional 127–8, 131–2; studies 30–1, 35, 52–3, 100, 106, 113, 117, 237; television and 201; traditional 7–8; trait 131; work 173, 270–1
Cunningham, Joseph Davey 153–6

Dalit autobiographies 65–6, 70, 85, 90
Dalit literature 25
Dalits 23, 66–7, 69, 71, 73, 76, 79–81
Dastan (Dil) 66, 70, 85–6
The Daughter of the East (1988) 69
death 28, 89, 120–1, 159–63, 175, 177, 191, 261, 275, 277
decolonization 19
Delhi 29, 83, 153, 184, 239, 241–2, 294
Denotified and Nomadic Tribes' Rights Action Group 28
denotified tribes (DNTs) 27, 30
Devi, Mahasweta 23, 26, 28, 224, 227

INDEX

Devy, G. N. 224, 225, 227
dharma 14
Didar Singh 159–60
digitization 266–7
Dil, Lal Singh 66, 85
discipline 4, 31, 36–7, 53–5, 113, 154, 273, 279–80, 286
The Discovery of India (Nehru) 100
discrimination 71–5, 80, 82, 84–5
distraction/co-option, discourses of 74–82
Division of Labour in Society (Durkheim) 109
Diwana, Mohan Singh 143
Doordarshan 204, 208–12

Elwin, Verrier 22–5
emancipatory project 110–13
emergent voice 22–6
The Empty Space (Brook) 229
English language 3, 5, 7; Indian tongues, cultural instruments 7; 'jeansification' of 4
English literature 3–5, 275
Erll, Astrid 266–7
Eros and Civilization: a Philosophical Inquiry into Freud (Marcuse) 105

false consciousness 39
families 14–17, 73, 79–80, 89, 101, 120, 179, 189–90, 202, 265–7, 269–71, 280
Farid, Shaikh 141, 143
filmmakers 248, 250, 253, 257, 259, 262
films 207–8, 213, 237–8, 247–62; studies 36, 250–1, 257, 260; theory 249
Fire (1996) 253, 260
Flueckiger, Joyce 177
folk 35, 46–8, 125–6, 134, 139–40, 170–7, 180–2, 184–9, 192, 237–41, 245; community 139–40; culture 47, 139, 148, 186; Islams 150; literature 139, 141; theatre 187; traditions 170–5, 182, 186–9, 192, 238

folklore 22, 139–41, 181, 226, 239
folk songs 26
Foucault, Michel 114
Freud, Sigmund 114, 249

Gaikwad, Laxman M. 25, 69
Gair Hazir Aadmi (Gorkhi) 66, 70, 73, 82
game 105, 111, 160, 213–14, 287–90, 292–3
Gargi, Balwant 188
gaze 52, 210; female 248, 255, 257–8; male 247–61
Geertz, Clifford 128
Gellner, Ernest 101
Ghori song 161–3
Ghosh, Amitav 273–83
globalization 50, 54, 57–8, 60, 100, 216–17, 262, 289
gods 11, 41, 130, 149–50, 175, 182
Goethe 273–5
Gorakhnath 175, 177, 189–90
Gor-Banjara 25
Gorkhi, Prem 66, 68–9, 77–8, 87–9
Gramsci, Antonio 39, 140
Great Tradition 127–8, 130–1, 133–4, 179
Greek cultures 9
Guga 170–1, 173–81, 184–5, 188–91; power of 190–1; tradition 170–93; worship of 171, 174–5, 182, 184–5
Guga Pir 170–1, 174
Guha, Ranajit 140
Gulamgiri (Phule) 90
Gurmukhi 142, 159, 185
gurudwaras 75–6, 80

Habitual Offenders' Act 28
Hans, Rajkumar 66
Hebraic culture 9
Hegel, George Wilhelm Friedrich 139
high culture 47, 126, 186
Hindi cinema/films 208, 210, 238, 241–2, 248, 252, 256
Hir-Ranjha 145–52
Hir Waris 145–52, 158

INDEX

historiography 139, 141, 143, 146, 157
history: national 102, 270–1; natural 274, 279; personal 83, 265, 267; popular 157; writing 265–6
History at the Limit of World-History 140
History of the Sikhs (Cunningham) 153
A History of the Sikhs from the Origin of the Nation to the Battle of Sutlej (Cunningham) 153
History of Sexuality (Foucault) 114
Holmes, Richard 275
Horkheimer, Max 105
human relationships 14, 16–17, 188

India: adivasi communities 24; cinema 252, 260–1; civilization 7, 127; classroom 49; culture 7, 47–8, 50, 117, 210; education 4, 5, 7, 9, 13; languages 3–4, 8, 24, 46, 186; literature 21–3; Muslims 143, 150; philosophy 14, 17; popular culture studies in 45, 47–50; sexuality in 17; society 18, 23, 27, 117, 123, 186, 214, 253, 261; subcontinent 58, 143, 265; television 201–2, 206, 210, 212, 215, 217; thought 11–12; traditions 15; woman 259, 261
Indian Constitution 20–1
Indian Cricket League (ICL) 288, 295
Indian history 133, 154
Indian Memory Project (IMP) 265–72
Indian minds 3, 8–9, 11–12
Indianness 99–100, 102–3, 106–13, 186, 216, 218; cognitive project 107–10; emancipatory project 110–13; item dances, social discourse 113–14
Indian People's Theatre Association (IPTA) 172, 186–8
Indian postal department 210–11
Indian Premier league (IPL) 286, 289–95
Indic cultural models 123–32

indigenization 215–18
International Monetary Fund 54
The Indus Saga: From Patliputra to Partition (Ahsan) 144
(in)visible publics 201–18
Islam 86–7, 141, 143–4, 146–8, 150–2, 173–4
Islamic culture 9

Jacobsson, Eve-Maria 258
Jainism 9
James, C. L. R. 288
Jini Rahi Mein Tooriya (Rahi) 82
Jini Rahi Mein Turiya (Rahi) 66
Jones, William 19
Judaic culture 9

Kakh Kande (Akida) 66, 70, 71, 73, 75, 84
Kamasutra (1996) 254
Kamble, Babytai 70
Kamble, Shantabai 70
Kanjar community 28
Kaplan, E. 260
Kapur, Geeta 192
Kashmir 117–23, 127, 131, 133, 144
Katal Hoya Hatth (Akida) 68
Kaur, Ajeet 70
Khalnayak (1993) 229
Khiangte, L. 26
knowledge: cultural 281; scientific 140, 273
Kocharethi (1988) 23
Kura Kabara (Kaur) 70

Lajmi, Kalpana 253
Lambert, Pierre 280, 282
language of liberation 3; *see also* English language
languages 4–5, 7–8, 14, 19–22, 24–6, 60, 65, 89, 91, 122, 124, 142, 152, 154–5, 258; of adivasi communities 24; diversity 20; epistemology of 20–1; tribal 23–4, 26
Lapsley, Robert 250
Latin American intellectuals 8

INDEX

Learning to Labour: How Working Class Kids Get Working Class Jobs (Willis) 106
leisure 211, 213, 286–7, 289–91, 293
liberal capitalism 54
liberalism 15
Limbale, Sarankumar 69
Linguistic monism 6
Linnaeus, Carl 280
literarization 134
literature 4–5, 20, 23–4, 26, 29–30, 65–6, 68, 140, 142, 145, 147, 162–4, 181, 247–8, 277
Llosa, Mario Vargas 258
Lokayatas 13

Macaulay, Lord 5–6
MacLeod, W. H. 152, 154, 157–8
MacLuhan, Marshall 49
Madhopuri, Balbir 66, 68, 71, 74, 77, 79, 81–2, 88, 90–1
male gaze 247–61
Mane, Laxman 25, 69
Mann, Gurdas 242
Marathi Dalit 65, 67, 69, 79, 87, 90–2
Marcuse, Herbert 105
marginalization 21–2
marriage 15–17, 127, 129, 148, 162–3, 175, 255, 259
marriage–martyrdom fusion 161–3
Marriot, Mckim 130
martyr 157, 161–3
Maruthal da Birakh (Madhopuri) 68
Marxism 55–7
mass culture 47–9, 286, 289, 291
Mastana, Asa Singh 245
Mazhabis 66
Mehndi, Daler 237–45
Mehta, Deepa 253, 260
Mehta, Vijaya 253
memories: citizenship 266, 269, 271–2; cultural 267–9, 272; cultures of 266–7, 269, 272; private 266; transcultural 267
Mishran, Suryamall 179
Mizo Literature 26

models, cultural 117, 123, 128–9
modern culture-work 181–5
Mohanty, Gopinath 23
Mulvey, Laura 248, 250–2, 257, 260
Murphy, Paula 251
The Muslim Community of the Indo-Pakistan Subcontinent (Qureshi) 143
Muslims 86, 133, 141–3, 149–52, 155–8, 176–7, 182–3
Myrdal, Gunnar 102

Nair, Meera 253, 254
Nanak, Guru 141, 142, 160
Nange Pairan da Safar (Tiwana) 70
Nation and Nationalism (Gellner) 101
national audience 207–9
Nehru, Jawaharlal 59, 100–2, 107–9, 111
Nilamata Purana (NP) 118–19, 121–2
Niyama 13
A Nomad Called Thief: Reflections on Adivasi Silence (2006) 225
nomads 25–6, 223–5
northern India 170

Ocean of Stories 23
On Method (Descartes) 10
operational dialectics 71–4
Orientalism (Said) 54

Pagan, culture 9
Painted Words (2002) 26
Pakistan 142–5, 174, 213, 265; people of 144
Pakistani Culture: A Profile (Abbasi) 144
parochialization 123, 130–1, 134
participatory culture 201, 205–6, 208, 210, 212, 215, 218
partition 141, 143–4, 157, 239
patriarchy 215, 247, 254, 259–60
Pawar, Daya 69, 70
performance studies 36, 231
Phule, Jotibha 90
pilgrimage 119–20, 122, 159
political beliefs 55

301

INDEX

politics, cultural 172, 175, 181
Pollock, Sheldon 131
popular culture 35, 45, 47–50, 104–5, 113, 213, 215, 293; ontology of 47; studies 36, 38–9, 42, 45, 49–50
pop videos 237–45
postcolonial theory 52–61
post-90s phenomenon 66–7
post-partition historiography 141–63
power-seeking state 104
Prakash, Atam 73, 84
Prison Notebooks (Gramsci) 140
Pritam, Amrita 70
private channels 212–15
protagonist 71–2, 75–6, 79, 81–5, 87, 92, 143, 147, 158, 262
'presidency' colleges 3
psychoanalysis 248–50, 255, 257, 260
Punjab 66–7, 73, 77, 79–81, 141–5, 151, 153–9, 162, 164, 171, 174–5, 179, 181, 184–5, 217; culture 143; Dalit literature 66–7; Dalits 65–71, 73–4, 76–82, 85, 87, 89–92; history 142, 147, 154; people 141, 145–6, 148, 158, 162, 184
Punjab, Muslims 145–6, 148, 151
Punjab: History, Art, Literature and Culture 142
Punjabi folk literature 139–64
Puri, Harish K. 73

Qissa 158–61
Qureshi, Ishtiaq Hussain 143

Rahi, Giani Gurbakhash Singh 66, 69, 82
Rajasthan 174–6, 178–9
Ram, Kanshi 66
Ram, Ronki 71
Randhawa, Mohinder Singh 142
Ranjhas 147–50
Rao Sahib (1986) 253
Rasidi Ticket (Pritam) 70
Rathod, Atmaram 25
Rawls, John 99
Razia Sultan (1983) 260

Reality TV 201, 209, 211, 213
Redfield, Robert 127
renaissance 9
resistance, literature 26–30
reverence 15
Romanticism 274–5, 278–9
Romantic science 275, 277–8
Roy, Raja Ram Mohan 3
Rudaali (1992) 253

Said, Edward 53, 59
Sanatana Dharma 9
Sansis 25
Sanskrit 122, 127, 129–31, 134
Sanskritization 67, 123, 129–31; process of 129–31, 134
sanyamaor sanjam 13
Sarvagod, Mukta 70
Schiach, Morag 46
science 8, 46, 107–8, 111, 273–9, 281, 283
scopophilic pleasure 250–1, 253, 255, 260
second language *see* English language
sexuality 17, 114, 173, 249, 252–4, 260
Sidhu, C. D. 191
Sikhs 9, 74, 76, 80, 133, 141–3, 152–8, 162, 175, 181–5, 241; history 157; people 154–5, 157
Singer, Milton 127
Singh, Baljinder 84
Singh, Bhagat 141, 158–61
Singh, Bhai Vir 182–4
Singh, Ganda 142
Singh, Giani Bhagwan 75
Singh, Giani Ditt 66
Singh, Giani Gurdit 174
Singh, Jeevan 66
Singh, Sadhu Wazir 66
social sciences 12, 99–100, 106, 110–11, 113, 117
social stereotype 27
space, cultural 117–18, 122, 133, 140, 162
SPARROW 265–6, 269–70
Spivak, Gayatri 53

302

INDEX

Srinivas, M. N 129, 134
subalterns 56, 104–6, 111–12, 170, 186, 191, 227, 229

television 201–2, 204–12, 214–15, 218, 239, 241, 245–6, 289
texts, cultural 38, 47–8, 152
Thapar, Romila 126
theatrical renditions 185–8
36 Chaowrangi Lane (1981) 253
Tiwana, Dilip Kaur 70
tradition 35, 37, 40, 43, 112–13, 162, 170–4, 176, 179, 181, 189, 191–2, 238, 243–5, 253; little 112–14, 127–8, 130, 133, 170, 181; pan-Indian 176, 180
transformative energy 222–36
transmission 128, 202
truths 11, 146, 225, 254; plurality of 11

Uberoi, J. P. S. 273–5
Uchalya (Gaikwad) 69
Upara (Mane) 69

valorization 181–5
vegetarianism 9

Vidyasagar, Ishvarachandra 3
villages 27, 71, 73, 80, 83, 89–90, 147, 149, 205, 239
Virilio, Paul 49
Visual Pleasures and Narrative Cinema (Mulvey) 248
Vividh Bharati 201, 206–8

Waris Shah 141, 145–6, 148–9, 151–8
The Way to Paradise (Llosa) 258
Western Christian culture 5
Western historians 154, 157
Western society 8, 14–15
Westlake, Michael 250
Williams, Raymond 38, 49
women 14, 16–17, 52, 60, 72, 82, 90, 175, 182, 184, 243–4, 247–54, 256–7, 259–60, 265
World Bank 54
The Wretched of the Earth (Sartre) 53
writers 29, 66, 68–9, 84, 90

Zindagi Na Milegi Dobara 247–62
Zoroashtrian culture 9